BARBRA S

D0201523

SHE LOVED THEM ALL—IN HER WAY

ELLIOTT GOULD—He was ready to walk out when she proposed. But the day came finally when he had to leave . . . to survive.

OMAR SHARIF—Sauve, sophisticated, he was the perfect revenge on a husband who was determined to come out from her shadow into a spotlight of his own.

RYAN O'NEAL—"I found her very sexy . . . a terrific girl . . . but I think she used me."

PIERRE TRUDEAU—Canada's dashing Prime Minister inspired fantasies on an even grander scale. But how could they make do on his salary?

WARREN BEATTY—Everywoman's man, he romanced her to headlines. But she had the last laugh—all the way to the bank.

JON PETERS—She met her match in the L.A. slum kid who made his fortune as a hairdresser and his fame as the protégé who changed her life and career. "I learned about real women from Barbra. I learned about power."

"A PRIMER OF ITS KIND, A CANDID BIOGRAPHY OF BOTH THE PROFESSIONAL AND PERSONAL SIDES OF THE DECIDEDLY OFFBEAT BROOKLYN GIRL WHO WENT FROM SINGING FOR HER SUPPER . . . TO A STAR MODEL FOR WOMEN EVERYWHERE."

—*Daily News* (New York)

"Provocative and hilarious."

—Liz Smith

BARBRA STREISAND

The Woman, The Myth, The Music

Shaun Considine

A DELL BOOK

Published by
Dell Publishing Co., Inc.
1 Dag Hammarskjold Plaza
New York, New York 10017

Dell ® TM 681510, Dell Publishing Co., Inc.

ISBN: 0-440-10464-5

Reprinted by arrangement with Delacorte Press

Printed in the United States of America

December 1986

10 9 8 7 6 5 4 3 2 1

WFH

To Saint Jude,
Patron Saint
of Hopeless Cases

Prologue

The year was 1962. A time for optimism. John F. Kennedy was President; John Glenn orbited the earth; and James Meredith became the first black to be enrolled at the University of Mississippi.

On April twenty-fourth of that year Barbra Streisand turned twenty. Though blessed with good health, a steady boyfriend, and her own apartment, she refused to celebrate.

A month previously she had made her debut on Broadway, in *I Can Get It for You Wholesale*. She'd gotten the best reviews, the leading man (Elliott Gould), and a Tony nomination. Rewards quite rare for one so young (in 1962 the age of twenty was still considered young), and for one so untrained. Yet still she frowned.

"If I'm such a hotshot singer," she asked her manager more than once, "why don't I have a recording contract?"

"Because we're going for all the bucks," the manager, Marty Erlichman, replied. "For you we need the biggest and the best; a record label strong enough to carry your talent." And to Erlichman the letters on that label read: COLUMBIA.

The biggest and the best? Columbia Records had always agreed with that assessment. In technology they were the leaders of contemporary sound. In marketing and sales they were also number one. Their prodigious catalogue of stars included Bessie Smith,

Billie Holiday, Frank Sinatra, Doris Day, Benny Goodman, Leonard Bernstein, Jo Stafford, Tony Bennett, Mitch Miller, Johnny Mathis, Miles Davis, Dave Brubeck, Johnny Cash, The Mormon Tabernacle Choir, and hundreds more.

Barbra Streisand joined the Columbia roster in 1962. Her entry was greeted with skepticism and bias, yet she soon became one of their brightest stars, eventually outlasting all others in terms of consistent popularity and revenue. This is the story of how she achieved and sustained that popularity for twenty-three years. It is a story of talent and genius, of originality and perfectionism. It also tells of power and temperament; of pandering and paranoia; of generosity and greed. It is a story of what contributed to her legend the most—her music; and it is told by the people—some two hundred strong—who were there, including this writer.

                                                    Shaun Considine

Part 1

Chapter 1

"Singing is no big deal. It's only wind and noise. I open my mouth and the sound comes out."

THE BEGINNING

It began in a gay bar, The Lion, on Ninth Street in Greenwich Village, New York. In June of 1960, to stimulate business for the slow summer months ahead, talent concerts were held each Thursday night. Four acts were chosen to perform, and the winner received fifteen dollars, a week's booking, and all the food and drink they could consume. It was the food that attracted Barbra Streisand· "In those days I could be had for a baked potato," she said in later years.

Singing in itself was no big deal to the eighteen-year-old. "It's only wind and noise," she claimed. "I open my mouth and the sound comes out." As a baby in Brooklyn she could sing before she could walk. She would hear a song on the radio and halfway through she could sing along. Not the words, but all the melody, in perfect pitch. Later, as a kid, she would sit on the stoop of her apartment house and sing with her friends. She took the lead and they sang the ooo-wahs on songs like "Have You Heard" and "Why Don't You Believe Me?," current hits by Joni James. Joni, who didn't have much of a voice, but who had this winsome, heartbreaking quality, was Barbra's favorite singer. At age ten she took the BMT subway to Manhattan, to visit Joni's record company, MGM, and to give them the first chance of discovering her. "I wore a blue dress from Abraham and Strauss, with white collar and cuffs," said Barbra. "I sang 'Have You Heard?' behind a glass booth. I felt sure they'd want me, but they just said thank you and that was it."

After that she stopped singing in public, except at school, in the choral group; but she was never given solos. "They never asked me. They had this other girl, an opera singer. She was going to be a big star, they said, so they gave her all the solos."

After high school Barbra moved to Manhattan to pursue an acting career. Her role models were Sarah Bernhardt, Eleanora Duse, and Anna Magnani. Determined to follow in their hallowed footsteps, she took acting lessons, not from one but three different teachers. She was in a hurry, you see. So much to learn and so much to do. Yet no one would give her a break. When she read in class, or auditioned at open calls, she was laughed at or ignored. "They had the power to treat me like an animal, as so much dirt," she said. Yet when she opened her mouth to sing, everyone listened. "I sang for one friend, and then another, and they'd go: 'Hey, Barbra, you sing real good.' And I'd say, 'Yeah, but that's *only* singing,' because in those days I thought to be called a singer was demeaning, that it was a second-class profession." In those days she was also broke. Her unemployment insurance had run out. "And my landlord had evicted me, so I thought, Okay, if I can get a job singing, I'll take it. I'll use it to open a few doors, then once inside I'll show them the real me. I'll act their ----- off."

Her competition that first night at The Lion, was a comic, an opera singer, and a baritone who performed the bouncy, familiar score from *Oklahoma!*. For her debut Barbra sang the subdued, lesser-known ballad "A Sleepin' Bee," from *House of Flowers*. By the second couplet she had stilled the room, and with the release of the final note from the song she was treated to her first ovation; and to her first victory.

After The Lion, Barbra moved one block over, to the Bon Soir on West Eighth Street—described by Phyllis Diller as "an underground oven *so* sophisticated, a nine-year-old boy came in the other night, and when he left he was thirty-eight." Barbra was second on the bill but drew the most attention from the cabaret-circuit set, and from the newspaper reviewers. Lavish praise was bestowed on her crystalline voice, her vintage wardrobe, and her natural, outrageous, spontaneous personality. That spontaneity, however, was viewed by some as being carefully calculated. A friend and fellow struggling actor, Dustin Hoffman, recalled his impressions of Streisand at this time. "We went to the same acting studio," said Dustin. "I got a scholarship by cleaning toilets, and Barbra used to baby-sit for the teachers. Then I saw her perform. . . . She was sitting on a stool, and before she sang her first song she took a wad of chewing gum out of her mouth and put it under the seat. I thought: 'What a smart girl.' It was a seemingly natural act but it had a method to its madness. It was quite provoking, and suddenly, out of this amiable anteater, came this *magic.*" She had artistry *and* the cunning of a heavyweight champion, Hoffman believed. "She did what a fighter does . . . she was feinting with her left when she put the gum under the seat. Then she knocked you out with her right when she sang."

From June to April of 1961 Streisand's star continued to rise. She was booked into clubs in Detroit and St. Louis, and she appeared on television guesting with Joe Franklin and Jack Paar. She also returned for three additional runs at the Bon Soir. But then the momentum stopped. In April of 1961, after finishing a seven-week run at the club, she learned she was out of a job, with no future bookings. A singer without a showcase, she was now one of the many up-and-coming young talents—including Joan Rivers, Woody Allen, and Lily Tomlin—who hustled for jobs at the Duplex or at Upstairs at the Downstairs. "Barbra was living at the Hotel Earle on Waverly Place, and I was playing at a club called Gatsby's on West Forty-eighth street," said pianist Neil Wolfe. "From time to time she used to come in and perform. She wasn't allowed to stand up and sing, so she would sit by me on the piano bench and we'd do four or five numbers together. Everyone loved her, but the owner would never feed her. He'd give her ten or twenty dollars, but he didn't want to give her dinner. That always made her angry."

"Picture a bunch of birds," said Dustin Hoffman. "There is the mother bird with the worm, and a bunch of baby birds with their mouths open, and somehow there's one straining more than the others to get that worm from the mother. Well, that would be Barbra."

In June of 1961 Barbra met a man who would supply the sustenance, energy, and encouragement to launch her career successfully and keep it in orbit for fifteen years. His name was Marty Erlichman, and he became her personal manager.

Erlichman was born in The Bronx and had worked as a time-log clerk at CBS Radio in the late fifties. When the folk music boom began in the early sixties, he and partner Lenny Rosenfeld managed blues singer Josh White and the Irish folk group the Clancy Brothers. "Marty discovered us," said Tommy Makem, a member of the group. "He was very constructive in knowing what should and shouldn't be. When we signed with him he locked us up in a rehearsal hall for three days. He made us sing all the songs we knew, and bits of poetry, all kinds of things. He would listen and say, 'That's good; that's too local; don't do it.' We recited a part of *Finnegans Wake* for him and he said, 'I like that. I don't know what it means, but I like it.' He had a good ear and a good visual sense too. It was his idea that we wear the white Irish sweaters onstage. We had them on in rehearsals, and he said, 'That's the look I want for you; the white sweaters, black pants, and black shoes.' And that kind of became our trademark."

Erlichman also had his eye out for new clients. He yearned for "the big one," the one superperformer who would put him in the league of star producers like George Scheck, who managed Connie Francis, and Colonel Tom Parker, who managed Elvis Presley. In June of 1961 Erlichman found his future in Barbra Streisand. Watching her rehearse for a local TV show he got "chills." "She was the most incredible performer I had ever seen, the wonder of my generation."

Barbra liked Marty too. "He told me I didn't have to change my name, my nose, nothing. I would become a big star just the way I was." He also offered to manage her on a nonformal deal without a contract, and he arranged for her to make an impromptu appearance at The Blue Angel, a chic supper-club on Manhattan's Upper East Side. "We were headlining at the club when Marty asked us if we'd mind cutting ten or fifteen minutes from our act so Barbra could sing a few songs," said Tommy Makem. "We were glad to. The musical director was Peter Matz. He had a trio in the room, and Bobby Short played in the lounge. When Barbra went on I could see she had something special. She was very good fun off-stage, too, very New Yorkese. At one point, between sets, I said to her, 'Well, I'm going upstairs to change my pants.' She said, 'Well, I'm not going to change mine.' I said, 'You're not?' 'No,' she said, and with that she lifted up her skirt and she was wearing pantaloons underneath—long, fire-engine-red pantaloons. She did it for the devilment."

Through the Clancy Brothers, Marty Erlichman had already established a good working relationship with their record label, Columbia. Autonomous from its corporate parent, the CBS Broadcasting System, the record label at that time was located at 799 Seventh Avenue, between Fiftieth and Fifty-first streets. The six-story building was old. Paint peeled off the inner walls; the pipes burst in the winter; and in the summer the toilets backed up and flooded the side hallways. Each floor was crammed with expanding staff, files, and furniture. Located in the basement were the mailroom, the record archives, and the purchasing department. On the top floors were the recording studios, and in between were the offices of the Art Department, A&R (Artists and Repertoire), Sales and Promotion, the Columbia Record Club, and Epic Records (the future home of Michael Jackson, but then a minor subsidiary label, set up to absorb Columbia's rock 'n' roll and rhythm and blues rejects). On the fourth floor, with its own separate reception area, was the office of Goddard Lieberson, the president of the entire company. Lieberson, who was born in England but educated in the United States, was an astute executive with an artist's ear and eye. A teacher, writer, and composer, he had begun in the classical division of the company, but it was his later expertise in the production of Columbia's Broadway Original Cast Recordings including *South Pacific, Camelot, The Sound of Music,* and *My Fair Lady*—that established his popular reputation. His nickname in the industry was "God," and his power, on vinyl, was equally omnipotent. He gambled on the new, the untried; and it was this daring that led Streisand's manager to believe that the executive would be eager to sign his new client.

Marty Erlichman and Goddard Lieberson were direct opposites in style and decorum. Lieberson was tall, distinguished, witty, and partial to pinstriped suits and pink shirts. Erlichman was short, overweight, gruff in manner, and his single suit of clothes looked as if it also served as pajamas at night. Barbra fussed over his health, but not for his appearance. How could she? Her own in those days was far from the pages of *Vogue* or *Harper's Bazaar.* At the time of her introduction to Goddard she was in the final stages of her so-called "kook phase." She wore a monkey-fur coat, a red velvet hat, full stage makeup, and her antique satin shoes which had been dyed purple, stained her feet, and company carpets, when it rained. "She made an *indelible* impression," said Lieberson. "I thought the meeting was a joke, set up by Marty. I kept waiting for the punch line."

Marty was not joking. As Barbra sat silently by his side, he ran through her credits for Goddard. He read her reviews and played a tape of her singing at the Bon Soir. "Listen to the applause," Erlichman exclaimed after each number. "They loved her. They gave her standing ovations, flowers, the works." Goddard listened politely, and Marty, knowing the man, and the haunting aftereffects of his client, did not push for an immediate decision. "Keep the tapes for a while," he urged Lieberson. "She's special. She needs close attention. Listen to her when the phones ain't ringing."

Goddard agreed to hold on to the tapes and promised an early answer. It came ten days later. He was not enthralled. Barbra had a legitimate voice, he felt, but it was best suited for the stage, not for popular records. "That's what everybody told us," said Erlichman, "she wasn't Annette Funicello or Connie Francis. They couldn't see that Barbra was going to break the mold for pop singers."

In August of 1961 Erlichman arranged for Barbra to audition for *Another Evening with Harry Stoones,* a revue due to open at the Gramercy Arts Theater on East Twenty-seventh Street. The director of the revue, Glenn Jordan, had seen Barbra before, reading a scene from *Separate Tables,* at Curt Conway's acting studio the previous year. He was not impressed with her acting. But at the audition when she sang "A Sleepin' Bee" and "I Stayed Too Long At The Fair," he found her "astonishing, absolutely extraordinary. I still remember that moment of hearing her for the first time—the absolute silence in the theater while this girl mesmerized us with the sound of her voice—absolutely unique. You didn't have to be smart to realize how good she was."

"She opened her mouth to sing and knocked us off our chairs," said the musical director, Abba Bogin. "We talked with her and she was genuinely funny and kooky."

But there was no part for Streisand in *Harry Stoones.* Her strong point was singing. She was weak on acting. Other performers were auditioned, until several weeks later the director announced he couldn't get "that singer" out of his mind. He spoke to the writer and they decided she was too good to let go. They would make a part for her. "And that's what we did," said Jordan. "We juggled the existing material around, recast it—since it was a revue we could do that—and made a part for her."

Streisand was marvelous in every performance, but a nightmare in rehearsals, Abba Bogin recalled. "She would be late five out of six days. She seemed to be spaced out half the time. She had definite ideas of her own as to how lines should be read, how songs should be sung, and how the music should be performed."

"When she did a song she seldom did it the same way twice," said Jordan, "and she took great idiosyncratic liberties with the tempo and phrasing. Barbra would say to Abba, 'Now, listen, at bar such and such, I'll be with you, but I have to get there however I want, and it's going to be different every time. But don't worry about it, because I'll be there.' And that was true."

"Her instincts were almost always right," Bogin agreed, "and often her way was the funniest, and most theatrical, and we went along with it."

On the night of October 21, 1961, *Another Evening with Harry Stoones* had its official opening. During the performance Streisand's songs and comedy sketches received the loudest applause, but the audience was hard pressed to find her name in the opening night's program. Through an error it was billed last and in type smaller than that of the rest of the cast. She didn't complain, but Marty Erlichman howled. Yet nothing could be done. New programs would not be printed, because *Harry Stoones* opened and closed the same night. "The newspaper reviewers killed the show," said Glenn Jordan. "A week later the magazine notices were raves, but by then we had closed and gone on to other things."

After *Harry Stoones,* Streisand auditioned for *New Faces of 1962* but that role went to Marian Mercer. She also auditioned for *Bravo Giovanni* and lost that part to Michelle Lee. Then in late November, the day after Thanksgiving, she walked on stage at the 55th Street Theater to try out for a new musical entitled *I Can Get It for You Wholesale.* "That was my first contact with Barbra," said the show's director, Arthur Laurents. "She walked on cold. We didn't know who she was. She started to sing and we all sat up in our seats. We had never heard anything like that. There was no part in the show for her. The role of Miss Marmelstein was for a fifty-year-old woman, and it was small. There weren't many lines. The woman was supposed to be unmarried, a spinster. I was determined to get her into the show, and when I did I kept giving her more and more musical stuff to do."

Laurents also called Goddard Lieberson at Columbia Records and urged him to reconsider signing Streisand to a contract. "Barbra and I knew nothing about that call," said Marty Erlichman. "Goddard contacted me and asked if I had placed her with another label. I said no, and he asked if I'd bring her by again. This time he wanted to put her into a studio and record her. He wanted to hear how she sounded professionally taped. Part of the deal I made with him is that we'd get to keep those tapes. And we weren't gonna sit forever for his decision. We'd record on a Friday, and he'd get back to us on Monday. I agreed. So we went up there—me, Barbra, and her accompanist, Peter Daniels."

"That second audition was held at Studio B, at 799 Seventh Avenue," said Goddard Lieberson. "Barbra arrived looking very odd indeed. She was dressed in a piano shawl, or maybe it was a piano."

Also sitting in for the audition was veteran producer John Hammond. "Goddard called and asked if I would listen with him," said Hammond. "She sang four or five songs for us, and later he asked me what I thought of her. I said, 'It's a wonderful voice, but she's coming on too young and too soon.' " He laughed. "Famous last words. But they were true. She was young and terribly brash. And Goddard said, 'Well, you're wrong. She is going to be the biggest star there is.' "

Lieberson, despite his prognostication, did not offer a recording contract to Streisand after that second audition. He called Erlichman the following Monday and told him that, regrettably, he was passing once more. Her appeal was too limited for records, he felt. "She was too eccentric," he said later. "She was too—the word they used then—far out."

"Goddard was a cultivated man," said Columbia Records publicist Peter Reilly. "He was very attracted to bright lights and famous names. He was a part of New York's Jewish aristocracy. He moved with the Stravinskys, the Leonard Bernsteins, the Moss Harts." And here was this brash kid from Brooklyn with the chewing gum and the yenta-like jokes and mannerisms. "She embarrassed Lieberson and his group. They didn't know it was an act with Barbra. To her it was all theater. Underneath she was Consuelo Vanderbilt, before she became the Duchess of Marlboro."

Goddard also felt threatened by Barbra," Reilly claimed. "She was a part of a generation that would soon leave him behind. She was also too strong for him. She reminded him of someone else. Of Fanny Brice. You see, years earlier he had been one of Fanny's young men."

"He was Mr. L. in her memoirs," Marty Erlichman confirmed.

"He saw many parallels between the two women," said another source, "and he was very fond of Barbra. But he preferred to keep her at a distance. It was easier for him that way. Perhaps he refused to see her future because of his past."

On April 1, 1962, Streisand and Lieberson met for the third time. But not for an audition. Barbra was at Columbia's Thirtieth Street studio to make her recording debut, on the cast LP of *I Can Get It for You Wholesale*. She was not the star of the show, but she had received the best reviews, and she behaved accordingly. Arriving late at the Sunday-morning session, she made an immediate impression on the assembled staff. While the other female cast members wore dresses, skirts, and high heels, Streisand wore dungarees, a ratty old sweater, and dirty white sneakers. She came in an hour after her scheduled call, and she went straight for Lieberson. "Goddard! Goddard!," she said. "I got a great idea for the album." She was only on a few cuts of the album, but she was ready to supervise the entire session.

"Goddard was a true gentleman," said musical director Lehman Engel. "He and I worked on a number of albums, and I was looking forward to see how he would handle Barbra. Oh, she could drive you nuts at times. David Merrick almost fired her from *Wholesale* during the tryouts, but Arthur Laurents interceded."

Recording her one solo in the show, "Miss Marmelstein," Barbra stopped midway. She didn't like the orchestration, she declared. "Goddard could have spoken to her over the intercom," said Lehman. "Instead he left the control room and walked over to her. He put his arm around her shoulders and gently led her away, to the sidelines. Out of earshot of the orchestra and the rest of the cast he spoke to her. I don't know what he said to her, but when she came back she sang the song as it was charted, straight through, in one amazing take."

According to legend, because of Streisand's outstanding performance on the *Wholesale* LP, and a second appearance on another Columbia album, *Pins and Needles,* she was immediately signed to a long-term contract by the label. This was not true. No contract was offered until four months later, and then it was tendered begrudgingly.

THE LONG WAIT

Throughout the summer of 1962 the future star continued to play a secondary role on Broadway. Her salary in *Wholesale* was raised to two hundred dollars a week. She was now making as much as the principals, but she was *bored.* Playing the same part eight times a week "was the pits." She tried to relieve the monotony of Xerox performances by adding new lines, new inflections, new tempos, to the songs, but the management objected. ("She altered 'Miss Marmelstein' in spite of us," said Engel, "and her nightly ovation stopped cold.") She asked to switch roles with the ingenue (Marilyn Cooper), the chorine (Sheree North), even the mother (Lillian Roth)—not permanently, just for a turn or two—but she was refused. And then there was the matter of her chewing gum.

"There was this stage manager," said Barbra. "She kept picking on me. She'd tell me not to chew gum onstage. So I'd provoke her. I'd stick it up in the roof of my mouth and go out there and chew. It bothered me because . . . listen, what does gum in your mouth matter if you're doing your job? And even if it did, maybe *that* character would chew gum. Sometimes gum is right. It's a defiance. Like, I'll always say, 'I'm not gonna do nothing.' And somebody will say, 'You mean *anything.*' And I'll say, 'No, I mean *nothing. I'm not gonna do nothing.*' "

For Barbra, *Wholesale* had only one redeeming asset—Elliott Gould, the six-foot-two droll but amiable leading man from Bensonhurst, Brooklyn. Gould had been acting since the age of eight. He was in the chorus of *Say, Darling* and *Irma La Douce* and was signed for *Wholesale* after Gene Kelly and Steve Lawrence turned down the role of the antihero, Harry Bogen. Described as "a doltish rascal" and "a big bear of a man," Elliott first spotted Streisand at the open auditions for Miss Marmelstein. He called her that night, said, "You were great," and then hung up.

"He did crazy things," said Barbra. "I liked him; he wasn't normal."

Encouraged by director Arthur Laurents and star Sheree North, the romance between the pair blossomed during the show's tryouts. Elliott had hitherto been known as a "chorus cocksman" and a gambler who spent Saturday night under the Fifty-ninth Street Bridge shooting dice. Soon Barbra got him to give up the gambling, and the chorus girls. She also persuaded him to move in with her. His reluctance had less to do with emotional commitment than with the smell of fish that pervaded her apartment.

"I lived over this fish restaurant on Third Avenue," she recalled. "The whole place stunk, but I didn't care. The place was cheap, and for the first time in my life I had my own apartment."

"The only window looked out on a black brick wall," said Elliott. "We used to eat on a sewing machine in the living room because a big rat named Oscar lived in the kitchen."

The couple fought frequently, alone and in front of company, including photographer Don Hunstein. "I was supposed to photograph Barbra in the hallway of her tenement. We took the photographs and afterwards she and Elliott and I went down the street to a Chinese restaurant. They were at odds with each other and fought throughout the whole meal. I never could figure out what they were arguing about, but it was pretty heavy shouting."

A close friend of Barbra's, Bob Schulenberg, recalled another dispute between the couple. One night after he and director Paul Bartel saw *Wholesale,* they went backstage to pay their respects. "Apparently she and Elliott were fighting," said Schulenberg. "She claimed he was flat on one of the last notes he hit in the show. She was really furious about that, because as regards voices hers was the gift to the world and around her people weren't supposed to ever make a mistake. So she wouldn't speak to him. He kept walking past her dressing room, calling out to the chorus girls, 'Well, Cindy or Mindy, are you going to be there later? Will I see you?' He was trying to make Barbra jealous, but she kept talking to us and taking off her makeup, ignoring him. Later the three of us went out to eat, without Elliott. After the meal we walked her home to her apartment over Oscar's on Third Avenue. We went upstairs with her, to talk some more and have coffee. She opened the door and there he was, sitting in front of the door, under a red spotlight. He was obviously angry. He adored her, but he had so little sense of himself. Barbra took care of him. She loved him. But a large part of that had to do with *her* position. For the first time in her life she had power over a man."

In July, Barbra worked a double shift, appearing in *Wholesale* each evening, and at The Blue Angel at midnight, with a new act staged by Arthur Laurents. "I introduced her to 'Down With Love,' which was a takeoff of all those love medleys," said Laurents. "The act was really a matter of not doing for Barbra. I believed, then and now, that less is more. Working on the show if you stand very still, and then move your hand, it means something. But in those days she moved her hands a lot. You know, she loved those fingernails."

That summer Streisand worked sporadically on weekends at Bill Hahn's resort hotel in Connecticut. She was on the bill with a group called The Four Young Men from Montana. Dick Riddle, one of the four young men, recalled those weekend excursions to the country. "We used to pick her up outside her apartment on the Upper East Side. She always had people with her: her mother, her kid sister, or Elliott. She also carried a lot of luggage, and everything she had smelled of fish."

They drove to Connecticut in a station wagon, with the men sitting in the front and the ladies in the second seat. "Barbra always sat in the rear jump-seat, with her back to everyone," said Riddle. "She worked on crosswords or played with puzzles. She was like a little girl. When Elliott was with her they sat back there holding hands and giggling like two teenagers. When her mother came along she would open these shopping bags, filled with food and aspirin. She gave you aspirin for everything. It always seemed liked it was raining. We'd get lost on the roads, wandering off on side streets. So at her mother's instigation we'd play twenty questions. Then Barbra would crawl over the backseat and come in the middle and insist on playing. When it was her turn, she'd always ask some dumb question. It had nothing to do with what was already asked. Eventually we'd tell her she couldn't play anymore, and she'd go back to the backseat, where she would yell things out at us, just to screw the whole thing up. Her mother would tell her to be quiet and open the window to air her out."

At the resort Barbra was the girl singer. "The comic came first," said Riddle. "His name was always Georgie or Jackie—there were a lot of those around, I recall. Then came Barbra. Everybody loved her, mainly because it was a Jewish sort of place. She was totally at ease with them. She'd giggle and laugh and they got everything. She had a tremendous stage presence. When she came on she was a different person. She had a sense of organization, a vocabulary; she was calm. At the end of the show Bill Hahn always made us get together to sing a closing number. He was like the MC. Beforehand we'd go down to this guesthouse, where he gave us the new closing song; something like 'On The Street Where You Live.' And Barbra would always louse it up. She would never practice. She'd stall by telling you a joke, and that was screwed up too. It never had a punch line. So consequently when we got onstage to do that last number, nobody knew what to do. So we'd tell her, 'You take the melody, and we'll harmonize around you.' So that's what we did, and she always stole the show. I'm not sure if she planned it that way. She thrived on confusion, on creating havoc for everyone else, so when she got onstage she was calm and ready to take over the show."

"She loved to play games, and sometimes they could be quite cruel," said Elly Stone, her understudy in *I Can Get It for You Wholesale*. "We had both auditioned for the role of Miss Marmelstein. It was between Barbra and me, and I hoped I wouldn't get it. I didn't like the show, I thought it was anti-Semitic. But I was as poor as a churchmouse in those days, and I didn't feel I had the right to turn anything down. But then Barbra was chosen, and later I was hired to understudy. When I saw her in the role I was amazed. Whereas I didn't much like her personally, when I watched her onstage I found myself adoring her; professionally I thought she was a genius. Offstage we weren't too friendly. I was really quite neutral, until one night, when I was scheduled to do a concert down at Cooper Union. I had told the producers of *Wholesale* about this date before they hired me to understudy. Everything looked okay until the morning of the show and Barbra called in sick, which meant I'd have to go on that night for her in *Wholesale*. All day we got reports from Elliott about her health. *I* was a wreck. The concert was very important to me, but if I didn't understudy for Barbra, I would be kicked out of Equity. At the half hour we found out she was okay. She came to the theater and we learned it was all a joke. She was never sick. This was one of her little games, and Elliott was a co-conspirator. Years afterwards he apologized to a friend of mine for the incident. He said Barbra did that a lot with him, and eventually it broke up their marriage. It made me physically ill. I did the concert, but I went on with the runs."

Throughout the summer of 1962 Streisand's manager continued to seek a contract for his client with Columbia Records. In June, after the third rebuff from Goddard Lieberson, Marty Erlichman began to concentrate on the executive staff below him. "He was promoting her day and night," said Peter Reilly. "He was always in the Ho-Ho (a Chinese bar and restaurant adjacent to the lobby of the record company), buying everyone drinks and telling them of Barbra's latest exploits."

Erlichman's main target was David Kapralik, an elfish and kinetic ex–circus performer, who was the director of Columbia's A&R department.

"Marty tried every which way to get David interested in Barbra," said Brett Bacchus, Kapralik's secretary. "He said he'd make me Barbra's road manager if I got David to go see her at the Bon Soir."

Kapralik, minus Erlichman, eventually discovered Streisand on his own time. On the night of May 29 he was at home watching the Garry Moore TV show when she appeared. She performed a standard that would become synonymous with her name. The song was "Happy Days Are Here Again." It had come to her attention through Ken Welch, the writer of special material for the Garry Moore hour. "My wife Mitzi saw Barbra first," said Welch. "She caught her down in the Village and came back saying she was the find of the century. Mitzi urged the talent people on the show to hire Barbra. Eventually they did.

"The format in those days was to book a star star, and a young up-and-coming talent. In this case the star was Robert Goulet, and the newcomer was Barbra."

The end of each show featured a "Wonderful Year" segment, which contained skits, dance numbers, and songs from one particular year. "There was a production finale already chosen for Goulet," said Welch. "The song was a Gershwin tune called "That Certain Thing," and the year it was associated with was 1929. It wasn't a very happy year because of the Wall Street crash, but I looked in the *Variety Cavalcade* and a song leaped out at me. It was "Happy Days Are Here Again." And I thought, wouldn't it be fun to do a dramatic version of that song? To put Barbra in a bar, coming into a speakeasy, very well dressed, with lots of jewelry on, and she's obviously lost everything in the crash. She sits down and orders champagne, but she has no money, so she pays for it by dropping her diamond earrings on the waiter's tray.

"When Barbra and Marty came in for the show I suggested it to them. Barbra had never heard of the song before. So I played it for her. 'Fine,' she said, 'do whatever you want to do.' So that night I wrote a special verse for the song. I called it 'Happy Champagne.' It set up the whole situation with her and the waiter, and it led into 'Happy Days.' The waiter, incidentally, was played by Bob Harris, who is the father of actor Ed Harris."

At rehearsals the next day Ken Welch explained the scene, then played the new verse and song for Barbra. "She cried," he said. "She loved it, learned it, and we scored it."

Standing in the wings when Barbra taped the song was Carol Burnett. She recalled her reaction: "When I heard that voice, I thought, That has got to be one of the most beautiful gifts God gave anyone."

"I remember I was at home watching the show when she came on," said David Kapralik. "And the hairs began to rise on the back of my neck. I was transfixed by this singer. Then I made the connection. This was the girl Marty was raving about. I found out she was down at the Blue Angel. I went there, to see her in person, to find out if she could set off the same electricity. She could, and she did. She absolutely destroyed me. No one since Edith Piaf affected me so. She had an *auteur,* a primal force about her. She went through the full spectrum of emotions. She put me in that special place between laughter and tears."

Kapralik, in his own words, became "a Streisand groupie," returning night after night to the Blue Angel, dragging friends and Columbia staff to witness this phenomenon. "I think I used to embarrass her," he said. "I always sat at a front table, and I laughed so hard at her jokes she would tell me to 'Stop it!' from the stage.

His enthusiasm, as hoped for, was relayed again to Goddard Lieberson. Streisand's name began to pop up regularly at company luncheons and executive staff meetings. Lieberson listened, Lieberson lingered. "He only moved," said a former associate, "when it favored *his* progression."

June passed, then July and August, and Barbra was still without a record label. She insisted that her manager talk to other companies. "We had some offers," said Erlichman. "I had a meeting with

Ahmet Ertegun of Atlantic Records. He wanted to sign her, but I told him his label was too small for Barbra. I still wanted Columbia."

In mid-September, in a final attempt to make a deal, Erlichman met with David Kapralik at the Ho-Ho bar. In conversation he casually mentioned that Alan Livingston, the president of Capitol Records, was coming in from L.A. that week to see and sign Barbra. Kapralik relayed this news once more to Lieberson, who at that moment was involved with litigation from the FTC against Columbia's record club. When apprised of Capitol's interest in Streisand, Lieberson parried, then asked Kapralik to make a decision.

"Should we sign her?" Goddard questioned.

"Yes," Kapralik replied.

"Then do it. But make the terms modest, and keep me out of the negotiations."

Chapter 2

THE CONTRACT

Over the decades from the beginning of musical recording, contracts with performers have changed considerably. In the beginning a flat fee—without royalties—was paid, usually in cash, at the actual sessions. In 1923 blues legend Bessie Smith received $125 for each *usable* side she recorded for Columbia (then the American Record Company). Her records eventually sold more than five million copies, but Bessie did not share in the riches. She died penniless in 1937 from injuries sustained in a car crash, and for thirty-three years afterward she lay buried in Philadelphia in an unmarked grave, until singer Janis Joplin paid for a tombstone. Columbia Records supplied the inscription on the stone, and they publicized its unveiling to coincide with their third reissue of her catalogue.

"In the thirties and forties it was considered an honor to be affiliated with a record label," said big-band singer Helen Forrest. "When your records were played on the radio, you got bookings in clubs and ballrooms. That's where the real money was—we were told. No one dreamed or mentioned that the sides we recorded for Columbia would be repackaged and reissued again and again—without our permission and, naturally, without pay."

Streisand's 1962 contract with Columbia gave her a beginner's royalty of five percent against ninety-eight percent of records sold.

This was to be paid after all recording costs were recouped. The length of the contract was also standard: five years, which in reality meant one year guaranteed, with four annual options to be renewed at Columbia's discretion. "We got a cash advance," said Erlichman. "It was small—twenty thousand dollars, I believe. We weren't interested in big front money. We waived that for other considerations, such as creative control, no coupling, and the right to choose her own material."

"I don't recall any problem with Barbra's request to choose her own songs," said David Kapralik. "We realized she had created a very successful nightclub career with material of her own. So we gave her that consent for records."

On October 1, 1962, the day of the contract signing, Barbra fussed over her appearance. She washed her hair and wore a dress, with pearls. In Lieberson's office she posed for the Columbia photographer. She sat with pen in hand at his desk, while Goddard stood on her right and Kapralik on her left. (When her star ascended he would no longer be mentioned or featured in the publicity pictures.)

"I still have that picture," said Kapralik. "Barbra has a wonderful cocky grin on her face. It's as if she were saying, 'You bastards, you made me wait a long time for this moment. Now I'm in and soon you're going to be waiting on me.'"

"She never forgot that they kept her dangling," said Bob Mersey. "And she paid them back, measure for measure."

After her contract was signed, Columbia looked among its staff for a producer to supervise her first recording sessions. Mitch Miller, who was responsible for a string of hits by Frank Sinatra, Rosemary Clooney, and Tony Bennett, among others, was approached to work with Streisand and turned the assignment down. "I had no desire to work with the lady," he said. "In those days we were making hit singles in forty minutes. We produced albums, beautiful historic albums by Percy Faith, and the early Johnny Mathis, in nine hours. To go beyond that amount of studio time meant we were amateurs. Barbra had an extraordinary talent, but a huge ego. I've always said that she had the ability to give you her life history in the word *the*. She needed special handling. She would have taken too much time away from the other artists, who were very, very productive."

Other staff producers balked at working with Barbra. "No one would go near her," said promotion manager Jim Brown. "They said she was another Judy Garland; that she'd appeal only to gays."

Eventually Mike Berniker, a twenty-four-year-old A&R producer, agreed to take the job. "I don't know why I was chosen," said Berniker. "David used to send me down to the Bon Soir to see her perform. I thought she was good, but I didn't know what I could do for her. I met with Marty, then with Barbra. I sent her a copy of a Tammy Grimes album I had just done. She listened to the album and said, 'Yeah, let's go.' "

On October sixteenth Barbra made her solo recording debut at Columbia's Thirtieth Street studio. "She was very nervous," remembers Berniker. "She was not used to working with a large orchestra—only trios—and we had something like thirty musicians assembled on the floor. Barbra kept looking out at them from the control room. 'I can't go out there,' she said. 'Let's stall them.' She was shaking. I had to take her by the hand and lead her onto the floor."

"Berniker is full of ----," said Peter Daniels, her accompanist. "Sure there was some degree of nervousness, but shaking? I think she was putting him on."

The session was for a single release. "Happy Days Are Here Again" and "When The Sun Comes Out" were two of four sides recorded. The arrangements and the orchestra were conducted by George Williams.

Long after the musicians were dismissed, Barbra remained in the studio listening to the playback of her performance. "It was the magic of the first time," said Berniker. "The elements were perfect . . . her voice, the arrangements . . . that was an exciting time for both of us."

Two weeks later the single was scheduled for release. Prior to shipment it was played at the company's weekly singles meeting. These meetings were classic, an adult parody of *American Bandstand*'s rate-the-record time. Each Tuesday morning key Columbia personnel gathered in the sixth-floor studio-conference room at 799 Seventh Avenue. Sitting at one side of the table were the executive sales staff, dressed in conservative suits and crew cuts. On the other side the promotional staff, hip and slick in Continental-cut mohair or sharkskin suits, with Slim-Jim ties, sat primed for perpetual motion. Their jobs depended on the enthusiasm they showed at these meetings. Ambidextrous hipsters, caught by "the beat," they snapped their fingers, shook their shoulders, and rolled their heads in rhythmic assessment of the records played. "Out of sight," "dynamite side," and "number one with a bullet" were some of their tabulated judgments. ("Lousy," "a bowwow," and "a stiff" were reviews seldom voiced until after the meeting had adjourned.)

The supreme, the final judgment at these meetings always came from the heavyset, florid-faced gentleman, Bill Gallagher, who sat at the head of the table. Since Goddard Lieberson (who claimed he was not eligible for these rituals, since he was unable to click his fingers and listen to music at the same time) was frequently absent, his place was claimed by Gallagher, the chief of Sales, who was personable, powerful, a giant in the record industry. In product placement and pricing Gallagher made the rules—and broke them when it suited his moves. He had set up Columbia's independent sales offices across the country. Within this network he had acquired friends and allies—loyal co-workers. He granted favors— lavish salaries, bonuses, incentives. Nothing was too good for a Gallagher man. In return he expected top performance, permanent fidelity, and total obeisance.

"He was called the Pope," said Clive Davis. "He had a Vatican-like following."

"They were the Irish mafia—a tight group," said Marty Erlichman.

Gallagher's taste in music was equally catholic. He liked talented, attractive, "pliable" singers—preferably white. The Brothers Four, Anita Bryant, and Robert Goulet were some of his current pets. With his blessing, and backing, they would go far. Acutely ambitious, he had plans for the future, big plans for himself and Columbia, plans that did not include Barbra Streisand or her ilk.

At that October Tuesday singles meeting, Barbra's "Happy Days Are Here Again" was one of nine songs introduced. The reaction from the group was laudatory (but second in yahoos to "Sleepin' At The Foot Of The Bed," the new country-and-western single from Anita Bryant). Bill Gallagher complimented Mike Berniker on his producing skills and predicted "Happy Days" would make a lot of noise in the market. However, the subsequent production order, which was based on future sales, contradicted his praises. Only five hundred copies of the single were to be pressed, Sales told Columbia's Manufacturing Department, and those were to be shipped to the New York market only. Furthermore, the single was *not* to be sent to any radio stations. "The reasons were clear. They did not want Barbra to succeed," said John Kurland. "She did not fit the company's wholesome image. They called her and Bob Dylan 'the two the fags and radicals brought in.' They ridiculed Barbra constantly. 'Why doesn't someone give her a bath, wash her hair, buy her a dress?' That was the welcome she got from Sales."

Despite the suppression, copies of "Happy Days Are Here Again" made it to various radio stations. Serviced by A&R, and publicity, the disc jockeys in New York, Philadelphia, Baltimore, and San Francisco began to play the record. But without a backup stock in stores the record died, as planned.*

Unaware of any resistance, and still anxious to launch his client, Marty Erlichman insisted that a second Streisand single follow as soon as possible. He was told that Barbra needed a more commercial sound, a gimmick, a trend topper. The charts were perused Suggestions were made. Name songs such as "Bobby's Girl" and "Johnny Get Angry" were big with girl singers. And then there was this brand-new dance called the bossa nova. It was going to be bigger than the twist or the Watusi. There was a song available, a bossa nova tune by Barry Mann and Cynthia Weill. Barbra should do it. Barbra refused. "I don't do dance records," she instructed. "People sit or stand when I sing."

Oddly enough, Streisand's next single came from Sales VP Bill Gallagher. Watching Perry Como's weekly TV show, he heard a cast member sing a ballad entitled "My Coloring Book." The following morning Gallagher called David Kapralik and suggested he contact the publisher and get a lead sheet and demo. Kapralik complied. He played the Kander and Ebb song, liked it, and submitted it to Streisand. She flipped. It had pathos, tragedy, despair. It was a miniature Greek play, she declared, and that was how she

---

* Upon the success of her first album the single would be rereleased. A year later it earned Barbra a Grammy for Best Vocal Performance.

intended to interpret it. Like Medea, proclaiming the death of her children: "Those are the hands that *held* them, that *touched* them . . . color them *gone!*"

On November ninth Streisand recorded "My Coloring Book." The song was arranged and conducted by Bob Mersey. "It was a rush session," said Mersey. "We were doing an album with a group called the Arena Brass, which was a cover of "The Lonely Bull" by Herb Alpert. So we sneaked Barbra in on that session, for the one song, and I will never forget it. At that time she was still a rag-bag lady. It was a hot day; there was no air conditioning. She's standing in front of the fan, and the brass players were downwind from her, as they played they started to grimace 'cause the smell was so bad."

The session was done in forty-five minutes—in two takes. Ten days later the record was released. On November twenty-third it was reviewed in *Billboard,* but placed *fourth,* behind three other versions of the same song. Kitty Kallen had recorded it on RCA, Sandy Stewart on Colpix, and George Chakiris on Capitol.

"We got screwed," said Marty Erlichman. "Columbia never told us of the other versions."

Nor did they back Streisand with promotion or advertising.

"That week, instead of pushing Barbra," said Marty, "they took a full-page ad for some singer I never heard of. She had this cockamamy song called "Shake Me I Rattle, Squeeze Me I Cry." I was furious when I saw it. I went storming into the Ho-Ho and slapped the copy of *Billboard* on Gallagher's table. I told him I'd match Barbra's career against anybody's. I'd bet my year's commission that she'd outsell, outlast, any of the people he was pushing. Gallagher laughed and said, 'Marty, take it easy, take it easy. You'll give yourself a coronary.' "

Airplay on "Coloring Book" was initially divided among Kitty Kallen, Sandy Stewart, and Streisand. Kallen and Stewart eventually left Barbra behind. She sold a poor sixty thousand copies. It was embarrassing. And to put a hammer to the hurt, another femme performer, and a newcomer to Columbia, Eydie Gorme, was galloping up the charts with a hit called "Blame It on the Bossa Nova." That was the dance record Streisand had turned down. Not that she cared, or considered Gorme competition. Eydie Gorme? From The Bronx? They almost met in Columbia's lobby one day. Barbra was alone. Eydie was with an entourage; her musicians, and a singing group, the Trio Los Panchos. Chattering in Spanish, they piled into the elevator, crowding everyone with their bulk and instruments. With little room to stand, Barbra backed off. Fluent in Spanish, she waved the group on. "That's okay," she told them. "I'll catch the next boat."

Barbra was in awe of only one other female performer—Barbara Harris. "She spoke about her a lot," said Peter Reilly. "She used to say, 'Well Barbara Harris can act; Barbara Harris can sing; Barbara Harris can do everything.'" Harris would also do *On a Clear Day You Can See Forever* on Broadway, and Streisand would claim the part for the silver screen.

On December 8, 1962, *I Can Get It for You Wholesale* closed on Broadway. "I'm free! I'm free!" said Barbra, running offstage before the final curtain had fallen.

With time to spare, and some political ground to cover, Marty Erlichman suggested that Barbra pay a social call on Columbia. Their annual Christmas party was coming up. A little cheer, a little politics—how could it hurt? Barbra refused to go.

"She hated that kind of socializing," said Marty. "But I got her to do one of everything. One awards dinner; one sales convention; and one Christmas party."

She balked at bringing gifts, however. No presents. No tinsel-wrapped bottles of booze. No Cartier pens or Tiffany key chains (Robert Goulet's offering that year), or gold-plated tie clasps (Anita Bryant's Christmas token). Barbra brought nothing.

"She never kissed ass," said David Kapralik.

Or hands or cheeks. At the party Streisand barely managed a civil hello to the Columbia staff. While the other celebrity guests cheerily popped in and out of the executive offices, Barbra stood in the hallways, dourly staring at the gold records that lined the walls.

"I went up to her at one point," said a trainee in the International Department. "I had seen her at the Blue Angel and on TV, and I couldn't wait to tell her how much I loved her. 'You don't love me,' she said angrily. 'You don't even *know* me.' It took me years to get over that."

A second encounter came with a production secretary who was a Streisand admirer, a bona-fide fan. Usually quiet and somewhat timid, the secretary, perhaps emboldened by the holiday spirit, approached Barbra, told her she was wonderful, then asked if it was at all possible to drop into the studio upstairs someday to watch her record. Barbra gave a curt no, and turned away.

Later she would explain the rebuff. "I don't ask to drop by to watch her type, do I?"

"Barbra was shy," said Peter Reilly.

"Barbra could be arrogant; sometimes thankless," said David Kapralik.

"Thanks? I hate that word," said Streisand. "I do my job, they do theirs. We both get paid, so why should we thank one another?"

Chapter 3

THE FIRST ALBUM

By mid-October, Marty Erlichman and Barbra felt that the fastest way to establish her recording career was not with singles but with an album. That move was vehemently opposed by some at Columbia. An album? Twelve songs from that oddball? Who would buy it? Furthermore, this was against company policy. Standard grooming for novices was as follows: During the first cycle of their one-year-with-options contract, all rookies were expected to warm up in the singles field. They went to bat two or four or six times, depending on the sides agreed to. Then, consistent with their sales performance—a home run (a million seller), or bases steadily covered (Top 100 charts placement), they were granted permission to record an album.

But if said novices failed with singles, if they struck out repeatedly, they were benched and gradually ostracized from the team. Once applauded and stroked, their calls to company "friends" went unanswered. At renewal time their options were allowed to lapse, and their tapes and dreams went into cold dark storage in Columbia's master vaults in Iron Mountain, New York.

In the industry the rate of performers dropped versus those renewed was fifty to one. Many were called but few were chosen, and only the strong survived. Including Neil Diamond. He was on the Columbia 1963 roster. He recorded three sides; two were released, and failed. Then, despite his lobbying for political favor downstairs at the Ho-Ho, the company bar, where he had cocktail napkins printed with his name and the title of his latest single placed under the executive's drinks, Neil was dropped at renewal time. He would return to Columbia ten years later, sweetly avenged to the tune of four hundred thousand dollars guaranteed as an advance for each album.

Back to Barbra. It was proven she couldn't sell singles. So who said she could have an album? Her contract decreed it, the opposition learned.

"One of the considerations I insisted upon when Barbra signed with Columbia was that we'd get an album within the first six months," said Erlichman. "The wording was that twenty sides, which meant two LPs, had to be recorded *and* released at six-month intervals that first year. I wanted to be sure that in the event she was dropped by the label she was first given every opportunity to succeed—our way, not theirs."

Much has been said and written about Streisand's first album—how it catapulted her to fame overnight and won every major music award. But in fact the very first album she recorded was inferior, and was never released. Had it been issued, her legend, they say, would not have been established so quickly, or in quite the same manner.

The idea was to record Barbra live, to capture the excitement and energy she transmitted in performance before an audience. The invitations, sent out by Columbia's publicist Peter Reilly, read: "Miss Marmelstein invites you to meet a very good friend of hers, Barbra Streisand, in concert at The Bon Soir, November 5, 1963." Attending that night's performance were members of the music trades, Columbia executives and their guests, and a team of engineers who wired the small room for remote recording. Among the songs recorded by Streisand that night were: "My Name Is Barbra" and "I Hate Music But I Love To Sing" (both written by Leonard Bernstein), "Napoleon" (from *Jamaica),* and "Much More" from *The Fantasticks.* All were taped, as were her performances on the sixth and seventh of November, but none of these tracks ever got beyond the editing stage.

Producer Mike Berniker defended Streisand's performance, which he called "just fine. But the quality of the recording was bad.

Remote in those days wasn't up to par." The engineers disagreed. The remote was perfect, Streisand wasn't. Her voice was shrill. She was showing off to an audience that was equally ostentatious and loud.

Peter Daniels, her accompanist, put some of the blame on her backup musicians. "Columbia refused to spend any money on that date," he said. "They insisted we use the musicians who played regularly at the Bon Soir. I didn't want to use Tiger Haynes or the Three Flames. Those guys always got a little something going for a performance, but for an album I felt we needed more. I wanted Barbra to go into a studio and do the job right."

Goddard Lieberson, upon hearing the Bon Soir tapes, agreed. He instructed Berniker to begin again, in a studio, with full facilities, and with new orchestral backing for Barbra. For the arrangements, Peter Matz was hired. Matz had worked with Marlene Dietrich and Noel Coward, and with Harold Arlen on *House of Flowers*. A framed sign on his wall read SIMPLE IS GOOD and he introduced Barbra to that credo. "We rehearsed at my apartment on West End Avenue," said Matz. "Barbra used to come over every day with her lunch in a brown paper bag. It was a delight to work with her. She didn't know how to read music, but she could follow it up and down on paper. With her instincts she didn't have to read. People credit me for those early arrangements, but really, most of the ideas and the songs came from Barbra and Peter. They made my job very easy."

"Most of the material was songs we had been doing for two and a half years," said Daniels. "It was a big compliment to me when Peter took our arrangements and expanded them for an orchestra. The collaboration was incredible."

"The budget from Columbia was small," said Matz, "so I couldn't have a big band. One session had a rhythm section and four trombones; another had a small string section. Columbia wouldn't pay for more. They really didn't know what they had with Barbra."

Contrary to published reports, that first studio album was not recorded in one day. The eleven songs were taped on three consecutive days, on January twenty-third, twenty-fourth, and twenty-fifth, in Studio A at 799 Seventh Avenue. Supervising the sound in the control room was one of Columbia's best engineers, Frank Laico, whose credits included "Chances Are" by Johnny Mathis, and most of Tony Bennett's hits. When he heard Streisand he "got goose bumps. When she stepped up to that microphone and began to sing . . . it was incredible to hear . . . a voice like that to come out of nowhere. She was nervous, but so was I. She concealed it. She acted like she had been doing this all of her life. And what was she? Nineteen or twenty?

"The arrangements by Peter were the best. His charts—the way he wrote, the coloring he gave—he put her in a perfect setting. She had some very harsh vocals going at times, but with his colors she sounded so great."

Laico recorded in stereo, but the playbacks for Streisand were in monaural. "Stereo was still new and no one understood it. Her sessions were done on three tracks: one for the vocals and two for the band. Barbra was a newcomer—I didn't want to confuse her by playing back the band, some to the left, some to her right, so I put the monaural tape on. That was a wise move, I found out later. The lady has amazing hearing. If she had heard herself in stereo we would still be recording today."

"Barbra's hearing was incredible," said Berniker. "It was unusual for a singer in the sense that most vocalists concentrate on themselves when they're recording. Barbra could do both. She was tuned into her own voice *and* to the orchestra. She'd hear things. We'd stop often to listen to her suggestions. There was a lot of give and take all around. She had signs of temperament, but I found the things that made her difficult also made her great."

THE COMPANY REACTION

Once the editing was completed on the first album, Mike Berniker made up studio reference dubs and hand-delivered them to the Columbia department heads. David Kapralik took his and ran from office to office, from floor to floor, playing selected cuts for anyone who would listen. Another copy went to Bill Gallagher, who passed it on to his secretary, who passed it on to the girls in the promotion pool, who played it nonstop until it vanished overnight from their hi-fi. A second dub replaced the first and that, too, disappeared, presumably lifted by some other Streisand admirer; her fans were slowly multiplying in number at the record label. (Later, in the midst of the company's move from 799 Seventh Avenue to the CBS Black Rock Building on Sixth Avenue, the missing dubs were found, dumped behind a wall of filing cabinets near the men's room.)

"The staff's reaction to that first album went to extremes," said Mary Jo Johnson, who worked on *Insight,* the company merchandising magazine. "People either loved it or hated it. Barbra was definitely an acquired taste. She wasn't the norm for pop singers at that time. Personally, I was partial to classical music, but when I heard that first album I stopped and said, 'Now, *who* is this?' She had substance and style beyond her years. She was peerless, also a professional. When it was decided to feature her in the company magazine she insisted on becoming involved. She sent her mother up to the office with photographs. She got her brother, Sheldon, who was in advertising, to draw some cartoons of her, which we used with the article."

Columbia's publicity department also rooted for the underdog. Its press chief, John Kurland, was an early Streisand advocate. Previously employed at RCA Records, his last assignment at that label had been to publicize singer-starlet Ann-Margret (then age twenty). "Ann-Margret was a sweet girl," Kurland recalled. "RCA brought her to New York to publicize her first album. I took her around to meet the disc jockeys and set up luncheons with columnists and magazine writers. She was very provocative with the press. We had to assign a chaperone to stay with her at the Warwick Hotel, just to keep the guys away."

When he and his assistant, Peter Reilly, met with Streisand, she told them the kind of press she *wasn't* interested in. She didn't want to be photographed on the Brooklyn Bridge, or in Times Square, with her skirts raised or her mouth half open (a pose Ann-Margret was partial to).

"Barbra knew she couldn't sell sex appeal or cuteness," said Peter Reilly. "She went with her instincts; she never knew how to bluff or be coy. Once at a luncheon meeting with a writer from *Holiday,* when he mispronounced her name as 'Barbra Streesand,' she took his name and turned the vowels around. She pronounced his name like that throughout the meal and he loved it. She was a natural. She couldn't be false if she tried. She always stressed the importance of writing the truth about her. 'Tell it like I am,' she used to say, and that made her very special to us."

"I don't recall Barbra as being very special or outstanding," said Myra Friedman another Columbia employee (and later the author of *Buried Alive*, the Janis Joplin biography). "I worked in publicity and I wasn't even aware that people thought she was different or eccentric. I wasn't the most conventional female myself, so I never looked at her and said, 'Oh, wow! What a freak.' She was the way I knew women to be. They didn't play female games. You're talking 1963—before Betty Friedan—when women acted like 'girls.' So Barbra was certainly different in that regard. But compared to Janis Joplin—who came much later—the reaction to Barbra was mild. Janis was like a meteorite that streaked across the sky in a brilliant flash. And then she died. Barbra has been up there for how long? Twenty-one, twenty-two years? She is an extraordinary talent, but in the same room, or on a stage, Janis would have blown her away."

THE FRONT COVER

The curtailment of cost for Streisand's album shot down her initial request for her cover photograph to be taken "by the guy who did the Tammy Grimes album"—Richard Avedon. He charged three thousand dollars a sitting, Barbra was told, whereupon she went to Times Square and had her likeness captured in a photo booth. Four shots for a quarter—two full face, two with left profile—were duly delivered to Columbia, with instructions that one was to be blown up and hand-tinted. When it was explained that a more professional image was needed, staff photographer Henry Parker was assigned to photograph Barbra in performance at the Bon Soir. The editing of the session was done by John Berg, who designed the first cover.

"I met Barbra in the office at seven ninety-nine after the edit," said Berg. "I picked one photograph and showed it to her and she said, 'Great!' This was her first record and she was willing to go with the flow. It was a very strange cover for that time insofar as one of her eyes was slightly crossed. But we both agreed it was a good performance shot. She also wanted to make sure that her first name was spelled correctly. And she choose the typeface. That was the first logo ever done for a recording artist, and she used it for years to come."

"Barbra was the first artist to ever come in and sit and work on her layouts," said art director Bob Cato. "Prior to her it was a closed-door policy with every art department in the world. But I wanted the performers and the managers to have an access—not to fight, but to participate in the design of their product. That really took them off guard, and they listened, and you both got something beautiful off the ground. So when Barbra said she wanted to come in, I said, 'Wonderful.' I had seen her at the Blue Angel. I brought Miles Davis to one show, and when he saw her he lost all of the cool game he used to play. He was abashed by her."

THE LINER NOTES

The backs of all Columbia albums, the liner notes, were usually assigned or written by editorial director Charlie Burr, who knew Barbra from *Pins and Needles,* the recreated cast LP which he coproduced. When they discussed who should write the introduction for her first album, she requested somebody big, somebody important. The top man at Columbia was Goddard Lieberson. Why couldn't he puff her praises? Charlie, a soft-spoken, erudite man, tried to explain that the president of the company could not show partiality by writing about individual performers. "Okay," Barbra replied, "then how about the President of the United States? Jack Kennedy could jot down a few words. We could pay him, or maybe give him a few albums?"

"I was never sure if Barbra was serious or not," said Charlie. "She presented herself with a very straight, earnest face."

The album notes were eventually written by composer Harold Arlen, who compared her to legends of the past. "Did you ever hear Helen Morgan sing?" he wrote. "Were you ever at the theater when Fanny Brice clowned in her classic comedic way—or when Beatrice Lillie deliciously poked fun at all the sham and pomp? Have you ever heard our top vocalists 'belt,' 'whisper,' or sing with that steady urgent beat behind them? Have you ever seen a painting by Modigliani? If you have, do not think the above has been ballooned out of proportion. I advise you to watch Barbra Streisand's career. This young lady—a mere twenty—has a stunning future."

"Is that it?" asked Streisand when she had read his salute. "So many dead people; couldn't we liven it up a little?"

THE TITLE

One obstacle, albeit a minor one, came with the selection of a title for Barbra's first LP. Titling albums was a serious business at Columbia. Once a month a two-hour meeting was called, specifically for this task. The creative representatives from each department assembled in a room and tapped their brains for compelling, captivating album appellations. The pontifications, when chaired by Goddard Lieberson, could sometimes be light. *"The Ineffable Tony Bennett,"* he read aloud at one meeting. "Who thought up that title? Edith Sitwell?"

Pop albums were usually titled after successful singles.

Therefore the first choice for Barbra's LP was *My Coloring Book.* It had consumer identification. Kitty Kallen and Sandy Stewart were using it to sell their albums, so why shouldn't Columbia capitalize?

"Because the song was not on Barbra's LP," they were informed. "At her firm request." No arguments. Creative control; remember?

Other titles mused upon were *And Here She Is! . . . Barbra Streisand; Hello! I'm Barbra Streisand; From Brooklyn to Broadway . . . Barbra Streisand;"* and the next-to-last ballot, and one almost used, was *Sweet and Saucy Streisand.*

"They loved that alliteration—*Sweet and Saucy Streisand . . .*" said Marty Erlichman. "When I suggested it to Barbra, she got nauseous. Together she and I came up with a great idea. Why not just call it *The Barbra Streisand Album?*"

Mike Berniker also puts his claim on that title. "I kept quiet about this for years," he said, "but that title was mine. I came up with it at a second meeting and I helped push it through. Everyone at Columbia said it was outrageous. Streisand was a nobody. How dare she assume that people would automatically know who she was without an introduction on the cover? They never saw the humor in it until years later when everyone started using it for records and TV specials."

THE PROMOTIONAL TOUR

Early in March, Streisand opened a three-week engagement at the Eden Roc Hotel in Miami Beach. This was to be the first stop on a cross-country tour to publicize her album. Barbra was second on the bill, which featured comedian Joe E. Lewis, and Italian singer Sergio Franchi. The audience was comprised of rich, elderly couples. The husbands, sporting tans, paunches, and pinky rings, chuckled at Lewis; the wives, encased in mink and diamonds ("the rocks and lox crowd," Barbra called them) swooned over Sergio. But the young female singer? They were a little baffled by her selection of tunes, which included "Who's Afraid Of The Big Bad Wolf?" and "Come To The Supermarket In Old Peking."

Crossing the hotel lobby one day, one amicable guest, dressed in a three-piece Cabana set and Harlequin sunglasses, stopped Barbra in mid-stride. Opening with a few niceties, the lady began to admonish Streisand on her choice of songs.

"With such a nice voice you should sing 'Moon River,' " she suggested.

"With such a nice song I should be sick," replied Streisand, and kept on walking.

From sunny Miami Beach, Barbra, Marty Erlichman, and Peter Daniels flew to snowbound Cleveland for a week on a new television program called *The Mike Douglas Show.*

"Mike had seen Barbra on *P.M. East,*" said Erlichman. "He called and asked me if she'd cohost with him for a week. 'A week?' I replied. 'In Cleveland? In winter? She'll kill me.' But the album was due out any minute and we needed some help, so I told him we'd do the show if he'd get us a nightclub booking for the same period. He agreed."

"The place they got us was a dump called the Chateau," said Peter Daniels. "There were two big pillars on each side of the room, and if you sat behind them you couldn't see Barbra. But there wasn't any audience. It was the height of winter, and the orchestra was the worst. Barbra was a little depressed. She'd sing for half an hour and the few people just sat there, with no reaction."

"Nobody knew what a Barbra Streisand was," said Mike Douglas. "This was particularly true of a couple of drunks who were heckling her. A few personal remarks were passed, and before you could say 'Muhammad Ali,' Marty was over at their table threatening to punch out the two of them."

The best part of the Cleveland stint was the daily TV show.

"Mike just flipped over her," said Daniels. "He kept plugging that first album. He made her sing every song from it. She was on something like three times during an hour and a half. By the end of the week there were over three thousand orders for the album in Cleveland alone. And Columbia up to that point had done nothing to promote it—absolutely nothing."

"The first that I knew something was wrong was after one of the TV shows," said Erlichman. "This tour had been deliberately set up to push the album. I had been offered places like the Fairmont Hotel in San Francisco and the Ambassador Hotel in Chicago for Barbra. They wanted to give us five thousand dollars a week, a sixteen-piece orchestra, and free room and board. I turned them down. Barbra thought I was crazy. She wanted to go with the money and the posh surroundings. I told her we didn't need a swank ancillary audience who would have dinner, see the show, and that's it. We were looking for an audience who would go out and buy her records. So I set up dates for her at the Hungry i, in San Francisco, and Mister Kelly's in Chicago. And here we are in Cleveland, ready to leave for those dates, and I find out Columbia is not behind us. The record stores couldn't sell her albums because they didn't *have* any. They got something like a hundred copies and that was it. Well, I blew. I went for the phones. I called Gallagher in New York and laid him out. I started yelling, 'How dare you do this to us? After we went out on a limb, taking less money, building a following, and you guys don't have records out there?' Barbra was creating all this excitement, people were going to stores, so where the fuck were her records?"

In Pitman, New Jersey, it turned out. At Columbia's pressing plant. The original production order, based on Marketing's low sales forecast, had been shipped and sold out in two days. Extra jackets, labels, and records were being made on double-time; all back orders were to ship air-express within five days.

"Columbia started to jump on the bandwagon," said Daniels. "They sent some guys out to San Francisco to work the album before we got there. There were lines around the door of the Hungry i before she opened."

Erlichman added to the excitement of opening night. "The club was jammed," said a witness, "and Marty called the police and the fire department. He told them it was a safety hazard. They arrived on the scene with the red lights flashing and the sirens screaming.

Naturally, it made the front pages the next day. All of San Francisco were talking about this new singer down at the Hungry i. They jammed the place for three weeks."

"It's funny," said Streisand. "I remember very little of what went on there. I used to do my show every night, and then I'd go to my dressing room. I never went out to the bar. I never socialized with the audience. It wasn't until years later I learned that Woody Allen was on the bill with me."

From San Francisco, Streisand headed home to New York, to open at Basin Street East, with Benny Goodman and his band.

Heady with the triumph of the tour and the success of her album, Barbra displayed the first open signs of temperament at this club. During her performance of "Cry Me A River" a musician played a wrong note. She wanted to fire him on the spot. She couldn't fire him, she was told. He didn't belong to her. He was one of Benny Goodman's band. "I guaranteed her he wouldn't play a wrong note again," said Peter Daniels. "And he didn't; not after I spoke to him."

Throughout the month of May *The Barbra Streisand Album* rose on *Billboard*'s best-selling charts from number forty-one to fifteen to the top five. The sweetest icing on the cake, however, came from Washington, D.C.—an invitation to sing for President John F. Kennedy, at the White House correspondents' dinner.

Different accounts of how that invitation came about were reported. One said that Kennedy himself had seen Streisand on television and asked that she appear. A second credits Merv Griffin (the MC of the night) as the catalyst. His agent, Murray Schwartz, lined up the entertainment, Griffin claimed. He booked Edie Adams, comedian Marty Brill, and the young unknown Barbra, whom Merv had turned down as a guest on his show. "I told Murray that John Kennedy liked bathing beauties," said Griffin, "a category Barbra didn't exactly fall into. But Murray persisted on Barbra's behalf, and I accepted the idea (thank God I'm not *too* stubborn)."

During the show, President Kennedy seemed pleased. Streisand, neatly coiffed and gowned, appeared next to closing, and stole the proceedings. She sang five songs, closing with "Happy Days Are Here Again," sung directly to the young President.

Post-performance, the talent gathered in a side room to meet

JFK. Everyone had been briefed by White House aides on the protocol. They were to stand in position as the President went down the line and spoke to each one. No personal touches, such as an embrace or a kiss, were to be tendered to the Chief-of-Staff; he was not to be detained.

Pausing in front of Streisand, President Kennedy asked how long she had been singing. "Just as long as you've been President," she replied; then added, "You're a doll."

"She also told him that her mother in Brooklyn would kill her if she didn't ask him for his autograph," said Peter Daniels, who stood by her side. "Kennedy laughed, he was delighted to oblige. He signed her program on *my* back. Talk about being thrilled."

The following morning at breakfast Merv Griffin complimented Barbra on her performance. "You were fabulous last night; you just floored everybody," he said. "But for God's sake, Barbra, did you *have* to stop the President for an autograph?"

"I wanted it," said Streisand.

"Well, I know," said Merv, "but they specifically asked us not to stop the President."

"But I wanted his autograph, Merv. How many times would I get the chance to have the President sign an autograph?"

"Well, did he write an inscription?"

"Yes. *Fuck you. The President.*"

Chapter 4

"When I sing, people shut up, what can I tell you."
                        Streisand to Newsweek, June 1963.

STARDOM, PHASE TWO

With her record career solidly established, Marty Erlichman concentrated on moving Streisand into the other areas of the entertainment business. That would require his undivided time and energy, and he decided to drop his other clients, the Clancy Brothers. The shedding proved painful for Erlichman. One account of the breakup had Marty visiting "The Boys" in Los Angeles after a concert. They were driving along the highway when he broke the news to them. They listened calmly, then opened the door of the car and tossed him out on the highway.

"It occurred on the East Coast," said Bob Mersey. "They were coming from Philadelphia and they threw him out of the car onto the Pennsylvania Turnpike."

"Lord, I don't remember that at all," laughed Makem, "but it could have happened. We had some wild times."

Dropping the Clancy Brothers was not the wisest of moves for Marty. With their departure went his commissions, then quite healthy. Barbra was making good money, but most of it went out to pay bills and musical expenses. "The first album had come out, but they were still broke," said Warren Vincent. "I was in the Ho-Ho one night and Marty came in. He told me he had just turned down a commercial for Barbra. They were offering him fifty thousand dollars and he needed the money, but he turned it down. 'She can't do commercials,' he said. 'She's too big.' "

What Marty needed was some financial advice, and backing. He found both in business manager Marty Bregman, who arranged the last stages of her transformation. Barbra needed star grooming. Her looks and her clothes had to be refined, and there was also the matter of that aroma. They eliminated the fish smell by moving their client from her apartment over Oscar's of the Sea to a rented duplex at 320 Central Park West. The new apartment came unfurnished, so Barbra brought along her $12.95 cot from Whelan's Drugstore. "If I get evicted," she said, "I can always hit the streets again with my bed on my back."

Streisand's looks and style had undergone some changes since her days in Brooklyn. A high school classmate, Florence Kaminsky, recalled Barbra as "different, always oddly dressed. If we wore shorter skirts, Barbra wore them long. When we wore sweaters, she wore a baggy blouse. She always did the opposite of everyone else. The only time she conformed was for the school pictures. Then they told you what to wear—a white blouse and a skirt, and neat hair. It's not like the kids today, who come in nude and they get their pictures taken. In the fifties you did what the teachers told you, or you were left out of the yearbook."

In school Barbra's looks were not the object of derision she imagined them to be. She had a long nose and a slight case of acne, but her eyes, a clear hostile blue, were striking, and she had a full, sensuous mouth. She also had at age fifteen the definite outline of a well-shaped body. With care she could be "passably" attractive, but she hated that word. She wanted to turn heads, to stand out in a crowd. And so, on graduation, she attacked her looks with a vengeance. She bleached her hair, then dyed it red, blue, and green. "I was punk before they even invented the word," she said. She wore purple lipstick and ghost-white makeup, and her clothes came from the closets of relatives and secondhand stores. "I wanted attention," she said, "so I made myself uglier than I was. I was outrageous. I never spoke softly. I was always loud, even in my thoughts. Of course I got attention, the *wrong* kind of attention, but at least I was noticed. I got their *eye.*"

Moving from Brooklyn to Greenwich Village, Barbra found she was ordinary once more, just one of a crowd. Beats and kooks and far-out oddities were the norm for the Village, and so she stepped back in time for another try at individuality. With the help of a new friend, designer Terry Leong, she discovered vintage clothing. "Barbra had just started to sing," said Terry. "She was poor and couldn't afford much. I brought her to the thrift shops uptown, on Ninth Avenue. She had a natural eye for style."

"Barbra didn't use the thrift-shop look for a gimmick," Peter Reilly said. "It was never a thing to create attention, it was her desire for quality. She could pick up a shoe, even if it wasn't her own size, and she'd say, 'Gee, they don't make shoes like that anymore.' She had never seen that kind of quality and she recognized it, because she was quality herself. It was like 'Gee, all this happened before me, but isn't it wonderful?' "

"We picked out a wonderful 1900 bodice," Leong continued. "It was gorgeous, all gun-metal sequins. I designed and made a velvet skirt for that. Another was a purple feathered bed-jacket. We did a taffeta sheath to go with it. We found accessories—belts, evening bags, a Juliet cap which she never wore. We couldn't afford jewelry, so we'd use a pin or a cameo brooch or a black velvet ribbon around her neck. We'd also go to fabric stores for remnants, or we'd get pieces from friends who dressed windows in department stores. I made the clothes at home. I had a sewing machine in my apartment on the Lower East Side. Barbra came down for fittings. She was terrible to fit. She wouldn't stand still. She was always running around the place looking at things. It got so bad I had to make her clothes on a dummy, from her measurements. In all there were six or seven original outfits I designed. She wore them at the Bon Soir. It was great fun. We were good friends."

After her wardrobe was designed, Barbra met a young illustrator who became her best friend and created her first professional facial makeover. Bob Schulenberg was a painting major from UCLA. He was introduced to Streisand on his first day in New York and was immediately taken with her. "Barbra was without a doubt the most talented, most driven person I have ever met in my life," he said. "I came from a secure family in California. My father was a lawyer. We had maids and all of the comforts and advantages that money could buy. Barbra came from nothing. So she had to pound the pavement and yell at people. She knew no one would do for her, so she went after everything on her own. She had no fear of anybody or anything. I was in open-mouthed awe of her. She taught me how to second-act plays on Broadway. We'd sneak into plays at intermission, carrying old programs and acting like we were there from the beginning. We must have seen *Gypsy* ten times. Ethel Merman was a seminal figure for Barbra; a bigger-than-life figure, and Barbra was interested in studying that personality. Her intelligence and grasp of the moment were extraordinary. She could see something or hear something and she'd turn it over in her mind, examining every facet. She could also filter out what she didn't want to see or hear from people. Her honesty was sharp and brutal at times. For example, she was of the mentality that if you say good morning to people, you have to mean it. Otherwise why say it? Another was 'It's nice to meet you.' If she felt it wasn't nice to meet someone she'd say 'It wasn't *nice,* so why should I pretend? Huh?' That kind of reasoning struck me as so basic, and so correct."

Less perfect to Schulenberg were Barbra's looks. "She knew nothing about makeup. I didn't want to say to her, 'Barbra, you look like ----' She was so easily deflated by those close to her. But she needed help. She didn't look suitable. She knew I had done the makeup for the stage productions in college. She was also interested in the idea that I was interested in working on her face. So one night after work I went over to her place. She had all this food laid out. We were going to have a picnic as we worked."

Schulenberg had studied photographs of Marlene Dietrich and Audrey Hepburn. He knew about Josef Von Sternberg's lighting and about the makeup tricks Hepburn had picked up from the models in Paris. "There is a way of doing your face, of making it attractive under any circumstances. If a flash bulb hits you, that look can't be taken away because the face is painted on. Barbra didn't know any of that. To me her face was an empty canvas. She had baby fat on her cheeks, so we shaded that. Her best features were her eyes and her mouth. Her worst was the nose. 'The nose is *there,'* I used to tell her. 'We'll ignore it and concentrate on the rest.'" That first transformation took three hours. Later the pair began to experiment with false eyelashes and different colors for her eyelids. "I taught her how to mix blue and yellow to make green. We also worked with sequins on the lids—clear glitter, then display glitter. She was willing to try everything. One night we took herring—we liked the way the fish skin looked—and we soaked it in cologne overnight. It took away the smell, but it also dissolved the silver on the scales."

Eventually the Streisand look was established, and paraded for the public to see. "First we had to coordinate the face to the wardrobe," said Schulenberg. "Barbra had some fabulous clothes, she loved clothes and had them stashed in apartments all over town, including mine. I was always afraid that people would open the door to my living-room closet, see the dresses and feather boas, and think I was a transvestite. One night after we did her face, I said to her: 'Okay, tonight we're going to the Brasserie and everything you wear will be red.' We picked red shoes, a red dress, a red belt—different shades so nothing clashed and over that we put a black trench coat. It was very Dietrich, and I said to her just before we entered the restaurant, 'I want you to act as if you had just awakened and put on these clothes.' I wanted her to appear uncontrived, even though it took three hours to put this show together. And she was perfect. When we walked down the steps into the restaurant, every head turned in her direction. One couple came up to our booth to pay their respects. The man said to her, 'We saw you at the Bone Swar, and you were marvelous! Where are you from?' And Barbra, very sultry, said, 'Smyrna.' She had picked that up from reading a box of prunes at Balducci's. And the woman was so impressed she got all flustered. 'Oh,' she said, 'my brother-in-law once went to Hong Kong.' Barbra smiled. She nodded. She was very world-weary of it all. And I was as proud as could be. As a production designer I felt I had designed the most successful production ever. I also knew right then that she could do it, that she was going to be charismatic forever."

With her face and wardrobe in place one major problem remained for Barbra—her hair. "She was very insecure about her hair," said Terry Leong. "She used to curse at it all the time."

"She told me her hair fell out when she was sixteen months old," said Schulenberg, "and apparently it never grew back right. It was very thin. She used to wear these Dynel hairpieces—Danish pastries, I used to call them—plopped on top of her head. She'd comb her bangs down to cover her teenage acne. I told her, 'We'll use heavier makeup to cover the acne, but get rid of the bangs. Comb your hair *over* that thing on top of your head. It'll look classier.' "

* * *

In May of 1963, prior to her appearance at the White House, Streisand brought her hair problem to Kenneth, the stylist to Jacqueline Kennedy and Babe Paley. Postwash, Kenneth personally cut and styled Barbra's hair in his upstairs private parlor on East Fifty-fourth Street. She was pleased with the results. Kenneth did a good job, but he was expensive, she learned, and very fussy about making house calls. He would travel for the First Lady, but not for Streisand, and certainly not for credit. "Screw 'im," said Marty Erlichman. "We'll take our business elsewhere."

In Chicago, while appearing at Mr. Kelly's, Barbra found the solution to her problem. She was introduced to a man who would work on her hair for the next seven years. His name was Fred Glaser and he owned the leading beauty salon in town.

Glaser, today a sculptor and artist, recalled that first meeting. "We were introduced by Arlyne Rothberg, who booked the acts for Mr. Kelly's. Arlyne mentioned that I was the best hairdresser in Chicago, and Barbra and Marty were very interested. They asked who some of my clients were. I told them Doris Duke, Paulette Goddard, Carol Channing, names like that. I invited Barbra to visit my place on Rush Street. Marty said they didn't have much money, but if things went well, he'd take care of me. I was amused by that, because I liked Barbra immediately. I knew she had enormous potential. I wanted to experiment with her. Her hair hid her face. ('That's so I can look out and no one can look in,' she explained.) It was also very fine, hard to control. What I did was bleach individual strands. Most people don't understand what that does. It bleaches the color out but makes the hair thicker. If it's done right it makes your hair much fuller."

And thus, said Glaser, began "the process of extraction." "Barbra constantly takes from people. She asks many questions. Most people are flattered to answer her because they like to talk about their work. She absorbs everything and then uses it. For stage she wanted her hair to move when she did, so I cut it that way. With each step I also photographed her. I had a photographer [Woody Kuzuomi] living rent free in the top floor of my building. He photographed most of my clients as I worked on them. I insisted on that. A mirror can show so much, but a photograph tells all. We had many sessions with Barbra. It went beyond just doing her hair.

I wanted to stylize her, to get a definitive look for her, which we eventually did through a long process of elimination."

In all, Glaser estimated they took over two hundred photographs of that first encounter. Streisand would choose one of these shots for the cover of her second album. It would also be the only cover in which her nose had been altered—straightened via airbrush surgery. Later she claimed it was done without her permission. The truth was that she granted not only permission but suggestions as to how it should be done.

Chapter 5

THE SECOND ALBUM

As sales on the first album continued to escalate, Columbia Records requested a second Streisand LP. Faithful to their contractual obligation of one album every six months, Barbra and Marty were glad to oblige. They were eager to keep her momentum going.

The same team were used for the production. They included Mike Berniker as producer, Frank Laico as engineer, Peter Matz as arranger-conductor, and Peter Daniels as her accompanist. Daniels would also help choose the repertoire.

"The format," he said, "was the same as the first LP. We started digging around for songs. It was a simple procedure, but nothing was taken for granted. And there were few disagreements. I'd go through things like 'Anyplace I Hang My Hat' and 'Right as the Rain'—songs I grew up with. And Barbra would say, 'Yes! I like that. Let's do that!'"

One new composition on the second album was "Gotta Move," written by Peter Matz. It was also scheduled for release as her second single. "I wrote it for her to do at the Blue Angel," said Matz. "She complained that she didn't have anything to get off with. I did the song, using her speech patterns. *Gotta move! Gotta get out! Gotta leave this place!* She started using it as her closing theme. We recorded it first with a small combo, and Columbia was going to release it as a single, but politics became involved. I had been signed to Columbia as the next Percy Faith. But I was also arranger-conductor for Barbra, and for Tony Bennett, who was fighting with Columbia because he thought Barbra was getting more attention than he. I was stuck in the middle, and in that position it's difficult to tell people to take a walk. So "Gotta Move" was never released as a single. It frustrated me at the time. But I don't think it was a single anyway, and Barbra performed it so much, I was satisfied."

Columbia's budget for the second LP was more generous, Matz believed. "They gave us a little more money, so I had a more luscious orchestra to arrange for. But in terms of studio time they continued to short her."

On June third, recording began at Studio A in the Columbia building. Before her arrival Frank Laico had the room carefully prepared for her performance. "I always placed her in the middle of the orchestra," he recalled, "and at the opening downbeat I was with her. I learned from the first album that the first notes out of Barbra's mouth were the best. She might do four or five takes, but quite often we went back to that first take."

At this second session Barbra began to interrogate Laico.

"It's like she got her feet wet with that first album," he said, "and *now* she was ready to take over. She came into the control room and started asking, 'Why don't you do this, why don't you do that?' I listened, then said, 'Hey, Barbra, you didn't know anything with that first album, and look how successful it's become. I'm still the same person. I have the same ears. I'm not going to let you down.'"

In three hours that afternoon only two songs were recorded. Barbra wanted to continue, but the studios and the musicians had already been booked for another session. She complained. She did not want to be limited by schedules; she wanted an indefinite closing time on her dates, and the musicians should remain until she felt she had given her definitive performance.

On June sixth three additional songs were done. Included were "Down With Love," "Anyplace I Hang My Hat Is Home," and "I Stayed Too Long At The Fair." During this session Frank Laico threatened to quit. Both Barbra and Marty were crowding him. "They stayed in the control room," he said. "One sat on my left shoulder, the other sat on my right. They kept giving me advice,

'Do this, do that.' It got so I couldn't move. I called Mike Berniker aside and told him either they let up or I was going on to another job. Mike said, 'We've got to be careful, we don't want to upset them.' *'Them?'* I replied. 'I got feelings too. Either they back off or I leave.' "

Word on the delays and extra costs drifted down to the executive offices. Bill Gallagher, who was still maneuvering for his takeover of the A&R department, decided to step into the breach. Although he had initially been opposed to the singer, he conceded she now had a future, and he needed her on his team. He would throw a bone to the girl by inviting her to Puerto Rico, to the company's annual sales convention.

These conventions were deluxe, expensive junkets, held each year in such glitzy, glamorous locales as Las Vegas, Hollywood, or Miami. Columbia distributors, dealers, key rack-jobbers, music-trade reporters, celebrity guests, and beautiful women (whose special touch usually had a price tag attached) were flown in for four days of wining and dining on the house. Product presentation meetings and seminars were conducted during the day, and at night gala dinner shows were hosted, with the entertainment supplied from Columbia's roster of stars, old and young. It was considered an honor and a boost to a new performer's career to be allowed to perform at these functions, so Gallagher met with Erlichman and gave him the good news. He and Barbra were invited to Puerto Rico, all expenses paid.

"Thanks, but no thanks," Erlichman replied. "We got club dates."

"Change them," said Gallagher.

"No can do," said Marty. Whereupon the Sales chief asked to meet directly with Barbra.

"Gallagher's trick in those days" said Peter Reilly, "was to gradually eliminate the manager by dealing with the artists directly. He would gain their trust and loyalty by promising to make them big stars, with special sales promotions and ad campaigns. He had the power, and most performers were vulnerable. They believed him."

But not Streisand. She refused to meet with Gallagher. "It was my job to keep her away from those guys," said Erlichman. "Barbra was uneasy with anything to do with selling."

Columbia, aware of Erlichman's nonformal deal with his singer, then planned to split them. David Rosner recalled one such attempt. "They called Helen Noga, Johnny Mathis's manager, and asked her if she was interested in taking on Barbra. Noga went to see Barbra perform, took one look at her, and said, 'She looks like a horse's ass' and refused to manage her."

Even if Noga had agreed to represent Streisand, it was unlikely Barbra would have left Erlichman. "Barbra and Marty were very close," said Peter Reilly. "He was a dear, sweet guy. He'd show up in my office full of booze and he'd say, 'Yeah, Barbra, she's nineteen going on eighty-one.' And Barbra treated him like a reprobate uncle. When he had a birthday she gave him the gift of a membership in a health club."

On August 4, 1963, Streisand began a two-week stand at the Riviera Hotel in Las Vegas. She opened the show for Liberace and came close to being replaced during the first week. "We found out very quickly," said Peter Daniels, "that Liberace's audience was not a Streisand audience. They didn't know what to make of her. We did two disastrous shows, then on the following day Liberace called a meeting in his suite. Barbra thought she was going to be fired. 'Here's what we're going to do,' Liberace said, and he changed the show around. Instead of Barbra opening for him, he went on first. He did five minutes and then he introduced Barbra as his discovery. It was like he was putting his seal of approval on her, and that was all right for them. They loved her after that."

From Vegas, Streisand, Daniels, and Marty Erlichman flew to Los Angeles for her first appearance in that city. The locale chosen for her Hollywood debut was carefully considered by Erlichman. Instead of The Troubadour II or The Whiskey A-Go-Go, Marty put Barbra in the Cocoanut Grove supper club, then part of the swank Ambassador Hotel. They needed this posh setting and its well-heeled clientele to showcase "the new *chic* Barbra." She and Marty were out to impress one particular couple from Bel-Air, The Starks: Ray, a former agent turned producer, and his wife, Fran, who was the daughter of the late Fanny Brice, the star subject of a forthcoming Broadway Show entitled *Funny Girl.*

Fanny Brice, née Borsch, was born on the Lower East Side of New York. Raised over her father's saloon, she displayed at an early age a natural talent for dialects and impressions. Married at eighteen, separated almost immediately, Fanny became a Ziegfeld Follies headliner at nineteen. She had neither beauty nor a great singing voice. What she did have was a natural comedic flair and an innate ethnic timing. During the forties she starred in a highly rated radio program. Upon her retirement in 1949 she was urged by gentleman friend, Goddard Lieberson, to dictate her memoirs into a new Columbia machine called a tape recorder.

In 1951 Fanny died of a cerebral hemorrhage and the book was finished by writer Norman Katkov. Advance copies were shipped to reviewers in 1953, but before the notices were printed, son-in-law Ray Stark pulled the book from circulation, reportedly paying fifty thousand dollars to have the plates destroyed. Young Frannie, it was said, objected to some of the revelations about her mother. They included details of Fanny's first marriage, and the blithe recollections of some of her friends, including Katharine Hepburn, who said, "Fanny didn't just swear; she created her own language. She sat like a queen and could swear like a truck driver."

Barbra Streisand was certainly equipped to play Fanny, many thought, including the composer of the *Funny Girl* score, Jule Styne. "I saw Barbra in *Wholesale,*" said Styne. "I climbed five flights of stairs to her dressing room and told her, 'I'd like to take you to dinner.' 'When?' she asked. 'Tonight,' I replied. 'Where?' she said. 'To Sardi's,' I told her. 'Will you get a good table,' she wanted to know, 'so everybody will see me?'"

Funny Girl was originally slated for Anne Bancroft, said Styne, "but I was secretly writing it for Barbra. I went to see her twenty-seven nights out of twenty-eight when she was at the Bon Soir. I took Ray Stark down to the club. I called Barbra beforehand and said, 'Look, don't open your mouth tonight except to sing. Forget the jokes. Forget the funny clothes. Come out with some elegance and let us hear your voice.' And she did. She was a good girl then."

Ray Stark was quite taken with Streisand and returned to the Bon Soir with his wife, but Barbra on this night was not forewarned. She came out looking and sounding like a banshee in heat. Fran Stark was clearly not amused. "That woman," she announced, "will *never* play my mother."

"Fran is a darling," said one Bel-Air neighbor, "but a trifle haughty. She worshiped her mother. When Fanny died, Fran and Ray set up a shrine to her image. Fanny became this very tasteful legend. 'She was the epitome of elegance,' that's what young Fran told *Harper's Bazaar*. 'Among my fondest childhood memories,' she recalled, 'were the many afternoons I spent with her at couturier fittings.' Sounds perfectly lovely, right? Well, fix that scene in your mind and superimpose the face and moxie of Barbra Streisand the night Fran saw her at the Bon Soir. Absolutely *not*."

The script of *Funny Girl* was then shuffled between Carol Burnett, Kaye Ballard, Mitzi Gaynor, and Eydie Gorme. None were signed, and so it circled back to Streisand. By the summer of 1963 she had become "stylized" and a national success with her first album. No longer an "unknown," she had become cool to the prospect of playing Fanny Brice. She had other offers to star on Broadway, her manager informed Ray Stark. She was up for *110 in the Shade*, the musical remake of *The Rainmaker* (she lost the part to Inga Swenson), and writer-director Arthur Laurents wanted her for his new musical, *Anyone Can Whistle*. "Stephen Sondheim and I wanted Barbra to play the nurse," said Laurents. "She turned us down and the role went to Lee Remick."

In August, Ray Stark and Jule Styne went to Las Vegas to see Streisand once more. "They played some of the new *Funny Girl* score for her, but neither side was making a firm commitment," said Peter Daniels.

On to Los Angeles, and her opening night at the chic Ambassador Hotel. In the first-night audience were Danny Kaye, Alan Jay Lerner, Natalie Wood, Rock Hudson, and the Starks. Backstage after the show Fran Stark embraced the "new Barbra," and later the two sat together at a gala supper party hosted by Sammy Cahn at the Bistro. Throughout the night Barbra was refinement personified. She spoke about her opening-night dress (a gingham creation she designed herself), about flowers, and fine china (a few pieces of which she had purchased during her thrift-shop days). And while the two ladies exchanged confidences, Ray Stark and Marty Erlichman had their heads down in deep conversation at the bar. It was obvious a deal was being struck. The following week the confirmation came in *Variety*. The paper announced that *Funny Girl*, the long-awaited musical of Fanny Brice's life, would open on Broadway in January. The leading role would be played by a newcomer: Barbra Streisand.

"Barbra was being managed before we met, and I didn't know one person from the other. There were a lot of bodies and very few people."

Elliott Gould

Since the closing of *Wholesale* the previous December, Elliott and Barbra had been parted professionally. In February he auditioned for the London production of *On the Town* and suggested Barbra for the role originally played by Nancy Walker. The producers agreed, and the decision was left to Streisand.

She wanted to work with Elliott again. They had made plans, to do the classics—Shakespeare, Molière, Chekhov. "They were serious," said a friend from that time. "Barbra was always saying that she and Elliott were going to be the next Lunt and Fontanne. With the billing reversed, no doubt."

These plans were put on a back burner when Barbra recorded her first album. Marty Erlichman insisted she tour and promote the record. "But Elly wants me in London," she wailed. "We're a team and I can't say no to him."

Marty arranged a meeting with the couple at Sardi's, and commenced yelling at Elliott. He was being selfish, he said, asking Barbra to take a secondary role in a revival of a play in a foreign country. Her career was just beginning in America, he had big deals, commitments, lined up for her.

Elliott yelled back that he didn't care about Marty's deals. "I just care about her welfare in relation to my soul."

He asked Barbra to make a decision. She decided to go with him. Elliott, grateful for her allegiance, then told her to stay. "You made the right decision," he said, "to come with me. But what you have to do is to pursue *your* career, because I can't do any more for you than you can do for yourself."

On the Town opened at the Prince of Wales Theatre in London on May 26, 1963. The reviews were tepid, and the show closed within weeks. When Elliott returned to New York, he found that Barbra was a star with her first album. While she toured he auditioned for work. Early in September, when she signed for *Funny Girl,* Elliott decided it was time to split up. Her career and retinue were destroying their relationship, he told her. He refused to become another figure on the landscape. He needed room to breathe, to assess his own career and future. They could still see each other from time to time, but for the moment he wanted out. "Barbra knew Elliott was serious, so *she* proposed marriage," said the friend. "She carried on about what good was a career and fame and fortune without Elliott to come home to. He came first, he was always first, she would give up everything if he told her to. In a way she *believed* that. Certainly they loved each other. They could make the marriage work. I mean, the girl thrived on challenges."

On September thirteenth, while Barbra was appearing with Liberace in Lake Tahoe, she and Elliott married in nearby Carson City. Their witnesses were Marty Erlichman and Marty Bregman. Before the ceremony Barbra asked that the marriage vows be rewritten. Instead of "Love, honor, and obey" she wanted to substitute the words "Love, honor, and *feed.*" "I mean food, nourishment; that's a very important exchange between people. It's as important as sex. You know?"

For a honeymoon Streisand and Elliott flew to L.A. and checked into the Beverly Hills Hotel. Barbra was there to work. She appeared for one night at the Hollywood Bowl (with Sammy Davis Jr.) and then began rehearsals for the Judy Garland TV show. That guest shot had been arranged for her by Judy's agents, David Begelman and Freddie Fields, who were anxious to add Barbra to their list of clients.

"David and Freddie had turned down Barbra before," said Marty Erlichman. "Then she hit it big and they changed their minds. They kept calling me, two, three times a day. I knew they booked the Garland show, so I said, 'Okay, you get us Judy's show and you got Barbra.' They did it, and we signed."

Taping on the series was done at the CBS TV studio in Hollywood. Judy, it was reported, had been a Streisand fan ever since she'd seen her onstage in Las Vegas. Erlichman denied this. "She never saw Barbra perform, anywhere. She heard her on records."

According to Mel Torme, Garland's TV director of special material, Judy was on her toes for the Streisand guest shot. The director and the crew expected a clash between the two singers. "I had never met Barbra," said Torme, "but rumors about her abounded. She was temperamental, she was unpredictable, she was foulmouthed, she was nuts. She was also one helluva singer."

Prior to rehearsals Judy stayed in her trailer listening to Barbra's single of "Happy Days Are Here Again." She called Torme in, and as she played the record, she sang along, in counterpoint, singing one of *her* signature songs, "Get Happy." The effect, said Torme, was electrifying. Garland, apprehensive of Streisand, asked Torme to make the duet *his* suggestion to Barbra. He did, and she accepted the idea immediately. She also admitted she was nervous and excited about working with Judy. The pair met and "it was instant warmth." "Judy was divine," said Barbra. "She was kind, sweet, frightened, clutching my hands, holding on to me. She was a very sweet, vulnerable lady."

Barbra's solo on the show, "Down With Love," was supposed to be followed by a light chat with her hostess, and then a duet between the pair. During the actual taping the rehearsed dialogue was diverted by Barbra, and cut in the editing. Peter Daniels recalled the scene. "Judy at one point said to Barbra, 'I'm so glad to have you on my show, and now that you've achieved so much success in so short a time, is there anything left in the world that you could possibly want?' And Barbra was supposed to say, 'Yes, to sing a duet with you, Judy.' But instead she said, 'Yes, there is. I'd like to take over *your* show.' There was a gasp from the audience. A couple of musicians dropped their fiddles. And Judy, who almost fell off her stool, steadied herself and said, 'Well, yes, dear, but *not* right now.' And then they did the duet as planned."

Following the duet Judy closed the hour with a medley of her hits, including "You Made Me Love You," "For Me And My Gal," and "The Trolley Song." She was in top competitive form; she was not about to relinquish her show or legend to this neophyte. When she came to the end of "The Trolley Song," singing, "With his hand holding mine, to the end of the line," the audience came to its feet, and Streisand led the ovation. "It was New Year's Eve," said Torme.

Leaving the CBS studio that evening, Streisand stopped by Judy's trailer. In what was an unusual gesture for her, she wanted to say good-bye and thanks for the good time. Garland was unwinding with champagne and her entourage. She jumped to her feet when she saw Streisand in the doorway. "She hugged me and wouldn't let go," Barbra later commented.

"We've got to keep in touch," said Judy. "You must meet Liza. . . . We must do another show together."

"Anytime," said Barbra.

They never did.

Without the help of a hit single, *The Second Barbra Streisand Album* came out and instantly made the best-seller charts. Throughout October and November it kept climbing until it reached the number-two position in *Billboard*. The number-one slot was held by *The Singing Nun,* and the Columbia Sales force in the field were told that Streisand's LP had to bump "Dominique." Being number one on the charts was important to Barbra, and to the label. It meant prestige, and extra cash to the Sales and Promotion team, and so one extra push was ordered.

On Friday, when the chart positions for the coming week were being tabulated at *Billboard,* a former employee recalled the day's events. "If you liked music and records at that time, Columbia was the only place to be. We walked, talked, lived, and breathed hit records. I remember it was lunchtime. I was in the basement, the lower level, where the mailroom and archives were. And this secretary, a beautiful black girl, Dorothy, came into the mailroom, and she started cursing and hitting the wall. 'We lost him,' she said, 'Dammit, he's gone.' Now, my mind was elsewhere. I knew Dorothy was a big Johnny Mathis fan, and I heard that morning that Johnny was leaving Columbia for Mercury Records, for more money. And I said to Dorothy, 'So what? He's gone, but we still have loads of his stuff on Columbia.' And Dorothy looked at me and said, 'What stuff?' I told her, 'His songs, his catalogue, we have enough in the vaults for ten more albums.' And she went, *'What in the hell* are you talking about? I began to mumble, 'Johnny Mathis . . .'—whereupon she started crying, *'Johnny Mathis?* You stupid jerk. I'm talking about *John F. Kennedy!* They shot him in Dallas this morning. He's *dead!"*

"I was in Marty Bregman's office, when I heard the news," said Marty Erlichman. "My first reaction was to call Barbra. She performed for him such a short time previous. She worshiped the guy."

"Jack Kennedy was like a movie star," Streisand recalled much later. "I swear—he had a ring around his head, a halo. He had an aura around him. There were girls screaming—it was his birthday when I sang for him. And there were like teenyboppers screaming for him—like for a movie star, 'We love you, Jack . . . aaah!' He was like, very charismatic. I enjoyed meeting him. I asked him for his autograph. I put it right down my dress and lost it. I couldn't believe it."

"The day he died we were rehearsing for a show at the St. Regis," said Peter Daniels. "There was Barbra and I and the orchestra. And when Barbra came to "Happy Days Are Here Again," the song she sang at the White House, she started to break down. That was the only time I ever saw her lose control onstage."

Chapter 6

PEProfile

PEOPLE

Early in December of 1963 Streisand performed at a series of concerts on the West Coast.

"That last tour was grueling," said Fred Glaser. "We went from San Francisco to Sacramento to San José. There were three of us in a rental car, Barbra, me, and Peter Daniels. It was hot and we had no air-conditioning. At every hotel we checked into there were new pages of *Funny Girl* waiting for Barbra. She learned the songs and the script in the car. Once she came across a scene where she had to roller-skate onstage. 'Roller-skate?' she said. 'Eight times a week? They gotta be kidding. I'm not breaking *my* bones for anyone.' "*

Rehearsals for *Funny Girl* began in New York on December tenth. Assembling the company on stage, director Garson Kanin told everyone that this was a time to experiment. Without mentioning Streisand by name he spoke of "this glorious girl, a consummate professional, with only one fault. She worries she's not good enough."

Kanin then instructed the cast to perform from the top. Barbra's first number came in the second scene. She played it sitting down,

---

* The roller-skate number was eliminated from the show but put back in for the movie version.

chewing gum. Kanin urged her to stand. She whined: "But I worked it all night."

"Please, darling," Kanin entreated.

Streisand stood, put down the script, took the wad of gum from her mouth, slapped it in Kanin's outstretched palm, and then began.

Reporter Stuart Little described the scene: "Wearing winter boots, a black sheath dress, and swinging rope-length pearls, Streisand stomped across the stage and attacked the song in full cry."

"It was an amazing performance," said actress Kay Medford, who played Fanny's mother. "Some of the cast were skeptical. Barbra was a newcomer—a novice, let's say. But she took that song and walloped our souls with it. You couldn't help but cheer for her."

Finished, Streisand retrieved her gum and her script, then sat down for the rest of the reading. "The way I prepare is not to prepare," she explained.

On the second day of rehearsals Ray Stark arrived in New York from Mexico, where he was producing *The Night of the Iguana* with Richard Burton and Ava Gardner. Unannounced, he sat in the back of the theater and watched the rehearsals. Streisand was still seized by inertia and Stark wanted to fire her on the spot. Garson Kanin intervened, explaining Streisand's rehearsal philosophy.

Later that day Stark met with his coproducer, David Merrick. Their partnership had become strained. Stark believed that Merrick was adding his name as a token gesture to the production. The bulk of his time and energies were elsewhere—namely in the supervision of six *other* shows, which included *Oliver* and the forthcoming *Hello, Dolly!* starring Carol Channing.

Stark and Merrick discussed their differences and then called in their lawyers. On December 13, an announcement appeared in the *Times*. Merrick, for an undisclosed sum of money, was withdrawing as coproducer. Ray Stark would produce *Funny Girl* alone.

But then he discovered that legally he had no leading lady for *Funny Girl*. Streisand's contract for the show had been with Merrick's office. With the split the paper became null and void. Stark therefore had to renegotiate Barbra's contract and salary, reportedly upped to ten thousand dollars a week.

"We asked for a few adjustments," said Marty Erlichman. "We got more money but no points, no share of the gross."

Their request for a limo and driver, plus her own hairdresser (Fred Glaser), was turned down, along with a "complimentary food" clause. The latter asked that free meals, for two, be supplied on matinee days from a restaurant of her choice.

"She has to eat," said Marty.

"No, she doesn't," said Stark. "She's fat enough."

Streisand's longtime accompanist, Peter Daniels, was also brought in under her contract. "My title was associate musical director," said Daniels. "What that meant was that I worked as a third party, as a go-between Barbra and the musical director and Jule Styne. It wasn't a good place to be. I got a lot of exercise running back and forth. And to add to the traffic and the hysteria of the place, Nicky Arnstein, the *real* Nicky Arnstein, used to come round the theater every few days trying to borrow a twenty from son-in-law Ray Stark. 'Fuck off,' Ray would tell him, 'I gave you a thousand last week.' "

In December, with the bulk of the music completed, composer Jule Styne concentrated on having some of the score recorded and released as singles, which would hopefully generate radio airplay and draw attention to the show.

There was nothing new in this promotional tactic. Jule Styne and Columbia had used it before—for *Bells Are Ringing* ("The Party's Over," sung by Tony Bennett) and for *Gypsy* ("Small World," by Johnny Mathis). However, *Funny Girl* was not a Columbia show. Goddard Lieberson had listened to the score in September and turned it down. He had also advised Barbra not to sign for the role of Fanny Brice.*

"*Funny Girl* at the time did not look so good," said Peter Daniels. "Some of the songs were okay, but the book was a mess."

What Columbia passed on, Capitol Records picked up. For a nominal investment they bought the rights to record the show. However, for the use of Barbra, Columbia retained the right to record four singles.

---

* When she did sign, Lieberson offered his mementos of Fanny to Barbra. They included personal effects and letters he had received from the comedienne.

These would be recorded and shipped at Columbia's discretion, preferably *after* the show opened and was a certified hit.

As a special favor Jule Styne called Goddard and asked if one single could be released before the out-of-town tryouts in Boston. "We needed the exposure from the airplay," said Styne, "and I was sure we had a hit with one song—'People.'"

"Now, get this right," Mr. Styne continued. "With 'People,' as with all of my songs, the melody came first. It was composed very early in the proceedings. I knew what the situation was in the show. I knew what the character was feeling; and knowing that I wrote the music. Then I gave the melody to the librettist [Bob Merrill] and he came up with the words."

The words to "People" came from a recurring line in the play's script, it was reported. Fanny Brice was described as "a very special person," and that word-image set the other lyrics in motion. "I don't recall that connection," said Bob Merrill, some twenty years after the fact. "The inspiration came from sitting long hours at the piano. The words were there. It took time to get them out."

To Merrill the most significant thing about "People" is that it was constantly out of the show. "Everyone said it didn't progress the story, which a show song should. I felt it was a good ballad, and it had a certain kind of magic, but none of the directors had any faith in it. As a matter of fact I had to promise Garson Kanin that I'd write a backup song immediately, before he would let it be performed."

"No one liked it," said Jule Styne. "Bob and I fought for it constantly. I knew when it was recorded it would be a smash."

When "People" was first played for Streisand, her reaction was less than thrilling. She felt that the message was too saccharine. "She wasn't crazy about any of the score," said Merrill, "but she went along with it. She had to. She didn't have that kind of power."

Publicist Peter Reilly recalled the first time he heard Barbra perform the song. "It was at a private party, at Marty Bregman's apartment. Various show-biz clients were there: Gloria DeHaven, Tuesday Weld, and Keith Mitchell, who sort of dazzled Barbra with his English accent and manners. Jule Styne was at the piano, and Barbra sat next to him and sang 'People.' She got a nice hand, but then Tuesday Weld sat next to Jule and she proceeded to sing, like *she* was the star performer. I was amused by that. It was always happening to Barbra. The first day of rehearsals for *Funny Girl* the director's wife, Ruth Gordon, came into the theater, and stood up against the proscenium and proceeded to sing the entire score of the show."

THE RECORDING

The first sides from *Funny Girl* were recorded in Studio A at 799 Seventh Avenue on Friday night, December 20, 1963. Present at the session were Jule Styne, Marty Erlichman, Mike Berniker, with Peter Daniels on piano, Peter Matz as arranger-conductor of the thirty musicians, and Frank Laico at the controls. Starting at eleven-thirty P.M. four songs were laid down. They were "You Are Woman," "Who Are You Now?," "Cornet Man," and "People."

"When 'People' was finished," said Daniels, "no one spoke. No one applauded. There was nothing but silence. When it was played back, Jule Styne almost broke down and wept. It was a very emotional moment."

"That song was done in one take," said producer Mike Berniker.

"No," said Peter Matz, "there were at least two takes. I know, because on the first take there was a mistake from the orchestra. There was a wrong note on the ninth bar in the French horn. We didn't fix it till the second time through."

"Maybe so," said Berniker. "What I remember best is that Marty and I got into a beaut of a fight over 'People.' There's a part in the song where Barbra sings out of tempo, with only the piano."

"It was called the interlude," said Peter Matz.

"It was a very important part of the song," said Berniker. "An esthetic change where she spoke the lyric over Peter Daniels's piano. It contributed enormously to the emotional impact of the piece. But Marty didn't want it. 'It's boring,' he said, 'it drags the record and makes it too long.'"

"Single records in those days had to be two-thirty or two forty-five," said Jule Styne.

"And 'People' ran close to four minutes. So Marty said, 'Shorten it, cut the chorus.' But Berniker refused. 'The chorus stays,' he said, 'or I'll walk off this date.'"

Streisand remained detached throughout the fracas. She didn't seem to care if the interlude stayed or not. "People" was still not her favorite. She preferred "Who Are You Now?"—the lyrics of which were closer to her own complexities. Furthermore, what did she know of timings for hit singles? She never had one.

"It was three o'clock in the morning," said Peter Daniels. "We had been rehearsing and recording for sixteen hours, so Barbra ended the session by saying, 'Hey guys, I'm tired. Good night.'"

The argument between Erlichman and Berniker continued past the door. "He kept yelling at me as we left the studio," said Berniker. "It went on in the elevator, in the lobby, and out on the street. He said he'd go to Goddard to have the record shortened. I told him, 'Fine, go.' And he did. But Goddard listened to the song and said, 'The interlude stays. It can't be cut.'"

On January 13, 1964, *Funny Girl* opened in the midst of a snowstorm in Boston. "People," which came late in the first act, stopped the show. Act Two, however, went on interminably and the curtain came down at 1:45 AM. Before dawn the reviews were read at a local restaurant. They were not kind in their assessment. "They massacred the show and wrote eulogies for Barbra," said Kay Medford. "She took it very hard."

"This was her first real flop, her first bad notice," said Peter Daniels, "and she was scared. She kept thinking, 'Whoa! What have I gotten myself into?' And Marty kept thinking of how he could drag her away from this wreck and back into nightclubs."

Ray Stark considered closing the show in Boston. He discussed it with his staff, and with wife Fran, who attended the opening. The entire production needed a lot of work, and more money. "I heard he casually flipped a coin," said a production assistant. "Heads we close, tails we stay open. But it didn't happen that way at all. Ray was a professional. Without him there wouldn't have been a *Funny Girl.* He worked hard. He was at rehearsals every day, hobbling around, his foot in a plaster cast. He had broken it while skiing over Christmas. At night his chauffeur would follow him into the theater, with a wooden stool, so he could prop it up on the aisle and watch the show."

Stark solicited more money to keep the show going. He hired a new writer for the book, and he sent to New York for Alan Miller, Barbra's former acting teacher. "He coached her during the day," said Peter Daniels. "She needed help, in the sense that she didn't know how to sustain a character throughout the play. By that time the story had very little to do with the script that was written, and it had very little to do with the life of Fanny Brice. Poor old Isabel Lennart. They ripped her scripts to shreds. They kept throwing scenes and numbers out. The bloody musical bill was over ninety-eight thousand dollars. In those days that was ridiculous for a Broadway show. Jule Styne was on the phone to Columbia in New York, begging them to release the single of 'People.' They were desperate for whatever help they could get." Columbia Records was in no hurry to release their single of "People." " 'Why should we push a Capitol Records show?' That was their reasoning," said merchandising executive David Rosner, who had heard the record at a company singles meeting, and planned a special promotion. "I loved the song. It really moved me, and usually in those days I would have to force myself to write anything about Columbia's singles. But with 'People' I filled an entire page, for a pink sheet, which was to go to all of the salesmen. Then I was told to kill the sheet. Sales did not want the record pushed. They had no intention of promoting the song. 'The quicker "People" is forgotten, the better,' that's the word I got."

On January twenty-first, while *Funny Girl* was still in Boston, Columbia Records put the single on the market. " 'People' was marked as the B side," said Ron Alexenburg, a promotion trainee. "I thought that was strange and questioned it, but the disc jockeys were told to go with the flip side, 'I Am Woman.' "

In actuality it didn't matter which side was up; the record, and all others released at that time, were buried by the debut of a brand-new British group called The Beatles. Their first single, "I Want to Hold Your Hand," and any other sides the DJs could beg, barter, or steal, were swamping the airwaves. "People" could barely get a courtesy spin, and Barbra could not, would not, understand the slight. She was at first confused, then angry. She had been fed this line. She had been told that "People" was "the quintessential ballad," that it would be a monstrous hit. And to have this group of foreigners, this odd-looking, odd-sounding foursome, impede her success? She would not forgive or forget their trespassing for a long time. She would outlast their popularity, she claimed. "I'm not a fad," she said. "I'm not singing rock 'n' roll, playing a strange instrument, or wearing my hair over my eye. My success is based on something real—talent."

On February 4, 1964, *Funny Girl* opened in Philadelphia. The reviews were more favorable than Boston's, but the show was still considered long and discombobulated. The following week *Life* magazine took a swipe at Streisand by deeming her "skittish, insecure, and oddly indifferent to her audience."

In a last, desperate attempt to salvage the production, Ray Stark brought in director/choreographer Jerome Robbins, who cast a cool and critical eye on the show and said, "It's going to be Barbra Streisand's show or nobody's."

Robbins told Stark he needed more time, and Stark postponed the New York opening. "We were supposed to be in Philly for three weeks," said Peter Daniels. "That was extended to five, then six, weeks. Jerry Robbins threw out fifty percent of Carol Haney's choreography. He threw out scenes, cut everyone's part, and concentrated totally on Barbra. She became the main focus of the play, and everything moved around her. He was tough with her. He knew what he wanted from her and he proceeded to get it."

Streisand thrived under Robbins's direction. She worked best, she said, "under battle conditions." Lyricist Bob Merrill recalled one minor skirmish. "She wanted a punch line in a song changed—to get a stronger laugh. I objected, and she said, 'Well, let me check this out with Marty.' I told her if she was going to start auditioning me with her manager I would never change another line for her. And her face went crimson. She understood that, and we never had any more trouble."

There was no particular warmth between them, the writer of "People" recalled. "We weren't particularly close. I didn't get along with her as well as Jule Styne. Jule seemed to be a personality she was more comfortable with. However, I felt she was a consummate artist. I have great respect for her work. The two most difficult people I worked with were Jackie Gleason and Barbra Streisand. Both demanded great things of themselves, and they demanded that other people come up to that level."

Jule Styne, meanwhile, refused to concede that his favorite song, "People," was a stiff. The British invasion be damned, he knew it was a good song, and if it wasn't going to be a hit with Streisand he would push it elsewhere. He shopped it around to his friends, including Frank Sinatra. "You screwed up," Frank told the composer. "You missed in the middle. After the first sixteen bars it rambles." After Sinatra's rejection the song went to Nat King Cole, who loved "People," and agreed to record it immediately.

When Marty Erlichman heard of Nat King Cole's interest in the song, his blood pressure shot up to 120. He didn't want *anyone* but Barbra to have a hit with the song. He called the Columbia distributor in Philadelphia and ordered two boxes of the "People" single to be delivered to his hotel overnight. The next day Marty took the 45's and distributed them one by one to every disc jockey and music programmer in the Philadelphia area. He also handed out complimentary tickets to the show. That night the first radio play on "People" came on WJRA. The second spin came an hour later, by request—from Marty. "He kept calling the stations, disguising his voice," recalled a bystander. "He handed out coins to the cast members of the show, to the stage hands, telling them, 'Call this number and tell 'em to play "People." ' " The campaign worked. Within a week "People" was a hit in Philadelphia. "The audiences at the show began to recognize the song," said Jule Styne. "They applauded it during the overture, also when Barbra began to sing it. It became so popular we had to add an encore."

The record was popular only in Philadelphia, and Columbia Records had no intention of rereleasing it nationally. The word at 799 was that *Funny Girl* was a bomb, that it would be a gigantic flop when it came to New York. The hit of the season would be *Anyone Can Whistle*, a Columbia show.

On Thursday night, March twenty-six, after three postponements, forty rewrites, three directors, and the elimination of twenty-six songs, *Funny Girl* opened on Broadway. "On the very last day things were being changed around," Jule Styne told writer Rene Alpert. "At ten minutes to seven Jerry Robbins was still rehearsing a new version of the last scene. Streisand and Sydney Chaplin had learned it that evening around six. When the critics saw that finale, it had never played before an audience before."

The finale—the farewell scene between Fanny Brice and Nicky Arnstein—came at 10 PM. Streisand was left alone, sitting stage left. Facing the audience, she began to sing the reprise of "Don't Rain On My Parade." Slowly at first, and then picking up speed, she "flung it in their souls." Her stage mother, Kay Medford, watched from the wings and recalled, "I got bumps on top of bumps. Barbra had the audience perched on the edge of their seats ready to fly with her." Her longtime accompanist, Peter Daniels, watched from the orchestra pit. "As she went for the last notes I felt this wave of relief roll over me. It was incredible. Everything had suddenly paid off. After so many months of sheer hell, we were home."

And then the ovations began. The audience screamed, yelled, whistled and clapped their hands raw. The curtain calls numbered twenty-three. Another ovation came at the opening-night party, at the Rainbow Room in Rockefeller Plaza, when Barbra came waltzing in with Elliott and Marty Erlichman, followed by her mother and Ray and Fran Stark, who bemoaned the unchicness of the room.

The following morning at Columbia Records Goddard Lieberson read the reviews for *Funny Girl.* He then buzzed his secretary, Liz Lauer, for an up-to-date report on the sales progress of their "People" single. There wasn't any progress beyond Philadelphia, he learned. Furthermore, staring up at him from that week's *Billboard* magazine was a full-page ad for "People" by Nat King Cole, on Capitol Records.

"Columbia looked like fools," said Peter Reilly. Capitol had it all—the Beatles; the original cast LP of *Funny Girl;* and now Nat King Cole was getting ready to take off with the single of "People."

Lieberson buzzed his Sales VP, Bill Gallagher. His order was brief. Capitol had to be stopped on the "People" single, at any cost. Gallagher called in his staff and promotion men. He wanted Streisand's single reserviced immediately to all radio stations, with special sleeves, in red.

The Columbia airplay for "People" began in New York early the next week. It soon spread to all major cities. Radio contests were inaugurated, store displays were placed, guarantees of 100% return privileges were given. Gradually the record began to move. On April 22, three months after the single of "People" was originally released, it showed up on *Billboard*'s charts, at Number 100. It went to 97, dropped back to 98, to 84, to 62, and following the Grammy Awards, where Barbra won for Best Female Vocalist and Best Single Performance, "People" entered the Top 10.

"It's popularity amazed me," said Peter Daniels (whose musical accompaniment on the piano netted him the grand sum of sixty-seven dollars), "Everywhere you went, in elevators, supermarkets, airports, you heard that song."

"It haunted me for years," said Peter Matz. "I'd hear it in a bar, on a jukebox, and I'd wince. You see, the version they released was the one with the wrong note on the French horn. Barbra's vocal on that first take was the best, so they went with it, flaws and all."

"People" also helped to sell one hundred thousand copies of Capitol's original cast LP, which stayed on the charts for over sixteen months. "That was like fingernails scratching across a board to Columbia," said a former executive. "Capitol had the hit album and Columbia kept calling Marty, pleading for *their* 'People' album. 'Barbra was busy, Barbra was tired,' that's all they heard. The bottom line was that Barbra *knew* that Columbia never pushed her single. They tried to shaft her once too often, but now the stick was in her hands, and she was going to use it."

Chapter 7

COLUMBIA WAITS FOR BARBRA

Movie stars, government figures, bankers, sports heroes, social movers and shakers flocked backstage each night at the Winter Garden, to pay tribute to Broadway's newest star, Barbra Streisand. On April tenth, a week before her twenty-second birthday, she appeared on the cover of *Time,* reportedly the youngest performer to be given that honor since Shirley Temple.

Time was one of the many major publications that called after the opening of the show. "We're talking cover stories only," her publicist told the press. *Time* agreed, as did *Life,* but she put the latter on hold because of the nasty swipe they had taken at her in Philadelphia during the tryouts.

To capture every nuance of Broadway's latest sensation, *Time* assigned a staff of twelve to observe the star. They included artist Henry Koerner, who painted her cover portrait in three sittings at her Central Park West apartment, "while interior decorators were coming in by the droves." After the portrait had been published, Streisand asked if she could have it to hang on her wall. When *Time* balked, because of company policy, she told them to keep it. It was "caca" anyway, and she intended to burn it.

Also on the *Time* team was reporter Ray Kennedy, who followed Barbra around New York City shopping for antiques, shoes, and Fudgsicles. While on the West Coast, correspondent Joyce Haber provided "a classic footnote to the story." Haber, with the aid of three police departments, the Nevada Gaming Control Board, the intelligence unit of the Treasury Department, lawyers, night-club owners, columnists, and several helpful hoodlums, tried to track down Fanny Brice's "former gangster husband, Nicky Arnstein." They found him in a seedy downtown Los Angeles hotel, but all that Haber and her posse could elicit from Nick was a "no comment." He was eighty-two, he had a bad heart, and his doctor told him not to get excited.

Streisand was far more loquacious with the press. In the first flush of success she was a journalist's delight. Her quotes were spontaneous and original. She had no guile, no tricks, no rehearsed public relations mush. She said whatever was on her mind. Brooklyn stood for "baseball, boring, and bad breath." She had to become a star; "I could never stay in the chorus because my mouth is too big." And success meant she couldn't shoplift "no more . . . because people recognize my face." Furthermore, the acclaim confused her. "What does it mean when people applaud?" she asked. "I don't know how to respond. Should I give 'em money? Say thank you? Lift up my dress?"

Such candor assured her friends that fame had not turned Barbra's head, or mellowed her personality. To some she appeared as negative and pessimistic as possible. "Happy? I'd be miserable if I were happy" was her standard reply. She still believed that behind every silver cloud lay a black lining. Her reviews for *Funny Girl* were not all raves, she learned. She insisted on seeing the pans. "Good reviews?" she said later. "I don't remember them. I remember only the bad." Another negative high came with the 1964 Tony awards. Streisand was nominated as Best Actress for *Funny Girl.* "I'm told I'll win all the major awards, the Grammy, the Tony, the Oscar," she said with a matter-of-fact assurance to writer Pete Hamill.

She won the Grammy that year, but not the Tony. It went instead to Carol Channing for *Hello, Dolly!* Streisand shrugged it off, but she cared. She was still sensitive to criticism, and not confident about her standing in the community. This insecurity led to fits of paranoia. "All right, what is it? Am I great or am I lousy? Huh? I need to know," she asked a *Time* reporter.

Her paradoxical moods extended to her fans also. During the opening weeks of *Funny Girl* the throngs waiting outside the stage door spilled onto Seventh Avenue. Streisand began to complain about their size and proximity. "Back! Back!" she growled upon exiting the theater, "I gotta breathe, don't I?" But when the crowds thinned out and moved a few blocks south, to the Lunt-Fontanne theater, where Richard Burton was appearing in *Hamlet,* Barbra felt abandoned. She still drew her regulars ("the crazies," she called them), but Burton was attracting *mobs,* and the mounted police. One principal attraction was Burton's new wife, the beautiful Elizabeth Taylor, who became a subject of curiosity to Streisand. "What does she have that's so hot?" she asked a friend of the star. "Nice eyes, big boobs, but what else?" When the classic shot of Taylor, wearing a Puerto Vallarta tan, and a pink towel wrapped around her head, appeared in *Life,* Streisand pounced upon the magazine. She held it up and announced: "They could have sold more copies if they had *me* on the cover." But one consolation came from Hedy Lamarr. After the former MGM star saw *Funny Girl,* she sent Barbra a note which pleased her so much, she taped it onto her dressing-room mirror. The note read:

> Dear Barbra,
> You made Elizabeth Taylor look like an old bag.
> Love Hedy

Streisand's pique did not extend to Taylor's husband, however. It was rumored that she had an affair with Burton. It was no secret she admired Burton's talent. "I wet my pants when he speaks," she said. But the actuality of an affair seemed unlikely to one local source. "Liz Taylor never let Burton out of her sight," said a female publicist. "She followed him everywhere, to the theater, to interviews, to the bathroom. I know, because I wanted to get to him too. In those days who didn't? One day by luck I heard he was recording *Hamlet* at Columbia Records, down on Thirtieth Street. I managed to put my name on the guest list at the door. It was a Sunday. I got there before noon and when Burton was recording, I deliberately put myself in his line of vision. I caught his eye and during a break we chatted. He invited me to share his lunch hour with him. We were just about to slip off for a little romp when the doors to the studio swung open and in walked Elizabeth Taylor. She was wearing a tweedy sort of suit, and this godawful hat with all these flowers thrown on top of it. Maybe it was Easter. Anyway she swept Burton off to lunch in her limo. She *knew* the scene. So if he and Barbra Streisand ever got it off, it had to be done over the phone, via heavy breathing."

In July, Columbia Records celebrated its fiftieth anniversary. The occasion coincided with Goddard Lieberson's twenty-fifth year with the company. The dual events were celebrated at a gala ceremony at the convention in Las Vegas. Included among the salutes were tributes from Laurence Olivier, Adlai Stevenson, Igor Stravinsky, Jacqueline Kennedy, and a note from Streisand, which read:

> Dear Goddard,
> The world is full of people. In the last few years I've met a lot of them. You are one of the few who has consistently offered me support in whatever I chose to do.
> P.S. *I also think you're good looking.*

"Barbra's relationship with Goddard was special," said Dave Wynshaw, director of artists relations at Columbia. "She got along well with all of the executives. I remember I used to visit her every Wednesday matinee day during *Funny Girl*. I brought her chicken pot pie. That was the deal we had. I brought her chicken pot pie every Wednesday.

"I also sent her flowers from time to time, for openings and stuff. And she inscribed a photo for me. It said: 'To David, who brings me flowers and food; what next?' "

"She sent me a note, from Vegas," said Peter Reilly, "thanking me for a press kit we sent out on her. Later, in Boston, when she was trying out in *Funny Girl*, we met in her hotel. Columbia was about to release her *Third Album*, and she wanted to know what publicity was planned for her. I was impressed, because the show was in terrible shape at that moment. But she was able to shut all that out and concentrate on the release of this album."

"Peter and John Kurland really worked hard for Barbra," said Myra Friedman. "Then after *Funny Girl* everything changed. I remember one day I came into my office at seven ninety-nine. I was in charge of sending out reviewers' albums, and she was down on her knees on the floor, raiding the cabinets for free records. There wasn't anything unusual about that, most of the artists did it. I also knew my boss, John Kurland, wanted to say hello to her. So I said, 'Barbra, when you've got a minute, John would love to see you.' And she looked up at me and said, 'John who?' "

"Barbra became remote after *Funny Girl,*" said Dave Kapralik. "She still dropped in, but there was a distance there. She could walk down a hall and not see the people she passed. Once in the lobby I stopped to introduce her to Muhammad Ali. He was Cassius Clay then and had just won the world's heavyweight championship. He had an album entitled *I Am the Greatest* on Columbia, so I introduced them. But Barbra pretended not to know who he was. 'I am the Greatest,' he told her. 'The greatest *what?*' she replied, and walked away."

During the July convention show in Las Vegas a series of Streisand slides were projected on the stage wall of the main room. The accompanying music was Barbra singing "People," and the announcement—the one that the Columbia sales force had been waiting five months for—was made. Their *People* album would be shipped with the August releases. That news, however, was premature—as of that moment the album was still not recorded.

"We had one meeting up at Columbia," said Peter Daniels. "Barbra was there, and Mike Berniker, and I think composer John Kander was in the room. We were all wondering what to put on the album. We sat there for about two and a half hours, tossing around ideas, until I said, with my offbeat Anglo humor, 'Now, look! All we have to do here is put together a bunch of songs and for the title we'll call it *More BS.*' Well, that went over like a lead balloon. No one laughed, and the meeting was adjourned."

In subsequent meetings between Barbra and Peter, twelve songs were selected. They included "Absent Minded Me" (a song dropped from the *Funny Girl* score), "Supper Time" by Irving Berlin, "When In Rome" (chosen by Streisand mainly because she could kibbitz in Italian), "Will He Like Me?," (from *She Loves Me),* "I'm All Smiles," and "Love Is A Bore," written by Sammy Cahn.

Cahn, the writer of "I'll Walk Alone," "Love and Marriage," "All the Way," and "I Fall in Love Too Easily," had met Streisand previously in Las Vegas. He and his partner, Jimmy Van Heusen, caught her show at the Riviera and went backstage to say hello. "She knocked us out," said Cahn. "She is an original, one of the special few, like Sinatra. I said to her, 'Jimmy and I would like nothing better than to write a song just for you.' She said, 'Please.' We tried to write something explosive for her. Writers have to be very careful when they write for Barbra. She is an incredibly talented creature. She makes everything sound so good. She can take a single line and make it magic. So we wrote with care."

Cahn and Van Heusen worked on "Love Is A Bore" for a month, then brought the song to Streisand when she was appearing in Hollywood at the Cocoanut Grove. "We met one night after the show, in the back room of the Villa Capri. Frank Sinatra went there a lot. They had a piano and we were ready. The demonstration of a song is the moment of truth. It's like walking into the bull ring. Barbra came in and sat down with Marty. And Jimmy said to her, 'We don't know if we've written you a hit, but if you sing this song it won't embarrass you, and it's a song that will stand the test of time.' So he played, and I sang the song. Not to her, but *at* her. It's a piece that takes staging. She could bite into the words . . . [He sings] . . . 'Love is a *bore!* . . . Love is a drag. . . . It's an I'll call you, it's a phone that never rings.' And Barbra sat there, smiling. And she recorded it. Of course we loved it. I wasn't surprised at how she made it sound. She is special, beyond special. I'm not paying her lip service, but she is unerring in her talent."

Prior to the recording of the *People* album Streisand tried out other songs at an outdoor concert in Forest Hills, New York. "We went out there on a Sunday afternoon," said Peter Daniels. "The rehearsals went well, but the first half of the show didn't."

"I was in the audience that night," said Kay Medford. "I really went out there, along with some of the guys from the show, to see if Barbra was a flash in the pan. When she came out a summer storm was starting up. A bolt of lightning lit up the sky and she looked up and said, 'Quiet down! I haven't done anything yet.' She was witty, very relaxed, like she was in her own living room. But there was too much of a distance between her and the audience. There was a wide stretch between the stage and the first seats. She wasn't reaching the people."

At intermission a fast meeting was held in Streisand's trailer.

"We changed the program for the second half," said Daniels. "We opened with 'People.' We had to get it in there fast. She walked off the stage—all the way down—right out to the center of the field—onto the wet grass. She was stringing the microphone cord behind her. She had been warned—she could have been electrocuted on the wet grass, but she did it anyway. She had to win back the crowd. And she did. They jumped to their feet after that number."

On July twenty-seventh the recording of the *People* album commenced at Columbia. There were two changes in the production ensemble. Arranger-conductor Ray Ellis stood in for Peter Matz, who was then commuting to the West Coast to work on the TV program *Hullabaloo;* and Bob Mersey replaced Mike Berniker, who had left Columbia for a better job at Kapp Records. Mersey was the new head of Columbia A&R, and he took the Streisand assignment reluctantly. "There was a lot of politics going on," he said. "The company had foreclosed on A&R, it seemed. They needed an album from Barbra, any album. They wanted someone who could wrestle with her and Marty. She was a horror to work with. She had a killer instinct. As soon as she sensed fear in anyone, she went for the throat. She was a real bully."

Mersey and Streisand had worked together on "My Coloring Book." "On one level she is a great talent" he said. "When she performed she was unbelievable. Offstage she was somebody else. Very disagreeable, with no charm or humor. I'll tell you a story. After the "Coloring Book" session I was talking to Andy Williams in L.A. Andy at this time had a very popular TV show. I had been riding him about using Aretha Franklin, who I thought was marvelous. But Andy said, 'No, I never heard of her, and who wants a black artist, and blah-blah-blah.' Then later I pitched Barbra to him. I told him, 'There's a girl, and she's turning New York upside down. Her name is Barbra Streisand and she is so phenomenal she could do nothing but light up your show if she were on it.' And Marty is standing there while I'm talking; but Andy says no again. He wants guests that his audiences recognize, and she's a nobody, et cetera. Okay. Time passes. Barbra explodes on records, then in *Funny Girl;* and Andy comes to New York. He *has* to see the show, because Barbra is the most wonderful thing he has heard in his life. I remind him he turned her down for the show, and he says, 'But she was a nobody then.' Still—Streisand *never* forgets. She has the memory of an elephant. But I get the tickets and Andy is dying to go backstage to meet her. I said, 'Okay, let's go.' We're in her dressing room and after I say, 'Barbra, I'd like you to meet Andy Williams,' there's this terrible pause. It's awkward beyond belief—because no one is saying anything. Finally Barbra says to Andy, 'You know, I hate all boy singers. I really hate 'em. But of all the ones I've heard, I hate you the worst.' Andy was open mouthed and speechless. He began to stutter, and I said, 'Hey, why don't we leave?' "

Streisand was serious, Mersey claimed. "The girl doesn't joke. You're always uncomfortable with her because she's basically a dull girl. Whereas somebody else, like a Bette Midler, is a lot of laughs, she laughs at herself. But not Miss Pitkin Avenue—she's serious; above it all. She knows everything that's possible to be known in the world. Like on the *People* album. Ask Frank Laico about the EQ episode. Somewhere, somebody, told her about equalization of the voice. It's a process used in recording. Now, she wasn't quite sure *what* it was, but if it was available she wanted ten pounds of it. [Laughter] Ask Frank."

"She wanted a *ton* of it," said Laico. "We were all set up for this session when she starts in on me. 'Frank,' she says, 'I want EQ, give me EQ.' I tell her, 'Barbra, you had equalization on all your albums.' But she wouldn't believe that."

"She kept it up," said Mersey. "She said to Erlichman, 'Marty, he isn't giving me EQ.' It became a ridiculous situation. She started yelling, 'I'm gonna tell Goddard Lieberson I'm not getting enough EQ.' All of a sudden Frank blew his top. He said to Marty, 'I've taken all the shit I'm gonna take from anybody. You can take your fucking songs and your fucking star and flush 'em both down the toilet, because I'm going home.' And Frank went stomping out of the studio, with Marty running after him, babbling like the yenta he is. It was wonderful—a real zoo—I can hardly remember anything I enjoyed more." Laico returned to the studio to complete the sessions for the *People* album (and for five subsequent LPs, of which Bob Mersey would produce four). "The game playing went on, from time to time," said Laico. "I think sometimes she did it from the little devil that is inside of her, to see how far she could go. She is a strong lady. I used to call her the barracuda. She'd eat you alive if you didn't push her off."

"I am hard to handle and hard to please," Streisand agreed. "And when I can't be handled I can destroy someone very easily."

"I never gave her the satisfaction of playing those power games," said Bob Mersey. "When she was great I told her, because how could you not? Her instincts and performances in the studio were marvelous to watch. But when she was idiotic, I let her know."

THE *PEOPLE* COVER

With the recording completed on the *People* LP, Barbra turned her attention to the cover art and the title of the album.* Visual suggestions had already been tendered to her by Columbia's Merchandising Department. The cover they envisioned was one of global unity, of international togetherness (and sales). They saw Barbra standing outside the United Nations building, surrounded by people and flags of all nations.

Barbra turned green when she heard that idea. She was not standing with anyone, anywhere. It was her cover art and she didn't intend to share it. She had already chosen the photo. It had been taken a year previously in Chicago, by Don Bronstein, a photographer for *Playboy* magazine.

Barbra was not posing nude, the company learned; in fact the only bare skin visible was that of her ankles and the back of her arms. Her face was not seen, because she had been photographed with her *back* to the camera.

"She brought that slide in," said John Berg. "Just the one photo —no selection, no alternatives."

"That shot was originally going to be on the back of the album," Bob Cato recalled. "That was how it originally went down. But when we looked at it we decided it should be on the front. There was no debate, no discussion. We loved it."

Columbia's marketing did not. The pose was offensive and would impede sales, they felt.

---

* After the *First, Second,* and *Third* Barbra Streisand albums were released, a sketch from Columbia's art department was circulated through the building and eventually made its way to the *New Yorker* magazine. The sketch showed Barbra, sitting in a rocking chair, à la Whistler's mother. The caption underneath read: BARBRA STREISAND: THE 74TH ALBUM. After that all numerals were dropped from her covers.

"There was a lot of excitement over the cover," said Bob Mersey, "but I said it wasn't such a bad idea—to see the queen of *menuvals*—that's Jewish for an ugly broad—turn her back to the camera. I thought it was an artistic landmark."

"That cover was unique, very unique," said Marty Erlichman. "It got a lot of awards because of the concept."

Concept? What concept?

"You know, . . ." said Erlichman, "Barbra . . . and people . . . and her hands on her hips, her back to the world."

"She did that quite often onstage," Peter Daniels recalled. "She'd be singing and she'd turn her back to the audience. The concept is the whole idea of looking into yourself—you know, people who need people but she's alone. Barbra became very closed in on herself after *Funny Girl* opened. She withdrew from the company, concentrating on herself and not caring too much about anyone else—which is the way it's supposed to be. You become a star and you've got to protect what you've got."

With fame came autonomy and the self-serving notion that Streisand alone was responsible for her success. Former friends and professional allies were gradually dropped. One of them, Terry Leong, who had designed her first stage wardrobe, found he was no longer welcome in her circle after *Funny Girl* opened. "She didn't need me," he said. "She had money and all the clothes she wanted from Seventh Avenue. I went to see the show and later went backstage. She was cordial, but very busy. It was like 'Hello, how are you, good-bye.' I was hurt and disappointed. I never saw or heard from her again." "Discarding the old for the new is not unusual when people become famous," said Fred Glaser. "There is always that problem of having people around who when they look in your eyes *know* from whence you've come. It's a chilling thing. So to eliminate that from your life you must get rid of that person."

Another seminal figure who reportedly was given a fast farewell in Streisand's dressing room was actor Barry Dennen. Although his name was seldom mentioned in interviews or press reports, Dennen was Barbra's first important mentor, and her first lover. Four years her senior, and a drama graduate from UCLA, he had met Barbra at an acting class in Manhattan in 1960. Not long after that she moved in with him. "Barry was rich, good looking, bright, and instinctive," said Bob Schulenberg. "Women, young women, young actresses, idolized him. To Barbra he was God on earth. He was the first person I knew who was a match for her. He was just as talented and devious as she was. She knew he had 'other romantic interests.' He used to hang out at Julius's a lot. And so did she. Back then, in the early sixties, it was considered bohemian. And Barry and Barbra were the Scott and Zelda of their day."

He was her first sexual experience; at age eighteen. "In my family sex was taboo," she confessed. "You don't screw anybody until you get married, you don't hold hands, you don't kiss, because you'll get a disease. It was all so awful I had to develop a fantasy."

Dennen also introduced her to music, to the songs and styling of Ruth Etting, Lee Wiley, and Mabel Mercer. When Barbra began to sing professionally, Barry coached her, picked her material, and spent hours taping her early performances. "Barry gave her enormous confidence," said Schulenberg, "but he also rode hard on her. He was a strong, brilliant director. He didn't stand for any foolishness from her. And she knew she could trust him, because he had such unerring taste."

The young couple considered marriage. "They told me they were thinking of eloping. They were sitting on the floor of Barry's apartment. He was massaging her feet and they were looking at each other as if no one else existed. When they told me their plans I thought, *Very interesting: Barry and Barbra, a married couple. It could work out, but then again it could be World War Three.*"

When Dennen went to California to visit his family, Barbra stayed in his apartment on West Ninth Street with strict instructions not to answer his phone. "He treated her badly," said Bob. "He stayed away too long and never contacted her. She was a true Taurus. She wanted one man, the home and the hearth. Barry wanted everything. When he came back the romance cooled. She said nothing. Barbra was never one to show her feelings, but when she sang 'Cry Me A River' in her act I understood everything. He was her focus for that song."

Even though they had parted, Barbra still relied on Dennen's musical judgment. When she was about to record *Pins and Needles* she asked and received his direction on the songs. She also made some "vague and ultimately unrealized promises" that he would work on her first album. At one point Barry swallowed his pride and called her to ask if she would introduce him to some people in the business. "She did nothing."

After *Funny Girl* opened, Barry Dennen and Bob Schulenberg went to see the show. Barbra supplied the tickets and extended an invitation to visit her backstage. But there was a hook to her hospitality. Wary in her greeting, and following some preliminary small talk, she got to the point. She asked Dennen about those early rehearsal tapes. She wanted them back. Dennen replied that he would be glad to play them for her whenever she wanted, but they had enormous sentimental value to him and he wouldn't give them up. The two began to argue. "It was a very awkward situation for me," said Bob Schulenberg. "I had set the meeting up. Neither of them would let the other side win. So they parted, coolly. Much later, after Barry was established in *Jesus Christ Superstar*, I received a postcard from Barbra. On it she wrote: 'What ever happened to Barry Dennen?' I never knew if she was joking or not."

"My mother eats, sleeps, and breathes—just like a normal human being."

Barbra Streisand, 1964

Streisand's banishment of old, familiar faces extended beyond professional friends to include a leading member of her family—her mother, who would be barred from the theater shortly after the opening of *Funny Girl.*

In her youth Diana Rosen, the daughter of a cantor who made leather coats in the garment district, had "visionary ideas" of becoming a famous performer. "I had a nice shape," said she, "I had a nice voice and face. I used to perform in front of the mirror, singing and kicking up my heels, y'know?" When she was twenty she traded in her fantasies of the footlights for the more tangible realization of love and romance. She met and married a dashing young English teacher, Emanuel Streisand. A son, Sheldon, was born in 1935 and, seven years later, a daughter, Barbara Joan, arrived. Fifteen months after that Emanuel Streisand died; of a cerebral hemorrhage, the neighbors were told.

To support her two children the young widow moved back to her family on Pulaski Street. She found work as a bookkeeper and Barbra was looked after each day by her grandparents. "My grandmother couldn't handle me," she told writer Dale Pollock. "She called me *fabrent* [Yiddish for 'on fire']. If I was sick with the chicken pox and I wanted to go out and play, I put on my clothes, climbed out the window, and went out to play." At age seven another trauma disrupted Barbra's world. Her mother remarried. The new husband was Louis Kind, a real estate agent whom Barbra preferred to call "a used-car salesman or something." In 1951 a beautiful, cherubic daughter, Rosalind, was born. Barbra was taken with the new baby, but when her stepfather began to refer to the two girls as "the beauty and the beast," she grew resentful, then combative, and in time, manipulative. She learned how to fight back. "It was always two against one," said one source, "or the world against Barbra. Her mother seldom took her side, and her brother had left for college. So Barbra learned how to scheme and disrupt things. All of the other little girls in the neighborhood were playing Heidi or Shirley Temple games, but Barbra was more attuned to Patty McCormack and *The Bad Seed*. She could be quite the little agitator."

In 1953, perhaps sensing defeat, Louis Kind left the apartment for the proverbial pack of cigarettes. When he failed to return, Barbra consoled her mother and then persuaded her to change the locks on the door.

Mrs. Kind never encouraged her acting career, Barbra often complained. "She said I wasn't pretty enough, not talented enough." When she was fifteen she wanted to go to the Malden Bridge Theater for the summer, her mother refused permission and the fare. "She was too young, and it was a hardship for me," said Mrs. Kind. "Rosalind and I were also going to the mountains for the summer, but in a different direction. I said to Barbra, 'How can you do this to me? I'm not gonna let you go alone.' She said, 'I have this friend, we're both going, but I need three hundred dollars.' I refused, but she was so insistent. She got the other girl, and the other girl's mother, to work on me, so I gave in."

"I could always manipulate my mother," said Barbra. "I could act rings around her. I made people believe what I wanted them to believe."

When Barbra graduated from high school her mother wanted her to become a secretary or a school clerk. "They get free vacations; summers off with pay, y'know?" she said. Barbra's reply was to grow her fingernails three inches long, and all talk of typing and filing was quashed. When her mother persisted with her plebeian plans, Barbra packed her clothes and books and moved to Manhattan. But Mama followed. She dogged her older daughter's every track. "Barbra moved about all the time," said Bob Schulenberg. "When I met her she was staying at Veronica Lake's apartment; but somehow her mother always found her."

"I was worried," said Mrs. Kind. "She caused me a lot of grief. Mothers don't get pleasure from knowing their daughters are traveling far from home. What if she wasn't eating right? What if she got sick? I didn't want my daughter dying in some stranger's apartment."

In 1960, hoping to win her mother's support, Barbra, age eighteen, invited her to watch her act at Alan Miller's workshop. After the performance Mrs. Kind remained silent, until she got her daughter alone. "She really let her have it," said one friend. "She told Barbra she was a fool, she was only kidding herself. She had no talent, and no one would ever pay good money to see her on a stage. Barbra listened to all this. She didn't cry or get angry. She let her mother attack her with all that negative criticism, and then, very calmly, she replied, 'You're *wrong*, Mama. Wait. You'll see.'"

With her success in *Wholesale*, and on records, Mrs. Kind's faith in her daughter's talent turned from disbelief to wonder, and then to self-homage. "She didn't fall from a tree," she told reporters. "She got her voice from *me*." In Boston, during the tryouts for *Funny Girl*, an assistant to Ray Stark recalled a visit from Mrs. Kind and daughter Rosalind. "Barbra's manager asked me if I'd join them for dinner," she said. "The five of us went to this restaurant not far from the theater, and most of the people there knew who Barbra was. She didn't acknowledge their attention, but her mother was practically standing up taking bows."

"You know what the situation reminded me of?" said another source. "It was like the Ethel Merman musical *Gypsy*, with Mama Rose and her two daughters—the younger, prettier Baby June, and the older, plainer Gypsy Rose Lee. To Mrs. Kind, Roslyn was the one with all the talent. She was amazed when Barbra started getting so much attention. When it happened, Mama wanted *her* turn in the spotlight."

After *Funny Girl* opened on Broadway and Streisand's celebrity was established nationally, Mrs. Kind attended every performance she could. She introduced herself to strangers at intermission, signed autographs for fans outside the stage door, and then, armed with her shopping bags filled with food, she visited her famous daughter backstage.

"Mrs. Kind was a typical Jewish mother," said actress Kay Medford. "She had a wonderful forthright personality, with two main concerns—your health and food. When you met her backstage, if you stood still long enough she'd feed you."

Barbra at this juncture had changed. She was not looking for encouragement or nourishment from her mother *or* the public. A shield of aloofness had been raised; familiarities with the cast, crew, fans, were verboten. She asked her mother to behave with the proper remoteness, to cool it with the shopping bags, the autographs, and so on. But Mrs. Kind, now over fifty, was having the time of her life. This was her first taste of celebrity albeit by proxy, and she had no intention of giving it up.

To further dissuade her mother's attention, Barbra cut down on her supply of free tickets to *Funny Girl.* When her mother still insisted on visiting backstage she had her name removed from the guest list posted at the door. Mrs. Kind was not discouraged, however. Peter Daniels recalled a surprise appearance during the preproduction of the *People* album. "We were having a meeting at my studio. No one had arrived when I heard a knock at the door. I opened it and there was Mrs. Kind, carrying a large paper bag filled with food. She headed for the kitchen and started laying out the corned beef, the pastrami, and the pickles. I knew Barbra had forbidden her mother to come anywhere near the stage door of *Funny Girl,* and how she found out about this meeting, I don't know.

"When Barbra walked in I thought she was going to have an apoplectic fit. She started screaming, 'I don't want you around. Get out! Get out!' She literally threw her mother out of my studio, out of my apartment, out of the house. It was a very awkward situation for all of us. Barbra came back, sat down, and she began discussing songs as if nothing had happened."*

---

* Upon the release of the hardcover edition of this book, Miss Streisand denied any differences with her mother. Yet, according to writer René Jordan, these early altercations would later become the basis for "the best nightmarish scene in her 1971 movie, *Up the Sandbox,* when the prying mama is not intimidated by a chain lock she proceeds to destroy with a giant wrench."

* * *

On August 21, 1964, Barbra completed the *People* album, recording "Fine And Dandy," "Autumn," and "I'm All Smiles." During the second week of September the LP was released and quickly rose to number one on the charts. It won Grammies for Peter Matz as Best Arranger, for Barbra as Best Female Vocalist, and the award for Best Album Cover went to art director John Berg. "That pleased her a lot," said Berg. "She chose the photo; she rode down the opposition to her being shown with her back to the camera. When it succeeded it was very hard for anyone at CBS to argue again with her about cover art. Visually, Barbra always knows what's best for Barbra."

Chapter 8

"I like very much what Barbra Streisand once said about being a star. I didn't hear this myself. It was on a talk show several years ago and someone quoted it to me. She was explaining to the host that people accused her of becoming a bitch since she became famous. 'It's not true,' she said. 'I was always a bitch.'"

Luciano Pavarotti*

MY NAME IS BARBRA

On January 16, 1965, Lyndon Baines Johnson was sworn in for his first full term as president. The previous night, Streisand had been one of the stars who performed at his Inaugural Eve gala.

The afternoon of the gala, because of security arrangements, Barbra was not given her proper allocation of rehearsal time. Consequently the show that night did not meet her professional standards. "Someone screwed up with her lighting," said Fred Glaser, who came in from Chicago to do her hair for the night. "The cues were off during one of her songs. No one really noticed except Barbra. When she came offstage she flew at me. Marty and Elliott must have known she was angry, because they were nowhere in sight. So I got her abuse. In the dressing room she began to curse and swear. I had never seen her like this before, but gradually I got her to simmer down. I told her I was going to make sure that the

---

* Luciano Pavarotti, with William Wright, Pavarotti: My Own Story (New York: Doubleday & Co., Inc., 1981)

lighting guy got fired, that he would never work again, and that seemed to calm her. She wanted *revenge.*"

Following the inaugural show, Barbra stood in line with the other stars—Johnny Carson, Ann-Margret, Carol Channing, and Rudolf Nureyev and Margot Fonteyn—to be presented to President Johnson, Lady Bird Johnson, and members of their cabinet. On this occasion, Streisand did not ask the President for an autograph. She could barely smile, except for the press.

"Barbra moved her head incessantly, trying to show the best side of her face to the cameras," said theater critic William Raidy, who attended the Inaugural Ball with the French ambassador and his wife, the Alphands. "Mme. Alphand was a big admirer of Barbra's, and she asked if she could meet her," said Raidy. "I knew Barbra from New York, so I made the introductions. Mme. Alphand told Barbra she was her favorite singer; that she played her records all the time at the embassy, and Barbra sort of raised one eyebrow and said: 'Oh, yeah'—like 'So what?'—and then she walked away. The Alphands were totally nonplused, and I was embarrassed. But thankfully I spotted Carol Channing nearby and I grabbed her. Carol did her entire 'Vive la France' act for the couple, and even sang a little song for them, which helped lighten their encounter with La Streisand."

Her rudeness was unintentional, Raidy believed. "She may have been overwhelmed by being in those surroundings. She didn't know what to say and was therefore totally inarticulate."

Publicist Pat Kelly offered another theory. "Barbra was not used to such large social gatherings, especially the kind of circuses they throw in Washington during Inaugural time. It must have been mind-boggling for her and Elliott to see all those important politicians in tuxedos and ballgowns and social types milling around like cattle. So eventually she said, 'Stop! Enough! Spare me this bullshit. I wanna go home.' "

By the end of January, Streisand had been appearing in *Funny Girl* for thirteen months, and that was twelve months too long, so far as she was concerned. Again she hated playing the same part, acting the same role, singing the same songs, eight times a week. "It's like being in prison," she complained, adding improvisations and tasteless bits of material to relieve the monotony. The changes threw off the orchestra and members of the cast. She was reprimanded by the stage manager, and by Ray Stark, who threatened to cancel one performance rather than subject the audience to an inferior show.

"Barbra would push Ray so far, then pull back," said a cast member. "When she knew he meant business, she got very sweet and playful. She still needed Stark. He was doing the movie of *Funny Girl* and he wasn't offering the role to her until her contract for the Broadway show was fulfilled."

On Monday, February 1, Barbra began to develop a cold, but she insisted on recording three new songs at Columbia Records. The following day her cold had become worse, but again she showed up at the Winter Garden and went on that night. The following morning, a Wednesday matinee day, she had laryngitis and could barely croak her instructions over the phone to Ray Stark. She couldn't go on, she told him, and wanted the theater closed while she was out. Stark refused. "There's absolutely no way I'll close the theater," he replied. "I don't give a damn if there's only two hundred people in the audience, the show must go on."

Streisand's understudy, Lainie Kazan, was notified that she would go on for the matinee and evening performances. Kazan, a statuesque chorus girl, with a Bachelor of Arts degree from Hofstra, had spent many nights anticipating stepping into Barbra's shoes. "She was always late, the little devil," Lainie told writer Michael Musto. "I'd be waiting in the wings all ripe and ready, and she'd come in at seven fifty-nine and go on. I cried a lot." On that matinee day, when her big break finally came, Kazan, in the best Eve Harrington tradition, went into pre-performance action. She called every critic and columnist in town and told them of her appearance. In turn she performed flawlessly at both the afternoon and evening shows and in all producer Ray Stark had only 125 tickets to refund.

The following morning the New York newspapers heralded the birth of a new star. The clamor and rejoicing reached the twenty-sixth floor of 320 Central Park West where Barbra lay in bed, eating her breakfast and reading the reviews. She grabbed the phone and began to shriek at the show's press agent.

"Barbra unfortunately believed in her own publicity," said Peter Daniels. "She thought no one could take over for Barbra Streisand, that she was irreplaceable, which is nonsense. It's not a question of whether Lainie did it as good as Barbra, or better. She did it differently, and it was just as acceptable."

Miraculously, that same day Streisand recovered her voice. She went on for that night's performance, then called a meeting with Ray Stark. Shortly thereafter Lainie Kazan left the show.

"They made Lainie's life very uncomfortable," said Daniels, "so she quit."

Daniels himself was also caught in the altercation. He was not only Barbra's accompanist, he was Lainie's lover. "We were running around at the time," he said. "That wasn't too smart. You want to talk about some of the bad moves you make in your career, that was one. Yes, we fell in love [and later married]. Once Barbra heard about it our friendship wasn't the same. That was partly my fault. Barbra and I continued to see each other every day, and I would take notes down, and sometimes conduct the first act. I played for her every night, but our relations were strained."

Early in March, after six years, the singer and her accompanist parted permanently. "It became a very trying time," said Daniels. *Funny Girl* had been a huge success, but it took its toll with so many people. There was so much gouging going on. So much acrimony and bitterness between the people who put the show on. Sydney Chaplin quit. Carol Haney (the choreographer) had died. She was found drunk down on the Bowery. She had too much to drink and no insulin. I had been torn between my role as associate musical director, between Barbra and everyone. There was too much sadness. I had to leave, to get some semblance of peace and normality. I took a two-week vacation. Before I left I called an old friend of mine, David Shire. I said 'David, this is what's going to happen. I'm splitting. Nobody knows it yet. I'm bringing you in as the pianist, and you'll take over my place. But don't say a word until the last of my two weeks' vacation.' "

There were no good-byes from Barbra; no farewell as friends. No one made any effort to have him stay. "It was all over by then," said Peter. "I had a wonderful time. It had been incredibly exciting for me, to see something happen to a person, to actually be there. The evolution of her rise to fame was fantastic to watch. She and Marty had made it. They were there, and I was out."

Another of Streisand's complaints, while in tenure on Broadway, was with the impermanence of theater. "Each night," she said, "after I finish a show, it's horrible thinking whatever special I did in that performance won't be retained."

In March of 1965 she would find a permanent keepsake for her work. It would come through the medium of television, which in one night would bring her a larger audience, and more money, than all her Broadway performances combined.

Since her opening in *Funny Girl* all three major TV networks had been interested in Streisand, for specials or for a comedy series, whatever she chose to do. The final bidding went to CBS and NBC. Agents David Begelman and Freddie Fields had no trouble negotiating the money (5 million dollars for one special a year during the next ten years); it was the subsidiary rights and controls that stalled the proceedings.

"It went back and forth for a while between CBS and NBC," said Marty Erlichman. "Then I had a fight with Begelman and Freddie. There were two open points in the contract. One was creative control, which CBS and NBC never gave to anybody. The closest CBS came was with Jackie Gleason, but he didn't have it in the *language* of the contract. I also wanted the right to do closed-circuit and pay TV, which were new at that time. Pat Weaver had just lost a referendum for cable TV in L.A., so Begelman and Fields said, that being the case, it was silly for me to ask something that was going to be ten years down the road anyway. I got angry at that. I didn't want to wake up one morning and have someone offer us a million dollars for Barbra to do a closed-circuit concert or a cable TV show, and I'd have to say, 'Sorry, I made a deal six or ten years ago that says she can't do that.' "

Erlichman told Begelman and Fields to put their priorities in order or to get out of the picture. They represented Barbra and *not* the TV networks. "I picked up and left L.A.," he said. "I came back to New York. I got a call two days later, saying that a conference call was being placed between Bill Paley and James Aubrey in New York, David Begelman and Freddie Fields in L.A., and me. It came down that Paley got on the phone last. Aubrey introduced everybody and Paley said, 'As I understand it, talking points are closed circuit and creative control. You have it.' And he hung up.

And everybody said, 'Congratulations.' But the truth of the matter is that I had Herb Schosser of NBC on the other line. I gave it to CBS because they were the first I had gone to and the first to say yes."*

Meetings for the first special, tentatively titled *The Barbra Streisand Show,* began in late January. Surrounding herself with the best staff possible—Dwight Hemion as director, Richard Lewine as producer, Joe Layton as staging director, and Peter Matz as arranger-conductor—Streisand also asked for Frank Laico to join the team to work on her sound. She wanted the same audio quality for TV as she had on her records, and the request for Laico went to Goddard Lieberson.

"They neglected to tell Goddard that they didn't want to pay me," said Laico. "I went over to the CBS rehearsal studios. Barbra and the rest of the guys were inside a room, talking. I stood in the doorway until I saw Marty. He beckoned to me to enter. I beckoned back. I wasn't setting foot inside until we came to an agreement. Barbra and Marty loved to make money, and more than that, they loved to keep it. I didn't believe I should give up my nights and my weekends for nothing. Marty came out and said, 'Sure you'll get paid. Write me a piece of paper, with your name and the amount you want, and I'll get it for you.' So I did. He took the paper, looked at the amount, and said, 'Yes. That's all right. Let's go to work.' So we did, but it took them a long time before they paid me. And the figure was low. I thought I was being smart, but they really had me."

Her first television special had to be different from all others, Streisand decided. The concept would be herself: her life story, from childhood, to adolescence, to young womanhood, and stardom. There would be no guests. No dancers, or backup singers; no announcer or other visible helpers. "Terrific," said a CBS programmer, "we'll call it *The Immaculate Conception Hour.*"

"Yeah, everyone said we were crazy," said Marty Erlichman. "CBS, Columbia Records, and Begelman were calling us, telling us we had to have at least one guest star on the show. Barbra was known on Broadway and on records, but to the vast TV audiences in the Midwest she was a nobody. Without name stars how would

---

* David Begelman, who had practically guaranteed Streisand to NBC, was because of the switch barred from dealing with the network for a number of years.

she attract them to the show? I told CBS, 'That's your job. You get them to us for the first few minutes and Barbra will hold them for the hour.' "

> *"When I heard her sing my song my reaction was: 'Oh, my God!' I didn't care what happened to the song after that, because hers was the performance."*
> **Mickey Leonard, the composer of**
> **"Why Did I Choose You?"**

By happenstance Mickey Leonard, a composer and vocal coach, was asked to contribute to the TV special. With lyricist Herbert Martin he was writing a Broadway musical based on *The Yearling,* and Barbra had recorded one of the songs, "I'm All Smiles," on her *People* LP. "A while later I ran into Marty Erlichman on the street. He mentioned that Barbra was going to do a TV special, and did I have anything she could see? He suggested I drop by their offices on Lexington Avenue. I went up there and played a song called 'My Pa,' for Elliott. He flipped for it. He called Barbra and made her come and listen to it. I never knew her attachment to her father at the time. I only knew that Emanuel was her father's name, and the name of her music company."

Streisand also loved "My Pa" and asked to hear more songs from the show. The composer played "Why Did I Choose You?" and "The Kind Of A Man A Woman Needs." "She decided she wanted to record all of them. It was unbelievable to me. To have your stuff done by Streisand is an absolute joy. We rehearsed up at her apartment. Bob Mersey, her record producer, asked me who I wanted to arrange and conduct. I said I wanted my hero, my guru, Don Costa. Barbra didn't know him, but Bob Mersey did, and said, 'You've got him.' "

Streisand did not take to Costa at their first meeting. She was used to Peter Matz. She felt uncomfortable with a stranger who didn't play the piano well. "Don played guitar," Leonard said. "On the piano he performed like a construction worker, with four fingers. Barbra was put off by that. But it all went pretty fast. We went over the songs, put on tags and endings, and that was it."

The songs were rehearsed at Columbia on the day Streisand came down with the cold that led to Lainie Kazan's replacement.

"Barbra wasn't going to record that day," said Leonard. "She was there to listen to Don Costa's arrangements. She had the sniffles, but when she saw the musicians and was told they were being paid, she decided to do one song. She took some chicken soup, literally, from a Thermos she had with her, and she began to record. She did 'Why Did I Choose You?' in two takes. 'The Kind Of A Man A Woman Needs,' which is a bitch to sing, she did in one or two takes also. 'My Pa' she wanted to hear the arrangement, but Don asked that she wait for another time, when she felt better. She persisted, however. He ran down the charts with her, they made a couple of changes, she rehearsed it once, then recorded it in one take.

" 'Why Did I Choose You?' was originally written in the show as a duet between the mother and father. It was called 'Why Did You Choose Me?' The mother wasn't attractive and she didn't know what the husband saw in her. We changed it for Barbra. All of her suggestions were good. She asked that we switch some lyrics around, which were hard to sing. In the line where she sings, 'And when I gave my heart to you, so many years ago, I gave it willingly and lovingly to you. . . .' 'willingly' is a closed sound, a very difficult word to sing up high; so she said, 'It's too hard, it'd be better if I switched the words and sang "lovingly" at first.' And that's the way she did it.

"You ask how I felt when I heard the playbacks? I'll tell you. You never forget an experience like that. When I heard her sing 'Why Did I Choose You?' my reaction was 'Oh, my God!' I didn't care what happened to the song after that because hers was *the* performance. She's like Sinatra and Judy Garland. 'Over The Rainbow' will always be Judy's song. 'People' is Barbra's song. It was the kiss of death for a publisher, though. After she recorded 'I'm All Smiles' and 'Why Did I Choose You?' no one would touch those songs for years. But I was happy. Who wouldn't be? It's a dream of every composer to have their songs recorded by Barbra Streisand."

The medley for the TV show came from a discussion among Joe Layton, Peter Matz, and Streisand. She wanted to model some high-fashion clothes, not on a runway or in a studio, but in a real-life setting—a department store. This would be her statement on success and acquisitions, but it had to be done in counterpoint to the usual rags-to-riches treatment. "Television was just getting into electronic editing," said Matz. "So we had the freedom of using different songs and different costumes and editing it down. We spoke about different songs. They had to lead from one moment to the next with a twist in the lyric." And thus a collection of songs suggesting the Great Depression—"Brother, Can You Spare A Dime?" "Nobody Knows You When You're Down and Out," and "I Got Plenty Of Nothin' "—were coupled with "Second Hand Rose" and "Give Me The Simple Life." "I worked on the songs at night," said Matz. "The next day Barbra would go over them. She'd say, 'That's good. This we change. Put this ahead of that.' We went through three or four drafts until it was perfect, and then I did the arrangements for the full orchestra."

Prior to the filming of the fashion sequence of the Bergdorf-Goodman store on Fifth Avenue, Barbra monitored each aspect of the sequence. She chose the clothes (by Bill Blass and Emeric Partos), the hats (by Halston), and the furs, which came from the private vaults of Bergdorf's. She supervised the choreography and the pretaping of the music; each facet had to be perfect. "This was essentially Barbra's film debut," said Fred Glaser. "She was determined to make herself as photogenic as possible. She lost weight and I cut most of her hair off.* She wanted to be as sleek and gorgeous as possible, to bury the 'kook' image forever. And it worked because she did it with such throwaway humor and elegance. In essence what she was saying with her romp through Bergdorf's was 'You want *chic*—well, here it is—and so *what!*' "

Leading into the opening of the fashion segment, Streisand talked on camera about material wealth. "Luxuries? Luxuries are meaningless. It's the simple things that are basic: food, shelter, and a few yards of cloth to protect you from the cold. Now, I'm like that—essentially a plain person. Simple. Very simple and unadorned." Fade to a medium shot of Barbra, dressed in a leather miniskirt and a fifteen-thousand-dollar full-length Somali leopard coat. She rides in a horse and carriage at dawn along a deserted Fifth Avenue. The carriage stops outside Bergdorf's. At the entrance is a liveried footman (Marty Erlichman). Singing "Give Me The Simple Life," Barbra sweeps into the store, then swoops from counter to counter, trying on jewelry, perfume, and hats. Cut to

---

* Her new hairdo, called "le Garçon," the boy look, was inspired by The Beatles, said Glaser. Streisand denied this. "Mine is shorter in the back," she said, "so what are *they* going to do now?"

Barbra vamping through the fur salon dressed in a floppy Halston hat and a hundred-thousand-dollar sable coat. She bumps and grinds through the archway, lowers the sable to show a backless dress, then stomps on the sable, all the while singing "I've Got Plenty Of Nothin'." This segues to Barbra, pre-Yentl, as a newsboy —dressed in white mink knickers, black velvet top, mink scarf, and white moiré cap—hawking newspapers. She grins and mugs and lip-syncs her way into "Nobody Knows You When You're Down And Out," wearing a floor-length crushed-velvet robe lined in mink. For the climax, and her exit from the store, she's in a white tailored riding outfit, with leather crop, and a matching brocade hunting hat, tied with yards of flowing tulle. Her musical adieu? "The Best Things In Life Are Free."

In the second week of April, after the show was edited, the CBS TV brass sat down to view the special. They were vitriolic in their judgment. "They hated it," said Marty Erlichman. "They said it had no beginning, no middle, no end. They wanted us to redo certain scenes. They said we had to insert a guest star—a Doris Day or an Andy Williams. I told 'em, 'No, it goes as it is.' "

Columbia Records were also discontent. Not with the show, but with the progress of the soundtrack album, which they intended to release. Barbra's last album had been the $2-million-selling *People*, released eight months ago. They needed the new TV album, but Barbra wasn't releasing the tapes. She told Columbia she was changing the format for the album. She was dropping some songs and adding new ones, songs that weren't on the special. First to be discarded was the Bergdorf medley. "Columbia panicked when they heard that," one executive recalled. "The medley was the highlight of the hour, it had to be on the album. They called in Marty and he told them the medley would be on a *second* TV album. The special was so great, he predicted CBS would show it again, and that way, by stretching the material, Columbia would get two albums, which meant double the income for everyone. They thought he was certifiably insane."

On April twenty-first, *My Name Is Barbra* was screened for the TV critics. CBS had hoped to postpone all showings until the day before the special aired, but *Time* magazine was running a story on Barbra and they insisted on seeing the show.

On Monday the reviews from *Time* and the advance notices

from the newspaper critics arrived at the publicity office of CBS. They were, in short, raves. "It is the most enchanting, tingling TV hour of the season," said *Time.* "A pinnacle moment in American show business, in any form, in any period," said UPI. And "Barbra Streisand, the delicious, offbeat song stylist, leaped upward in her meteoric and still-rising young career," said the New York *Herald Tribune.*

On the night of the show's telecast Andrew Goodman, co-owner of Bergdorf-Goodman, hosted a special telecast-party at his penthouse apartment atop the store. Invited were Bill Paley, Frank Stanton, and Goddard Lieberson of Columbia Records, plus assorted celebrities, columnists, and social figures. Barbra attended with Elliott and Marty Erlichman. Following the telecast she was virtually jammed into a corner of the Goodmans' living room by guests who wanted to talk to her, to touch her, to take home some keepsake, verbal or otherwise, of her evening's triumph. "She was positively glowing," said a guest. "This night meant more to her than her opening in *Funny Girl.* I told her that twenty-five million people had watched the show, and she replied, 'Wouldn't it be nice if they all wrote in and sent money?' "

On the day after the telecast Frank Stanton called Goddard Lieberson to inquire where his copy of the soundtrack LP was. Lieberson had to explain there were no albums available, because the star of the TV show had still not recorded her "new format."

"She had them by the balls," said Bob Mersey, "and she loved to apply pressure."

On the afternoon of Friday, the thirtieth of April, two days after the TV special was shown, Streisand strolled into Studio A at Columbia with three new songs that met her approval. They were "I Can See It," from *The Fantasticks;* "Jenny Rebecca," written by Carol Hall; and "I've Got No Strings," from *Pinocchio.*

"The schedule for that session was hell," said Warren Vincent, Columbia's supervisor of editing. "Barbra was recording in one room and we were editing in the other. The word had come from Stanton, via Lieberson, that if the album wasn't out the following week, heads would roll."

After recording her songs Barbra listened to the playbacks, then departed. Warren and the engineers worked through Saturday and Sunday editing the complete album. Late Sunday night the lacquers went by messenger to the pressing plant in Pitman, New

Jersey, where a special work-shift waited to make the mothers and press the records. "We had fifty records made by hand," said a production supervisor. "They were put into special sleeves, jacketed, and the messenger brought them back to New York. On Monday morning five copies were put on Dr. Stanton's desk; another batch went to Lieberson and his staff; and the rest were delivered to Streisand's apartment. By noon that day Sam Goody's and Doubleday's had the first copies for sale in their windows."

"We truly set a record for speed on that album," said Warren Vincent. "We worked nonstop for seventy-two hours. But no one was impressed; least of all Barbra. I remember I said to her later in the week: 'Well, how about that new album? What did you think of it?' And she said 'Warren! Don't depress me. I never play my records.' "

Chapter 9

"I worked myself up from nothing, to a state of extreme poverty."

Barbra Streisand, 1965

SAVING PENNIES

Beyond the lofty ratings and critical acclaim for her first TV show, Streisand was doubly pleased with the consensus on her new looks. In one night she banished her kook image; she was now considered chic, an arbiter of style. Her short hairdo was copied in beauty parlors across the country. "Give me the Streisand look," one patron told her hairdresser, whereupon he took his brush and broke her nose. The jokes continued, but laughing loudest was Streisand, not at herself but at the fashion and beauty manufacturers clamoring for her endorsement. Her press office, Solters, Sabinson and Roskin, were besieged by calls from editors and columnists pleading for interviews, beauty secrets, and photographs of "Bar-bra." *Vogue* magazine a year previously had run her photo inside the magazine with the caption "Nobody looks at her twice except in sympathy." Now they offered her the cover, with Avedon and the makeup, hair, hands, and foot person of her choice. The clothes would come from whatever designer she'd care to appoint. The doors on Seventh Avenue were open to her twenty-two hours a day. But Barbra seldom went downtown, they learned. She wasn't keen on fashion shows or fittings. If the designers wanted her to wear their clothes, they would have to haute-couture themselves and their goods up to her apartment. Dresses, evening gowns, suits, furs, hats, gloves, shoes, boots, and jewelry arrived at her door by the hour. Most of it came wholesale, some of it free.

Free, along with *food,* were two of Barbra's favorite four-letter words. Never shy about haggling or shopping for bargains, she was ecstatic when she got anything—a sample of toothpaste or a fur coat—for nothing. The stories of her frugality matched the tales of her genius. A classmate recalled how, as a teenager at Erasmus High, "Barbra would waltz into the cafeteria, eat heartily, then make a dramatic and belligerent refusal to pay." Joe Franklin, a local TV host, recalled that, as a budding performer, Barbra would take a cab to his TV studio and "then tell the driver she had to break a hundred-dollar bill and hide in a store around the corner till the guy got disgusted and drove away."

In the early days she was broke, she told everyone. Yet one source from that time recalled that Barbra always had a secret hoard of money. "She had this bank book. I saw it once. She had hundreds of dollars accumulating interest in this savings account. Money she got from baby-sitting and other jobs; even her unemployment benefits went into that account.

In 1965, while making ten thousand dollars a week from Broadway, TV, and her records, Barbra still felt the need to economize. She clipped coupons and kept track of sales at supermarkets and department stores.* When mini-skirts came into fashion she hired a seamstress to chop off the bottoms from her old dresses. Nothing was wasted or thrown out, including the green brocade fabric that covered the walls of her library. With material to spare she upholstered a sofa, and had enough left over to make a sleeveless dress. (She posed on and in both for *Look* magazine.) And then there were the tales of her Christmas frugality. "She made Scrooge seem like a spendthrift," said one associate. "During *Funny Girl,* as a gift to the doormen and the elevator operators in her building she gave each one a copy of her *People* album, unwrapped. The mailmen and delivery boys got copies of her latest single."

The classic token of seasonal greeting went to the staff of Columbia Records. To those she liked she sent a recycled Christmas card. "What she did," said one producer, "was save the cards she got the

---

* Especially at Saks Fifth Avenue, where Mrs. Goldstein, Elliott's mother, worked in the girdle department, and could purchase special merchandise at employee discount for her famous daughter-in-law.

year before. She'd cross out the sender's name, write in her own, and mail it out."

"They're collector's items," said Frank Laico, "but unfortunately I threw mine away."

Each week, included in her paycheck from *Funny Girl,* there was a sum designated for "traveling expenses." This could be used for a limo to take Barbra to and from the theater; or as she preferred, a taxi, which was twelve dollars a week cheaper, and she could pocket the difference. Some days she got to save the fare entirely by hitching rides to the theater from friends, or strangers, or from a passing squad car. "I'm always late," she told the police. "It's kind of like a game for me, racing against the clock."

With the escalation of her success, and her new chic image, Barbra decided it was time to buy a car and hire a chauffeur. Shopping for a bargain, she found a used Rolls-Royce. It stalled, then exploded, on Seventh Avenue one night, and was replaced by a 1961 beige Bentley (the backseat of which was soon covered with grease stains from the drippings of the hot dogs and White Tower hamburgers Barbra munched on the way home from the theater each night).

The chauffeur would also displease her. "He washed his socks in the kitchen sink and took baths in our bathroom when we were out," she grieved. "And one evening, when they were entertaining guests on the terrace," said one reporter, "the chauffeur, doubling as a butler, came out to serve blueberry pie. Even in the soft fading light it was impossible to miss one blueberry—lone, plump, condemning—that hung suspended at the corner of his mouth."

The next day the chauffeur was fired, and Barbra, or her best friend, Sis Corman, took turns driving the Bentley, except on days when she insisted on playing the star. "Barbra had become this big *mahah,* the big wheeler-dealer," said Bob Mersey, "and Elliott was nothing next to her. So she made him put on the chauffeur's cap to drive her around."

"Elliott indulged Barbra's little games," said a witness. "He worshiped her and she, in her own way, loved him. But at times she completely ignored him. Her favorite subject was always Barbra. She would get so involved with herself that no one else existed."

Columbia Art Director John Berg recalled one humorous incident of self-absorption. "I went up to their apartment with some slides and a light box—a viewer. We had to choose one photo, I'm not sure if it was for an album or not. Anyway Barbra greeted me dressed in a housecoat. She and Elliott were due for dinner at Richard Rodgers's house. We went into the library, the study, to make the final selection. After a while Elliott came into the room naked, except for his jockey shorts, and he said, 'Barbra, we got to get dressed to go out.' And she said, 'Elliott, don't worry, we've got plenty of time.' Then seven P.M. comes round and we're still editing. Marty Erlichman rolls in from somewhere, carrying a bottle of Dewar's Scotch, which he proceeds to open and drink by himself in a corner. Elliott comes in dressed in a shirt, his shorts, and socks, and says, 'Barbra, come on, now.' She kept looking at her photos—yes to this, no to that—and eight P.M. comes around. Marty is still drinking alone in the corner. Elliott is beginning to rage. Barbra's still looking at the slides, and says, 'Just a minute, hon, just a minute.' And she means that! She thinks it's just a minute, but Elliott is completely tuxed up, and it's nine o'clock. I'm beat, worn out. Marty is drunk. And Elliott is thoroughly pissed off. He's going around the apartment yelling, kicking the furniture. Until finally Barbra holds up one slide and says, 'John, this is it! I've decided. This is the one.' She's happy. She has chosen her photo. She also gets to keep the viewer. She sweeps off to change for dinner, oblivious to the fact that she just spent four hours of time; or that Elliott was angry."

"With Barbra it was a clear-cut situation," said Elliott. "She was committed to the work long before I was. I had to develop my self-respect before I could do anything. So we made Barbra a star before me—because that was more important to her."

In June of 1965 Elliott was signed for *Drat! The Cat!* a musical about a policeman and a jewel thief, set in the early nineteen hundreds. The role of the policeman was described by writer Ira Levin *(No Time for Sergeants)* as "the youngest, dumbest flatfoot on the force." The first actor considered for the part was actor Alan Alda. "Alan auditioned and was marvelous," said the show's composer, Milton Schafer. "He had the right intensity and charm, and a wonderful sense of paranoia. We wanted him, but then the original producer dropped his option." A subsequent producer, Norman Rosemont, managed Robert Goulet, who was given the role but dropped out after he was offered a TV series. Elliott Gould was then hired, and the leading lady, Joey Heatherton, departed. "I'm not sure if she was opposed to Elliott," said Schafer. "I only know she wasn't right for the cat. When she left, we got Lesley Ann Warren, who was lovely and properly feline."

The show was budgeted at four hundred thousand dollars. Among its investors were Columbia Records, Robert Goulet (whose Rogo Productions owned half), and Elliott and Barbra Streisand Gould, who put in fifty thousand dollars, followed by another fifty thousand dollars when the budget went into overcall.

Composer Milton Schafer had known Barbra since 1962, when she lost a role in *Bravo Giovanni* to Michelle Lee. "I never understood that situation," he said. "She came to the theater and sang two songs from the score, 'I'm All I've Got' and 'Here I Am.' It was really quite thrilling. She came on like a skylark. She then read a scene. I didn't see anything wrong with it, except maybe she looked a little incongruous with the leading man, Cesare Siepi. She was supposed to be a nineteen-year-old Italian girl, and maybe that wasn't a convincing image. Anyway the director ruled her out, and they flew in Michelle Lee from California. She looked right, I guess, and was hired."

To help promote *Drat! The Cat!* Robert Goulet, then Streisand, recorded two songs from the score. One of these, "He Touched Me," would soon become a Streisand standard.

"That song," said composer Schafer, "was a piece of luck. It was a replacement for another song that wasn't working, for Elliott. A song called 'She's Roses.' It was supposed to be a comic song, because he and Lesley had just met at a masked ball, where they danced together. He was a policeman and she was the cat burglar, but he didn't know it. He's enraptured with her, he says, 'She touched me.' That's how the lyric came. Very quickly. It was written in rehearsals."

Goulet recorded the song first, with a very different interpretation. "Because the song was in a funny situation, the first thinking that people had was that it should be upbeat," said Schafer. "The pop demo was done that way, and Goulet did it uptempo, very slick. He was a Copacabana kid, very Las Vegas."

Streisand preferred to treat the song as a ballad. "She goes way beneath the surface of anything," said Schafer. "She felt the pathos of the song and decided it should be done slowly. Originally, with 'She's Roses,' I thought it should be sung in the show by an Irish tenor—with pure, high notes. That's how I thought the emotion of the character at that moment should be expressed. Well, Barbra certainly conveyed that, and more."

The first copies of "He Touched Me" by Streisand were released the second week of September, 1965, when the show was in previews in Philadelphia. Neither the composer nor the cast was aware that Streisand had recorded the song. "We were rehearsing one night," said Schafer, "and everybody was kind of down in the nose, which often happens out of town. The producer called everybody into the lobby about midnight. He said he had something he wanted to talk about. No one knew Barbra was involved; then he brought the record out and played it for us. We were all thrilled. It helped the show a lot. The DJs played it all the time. There was a lot of good reaction from important people."

Including Glenn Gould. One night when the celebrated classical pianist was recording with Leopold Stokowski, Barbra was in the adjacent studio, editing her sixth album. "Glenn was very eccentric," said Warren Vincent. "He was always cold. [In summers he wore sweaters and a topcoat, and there was always a rug under his feet when he performed in concert.] And this night one of the engineers, Stan Weiss, who had a wicked sense of humor, came in and said to Barbra, 'Hey, Barbra, do you know who's next door to us? Did you ever hear of Glenn Gould, that great piano player?' And she said, 'Yeah! yeah!' very excited. She knew who he was. And Stan turned to me and said, 'Maybe later on we can introduce Barbra to him.' Then to Barbra, he cautioned, 'But don't be upset if his fly is open, because he'll have at least one extra pair of pants on underneath.' "

The two legends did meet that night. Streisand timidly knocked on Gould's door. "Hi," she said, "I just wanted to say hello, because I'm a fan, and since we were here, I thought I'd stop by and tell you that and I . . ."

"She was very shy with Glenn," said Warren. "She was actually awed by him."

"And I," said Glenn, "to my eternal embarrassment, contributed the most maladroit moment of that or any other conversation, by saying, 'I know.' "

He was an unabashed admirer of the singer, he subsequently told *Rolling Stone*. He considered her "the greatest singing-actress since Maria Callas, and I hyphenate very carefully, in the sense of 'singing-actress.'" Her choice of material was often impeccable, "For instance, I can take a song that is full of rubato like 'He Touched Me'—which is a magnificent structure harmonically, by the way, I mean it's as good as anything Fauré ever wrote."

The opening night for *Drat! The Cat!* in New York was scheduled for Saturday, October 9, 1965. It was then postponed until Sunday, so Streisand could attend on her night off from *Funny Girl.* "Barbra saw the show in Philadelphia," said Schafer. "She was rooting for Elliott, for all of us. On opening night Hoagy Carmichael showed up, and Goulet, and Goddard Lieberson and his wife. Everyone thought we had a smash hit. I know Walter Kerr loved the score, but his review never appeared in the New York *Times* because the city was locked in the middle of a newspaper strike."

Drat! The Cat! limped along for five performances, then closed at a loss of five hundred thousand dollars. "Talk about bad luck and rotten timing," said one agent. "First Elliott had to deal with a press strike and the closing of his show. Then a week later he had to contend with his wife's success again. CBS television repeated her special *My Name Is Barbra.* Columbia Records released a second album, with *his* song, 'He Touched Me,' on it. The album sold like hotcakes. She won the Emmy. It seemed everything Barbra touched turned to gold, everything but Elliott."

Streisand was miserable about Elliott's misfortune. She wanted a big success for him. She also wanted a big return on their investment. "When the show closed she and Elliott tried to deny that they had any large financial stake in it," said a co-worker. "Elliott told one reporter their investment came to $850, not $100,000. That made the situation worse. Barbra was very unpopular with the cast and the backstage crew of *Funny Girl,* so whatever opportunity they could get to rile her, they used it. They said, 'Oh, she tried to use her name and money to boost her husband's career,' real nasty stuff, because Elliott took the brunt of it. He was a nice guy. Very talented. He had enough to put up with without their nastiness."

Throughout November, as Elliott continued to brood over the closing of *Drat! The Cat!,* Barbra, at first empathetic, became angry with her husband. "Elliott has no sense of himself," she said. "He does imitations of Alan Arkin and I tell him, 'No, no; be *you.*'"

She had no doubts about her own original talent or worth: "What does it matter what critics or people say? If you felt you did good, then fuck 'em.'

She continued to record. One session was a guest appearance on an album of songs sung by Harold Arlen. He had written the songs for *The Wizard of Oz* and *A Star Is Born*. Barbra recorded seven of his songs on her first three albums. She regarded him as her favorite composer and a close friend.

The producer of the Arlen LP was Thomas Z. Sheppard, who later produced the original cast albums of *Sweeney Todd* and *Sunday in the Park with George.* Sheppard recalled: "The Arlen LP came about by accident. He had done an album for another company and he sent it to Goddard, who said, 'We could do this better ourselves.' Goddard didn't mean we should do it, but somehow messages that are passed on get tangled, and it was interpreted to me as 'Let's do it.' I got very excited. I was an admirer of Arlen's. This was a good excuse for me to meet him and learn his catalogue. And I wanted to work with Peter Matz."

Barbra's involvement came from Arlen's suggestion. "It was one of those pipe dreams," said Sheppard. "We all wanted her but didn't believe she would do it. I felt it would be a definite plus, because we needed more than just a composer singing his songs."

Marty Erlichman was contacted. He liked the idea. The exposure would be good for Barbra. But her services would not come cheap, not even for the sweet cause of friendship. For singing one solo and one duet with Arlen, Erlichman and Barbra asked for *half* of Harold Arlen's royalties for the entire LP. "I felt they were being rotten," said Sheppard, "but Harold said okay. He was so pleased to get the recognition and attention that he didn't mind giving up his royalties."

Streisand's two songs on the Arlen LP were recorded on November twenty-second and twenty-fourth. "I didn't know Barbra," said Sheppard, "so I didn't know enough to have any problems with her. She was very professional. She listened real hard to the band. These were live sessions, not pretracks, so she paid a lot of attention to what went on behind her."

She also coached Arlen on his numbers. "She made suggestions," said one of the engineers. "It was funny. Here was a guy who had written 'Over The Rainbow' and 'The Man That Got Away,' and she was telling him *how* to sing his songs. But he didn't mind. He and his wife adored Barbra. They were obviously good friends. But friendship aside, if her talent was involved, she wanted the work not to be good, but great."

In December, Streisand played out her final weeks on Broadway. During that last month her dedication to *Funny Girl* vacillated between professional concern and blithe indifference. Offstage, in her dressing room, while one hand was writing notes of correction to the stage manager, the other was impatiently crossing off the days on a calendar.

Her onstage performance mirrored a similar schizophrenia. Some nights she was breathtakingly brilliant; on others she was indolently amateur. Screenwriter and novelist William Goldman recalled seeing her late in the show's run. "Her performance," he said, "was indistinguishable in all ways from what Jerry Lewis would have done with the part, and I mean that. She moved like Jerry Lewis, mugged like Jerry Lewis, and except when she sang, sounded like him. She was dying of boredom and very clearly didn't care about her performance, and it very clearly didn't matter to the audience, who loved her."

Her final performance came on the night of December seventeenth. One day prior to this it had been announced that she would indeed appear in the movie version of *Funny Girl*. This fillip, perhaps, gave her the energy or inspiration to make her closing at the Winter Garden as memorable as possible. That performance—her last ever on Broadway—was described by one critic as "sublime, one of the more incandescent of Streisand's career."

Barbra recalled singing "People" for that closing show. "It was as if I had just discovered the meaning of the song. As I sang it I deliberately looked out into the audience. That used to frighten me before, but this night, it was like farewell, and I sang the song to them. I got very emotional. . . ."

"All of a sudden life and art came together—and she started to weep," said Elliott Gould. "All I wanted her to do was to get through. She started to weep because of the reality of what was going on got to her, penetrated. When the show was over she got this standing ovation, but I was still sitting in the front row thinking about that line, 'People who need people are the luckiest people in the world.' No one is alone. Everybody was with her. Everybody was pulling for her. All of a sudden something got through to her."

Chapter 10

"I am a bit coarse, a bit low, a bit vulgar, and a bit igno-rant. I am also part princess, sophisticate, elegant and controlled. I appeal to everyone."

Streisand to Life magazine, 1966

COLOR ME BARBRA

New Year's Day in New York brought a transit strike. All subways and buses were immobilized and producer Ray Stark sued Mike Quill, the president of the transit union, for $570,000, the losses he incurred from the drop in income for *Funny Girl,* now starring Mimi Hines.

Barbra was delighted. She had just been voted one of the World's Best Dressed Women. Cited for her "extraordinary individuality and infallible fashion instinct," the former kook gave this quote: "If you asked my mother who Balenciaga was, she would have thought it was a grocery store in Brooklyn."

After *Funny Girl* Streisand planned to rest, to stay in bed for a month, watching TV, and gorge herself on brownies and coffee ice cream. She grew tired of that ritual after two days. She had to keep busy, and she couldn't gain weight because filming of her second TV special was about to begin.

On January seventh she recorded "Where Am I Going?" which would be included in the special and released as a single. The song was from the forthcoming Broadway show *Sweet Charity.* The cast LP was on Columbia, and Goddard Lieberson, anxious to recoup the company's losses on such flops as *Do I Hear A Waltz?, The Girl Who Came to Supper, Bajour,* and *It's a Bird, It's a Plane, It's*

Superman, personally requested that his top artists help by recording songs from the show's score. Tony Bennett obliged with "Baby Dream Your Dream"; Steve and Eydie sang "If My Friends Could See Me Now"; Jerry Vale recorded "Too Many Tomorrows"; and to Barbra fell the plum of the score: "Where Am I Going?" There were two separate recording sessions on the song. The first was done on December 14, 1965. This date was scrapped, reportedly when one of the jazz musicians, who had been smoking pot, began to improvise musical riffs *during* Barbra's vocal performance. "She didn't know what in hell was going on with the guy," said a witness. "He kept playing while she kept saying, 'Stop! Stop!' She couldn't understand why he was grinning from ear to ear. When he was thrown out of the studio she was told that he'd been smoking marijuana, and the blood went out of her face. She was shocked. Drugs at one of her sessions? She was super-square back then. She said, 'Shouldn't he be arrested or something?'"

The second taping of the song was arranged and produced by Bob Mersey. "That was a good night," said editor Warren Vincent. "I remember she was having a great time with the band, who also dug her. At that time the musicians loved her; they thought she was a gas. I've seen them jump up in the air and start applauding. She joked with them and had fun. I never saw her pick on anyone, except maybe once; I didn't like what she did with Don Costa. One day she started picking on him in front of everyone. He was calm. He went over to the drummer, who was a friend of his, and he sat down and said to Barbra, 'Okay, go ahead; have fun; you run the session.'

"Anyway, where were we? Yes, 'Where Am I Going?' That night she completed the song in a half hour and the session was booked for three. And we were paying these great musicians, some of the great jazz players in New York . . . I don't remember names . . ."

"Ellis Larkins was one of them," Bob Mersey recalled. "He played a lot with Ella Fitzgerald."

". . . So I said to Barbra, 'Why don't you do a few numbers with these guys?' And she said, 'I don't have any sheet music.' But the Colony Record Store was across the street. I told her, why not call them? She did. She got on the phone and said, 'This is Barbra Streisand, I'd like this song and that one, and I'm sending someone over to get them.' Marty went over, got the sheet music, and that night she did four or five numbers, including 'When Sunny Gets Blue.' When she was finished she said to the musicians, 'Great work, boys. Now I'm going home.' And she called to Erlichman: 'Marty,' she said, 'here are the song sheets. Take them back to the Colony and get our money back.'"

"She was a beauty," said Mersey. "She never changed. She had incredible success, and I really believed it was in spite of herself."

The single of "Where Am I Going?" was released on January 17, 1966, with a "unique" Columbia merchandising campaign. Life-size Kleen-Stik stickers of Streisand's feet were tracked on the streets of New York City. The stickers showed her name, the title of the single, and the company catalogue number.

The record, however, received only moderate airplay and was not a big seller. It was a difficult song to sing (and often dropped from the show by its star, Gwen Verdon); but furthermore, Streisand's interpretation was considered "too dramatic." At the finale of the song, as she had done on "Happy Days," she began to shriek. "My *geshrey*ing," she called it. She screamed the question "Where am I going?" so long and so loud, that one L.A. disc jockey answered, "I don't know, Barbra, but I wish you'd get there; you're giving everyone a headache."

By the third week in January rehearsals for her second TV special were under way at the CBS studios on East Seventy-sixth Street. This would be Streisand's first show in color, a process then new to television. One idea for the musical skein of the show was that the songs be hue oriented. Titles such as "Blue Moon," "Green Eyes," "Red Sails In The Sunset," and "Mood Indigo" were tossed to Barbra. She promptly tossed them right back. The idea was "old hat" she declared. The colors would come from the sets, props, and costumes, which she would help design.

The title of the show—*Color Me Barbra*—led to the idea for the opening animated sequence. In her first special Barbra had played a kid of five drawing with a giant Crayola. Reluctant to repeat this character, she suggested that a child be shown in animation. It was created by graphic artist Elinor Bunin.

"I met with Barbra a few times," said Elinor. "She had some wonderful ideas. She didn't want the child to resemble her. She wanted it to look like a typical mischievous kid. The drawings also had to look like they were done by a child. In my studio I looked at many sketches by schoolchildren. It had been years since I was that young. I no longer had that free, awkward spirit, so I began to draw with my left hand. And that's how the storyboards came about. One of them became the logo for the show, and it was used on the album cover." It also appeared in the hieroglyphics above an archway in the Philadelphia Museum which was used as a location for another of Barbra's musical adventures.

Extending the color motif of the show, the names of master painters—Van Gogh, Chagall, Monet—were suggested. Why not use them? Not only as a backdrop for certain musical numbers, but from time to time Barbra herself could appear as a recreation of a painting.

The location sought for filming was the Metropolitan Museum on Fifth Avenue in New York. Permission to film there was flatly refused, and the second suitable site was the Museum of Art in Philadelphia. Their board of directors were more amenable to the filming, provided it be done on weekends, and that Barbra and CBS be held personally responsible for all damages, breakage, or theft of their priceless paintings, sculptures, and tapestries.

Preparations for the museum filming began on a Saturday at noon in Barbra's Philadelphia hotel suite. After a final fitting of her wardrobe she began to apply red and blue and silver sequins to her eyelids. This was for the opening op-art scene, wherein she appeared surrounded by Picassos and Mirós, wearing purple plastic triangular earrings and a dress of electric colors. The eye makeup took three hours. "Listen," she said, "they wanted me to use Pablo of Elizabeth Arden, but he takes five hours, and I can't sit that long." When an aide complimented her on her Liz Taylor/Cleopatra eye-look, she snapped, "It's *my* look. I don't copy fake Jews."

For the next thirty-six hours she worked the museum, running up and down stairs, dusting statues, straightening paintings, repeating songs, changing costumes, all for eight minutes of film.

In between takes, as the long night wore on, Barbra fortified herself with neck massages from Elliott, and with food. Standing nearby, a reporter from *Look* made an inventory of each morsel that went into the star's mouth. "Hour by hour," he said, "she ate pretzels, potato chips, peppermint sour balls, a hero sandwich, pickles, stuffed derma, a corned-beef sandwich, coffee ice cream, roast beef on rye, Swiss cheese on white, hamburger, Danish, and petits four." Wiping her hands with tissues, Barbra was chastized by a museum guard when she leaned against Renoir's *The Bather*. "Cheez," she retorted, "just like New York. Pardon me for breathing."

With one day to rest a second marathon medley was taped in New York. The inspiration for this—a circus scene—came from Barbra's constant companion, her poodle Sadie. The dog was a gift from the *Funny Girl* cast. "I remember I put my hand in the box and I thought, 'Terrific. A warm hat!'"

Talk of Sadie led to the possibility of using other animals: monkeys, tigers, elephants, and guppies. "I like guppies," said Barbra, "because the male guppy dances around the female during courtship, and that's always nice."

"We found out what animals were available," said Peter Matz, "and wrote a medley that would fit. And *that* was the easy part." Wearing a two-thousand-dollar Day-Glo orange clown-suit, Barbra acted as the ringmaster of the circus. The thirty hours of filming was filled with mishaps. The baby elephant got tired and went to sleep on camera. The pony pranced backward and left do-do on the star's three-hundred-dollar orange leather boots; the monkey almost bit her finger off; and one of the penguins died under the hot lights. "We were fools," Barbra groaned, "thinking we could pull this thing off."

On Friday night the concert finale was taped before a live audience at the CBS West Side studios. The guests had been recruited from Barbra's fan clubs and were therefore considered "friendly." She sang five numbers for them and then fled to the control room. She disliked two of the songs and asked that they be redone. She also insisted that the audience leave. "Tell them to go away," she said to Marty Erlichman. "I hate them. I hate them."

Erlichman and the director persuaded her that they needed the fans' live reaction for the soundtrack. Streisand relented, returned to the stage, finished the two songs, thanked the audience for staying, then returned to the control room and watched herself for four hours, on three monitors, in playbacks of the show. "I know this is a better show than the first," said Barbra. "But they are waiting for it to bomb. They always are. People say, 'Go and see this terrific girl.' But most of them come thinking, 'Nah, she can't be that great.' It makes me feel they're the monster and I'm their victim."

* * *

A week after the completion of the TV special Barbra and Elliott flew to Europe for a second honeymoon. For the trip she brought along six suitcases, monogrammed BSG, and wrapped in red velvet scuff covers which were held together with safety pins. "I kept the bags packed in Venice," she explained. "I can't bear packing and unpacking. I opened only one bag, which was great. I wore only two different outfits. I just washed out my stuff each night and put it on next day."

Arriving in Paris, Barbra purchased three more suitcases, and two travel bags, to carry home the loot she planned to acquire at the latest couture showings. "I'm here," she told the press, "to purchase the wardrobe for my next TV special. Cost is no object because my sponsor [Chemstrand] is picking up the tab [twelve thousand dollars for six dresses]."

As an honored guest she delayed the Dior show fifteen minutes by arriving late. Then, sitting ramrod straight, dressed in a jaguar-skin suit and matching derby, she looked neither left nor right at the other celebrities in the front row. One of them was the legendary Marlene Dietrich, who, anxious to meet Streisand, said, "I vanted to vave at her, to say a few happy words, because the poor thing looked sooo sad."

"I am ill," said Streisand, "from too much French food and too much French fashion." The latter was "nice," she added, "but not for me." Privately she added, "It stinks."

In her hotel, while Barbra was changing into purple slacks, alligator boots, and a black mink coat, Elliott was dispatched to find some chicken soup for his wife. Fortified, she was then driven to a photo studio, for a special *Vogue* layout with Richard Avedon. Caressed and soothed and appraised by stylists, makeup artists, and by Parisian hair designer Alexandre, the ailing star was soon transformed into a high-gloss model of couture perfection. Further inspired by the sound of her own voice, coming from a stereo system, Barbra glided through the studio wearing tussah pants, a Gres poncho, and ballooning chiffon pajamas. For the finale she stepped into Yves Saint Laurent's heavenly bridal confection. Encased in the white wedding gown, Streisand raised her arms, looked in a mirror, and asked, "Imagine if I should throw up now?"

In parting, Alexandre presented Barbra with a free hairpiece.

Accepting, she squealed: "C'est uncreeedable. One of those things I've always wanted and never had. Can I wear it in the street? Yeah, and then personne ne me will not be recognized."

Back in New York, in March, the *Vogue* photos appeared in a six-page salute to spring, with Barbra on the cover with a daffodil stuck in her mouth. These pictures, she declared, were the best she had ever seen of herself; but the accompanying text perplexed her. The article, written by Polly Devlin, was so cleverly worded, Streisand had to read it twice to understand it. Devlin wrote of "an ego that can't be sated, a strange vanity, and frantic pride." And then there was the line about the "poison." If it meant what Barbra thought it meant, she was not too happy. "What is alarming," said Devlin, "is that when she is being bothered—or thinks she is being bothered—she doesn't allow irritation to show; she simply darts out a beam of pure poison from her eyes and lodges it in the annoyer."

In rapid succession that same month Streisand's face appeared on the covers of *Life* and *Look,* and she received full-page write-ups in *Newsweek* and *Time.* This coverage was arranged to coincide with tele-showing of *Color Me Barbra* on March thirtieth. The articles and reviews were the regular, run-of-the-mill raves, and she breezed through them until she came to *Time,* when her reading slowed down and her pulse quickened. The magazine actually *panned* her and the show. They said the publicity buildup for the special made it sound like "the Second Coming." That the show was "overcute, overwrought, and suffocatingly overproduced. If anything," *Time* concluded, "it proved that one full hour of Streisand's peculiarly nasal voice is about 45 minutes too much, and her choice of songs ("Sam, You Made The Pants Too Long" and "Animal Crackers") can be appalling. The Streisand talent is considerable, but it is getting lost in a myth."

On the last Sunday of the month, prior to the showing of the special, the *Time* review was a bouquet compared to what appeared in the "Arts and Leisure" section of *The New York Times.* An interview, granted by Streisand in Philadelphia during the taping of the museum, was published. It was written by a relatively new writer, Rex Reed.

Reed—who at the age of two appeared on TV reciting the alphabet—was a former actor, singer, and pancake cook. He got into print, not unlike other celebrity journalists, by hustling an interview with a star—Buster Keaton. He went on to sharpen his quill and expand his reputation with corrosive but brilliant profiles of Ava Gardner and Warren Beatty.

His intentions with Barbra were pure, he claimed, and he can be believed. Rex Reed loved stars. He grew up worshiping at the celluloid feet of Betty Grable and Tyrone Power. He related to actors: "Show me one," he said, "who hasn't clawed his way to the top and I'll show you one who really isn't an actor"—and to celebrities: "I have an empathy for their pain, which often leads them to tell me more than they realize."

Streisand told him less than he desired and therefore got skewered to the bone. Why? For openers she kept him waiting in Philadelphia for three and a half hours while she did her eyes for the op art sequence. Then she was rude. She swept into the CBS publicity suite, plotzed herself in a chair, with her legs spread out, tore open a basket of fruit, bit into a green banana, and barked to Rex: "Okay, you got twenty minutes, whaddya wanna know?"

Polite and professional, Reed asked what the new show was like. Curt and informative, she told him: "Like the old one. They're book ends. The first one was great, ya know? So this one's gonna be close as it can be. Whadda I know from TV? I hire the best people in the business, then I let them do everything for me. I don't take chances. I'm payin' the bill, it's my problem, right? I coulda got Frank Sinatra and Dean Martin to clown around like everybody else does on their specials, but who needs it? I got complete control here, so I do it my way, right?"

The interview continued, terse and uncomfortable. Rex listened as Streisand complained about her stardom, her lunatic fans, and the dirt and soot up on the twenty-sixth floor of her New York duplex apartment. When his twenty minutes were up, the star stalked out of the suite, leaving Rex with half a story and a fully deflated ego.

"Poor Rex," another reporter sympathized. "He wasn't used to such shabby treatment. Like most of us he thought he had the power of the press behind him. Also he had just acquired a semblance of celebrity himself. He was a big fan of Barbra's and he had the usual fantasy of their becoming instant friends for life. But she treated him like a messenger and she didn't even bother to find out his name."

There was nothing gratuitous in Streisand's behavior, others felt.

That was just Barbra. She had no tact, she had work to do, and interviewers had become a bore. They had been useful when she first needed them, for free publicity and a hot meal. But now she was a star and she had no need of the press except when it was time to push her latest product. It was a two-way deal, she believed. Her face sold their magazines and newspapers, and in turn she expected favorable write-ups. Rex Reed and the *Times* violated that code, and she wouldn't forget the wretches for years to come.

Chapter 11

"This is Miss Streisand's first appearance in a foreign country. Luckily she speaks English fairly well."
Program notes for London production of Funny Girl

BARBRA IN LONDON

In England, for the limited run of *Funny Girl,* Streisand decided to cancel all requests for interviews. She would hold an open press conference at the Savoy Hotel, come one, come all, like it or leave it.

On the night she arrived in London she placed a call to the show's publicity agent. She was told the agent had been married that day and was spending his nuptial night at a nearby hotel. Streisand rang the hotel and insisted on being put through to the honeymoon suite. She didn't care about the circumstances, she wanted to see the groom, *now.* The man did what he was told and went to see the star. Three hours later, after she had given specific details on how her press should be handled, he was allowed to return to his bride.

The following day Streisand inspected the Prince of Wales Theatre, where she was scheduled to appear. She gave notes to the stage manager, the lighting man, the electricians, and to the head usher. Moving to the backstage area, she took one look at her dressing room, promptly turned on her heel, and left the theater. The British producer, Bernard Delfont, was later called and notified that Miss Streisand did not intend to return until she had proper living quarters. "A few walls were broken down," said Sheilah Graham, "some fancy furniture hastily collected, and the Star returned. The back staircase was reserved for her exclusive use, and no one was allowed to dress on the same floor."

On April thirteenth *Funny Girl* opened. Attending the premiere were Rex Harrison, Rachel Roberts, Peter Sellers, Britt Ekland, Ursula Andress, Elsa Martinelli, and Leslie Caron, with her boyfriend, Warren Beatty.

Elliott Gould was also in the audience that night, standing at the back of the stalls. He, and Barbra, and Ray Stark, were apprehensive about the reception of the show in England. Elliott's *On the Town* had failed at this same theater, and American musicals didn't always travel well. The name of Fanny Brice, let alone her life story, meant nothing to the British. Barbra Streisand they knew of, from her records and TV specials, but in person, onstage, she had to prove herself.

The reviewers by and large panned the show but praised Streisand's performance. "The show is Barbra Streisand," said the *Daily Mail.* "Take away this pulsating dynamo with the thousand-volt voice and there would not be enough glow to light up your programme."

"She makes every song she sings sound like a hymn, and rouses her audiences to ecstasy," the *Sunday Citizen* declared.

Streisand's comedic skills and projection were singularly examined by the *Sunday Times.* "Miss Streisand has a neat, pocket-size humor, expressing itself in small, mocking gestures, and alarming fingernails that would interest a vampire," said Harold Hobson. "The battery of microphones enables the front rows to hear her when she speaks, and the back when she sings. The rich and leisured can thus get the entire show at two visits if they arrange their seats properly."

Writer Hugh Leonard also questioned the actress's dramatic ability. "Only when straight acting is demanded does she come a cropper," said Leonard in *Plays and Players,* "for while Miss Streisand can send up like nobody's business, she cannot simply *send.* Two emotional scenes occur towards the end of the show: she deals with one of these by turning her back to the audience, and with the other by crashing her face down on the surface of a dressing table and staying there until the coast is clear."

Leonard went on to surmise that this defect was due perhaps to the actress's lack of technique. "There seems to be an icy hardness in Miss Streisand's personality which needs comedy as a mask, and this may be why she avoids, or cannot cope with, pathos."

Regardless of its defects the public flocked to see the show. The day after its opening *Funny Girl* sold out for its entire fourteen-week run. Barbra became the toast of the town. Invitations to high teas and late-night suppers arrived daily at her door, but she declined to dine with many, including Princess Margaret.

The Queen's younger sister was an enormous Streisand fan. Copies of her first albums had been sent to her by Sharman Douglas and her American friends. When she'd visited the colonies the previous November Princess Margaret had expressed the desire to meet the performer. This was arranged by director Josh Logan, who invited Barbra to a black-tie buffet dinner for the Princess, held in his apartment at River House. The other guests included Rosalind Russell, Alan Jay Lerner, and Sammy Davis Jr., all of whom were delighted to perform for the royal guest and her husband, Lord Snowdon. But not Barbra. She refused to get up. "She sat in a corner," said Logan, "spooning food into her mouth as fast as she could. She told me she didn't come to sing, she came to eat."

In London, following the opening of *Funny Girl,* Princess Margaret and Lord Snowdon attended a Command Performance of the show for charity. They showed up backstage to meet the star and the cast, and later an invitation to visit the Snowdons, in residence at Kensington Palace, was sent to the Goulds. Barbra gave regrets.

"More's the pity for her," said a friend of the Royals. "Princess Margaret was a marvelous hostess. She held these wonderful musical evenings where Peter Sellers performed and she played the piano. She knew Barbra's music and would have accompanied her. But can you see it if the Princess erred, if she played a wrong note? It would have been Anne Boleyn all over again. Streisand would have sent her to the Tower. She was unforgiving and took no stock in royalty. She once asked me, 'Why should I curtsy? Why should I call her Ma'am, or Your Highness? She's not *my* highness.' She had absolutely no propriety for the customs of society. *She* was the top and that was it, duckie. And more's the pity, because she didn't know how to have a good time. I hear she's changed. I hope so. To have all that talent and no fun. Well . . . [A pause] I wish I could tell you something witty or wicked about Barbra. But it didn't happen. Back then she was really quite a *lump.*"

Streisand was not interested in sight-seeing either. She had been to England before, she told reporters. That was in 1963, and on that visit she had spent most of her time indoors. "We were in Oxford together," said Bob Schulenberg. "Barbra was visiting Elliott, who was doing *On the Town* in tryouts. I was living in Paris then; working for Condé Nast; and Barbra wrote and asked me to come see her. I arrived with a friend and every day we went out touring. Oxford is a beautiful place, there was so much to see. Every morning we'd ask Barbra to join us. She'd say, 'Uh, no, not today. I'll stay in the hotel room, and I'll see you guys later.' Every night we'd go to the same Chinese restaurants, and she and Elliott would have Pepsi-Cola, like they were back in Brooklyn. One night we went to the movies, to see *Come Fly with Me.* It was a movie about airline stewardesses. We bought nuts and raisins and sat in the balcony. When the shots of the Champs Elysées and the Swiss Alps appeared, Barbra whispered to me, 'Wouldn't it be great to go to those places sometime and see them.' I said, 'Barbra, you're in Oxford right *now,* and you're not seeing it. When does it start?' "

"She never went anywhere," said Ettore Stratta, who recorded Streisand in London during her run in *Funny Girl.* "She went from her flat to the theater and back again. One day she asked me, 'Are there any good restaurants in London? I said, 'Are you crazy? There are fabulous restaurants in London.' She had never been anywhere, not even the countryside, until one day Dirk Bogarde, who became a friend of hers—he took her out in his car to the country. She loved it. She told me about it. It was so beautiful and green. It was as if she had never been outdoors in her life."

Barbra missed New York, and more than that she missed her dog, Sadie. Because of the English quarantine laws Sadie could not be brought into the country. "She died for the dog," said Stratta. "She used to call me in New York and say, 'Hey, Ettore, how about if you and Elliott give Sadie a sleeping shot, put her in a bag, and bring her over to London.' 'Are you out of your mind?' I said. 'That's illegal. Suppose the dog dies. Suppose they catch us in customs?' But she wouldn't give up. She would get bored or lonely and she would call again. 'When are you coming over?' she'd ask, then she'd bring up Sadie again. Once she said, 'I've got it! You two go to Paris, then bring it by boat to London.' I told her no way. She was so upset. She missed the dog so much. I think she missed Sadie more than she missed Elliott."

Elliott, who was in London for the opening, was described as

"Barbra's manager." This he refuted. "I wouldn't dream of becoming Barbra's manager," he said. "I don't believe in husbands managing wives. I'm here when she needs me."

He had turned down two TV shows, and a possible movie, to be with his wife, yet at times Barbra was not aware of his existence.

"He'd be with her backstage when the stars and other celebrities came to call," said Fred Glaser, "and she wouldn't introduce him. She ignored him. She was so elated by her own performance she didn't know there was anyone in the room but herself."

"Elliott was very supportive, very bright, very nice, a lot of fun," said Ettore Stratta. "I don't think Barbra was a good wife for him in those days. And that's a shame. He had a lot going, and they were good together. They were in love, I think, but she was so wrapped up in her own career there was no room for anyone else. The only way for somebody to make it as big as she did was to be totally involved with herself. It's self-centeredness to the maximum degree. It has to be like that. You can't do it any other way. I remember, from the moment she got up in the morning to the moment she went to bed at night it was me-me-me-me. It sounds egocentric, but that's what it was. In those days Barbra was also very insecure, and very shy. Very afraid of people. Afraid of people just looking at her in any way."

Elliott, and only Elliott, not her manager, her agents, family, or friends, was capable of reaching Barbra when she flew off on her flights of superstardom. His words, delivered calmly, or in anger, could eventually reach her and bring her back to earth. On one such reentry, in London, he made her pregnant, "and I may say that was the best bit of talking I have ever done," he told writer Donald Zec.

"Well, by then, the star thing was really going very hard. And I really had to talk her down," said Gould. "I talked her all the way down through all the whole encounter, not ever dreaming we would have a child. But also knowing it was the best thing. Also knowing that I was being irresponsible and inconsiderate of my son, not thinking of him or myself. I was thinking of Barbra. The best thing I could give her was a child . . . a son . . . my son— to be her friend so she could understand more about where I was coming from . . . bringing her mind back down into life. And, as the Lord deemed fit, we made a child that night."

* * *

When the news of Streisand's pregnancy hit the newspapers it was headlined "Barbra's Million Dollar Baby!" That was the sum she would forfeit because of the cancellation of her forthcoming summer tour. With some hasty adjustments, however, manager Marty Erlichman announced that the tour would still go on, but instead of twenty-six cities, Barbra would appear in twelve. This was later cut to four.

"The producers of the tour, Alan King and his partner, really took a beating on that deal," said an agent. "They had a lot of the locations booked in advance." They made concessions to local promoters, and to Barbra. Her contract with them totaled thirty-two pages. She had to have her own staff traveling with her, in her own private jet; and she wouldn't travel more than two hours at a time. Real superstar stuff; and you must remember *no one* was doing this at the time, except the Beatles. "I am getting *more* than the Beatles," Barbra corrected Sheilah Graham. "I get as much for me, one person, as they do for the four. I was offered the same as they were paid for Shea Stadium, but I turned it down. I make as much as Liz Taylor receives. A million dollars. But she has to spend three to five months on a picture. I get that for less than three weeks."

Local contractors, printers, and sound technicians had to be notified of the cancellation. "They built this special set for her," said the agent. "A backdrop of lights—it was forty by forty, it changed colors and patterns with each song, and cost a hundred fifty thousand dollars. Alan King was chewing and spitting out his cigar. But what could he do? Pregnancy is an act of God."

Barbra *enceinte* was a changed person, it was said. She was nicer, softer; she even spoke to her understudy in London, and to one interviewer.

"I get so self-involved, too focused on my own problems," she told writer Gloria Steinem, "but when I think of what's growing inside me, it's a miracle."

Steinem had been assigned by the *Ladies' Home Journal* to go to London and talk to the new mother-to-be. Barbra, wearing a $190 maternity outfit (which had to be adjusted and augmented with padding to give her a more pregnant look), posed for photographs in Hyde Park and Ennismore Gardens, surrounded by British nannies and schoolchildren. She chatted to Steinem about natural childbirth, about knitting "a baby blanket of orange, blue, and pink" (which she dropped after the first ten rows and gave to her dresser to finish), and about the name she would choose should the baby be a girl—Samantha. Steinem, looking for an angle of contrast, commented on the rich and luxurious life-style the future child would have compared to the poor childhood of its mother. "Well, I can't suddenly get poor for him or her, can I?" Barbra snapped.

In June, Streisand began to socialize. She invited friends to her flat in Belgravia, and ventured forth in public on special occasions. She went to the American embassy and performed for a special Independence Day celebration. Introduced by the ambassador, and by composer Cy Coleman, she sang "Where Am I Going?" followed by "I Got Plenty Of Nothin'," "I Loves You, Porgy," "It Ain't Necessarily So," and "Porgy, I'se Your Woman Now." Her performance was taped by Columbia Records but never released.

Also in London, Streisand recorded four Christmas songs at Olympia Sound Studios. This session was for a special album to be released in November by the American Premiums Division of Columbia. (The album of Christmas songs, by various artists, was not for sale in stores, but was to be given away by the Goodyear Rubber Company in gas stations and other outlets. The order was a guaranteed 2 million, and Barbra would receive royalties and a share of the publishing.)

"I'm not sure who chose the Christmas songs," said producer Ettore Stratta. "I know Ray Ellis did the arrangements, and that Barbra was insistent that her interpretation be different. She didn't want any traditional arrangements."

Silent Night was singled out for a radical change. Usually the song was performed as written—as a hymn. Barbra changed the format. She would do the first verse straight, then add her own interpretation for the second.

On June 24, three other songs—"The Lord's Prayer," "I Wonder As I Wander," and Gounod's "Ave Maria," were recorded, the latter in Latin. "That was also Barbra's first recording of a semiclassical song," said Stratta. "Her voice was perfect for it. It was thrilling to see and hear her. She was so happy—she was having a baby—and she would soon be going home. It was a very good time for her."

Chapter 12

"Blessed is the merchant who can read the fads of the day, and ride them carefully to what can be a sizable fortune. America's Fountain of Youth is an ever-changing market, and the man who sells successfully to this market must understand it, hunt out its fads, and read its new trends while they are still in the making. He must stay hip, aware, keen as the teen."

*A merchandizing message to
Columbia Records salesmen, 1966*

COLUMBIA ROCKS AND ROLLS

Since 1963, in the three years since Barbra Streisand had risen from the "least likely to succeed," to become the number-one female vocalist in the country, Columbia Records had undergone sizable expansion. Once known as a company that made and sold only records, they expanded into the manufacture and sale of phonographs, educational toys, guitars, drums, and acoustical speakers; they owned and operated two music-publishing firms; and they opened sales offices and pressing plants in the major foreign markets.

By 1965 all of this had become too much for one man—Goddard Lieberson—to handle effectively on a direct day-to-day basis. And so, following a lengthy in-company analysis by the Harvard Business School, the company was reorganized and renamed the Columbia/CBS Group. It was housed in the new CBS headquarters at Black Rock, 51 West Fifty-second Street, and headed by

Goddard. The new subdivisions were called CBS Records, CBS International, CBS Direct Marketing Services (the Record Club), CBS Musical Instruments, and CBS Educational Services.

In the domestic records division Goddard promoted Bill Gallagher to vice president of both Marketing and A&R, the territory he had avidly coveted. But placed slightly above Gallagher, as administrative vice president, was a relatively new, bright, equally ambitious and shrewd lawyer named Clive Davis; and he and Gallagher clashed immediately.

"The nature of the confrontation was clear," said Davis. "Lieberson had structured company operations so that he could lie back and take a rest while his underlings struggled for position and power."

"Goddard also wanted *out* of the pop music business," said Bob Mersey. "He wasn't a fan of rock 'n' roll ("Prepubertal singing about postpubertal problems," he called it) and that was clearly where the market was going."

The days of Jo Stafford and Doris Day were clearly over. With the advent of the Beatles (whose first three singles were turned down for distribution by Columbia) and the continued onslaught of other successful British acts, the industry learned that rock 'n' roll was here to stay. It also learned that an entire new audience was actively buying records. They were the American teenagers— 24 million strong in America alone, and growing by 600,000 each year. This group spent a total of $13 billion a year on records, record players, transistor radios, encyclopedias, cars, weights, guitars, motorbikes, perfume, patterned stockings, hair driers, and high boots, in *that* order, and Columbia (or CBS Records as they now preferred to be called) wanted the lead for slot number one.

"The company was late getting into the teenage market," said vice president Bruce Lundvall, "but when they did, it was with all cylinders blasting."

Anything that had long hair and could sing and play a guitar was signed to the label. The Creatures, an Irish group found in the Cave, a Dublin cellar club, were introduced as the next Beatles. And then came The Blacksheep, The Magicians, Pogan, Pogan and Regan, The James Boys, Arnie Corrado, Donna Lee, Mattie Moultrie, Susan Christie, Linda Andal, Kui Lee ("Singer! Songwriter! Guitarist! Pianist! Bass Player! Dancer! Choreographer! Nightclub Entertainer! TV Performer! Surfer! Ten Men Rolled into One"),

Tim Rose ("is happening, and Columbia's helping. Like always, like everywhere"); and singers acquired from other labels: Jan and Dean, Lou Christie, Gene McDaniels, and Shirley Ellis.

CBS Records also let some promising talents get away, including Jim Morrison ("I was with a group called Rick and the Ravens. We were at Columbia for six months; no one knew what to do with us, so we left"); and Carly Simon ("I was told I was going to be the next Bob Dylan. I taped some songs, listened to a lot of talk, and then, nothing").

"It was the Lawyer (Clive Davis) versus the Salesman (Bill Gallagher)," said Bob Mersey. "Neither one knew anything about producing music. The release philosophy at Columbia was 'Let's throw them all up on the wall and see which one sticks.'" Occasionally that principle worked. Hits came in from Paul Revere and the Raiders, The Buckinghams ("Hey Baby, They're Playing Our Song"), The Cyrkle ("Red Rubber Ball"), Billy Joe Royal ("Down In The Boondocks), and The Byrds ("Mr. Tambourine Man").

On July 21, 1966, Columbia held its sales convention at the Sahara Hotel in Las Vegas. Its theme was "Total Participation," and before an audience of six hundred employees and guests Goddard Lieberson spoke of his continued devotion to the record business— "It is my first and abiding love." Clive Davis gave the group some figures—200 million records pressed that year compared to 60 million in 1960. Bill Gallagher congratulated his men on the renewed success of the company, but reminded them, "We have yet to strike fully the shimmering, glimmering teenage lode."

The theme of the convention shows was similarly youth oriented. At the opening night's dinner, young girls in silver lame mini-skirts and white boots danced atop tables. Incorporating the entertainment with the Italian meal and theme, the evening was called "Dago A-Go-Go."

On the final night of the convention the dinner show combined the new—Chad and Jeremy, John Davidson, and Van McCoy— with the proven—Tony Bennett, who closed his act with the propitious "I Wanna Be Around."

As Tony Bennett exited, Goddard Lieberson appeared onstage. He announced an unscheduled extra attraction. Another Columbia talent had come to Las Vegas to say hello to the conventioneers and to sing a few songs. He introduced the mystery artist not by name but by the catalogue number of her latest album—CS 9278, *Color Me Barbra.*

"When Barbra appeared onstage the entire room of six hundred people went wild," said merchandising director Tommy Noonan. "She had never done a convention before, so most of these guys had never seen her in person. It was great. Forget the rock 'n' roll and all the rest of the talent they had seen. *This* was Barbra Streisand! A *real* star. They spoke about it for months."

On the morning of July thirtieth Barbra flew in her private jet to Newport, Rhode Island, to begin the first date of her summer tour. Traveling with her were Elliott; her manager, Marty Erlichman; hair stylist Fred Glaser; and Dr. Harvey Corman, with his wife, Sis.

Barbra rehearsed for two hours that afternoon in Newport, with Peter Matz and a thirty-one-piece orchestra. She then checked the 143 light cues in the backdrop and took a preperformance nap guarded by Elliott in her dressing room.

That night, thirty minutes late, the show's overture was played, and Barbra glided onstage wearing her "split-personality dress." The chiffon gown had two different-colored panels—the left side orange, the right side brown—with different shoes and earrings to match. During the eighty-minute set, she stuck to familiar musical ground. She sang her standards "Down with Love," "Cry Me A River," "Who Will Buy?," "People," and "The Music That Makes Me Dance" from *Funny Girl,* (which would be reviewed in *Variety* the following week as "The Music That Makes Me Mad" from *Funny Face).*

For her first encore in Newport, Barbra defied the month and the tradition by singing "Silent Night."

"Only she would dare to try and hush a crowd of seventeen thousand with *Silent Night,*" said writer Bruce McCabe. "But there we were on July thirtieth, listening to her sing it with cathedral softness. Barbra the mother . . ."

"I was at that concert," said Phyllis Brady, a musician, "and the show up to that point was good, very good. But with that song Barbra put it over the top. She had that genius of giving you one perfect timeless moment. You forgot everything that came before it or after it. And for the joy you felt, you could forgive her anything."

Returning to New York that night by jet, the singer was also jubilant. The box-office gross that night came to $121,000. This was $41,000 more than Frank Sinatra had taken at the same location the previous summer. "There was this strange rivalry going on with Sinatra," said Fred Glaser. "I never understood it. Sinatra wasn't fit to put manure on her lawn."

With three stops to go on the tour, in larger arenas, it was estimated that Streisand's mini-tour would gross half a million dollars. The eventual take was much lower, but still impressive. In Philadelphia, at the JFK stadium, she drew 18,144 people (against 7,500 for Andy Williams, in concert the same night at Convention Hall) for a take of $108,000.

The third date in Atlanta, at the Sports Stadium, was almost canceled because of rain. Fifty minutes past showtime, when 11,273 fans remained sitting in the mud, Streisand appeared on-stage, carrying an umbrella, and wearing a yellow rain-slicker and galoshes. Stripping off the rain gear, she revealed a slinky black sequined dress with apron pockets. She began to sing, then stopped seconds later when her voice bounced back from audio feedback.

"It's so great with this echo," Barbra quipped. "I feel like Patti Page."

"We love you, Barbra!" a voice yelled out from the night.

"See!" she said cockily to the band. "Did you hear *that!*"

The fourth and final concert was given in Chicago on August ninth. This time with clear skies and no competition (except the sound of a train whistle from a nearby track—"it's got poifect pitch") Streisand drew 14,220 people to Soldier Field. She filled half the stadium and took in "a sizzling $98,754" for a total take of $406,618, half of which reportedly went to the Streisand.

In Chicago, at a postperformance party, the principals toasted each other and agreed that the following Summer, when the balance of twenty-two dates were filled, Barbra would break all records.

This never happened. With the exception of one New York concert, it would be eleven years before Barbra would sing in public again.

Back home, Barbra remained blissfully barefoot and pregnant for the remainder of the summer. Far from performances and crowds, she and Elliott rented a cottage on Long Island. They went to the beach, walked on the sand, and Barbra worked on her tan. She played with Sadie, shopped for groceries, and learned to cook. Once only, while antique hunting in Bridgehampton—wearing a gingham dress, a matching hat, and sunglasses—was she recognized. "Take off the shades," Elliott told her, "and no one will bother you." She did, and they didn't.

JE M'APPELLE BARBRA

In New York City in September, the singer resumed work on her new Columbia album. Within certain circles of the company this was jocularly referred to as "the Streisand *mishugass.*" It was a collection of songs sung in French and originally intended for release in France only.

The French venture had begun a year earlier when Nat Shapiro, the director of Columbia's International Department, called Barbra to discuss expanding her sales and popularity in the European market. Many of Columbia's top artists were already recording in foreign languages (including Andy Williams in German and Steve Lawrence and Eydie Gorme in Italian; Eydie on her own was enormously successful in the Spanish market with her Trio Los Panchos albums).

Barbra told Nat Shapiro she was definitely interested in expanding her sales and popularity. But more than that she was eager to alter and upgrade the public's perception of her on the homefront. Audiences, she complained, only saw her as a funny girl, as a "People" pop singer, and "that's wrong, *so* wrong," she said. "I'm an artist, a *serious* artist. I refuse to be locked into anyone's limited perception of me." She told Shapiro she spoke Spanish, and was learning Italian, but Shapiro turned her attention to the French market. "She agreed with me that French was classier than Italian," said Nat. "They had more sophisticated songs and songwriters. Also we had a much more active company in France. Another strong factor was Michel Legrand. He was one of the best composers and orchestrators in the world. He had just written the music for *The Umbrellas of Cherbourg.* It won the Academy Award. That appealed to Barbra."

Legrand knew of Streisand. "Nat had sent me most of her albums," he said. "I received a plane ticket to come to New York to meet and talk with her. We got along famously. She was in *Funny Girl* at the time, and we would meet in the theater after the show was finished. There was only Barbra and I. We worked backstage, where there was a piano. We talked and laughed until four, sometimes five, o'clock in the morning, which did not make Elliott too happy, I think."

Before she could record in French, Barbra had to learn the language. She hired a tutor, and was coached by Legrand, and by Ettore Stratta, who would produce the sessions.

"She had a good phonetic sound," said Stratta. "She had to work hard because she never spoke the language before."

"Her French was good," said Nat Shapiro, "but she spoke it with a Brooklyn accent."

The songs for the project were commissioned by Shapiro. "They were written by writers I knew in France. We were only looking for four songs because the intention was to release an EP only, not an album. Then the songs came in. . . . There was, let's see . . . "Non c'est rien," which later became "Free Again"; and "Le Mur"; and two songs that Michel and a guy named Eddie Marnay wrote, one was called "Et la mer," but the other ["Les Enfants qui pleurent"] I don't remember. We recorded those four, then some more came in, and Barbra loved them. She wanted to keep going. We didn't tell Columbia what we were doing. No one knew, except Goddard. The rest of the people thought we were doing the stuff for France, but we were actually beginning to compile an American album."

During Christmas of 1965 Michel Legrand returned to France for the holidays, and work on the album was postponed until his return. On the evening of January thirteenth, after rehearsing all day for her second TV special, Barbra resumed recording the French songs. It was here that Streisand the perfectionist, also known as Streisand the insecure, and Streisand the megalomaniac, came into full bloom. The session ran from nine o'clock at night to six o'clock in the morning, and for one song alone she insisted on twenty-eight takes over a period of three and a half hours.

The song—"Autumn Leaves"—was done at the request of Michel Legrand. It was sung without the orchestra; she was accompanied by a lone viola. "The viola was played by Emanuel Vardi," said Ettore Stratta. "I thought it was a sensation."

The 28 takes were necessary, Legrand believed, "because Barbra wouldn't quit. She loved the song so much, she said to me, 'Let's do it again for the pleasure.' I loved her attitude of redoing it for pleasure."

After the song was completed to Streisand's satisfaction, "and after recording all the other numbers," said Diane Lurie in *Life*, "correcting every phrase, word, or syllable she disliked and could get the conductor and the director to alter—she was ready for the more arduous ritual of second-guessing. 'Please replay the tapes from the beginning,' she said. And they did. Four hours later she leaned back in the chair. 'Yeah,' she said, exhausted. 'I love it.'"

The following day the tapes were turned over to Columbia engineer Stan Weiss, who was assigned the task of mixing and balancing the sound. Weiss, unaware of the secrecy of the project, called in Bob Mersey, the director of pop A&R.

"They were doing this on the sly," said Mersey. "It was supposed to be a big surprise, and Stan called me. He didn't know what to do with the 'Autumn Leaves' song. He went frantically through each take, trying to find the rest of the orchestra. He called me, and I went up to see him. 'Listen to this,' he said. 'I can't find the orchestra.' So I listened to the tape, to herself and the viola, and I said to him, 'Stanley, your problem is you don't know art. *This* is being artistic, you lowbrow piece of — . Something great is happening here and you don't know it.'"

Weiss, with no help from the irreverent Mersey, proceeded to mix the tape on his own. "We didn't know what was going to happen," said Mersey, "but what he proceeded to make turned out to be the funniest thing I've ever heard on record. You know, stereo was still new at that time. So he had Streisand on the left speaker, and the viola on the right. Then he edged the viola over to her, and if she didn't like it she went to the other side. [Laughter] He had them chasing each other around the room. I heard it and got hysterical. I said to Stan, 'Make me a copy, I want to play it for her.' Which he did and I called Barbra. She came to the editing room but before I played the tape I started putting her on by saying, 'Oh, Barbra, there's not enough brass in this session.' Then we played it for her. And meantime other people, including Robert Goulet's manager, Norman Rosemont, had wandered in. Well, they were falling off their feet laughing. And she was livid. She didn't see the humor in it. Not one bit. The girl never knew how to laugh at herself."

Following this embarrassment, the French album was put on hold, postponed for seven months. Barbra played *Funny Girl* in London; then she went on her concert tour. When the summer was over she was ready to pick up the project again. But she requested that Mersey and Weiss and their ilk be kept away from her and the studio. Throughout September and early October with Legrand and Stratta she recorded seven additional songs for the LP. Included were "Autumn Leaves," repeated with *full* orchestra, and a song which became known as Streisand's first composition, "Ma Première Chanson."

"There is an interesting story behind that song, that people don't know," said Stratta. "I actually cowrote that song with her, but my name is not on it. It happened in London. We were in the studio doing the Christmas songs and she said, 'I have a tune that I want you to write down.' She began to whistle, but she really didn't have a tune. She had this melody, it was small and uninteresting. But as she whistled it, I rewrote it, harmonized it, and then made a demo of it with her singing. I sent it to Eddie Marnay, who wrote the French lyrics, and it ended up as "Ma Première Chanson," which is listed on the album as written by Barbra. But I made it better; I collaborated on it. I never asked for credit. Today I would. But back then I was either too naive, or I didn't think it was that important. In those days they were reluctant to even give credit to producers. They'd put it on the album, but it was so small sometimes you couldn't find it."

The mixing and the reediting of the French album went to Warren Vincent. "It came to me after Ettore," said Vincent. "Barbra had a lot of doubts and mixed feelings about releasing it, but the Sales Department needed product. They didn't care what she thought, they wanted an album. I didn't like the thing, not one bit. I really felt it wasn't up to par with her other stuff. But I worked on it, and worked on it, until Barbra and I had a falling out. She was beating the thing to death. It got to the point where there were a lot of other artists recording—a lot of other records to be made—and she was making this a lifelong project. The list of changes she wanted was so long you'd have to write them on a roll of toilet paper. And eventually we had a blowup. Barbra doesn't like bullshit. She knew she could get the truth from any of the guys in the control room. She asked me what I thought of the French album, and I told her I hated it. I also told her to get someone else to work on it. After that I didn't hear from her again until the movie of *Funny Girl.*"

Je m'appelle Barbra was completed and released the fourth week of October 1967. The reviews were generally kind. "Among the best tracks," said Gene Lees of *High Fidelity,* "are 'Free Again,' 'Martina,' 'Autumn Leaves,' and 'Clopin Clopant.' Unfortunately, Miss Streisand insists on screaming her way out of 'I Wish You Love' and 'What Now, My Love?' lowering an otherwise tasteful level. In her soft moments, however, she never sounded better."

"The thing that I was sorry about, and Barbra admitted later that she was wrong, was that her voice was too loud on the entire album," said producer Stratta. "Like most artists, they felt the orchestra was too present, too loud. At the beginning all they want to hear is themselves. Barbra wanted to make sure everything was her. She was insecure. So she made me lower the orchestra, and a year later she came to me and said, 'You were right. I miss the orchestra.' By then she was beginning to believe that the impact, the dramatics, the whole voice, is much better when it's an integral part. But as an experiment for her, it worked. The album sold close to 500,000 copies worldwide, and it's still in her catalogue."

In early December, with her baby due just weeks away, Barbra had one important decision to thresh out. It had to do with her nose.

Although Streisand frequently claimed she was opposed to changing her appearance, in the early sixties she seriously considered having her nose altered. She spoke about it to the wife of Alan Miller, her acting teacher, and to illustrator Bob Schulenberg. "She brought it up frequently," the latter said. "We'd be in her apartment or at a restaurant and she'd stop everything to play with her nose. She'd push the tip of it up with her middle finger and say, 'See . . . this is how I want it to look. What do you think?' I'd tell her, 'I can't see anything with your hand in front of your face; leave your nose alone.'"

"I would have liked to look like Catherine Deneuve," said Barbra. "If I could do it myself with a mirror I would straighten my nose and take off that little piece of cartilage from the tip."

"I tried to convince her that her nose was original," Schulenberg continued. "It was classic in the Italian and French tradition. I showed her photographs of Eleanora Duse and Jacqueline de Ribes, who both had big noses. Years afterwards when Barbra was famous, Jacqueline de Ribes said to her, 'People always say you resemble me.' She was haughty about it, which I found amusing, because to me it was like the worm turning back on itself."

At the start of her career Streisand didn't have the money for an operation; later she didn't have the time. In the winter of 1966 she had both, but if her nose was to be fixed it had to be done pronto, before she commenced filming on *Funny Girl* the following May. "Barbra was terrified of making her first movie," said an associate. "Television wasn't a problem because the screen was small. But in movie theaters, in close-ups her face would be magnified to twenty feet. She kept worrying, 'All you'll see are my cross-eyes and my big nose.' She refused point blank to do a screen test for producer Ray Stark."

"Ray Stark asked her to test again and again," said Marty Erlichman. "He offered us twenty-five thousand dollars and actually went up to seventy-five thousand if she'd do the test. I said, 'Hey, for a couple of dollars more you've got her for the whole picture.' But no test—we didn't want that."

Barbra talked to surgeons, and all made the same diagnosis. They could give her a perfect nose, but they couldn't guarantee it wouldn't alter the sound of her voice. Her nasal sound was distinct, unique. Did she want to trade it for conventional beauty? The decision she made was no. "Having my nose fixed would have been not really who I was," she admitted. "I was also afraid it would change the sound of my voice. And I didn't trust doctors too much. And I don't like pain. But there's something I wouldn't like about myself if I did it."

On December 28, 1966, Barbra checked into Mt. Sinai Hospital, registering under the name of Angelina Scarangella. At six A.M. the following morning her labor pains began. Nine hours later Jason Emanuel Gould was born. "He cried when they cut the umbilical cord," Barbra said proudly. He weighed seven pounds, three ounces, and had his father's dark hair. "But his eyes are the brightest, bluest, flashingest—just like hers," Elliott told reporters.

Chapter 13

AND JASON MAKES THREE

After the birth of her son Streisand took two months off to devote her full time to his care. "She became totally absorbed with the kid," said one visitor. "It was as if she had never seen a baby before. She used to dress him up, then lay him down on the carpet in her bedroom. She and her dog Sadie would sit on the edge of the bed, looking down at Jason. They kept staring at the kid for hours, expecting it to talk or bark or do something. One day Jason smiled and gurgled and Barbra went nuts. She began cheering, and the dog started to bark. They were both thrilled at this new development."

Barbra during this time grew closer to her own mother. When she realized that no amount of pleading or stern caution would inhibit her mother, a truce was discussed. Mrs. Kind could still visit, and bring food, and fuss over Barbra and the baby's welfare, but she was asked not to talk openly about her famous daughter to strangers or to the press. "Strangers? The Press?" her mother replied. "I should ask the world for identification when they inquire about my daughter's health?"

In January, Streisand allowed two publications to visit: *Look* magazine, which was still in her favor, and the *Christian Science Monitor. CSM* writer June Carroll even rated an invitation to dine on pink roast beef and horseradish sauce (from London), served from a sideboard by Barbra herself, dressed in a brown lace gown, with a huge brown diamond on her finger, "as she burped the baby."

Look photographed Barbra holding and feeding the baby. She was dressed in designer's knits and bibs, her hair artfully coiffed, and her elongated nails buffed and polished. The length of the nails prompted one reader to inquire how Barbra could possibly bathe or caress the child without harming his tender skin. Or did she wear long gloves for these duties?

As baby made three, Barbra and Elliott decided they needed more living space. His nursery was her former sewing room. In late January they bought the apartment next door, but after the purchase they learned they were not permitted to knock down the connecting wall. The noise and the devaluation of the unit (should they decide to resell) were prohibited by the building's board of directors.

After an appeal, and a promise from their star tenant that the work would be done rapidly and as silently as possible, and that they would rebuild the wall at their own expense if they should decide to move, permission was granted. "Can you imagine the psychological damage that would have caused the kid," said Barbra, "to live in a separate apartment from his parents? His shrink bills would have been enormous."

In early March, Streisand began rehearsals for her third TV special, which was overdue and had to be completed before she left for Hollywood to film *Funny Girl.*

The new TV show, entitled *The Belle of 14th Street,* was initially described as "set in the Belle Époque period." In actuality it was to be a re-creation of a nineteen hundreds vaudevillian troupe, with the songs and costumes of that era. "We weren't looking to make fun of it, but do it as they did," said Barbra.

Breaking her precedent of "no guests," Jason Robards was hired as her singing-dancing-Shakespearean actor costar. Streisand originally asked for Marlon Brando or Richard Burton, but she was told (a) their fees were higher than her whole budget, and (b) they didn't do television.

"Barbra had the perfect actor under her nose all the time and never used him," said a casting agent. "Elliott would have been perfect for the part, and he would have brought some degree of control to the project."

Elliott allegedly would not work with Barbra, especially after he'd been bypassed for *Funny Girl.* He had wanted to play Nicky Arnstein in the original Broadway production, but no one had asked him. "At the time," he said, "I couldn't get the job. And I'm more talented than all the guys who played Nicky Arnstein put together. Later they asked if I'd play it with Barbra in London and I refused."

The Belle of 14th Street, written by Robert Emmett, seemed to be a perfect comic and theatrical outing for Streisand. It enabled her to play seven different roles (all of the women and two of the boys) and to use different dialects. One of these was the Irish immigrant mother of a singing quartet called the Dancing Duncans. Dressed in red, white, and blue, with her young daughter by her side, Mrs. Duncan (Barbra) talks of her good fortune in America. "Sure, it's people like me," she said in a thick Irish brogue, "born of poor Irish stock—a small potato in the great melting pot. Me. Being able to come here and sing and dance for wonderful people like you. An opportunity for a family like us to march together down the road of life, liberty, and the pursuit of happiness. . . . You can pull yourself up by the bootstraps and become, who knows? [She looks down at her earnest daughter] Maybe the secretary to the President of the United States!"

A second highlight—which the *Hollywood Reporter* would refer to as "deviation to bad taste with unnecessary anti-German slurs" —presented Streisand as the Nuremburg Nightingale—Madame Schmausen-Schmidt, the daughter of Germany, the mother of six, and the wife of Otto Van Schmidt. Hands clasped across an ample bosom, she gave a mock Teutonic rendition of "Liebestraum," then addressed the audience:

"Oh, danke, danke. Thank you very much. As you know, this is the first performance I make on my triumphant tour of your country. I was just now coming from Berlin where I was singing lieder for the Kaiser—jah. Oh, the Kaiser, he loves America . . . like it was his very own. Und, I would just like to say that we shall march . . . all over your country . . . singing the beautiful songs of the old world. For music is the universal language . . . of Germany. You like Brahms? He was German, you know. Und Beethoven . . . Wagner . . . und Franz Liszt, the man with whom, which I sang now the song: he was German. Well; on his mother's side. Und now for your immense enjoyment, I would like to sing one of your popular songs I learned when I was perfecting my English. If I forget some place the words you will speak it up to me, jah?"

Madame Schmidt launched into "Mother Machree" and was soon joined by a tenor voice from the audience. A young boy dressed in Lord Fauntleroy velvet knickers stood in a front box and commenced to sing along. The boy was Streisand—and the duet (her serious intentions withstanding) was both high camp and glorious entertainment.

On paper—with other skits and backstage theatrics—*The Belle of 14th Street* was first class; but in action, in its execution, it died. "Everyone had the best intentions," said Fred Glaser, who created the hair styles for the show, "but somehow the magic of the other two specials was missing. Barbra didn't seem to have the same dedication. She seemed anxious to get everything done fast, so she could leave for Hollywood. In essence she was using this show as a rehearsal for the movies she planned to make. *The Belle of 14th Street* later became parts of *Funny Girl* and *Hello, Dolly!*"

> *"Hollywood is my newest challenge. I'll be the brightest star they ever had."*
> *Barbra Streisand to reporters in L.A., 1967*

On May 10, 1967, Streisand arrived in Los Angeles for the *Funny Girl* filming, accompanied by Elliott, Jason, and Sadie.

For the duration of the movie production she rented Greta Garbo's former home, and with the lease came the Swede's dictate for privacy and aloofness.

On Sunday night, May 14, Fran and Ray Stark threw a welcome-to-Hollywood party for Barbra, and Elliott, at their Bel Air home, once owned by Humphrey Bogart and Lauren Bacall. The guest list was culled from column A of the movie colony: Merle Oberon, John Wayne, Marlon Brando, Gregory and Veronique Peck, Jimmy and Gloria Stewart, Robert Mitchum, Steve McQueen, and Natalie Wood.

Barbra arrived an hour late, then stood in the hallway and announced to her hostess that the lighting in her home wasn't right for her. Sweeping through the living room, she paused briefly to greet her idol, Marlon Brando, with "What are *you* doing here?" Then she settled in the Starks' library and wouldn't budge for the evening. Those who wanted to meet and talk had to move in her direction.

"That arrogance was a cover-up," said one guest. "Barbra was really shy and a little in awe of those big names. She was also a wee bit defensive and defiant. Hollywood was still a town preoccupied with sex and beauty. The all-American ideal was the blond, blue-eyed Sandra Dee. Barbra's currency was talent. She was hired for that, and she didn't intend to spend a lot of time socializing. She was there to work, not play, and she was very direct about it. She could barely get past the "Hello-how-are-you's" to people like Rosalind Russell, Natalie Wood, and Cary Grant before she asked them about their tricks before the camera. She asked Cary Grant about the cleft in his chin; if it always showed up on camera."

"She used to pick my brain about things like lighting and makeup and hair and angles," said actress Joan Collins. "She's an absolute sponge. She and Brando are very similar. He's a sponge too. They soak things up. I'm a sieve—things go in and they go out immediately."

Throughout the months of April and May, in between rehearsals for the *Funny Girl* musical numbers, Barbra was fitted and tested for wardrobe, hair, and makeup shots. "Barbra adored clothes," said designer Irene Sharaff, "and she wore them with flair. She liked to vary the size of the padding in her bras, which I found amusing, but which was maddening to the fitters."

"There was also a union problem about her hair," said a production aide. "The studio had assigned two people to design the many wigs and different hairstyles she wore, but she didn't want to work with these people. She brought in her own guy [Fred Glaser] and hid him in her dressing room. When the union found out, they bounced him from the studio. So Barbra put him in a trailer outside the studio gates, and she'd sneak out during lunchtime, carrying sketches and swatches of hair."

"I never worked in a trailer," said Fred Glaser. "When the studio prohibited me on the grounds I worked with Barbra at her home."

Sidney Lumet was originally assigned to direct *Funny Girl.* He met with Streisand frequently in New York and London, and then he withdrew from the project. "Sidney wanted to film the first twenty minutes in a montage," said Marty Erlichman. "Me and Barbra disagreed."

Streisand's alternates for director were Mike Nichols (who chose *Who's Afraid of Virginia Woolf?* for his directorial debut) and George Roy Hill, who directed *Thoroughly Modern Millie.* She had never heard of William Wyler. "What's he done?" she asked. *"Ben-Hur,"* she was told. "Chariots!" she replied. "How is he with people, like women? Is he any good with actresses?"

Wyler was good with women, she was informed. He had directed Bette Davis in *Jezebel,* Merle Oberon in *Wuthering Heights,* and Greer Garson in *Mrs. Miniver.* "Yeah," said Barbra, "but that's years ago; gimme someone recent."

Audrey Hepburn in *Roman Holiday* was mentioned. Directed by Wyler, she won an Oscar for the role. "Audrey's okay," said Barbra. "I saw her in *Sabrina.* She wore flats a lot. How tall is she?"

Appraising actors for the role opposite Streisand was equally thorough. "We looked at a lot of guys," said Marty Erlichman. "David Janssen was up for the role, and so was Sean Connery and Gregory Peck. I remember Ray Stark ran a screening of *The Americanization of Emily* in his home for us. He wanted to know what Barbra thought of James Garner."

Garner was not chosen, nor was Frank Sinatra. "I wanted Frank," said Jule Styne. "What a powerhouse bill that would be. Streisand and Sinatra together. Frank was interested, if I expanded the role and wrote a few new songs for him. I called Ray Stark. Ray said Sinatra was too old, that they needed someone with more class. So who do they pick? Omar Sharif, who couldn't sing and was an Arab. You figure it out. That's Hollywood."

SATURDAY IN THE PARK WITH BARBRA

On Friday evening, June 16, after rehearsing all day at Columbia Pictures' Gower Street studio, Streisand was driven by limo to the L.A. International airport, where she boarded a jet for New York.

Arriving at Kennedy airport at two in the morning, she was greeted by New York Parks Commissioner, August Heckscher; who whisked her by helicopter to Central Park in mid-Manhattan, where she was to give a free concert the following night.

The producer-director of the concert and subsequent TV special was Robert Scheerer, who had recently directed the Danny Kaye series. He was waiting for Streisand in the park, and upon her arrival they began rehearsals with the orchestra for the TV cameras. "That night we only had time to block out four or five numbers," said Scheerer. "We knew the preparation time would be minimal. So in a situation like that you solve as many problems as you can going in, and then you pray you get by."

On Saturday afternoon after four hours sleep in her apartment, Streisand returned to the park with Elliott and her sister, Rosalind. The fans had already gathered behind the barricades and applauded the star's arrival. What ensued "was one of the more exciting moments of my life," said the director. "I was standing on the stage. Mort Lindsay was running through some of the songs, and Barbra started singing "Second Hand Rose." Four or five hundred of her staunch fans were hanging round the stage, and she got into maybe eight bars of the song when she realized that they were singing the song to her. And she stopped singing. She stood there smiling and listening to them. She was thrilled. It was wonderful; an electrifying moment. We tried to capture it again that night on the TV cameras, but it wasn't the same."

In all, 7 cameras were used to film the open-air event, including one on a helicopter, and one on a crane connected to a two-hundred-foot ramp. For audio, twenty-eight microphones and twelve speakers were placed, with two direct feeds, one to the TV facility, and another to Columbia Records' remote truck. "Columbia was recording the album and wanted their own feed," said Scheerer, "but that was impossible with this schedule. As it was, Phil Ramone, who supervised the sound, did a mammoth job. He was ready to project Barbra's voice over the meadow, up as far as Eighty-sixth Street. That way the people on both sides of the park could listen to the concert from their apartments on Fifth Avenue and Central Park West. That was an amazing feat in those days."

At seven P.M., even with the threat of rain, Central Park was jammed. Over 135,000 people of every age and ethnic background had gathered in the Sheep Meadow for the concert. By eight-thirty they were growing restive. Chants of "Barbra! Barbra! We want Barbra!" filled the air. "We had to wait until dark for the television tubes," said Scheerer, "and the delay caused a bit of a stir."

"Some fences were knocked down," said Ed Graham of Columbia, "and one guy almost got electrocuted by walking too close to the open cables. But for the most part the people were calm."

Streisand, however, was petrified, "literally terrified of appearing before so many people," said Scheerer. "Her main fear was the spotlight. She felt it was a perfect target for someone with a weapon. Everyone was saying how symbolic that was of her fears —but a few weeks later, when she did a similar concert in the Hollywood Bowl, the police pulled some guy out of the audience with a forty-five revolver. So it wasn't so symbolic after all. Her fear was legitimate."

The security for the event was also lax. Bob Schulenberg recalled going by the meadow earlier that day and he found only one guard on duty outside the cluster of trailers. "I told him I was a friend of Barbra's and I walked past him. No one stopped me. I went right into her dressing room. I left a note. For all anybody knew I could have left a bomb."

That night, minutes before the concert was to begin, the director ordered that the red lights on all the TV cameras be turned off. "I didn't want her to know where the cameras were," said Scheerer. "That way she'd be as loose as possible when she came out." He relayed the first camera cue to a helicopter hovering over Battery Park in lower Manhattan. It flew uptown, photographing the city, then closed in on Central Park. That was Barbra's cue to appear. "She wouldn't move," said Fred Glaser. "She had to be helped up the stairs and then pushed onstage."

Walking down the clear Plexiglas runway, dressed in a pink Irene Sharaff chiffon gown, Barbra was momentarily stunned by the roar of the crowd and the flash from thousands of Instamatics. "I didn't do nothin' yet!" she said, admonishing the audience, and then she began to sing "Anyplace I Hang My Hat Is Home."

"That opening portion was no good," said Scheerer. "Barbra was too tight, still nervous. It took four or five songs to get her warmed up, and we couldn't use any of those for the TV special. But we planned on being over anyway, just so we could be more selective."

There was also an intermission, which CBS asked be eliminated. "We wanted continuity. If there were problems we could then intercut. But that wasn't possible if she was wearing a different outfit. But she insisted on changing gowns and hairstyles. She obviously wanted to have a second entrance."

"She was in a foul mood during the break," said Fred Glaser. "The air was humid, her hairpiece wouldn't stay on, she began cursing and swearing at people in her trailer. Everyone fled and left me with her. It was like the night of Johnson's inauguration. I was the only one there to take her abuse. I remember I got her out of the trailer and we drove in a golf cart to the back of the stage. She continued to rant and rave. She said the crowd had moved too close to the stage."

"Move them back! Move them back!" she ordered the security guards. "I don't want to see their faces, I don't want to hear them talking."

"There was no way for the crowds to go back, only forward," said Glaser. "And then the wind blew up and she got something in her eye. As she stood behind a rock I had to run back to the trailer for a Q-Tip. On the way back I fell and put my knee out in my new slacks. The TV crew applauded and she snapped, 'Never mind, it's gone now, leave me alone.' Then she sailed onstage to another ovation."

Total time for the concert was two and a half hours, with thirty-five songs performed. "Two of those songs I wasn't prepared for," said the director. "I never heard them before and didn't know the timing, so when I say we winged it, it's no understatement."

As she closed with "Happy Days Are Here Again," one camera pulled back for a long shot of Streisand, which dissolved to a sky-view of the entire meadow. "I had this two-hundred-foot ramp built and waiting in front of her," said Scherrer. "At one point in the show she saw the crane and said out loud, 'What's that?' It was really quite funny because she had forgotten about the shot and thought something was wrong. So did CBS. Throughout the concert they kept asking, 'When are you going to use the ramp we built?' They thought I had wasted their money. Then as she was closing with "Happy Days Are Here Again" I gave the cue to the guys on the crane. The camera drew back from Barbra—very slowly—up into the air, and over the park. We watched it on the TV monitor. It was really quite a moment. And the guys from CBS said, 'Oh yes, we see, we see.' "

"When Barbra came off," said Glaser, "everyone was cheering. All of the phonies surrounded her. I fled. The crowds everywhere were so happy and I felt miserable. I did. I felt like the loneliest guy in town. She made me feel worthless. Then I bumped into this friend of mine, Monti Rock, and he said, 'Why the long face?' I told him and he said, 'Oh, ----, she's only a star, let's go to a party.' And I did, and got ripped. The following morning the phone rang in my hotel room. It was Barbra, apologizing. I remember it vividly because in our seven years together that was the *only* time she said 'I'm sorry.' "

In Los Angeles prerecording of the songs from *Funny Girl* began in July. The orchestra, under the direction of Walter Scharf, varied in size from eighty musicians for "People," to seven for "Roller Skate Rag" and "I'd Rather Be Blue Over You." Scharf, a seasoned composer-conductor *(Hans Christian Andersen),* had been briefed on Streisand. "They warned me she was temperamental and stubborn," he said. "She was, but she was also one of the most original and gifted artists I have ever encountered." "People," which Streisand had sung an estimated 950 times onstage in New York and London, required extensive takes for the movie version. "It sounded great on the first playback," said publicist Jack Brodsky, "but she made a face. She didn't like a phrase, and went over it with the conductor. She did it again, and again. They worked for hours. I couldn't tell the difference between take one and take two, but I *could* tell the difference between take one and take ten."

"It differed from the original version in that it wasn't as good," said composer Jule Styne, who was in Los Angeles for the recording session. "I was upset with the orchestrations for the entire movie. They were going for pop arrangements. "My Man," which wasn't in the show, and didn't belong in the movie, was like a Las Vegas arrangement. They dropped eight songs from the Broadway show and we were asked to write some new ones. They didn't want to go with success. It was the old-fashioned MGM Hollywood way of doing a musical. They always change things to their way of vision, and they always do it wrong. But, of all my musicals they screwed up, *Funny Girl* came out the best."

Throughout rehearsals and the early shooting of the film, Elliott Gould stayed by Barbra's side to add support and, sometimes, a needed discipline. Codirector Herb Ross, who staged the film's musical numbers, told of one incident: "During a rehearsal Barbra got tired and said she wanted to go home. But Elliott pointed to the chorus and told her, 'They're getting three hundred dollars for doing what they're doing, you're getting five hundred thousand. So get back up there and do it.' "

On his own in Hollywood, Gould was uncomfortable. The town had never been overly solicitous or respectful of consorts or husbands, especially those with acting aspirations of their own. True, they gave him court. Calls for Elliott came in from studio executives and casting agents, but no amount of sweet banter or hip endearments could camouflage the fact he was being patronized for his proximity to Streisand.

That August, while appearing in a stock production of *Luv*, with Shelley Winters, Elliott was visited by director William Friedkin, who offered Gould a role in his forthcoming movie *The Night They Raided Minsky's*. It was only the eighth lead, and it was to be filmed on location in New York, but pleased to be accepted for his own worth, Elliott took the job.

"That was a big mistake as far as Barbra was concerned," a friend of the couple reported. "She wanted Elliott in Hollywood. She wanted *everyone* in Hollywood. She had Marty Erlichman flying back and forth from New York; she had her best friend, Sis Corman, in the chorus of *Funny Girl;* and David Begelman and Freddie Fields were holding her hand between scenes. Elliott knew he had to get away from her. He had to establish a career on his own. So he left, and Barbra got very peeved. She was like a spoiled child—immensely talented, but spoiled. And for spite, she took up with Omar Sharif."

In Hollywood the ritual of actresses falling in love with their leading men was as old as the medium itself. In the 1920s it was Garbo and John Gilbert; then Joan Crawford and Clark Gable, Lauren Bacall and Humphrey Bogart, Lana Turner and Fernando Lamas, Natalie Wood and Warren Beatty; and by 1967 Barbra Streisand and Omar Sharif were ripe to join the group. Sharif, after *Lawrence of Arabia* and *Doctor Zhivago,* was the "hot hunk" of the day, the male fantasy figure for millions of women. He had smoldering dark looks and a calculated Continental charm. When he first met Streisand he kissed her hand and told her that of all the women in Hollywood he wanted to meet, she was number one. That line got him the part of Nicky Arnstein; it also got him into her bed.

According to Sharif's biography, *The Eternal Male,* his and Barbra's real-life affair was "a wonderful love story." At first he thought she was ugly, but gradually she put a spell on him. "I fell madly in love with her," he confessed. "The feeling was mutual for four months, the time it took to shoot the picture."

They spent evenings together and sometimes weekends at her Holmby Hills mansion, while his wife and family were lodged nearby in a rented house. He taught Barbra how to play cards, and cooked Italian meals for her. She made TV dinners and coached him on his solo song, "Pink Velvet Jail," which was later cut from the movie. "Our affair was discreet," said Sharif. Few people knew about it besides Ray Stark, Sheilah Graham, and Omar's male buddies at the Daisy discotheque, to whom he confided he was seriously thinking of becoming circumcised for Barbra. Sheilah Graham reported the couple were seen at a fashion show, and later went for dinner at The Factory. Her column was read by Elliott in New York, he responded, "Nothing to it. I was out of town making a movie, and Barbra is cheap. The tickets to the show cost two hundred fifty dollars each, and she hates to buy her own meals. Sharif was just somebody to pick up the tab."

"Fine," said Hollywood columnist Jim Bacon, "except that most of the dinners were in Omar's suite in the Beverly Wilshire Hotel. I used to report them regularly, even naming the brand and vintage of the wine, not to mention the main course. Barbra always wondered how I knew those things."

On December twenty-first filming ended on *Funny Girl,* and with it the affair with Omar. The playacting for Barbra was over and she returned to Elliott. To a reporter she described Sharif as "luminous, a charismatic star." He was not as gallant after they parted. "She's a monster," he told Rex Reed. "I had nothing to do but stand around. But she's a fascinating monster. Sometimes I just stood on the sidelines and watched her. I think her biggest problem is that she wants to be a woman and she wants to be beautiful and she is neither."

During the period Streisand was filming *Funny Girl,* her contract with Columbia Records expired. Though other major labels were bidding for her vocal talent, she agreed to give Columbia first refusal. But the days of "modest advances" were over. Prior to negotiations she instructed Marty Erlichman to nail Columbia for every control and dollar they could get.

With his boost upstairs at CBS, Goddard Lieberson had adroitly removed himself from the wheeling and dealing of the record business. Negotiations for Streisand's new contract were handled by Clive Davis, who was also renegotiating the contracts of Andy Williams and Bob Dylan. Williams, the largest seller of the three, received a guarantee of $1.5 million, for ten albums, over a period of five years. Bob Dylan asked for no money up front but a ten-percent royalty on all retail sales, with no minimum product. Streisand, who stood between Williams and Dylan, saleswise, wanted what the other two got combined. She asked for Andy's advance and Dylan's royalty, and it was up to Clive to say no.

"The Streisand negotiations were volatile," he said. "Erlichman would pound the desk and storm out of the office periodically, and then not call back for three or four weeks. My general technique was to avoid returning emotion for emotion; you can't take these things personally. It's business."

When Erlichman stormed out of his office, Clive usually conferred with Walter Dean, the head of business affairs at Columbia. Both agreed it was best to wait for things to cool off, then to call Marty. "It was sometimes quite upsetting," said Davis. "I'd sit in my chair and grind my teeth, thinking: *I can't close this goddamn deal.*"

Marty, of course, relayed each move to Streisand who told her manager to wait out the situation and not budge an inch. "Finally," said Davis, "after having my back against the wall for what seemed an eternity, we came to terms." She was offered a sliding-scale royalty, higher if she would accept a lower guarantee of one million dollars.

Barbra and Marty accepted.

"The guarantee was not quite a million," said Erlichman.

"It was eight hundred fifty thousand dollars," said a Columbia executive, "with one sixth payable on signing, and one sixth due on the September thirtieth of each year. Her royalty rate was forty cents an album [which was one penny more than the Beatles were getting at that time] and ten cents per single."

"In those days," said Erlichman, "most of the deals they were making were against percentages of wholesale prices. But they could change those prices to different distributors, and you got paid on the lower figure. I said, 'No wholesale, we want our royalty against retail prices, and if they go up we get the higher rate too.' Her royalty was never less than ten percent."

The number of Streisand albums promised was fifteen, over the five-year period. She would later regret this obligation, blasting the label for the workload, but the money at the time blinded all foresight.

Also guaranteed by Columbia was an outlay of $125,000 to be used specifically for the promotion and advertising of the Streisand product. "We didn't want her lumped with everyone else in the company's promotion pool," said Erlichman. "When she had an album coming out we wanted to be able to say, 'Okay, we want a full page in *TV Guide,* a half a page in *Life.*' It was our money to spend. We could use it at our discretion and not wait for some advertising executive to do us a favor."

Other inserted clauses included: no couplings on songs or compilations, no premium albums or budget reissues; full consultation and approval on all packaging components, from album-cover art to the color and type on record labels; plus approval of all producers, arrangers, conductors, musicians, engineers, and editors; and at each recording session a company guard was to be posted at the door, barring all visitors to the studio.

In November, upon the signing of the contract, two new Streisand LPs were released. One was *Simply Streisand,* a collection of standards which sold poorly.

The second LP was *A Christmas Album.* It contained the four songs she had recorded in London the previous summer, and seven new selections recorded in Los Angeles on the ninth and sixteenth of September 1967. The producer on the new Christmas sides was Jack Gold; the arranger-conductor was Marty Paich, who had worked previously with Frank Sinatra, Lena Horne, and Ray Charles. "I met with Barbra in the house she was renting in Beverly Hills, the one off Sunset Boulevard," Paich recalled. "Elliott was there, and the new baby. It was a very pleasant meeting. Later we discussed the LP in Jack Gold's office, and Barbra also sent me a tape on which she put down a few musical ideas."

She was quite taken, she said, with Judy Garland's performance of "Have Yourself A Merry Little Christmas," from the classic MGM musical *Meet Me in St. Louis.* She suggested they intensify the poignancy of Judy's version by adding an arrangement similar to the one Barbra used on "Happy Days Are Here Again." "We opened with a brass fanfare," said Marty Paich. "We had three

French horns, three trumpets, and two trombones. There was also a harp, a rhythm section, and thirty-five strings."

The last song recorded, and one resisted at first by Streisand, was "White Christmas." "She didn't want to do it because it was too closely associated with Bing Crosby," said Jack Gold. "I remembered that it had a special verse, an introduction that Irving Berlin wrote about being stranded in Beverly Hills on Christmas Eve, with the sunshine and palm trees. Few people knew of the introduction because it wasn't usually sung. It was late at night, past midnight, and Barbra had an early call at the movie studio the following morning. She was making *Funny Girl* by day and recording the Christmas album at night. I asked her to listen to the 'White Christmas' verse before she left. She listened to it and we recorded the song the next night."

Barbra was stubborn; she liked to have her own way, Gold reported. "I used to think her way was as good as anyone else's, but I came to know in many instances her way was better. I have regrets about Streisand sessions. Not about her, but about myself. I wasn't well at the time. I was in the early stage of an illness I didn't understand. I was insecure about my ability to get up and talk to her from the control room. I didn't want to do it over the system. I wanted to correct her, to give her ideas. She was looking for that, for strong direction, and I failed to give it. Oh, I got my points across okay, but I wanted to do one great session with her. She was a true artist. Later on Marty called me to do "The Way We Were." But I wasn't up to it. I knew I couldn't hack it, so I turned it down. When I heard the song on the radio I thought she was exceptional."

First and foremost she is a singer, Marty Paich agreed. "As a singer she is tops. And though the rest of her talents are incredible, they are secondary. Her voice is her first gift, and always will be."

Because of her schedule with *Funny Girl* there was no time for a Christmas photo sitting. The cover photograph chosen by John Berg and approved by Barbra was a shot of her taken on the night of the rehearsals for the Central Park concert. The liner notes on the back of the album were a personal greeting. "Originally we wanted to use one of Barbra's recycled Christmas cards," said Charlie Burr, then director of Literary Services. "But no one had the courage to suggest it to her. She was beyond second-hand cards, we were told. Instead, she sent us a pink sheet of Tiffanyembossed stationery. She wrote: *Season's Greetings, Barbra Streisand.* She also sent us a bill. She charged us fifty dollars to use it."

After Thanksgiving, with the album placed in stores, it was mandatory for a single to be released, to generate airplay and album sales. No one at Columbia could decide which of the eight new sides ("Silent Night" and "Ave Maria" had been released as a single the previous year) to choose, so the decision went to Barbra. Within days the word came back. She wanted *all eight* sides released. "They didn't say boo," said one executive. "Whatever Barbra wanted, Barbra got. If she wanted four singles pressed on red and green vinyl, they did it. If she wanted Santa Claus and his seven dwarfs to deliver them to the disc jockeys, they called the North Pole. It was hysterical. People jumped when her name came up. It was always 'Well, Barbra wants this, and Andy [Williams] wants that.' He was as demanding as she was. Once, the blue in his eyes didn't match the blue in the sweater on his album cover and Clive called an emergency meeting in his office.

"On 'Silent Night' Barbra thought her interpretation transcended time, transcended Christmas itself. She wanted it re-released as a nonseasonal single, and Columbia *agreed* with her. Christmas was over, it was January, and they took out full-page ads in the trades for her and the song. 'Destined to be a timeless classic,' they said. Sheer stupidity. I sometimes wondered if she *knew* what she was up to. If she wasn't laughing behind their backs and saying, 'You dumb ----s. Just wait until you see the next hurdle I'll make you jump.' "

Chapter 14

"Dolly is not the kind of thing I'm interested in. I'm interested in real life, real people—and in playing Medea. Dolly takes place in an age before people realized they hated their mothers—the whole Freudian thing."

Barbra Streisand, 1968

HELLO, DOLLY!

In January of 1968 Streisand was served with an injunction from Ray Stark. The crux of the lawsuit was this: When she signed for *Funny Girl*, the movie, she was eager for the role and agreed to do three more pictures for Stark. There was no fixed date for these follow-up movies. The producer assumed that once *Funny Girl* was successfully completed, Streisand would be amenable to do any film he offered to her. He submitted two scripts to her: *Two for the Seesaw* and *Wait Till the Sun Shines, Nellie*. She passed on both projects. She was about to begin filming of *Hello, Dolly!* to be followed by *On a Clear Day You Can See Forever*, and after that there was a possibility of her doing *The Fantasticks* for MGM pictures. Stark knew that by the time she honored her commitments to him he would be old and gray. And so, he sued.

He asked the court to "order" Streisand to make a film for him. Furthermore he claimed she had breached her agreement with him by working for other employers (CBS TV) while filming was in progress on *Funny Girl*. He wanted a full accounting of all monies earned by Barbra in her Central Park and Hollywood Bowl concerts.

"Barbra underestimated Ray Stark," said an agent. He was adept "at playing games of wit, control, and confusion," said director John Huston, "and he refused to be intimidated, even by himself." The agent added, "Barbra thought she could dispense with him and his contract as soon as she had *Funny Girl* under her belt. He knew she was going to be a big star, he had given her the big break, and he wanted his future share. So he took her to court."

"Barbra was willing to work for Stark again," said Marty Erlichman. "We told him, 'When you've got a good script, call us.' "

In the meantime she would proceed with her next blockbuster movie, *Hello, Dolly!* which, budgeted at $20-million became the most expensive musical ever made.

"It's lightweight, a piece of fluff," Streisand said of the play when she was in competition with Carol Channing for the Tony Award. Channing won the prize and was the strong contender for the movie version until her appearance in *Thoroughly Modern Millie.* That was supposed to be her screen test for Dolly, but according to producer Ernest Lehman he couldn't "take a whole movie in which Carol was in practically every scene. Her personality is just too much for the cameras to contain."

Other stars considered for Dolly were Lucille Ball and Elizabeth Taylor. "Liz should play the role," Barbra said sweetly. "The part calls for an older woman."

Elizabeth Taylor was in fact considered by producer Lehman. "I talked to Elizabeth when we were on the final stages of *Virginia Woolf,*" he said. "I casually asked her whether she'd ever thought of doing a musical. She got quite excited at the prospect, and a couple of years later, when I came to cast the picture, her agent rang me up and told me Elizabeth really wanted to play Dolly. And I must admit I felt very guilty at having ever mentioned it to her, because it was a thoroughly rotten notion of mine. At least I *think* it was. In this business you can never ever tell until after the event."

Streisand had the right vocal quality, Lehman decided, and she was sure to be a star when *Funny Girl* was released. So he approached her through David Begelman. She resisted; the play was silly, infantile. He persisted; the script was being rewritten. It was a one-song show, Streisand countered. New songs would be put in, he assured her. The cons, the pros, the promises, went back and forth, until Barbra, true to form in work situations like these, asked for an impossible sum of money. She wanted Liz Taylor's fee per picture, she named her favorite sum—one million dollars. "Agreed," said Lehman, and the new Dolly was signed.

To Streisand the project now took on a new significance. With the money she saw the role in a different perspective. She told a reporter that Dolly was "the story of any woman who has loved and lost and has to make that important decision whether to live the rest of her life or just dwell on the past and memories. And that's a very unusual problem for women of all ages."

"Well look at that," the reporter replied. "And I just thought it was the story of a woman who arranges things, a matchmaker."

To direct *Dolly* Ernest Lehman chose Gene Kelly, with Michael Kidd hired to choreograph. Kelly's experience in musicals *(Singin' in the Rain* and *An American in Paris)* was prodigious. He also possessed, according to Lehman, "tremendous energy and vitality, and a maddening cheerfulness."

Apprehensive of Streisand, Kelly flew to New York and met with her and David Begelman in the Oak Room of the Plaza Hotel. He reported: "I came right out with it and said, 'Barbra, is there any truth to all these stories that you don't want to rehearse and that you're difficult?' And to that she said no. All she needed, she said, was a director to guide her, and that she was dying to do the role, and that I could count on her. I told her she would have to work damn hard, because the part called for a matron and she was still a young and blooming woman. She agreed with me and said she would."

By mid-March of 1968 Streisand was back in Hollywood rehearsing and being fitted for her half-million-dollar wardrobe as Dolly Levi. To enhance her image within the movie community she also agreed to make some social appearances. She showed up at the home of Joanne Woodward and Paul Newman for a cocktail party in honor of Senator Eugene McCarthy, and though she was only one of several big stars in attendance, she had the honor of leaving, and driving off with, the presidential candidate. On April tenth she made an appearance on the annual Academy Award telecast. She presented the Oscar for Best Song to Sammy Davis, Jr., and the following morning she found out she had received a citation too. The assembled critics had voted her "the worst dressed and coiffed [she had worn an Afro wig] presenter" of the evening. "They were right," said the litigious Ray Stark. "She looked like a cartoon."

On May twentieth a second attack came from a leading member of the Hollywood press. A profile of Barbra, written by Joyce Haber, appeared in *New York Magazine.* In the piece Miss Haber examined Streisand's behavior during the filming of *Funny Girl* and asked the industry question: Was the new superstar "a bore or a monster?"

"She might have opted to be a bore," said Haber. "There is evidence that she has talent in that direction. But the department of dullness, saintly dullness, has been preempted by Julie Andrews. Julie is so solidly entrenched there that she could be living at the Beverly Hills Hotel with two Viet Cong guerillas and a Chinese gigolo without disturbing her public image of good-sweet-jolly-dull girl."

Barbra was partly sexy, "stacked in a lingerie-counter sort of way," Haber continued. She was also a staged eccentric, who was bossy, frequently bored ("which she tends to be whenever people are not talking about *her"),* and determined that the town's legends (i.e., William Wyler) know their place in her presence

Because of the Haber article all reporters requesting access to the *Hello, Dolly!* set were carefully screened by publicist Pat Newcomb. Newcomb, the daughter of an Army judge advocate, was soft spoken and skillful. She had been Marilyn Monroe's personal press agent. She had been with her on the evening she died. And the fact that, subsequently, she never once spoke to the press about Marilyn or her death was proof of the protection she offered her clients.

Liz Smith was a free-lance writer in those days, and along with John Gregory Dunne (of *Life),* she was allowed to visit the *Hello, Dolly!* set. "I had interviewed Barbra for *Cosmopolitan* a few years previous," said Liz. "I liked her, and I think she liked me also. She wasn't as wary or nervous; and Pat Newcomb also said, 'Hey, look, this is someone you can trust.' So I arranged to interview her for *The New York Times.*

Streisand was slightly crazed during the filming of *Hello, Dolly!,* Liz recalled. "She was way in over her head. The movie was costing millions each day. She was too young for the role. And the pressures were enormous. She had also gone Hollywood in a huge way. At night we would sometimes go to her house for dinner.

And later she would show us still pictures of herself from *Funny Girl,* which wasn't released yet. She would ask me what I thought of each one. I knew she needed a more astute opinion than mine, and she would get exasperated when I'd say, 'That one is okay, that's nice,' and on and on. It was too bizarre. It was all *her.* The idea that you are so fascinating that people would be happy to stay up until three in the morning looking at pictures of yourself, seemed so *strange* to me; sort of like Norma Desmond. Of course I was also fascinated, because I was doing a story and this was wonderful material."

That material never made it into print, however. "Barbra had asked for quote approval," said Liz, "and I foolishly said okay. I don't know what the policy was at the *Times,* but I figured if it was a good story they'd run it. But she screwed around with the piece and really vitiated it. She cleaned it all up until it didn't resemble anything. I lost control of my own story, and that's a position I tried not to put myself in again. Of course the *Times* turned the piece down. It was too ass-kissing, they believed. And they were right. But I couldn't argue with Barbra. I wasn't strong enough with her then. So we both lost out. But to this day she always tells me, 'You know, Liz, the best story ever written about me was by you. And *The New York Times* never printed it.' "

To add to the chaos a feud erupted on the *Hello, Dolly!* set between Streisand and her leading man, Walter Matthau. Matthau, a gambler, raconteur, and a man of irascible wit had met Barbra a few months before at a theater opening back East. "I know you," he greeted her. "You're Barbara Harris. I see you've had your nose fixed." Streisand was *not* amused.

In Hollywood their first publicized flare-up came on stage fourteen, where the $375,000 Harmonia Gardens was recreated for the *Hello, Dolly!* title number. The set was closed to the press, but two reporters, columnist Earl Wilson and journalist John Gregory Dunne were allowed to stand on the sidelines and watch the rehearsals.

"Barbra stood on top of the staircase and chewed on a hangnail," said Dunne. She ran through the song and dance and continued to trip over her fifty-thousand-dollar, twenty-pound beaded dress. After a break she gathered son Jason in her arms and swept off the soundstage to her limousine parked outside. Earl Wilson followed.

"Walter Matthau came out and started talking to Jason," Wilson reported. "The kid seemed terrified of him. 'One way to bring up kids,' Matthau kept snorting kiddingly, 'is to talk baby talk to 'em and beat 'em.' Barbra said nervously she was taking Jason for a ride in the car. 'Gonna make poo-poo in the car, Jason?' Matthau said, and the kid seemed happy to get away."

In the weeks that followed, Streisand got her marks in on Matthau. She stepped on his lines and told him how to act. She also gave lessons in directing, cinematography, and orchestration to Gene Kelly and to musical director Lennie Hayton (who had conducted the major MGM musicals).

"The trouble with Barbra," said Matthau, "is she became a star long before she became an actress. Which is a pity, because if she learned her trade properly she might become a competent actress instead of a freak attraction—like a boa constrictor. The thing about working with her was that you never knew what she was going to do next and you were afraid that she'd do it."

Matthau developed an ulcer and went to studio head Darryl Zanuck for commiseration. "I'd like to help you out," said Zanuck, "but the film is not called *Hello, Walter!*"

"Who needs her?" producer Lehman would later ask. "To her, midnight isn't too late to phone the screenwriter and discuss line changes. If he happens to be the producer, too, even one o'clock in the morning is all right. But to talk to him for an hour? . . . Two hours? . . . just to make a few scenes better . . . she'll stay up till four in the morning figuring out how to make it better while she's doing her nails and eating too much chocolate ice cream."

"I'm supposed to be Rubenesque in this film," Streisand confessed to writer Nora Ephron, "and let's face it, I'm fat! But I learned a trick from Liz Taylor's cameraman. If they shoot you from a high angle the double chins won't show."

In June outdoor location scenes began shooting in Garrison, New York, where part of Yonkers, turn of the century, was rebuilt. Garrison, a small village of one thousand people, had no hotels or motels, so every available house was rented to the cast and crew. Barbra got *two* houses—one to live in, and one to serve as a dressing room.

In Garrison the star did not make many new friends among the townspeople. She refused to talk, mingle, or give autographs.

"I said hello to her on the street," one lady told a reporter, "and she grunted."

"I heard her cursing," said another citizen. "It wasn't any big deal. I had heard most of the words before, but you don't expect them to come from the mouth of a movie star."

To whitewash the negative reports the Fox press office sent out pastel-colored press releases describing scenes of Streisand frolicking with the natives and playing Frisbee with their children.

Helene K. Remer, the mother of two children hired as extras, recalled a different panorama. "Walter Matthau and Gene Kelly were perfectly wonderful to all the children," Mrs. Remer said. "Barbra Streisand had nothing to do with them, and was generally hostile to everyone involved with the movie or the arrangements.

"We had a special kind of baby-sitter in Garrison," Mrs. Remer continued, "who would take your children into her home for a day, a weekend, or a week. Barbra found out about Helmi Saunders, which was the woman's name, and called her to see if she would come and take care of Jason. Helmi said she would be happy to look after Jason if he would come to her house like the other children. Barbra said that perhaps Jason could come, but only if he was the only child there. Helmi refused to agree to this, so it was a standoff."

"She used to suffocate that kid," said Fred Glaser. "Jason was a live wire, full of energy and mischief, but Barbra didn't want him to be exposed to other kids. She even kept him away from me. She told me once, 'I don't want you becoming too friendly with Jason,' as if being a hairdresser was contagious."

On June fifth, the day Robert Kennedy was assassinated in Los Angeles, the rancor between Streisand and Matthau came to a head. The weather was hot and humid, the mosquitoes were lunching on the crew, and "if the elements were not enough," said Matthau, "Barbra kept asking Gene whether he didn't think it would be better if I did this on this line, and that on the other, et cetera, et cetera—and I told her to stop directing the fucking picture, which she took exception to, and there was a blowup in which I also told her she was a pipsqueak who didn't have the talent of a butterfly's fart. To which she replied I was jealous because I wasn't as good as she was. I'm not the most diplomatic man in the world, and we began a slanging match like a couple of kids from the ghetto. I think Gene thought one of us was going to die of apoplexy or something, or that I'd belt her, or maybe she'd scratch my eyes out—or worse, that we'd walk off, leaving twenty million dollars' worth of movie to go down the drain."

Before the day ended, a tentative truce was called. Neither side apologized, though Matthau later claimed it was probably his fault. "It was exaggerated," he claimed, "a momentary clash of egos." His mother visited him from Manhattan later that week, and she requested to meet Streisand. "You look lovely," Mrs. Matthau told Streisand. "So how come you're fighting my son?"

"He told me he fights with you a lot," Barbra shot back, "so I guess he fights with people he loves."

THE RELEASE OF THE *FUNNY GIRL* ALBUM

While still in Garrison, Streisand was visited by a contingent of executives from Columbia Records that included Clive Davis, business vice-president Walter Dean, and art director John Berg.

"I went up on my own," said Berg, "in a limo that Barbra had sent for me. I remember I passed Clive and Walter on the Thruway and I saluted them from the back of my car."

Berg carried with him the completed artwork for the soundtrack LP of *Funny Girl.* The movie had had its first sneak preview in Milwaukee the week before, and the response from the audience was rapturous. The buzz in the business was that the movie was going to be a blockbuster, and Columbia Records was pleased. This time around they had the rights to the soundtrack, and no expense was to be spared in its packaging and promotion; or in pleasing Barbra.

"I was showing the artwork to her when Clive arrived," said Berg. "I was surprised when Marty introduced them. Clive had never met Streisand till then."

"Clive kept calling me, asking to meet her," said Erlichman, "and Barbra kept putting him off. Then one day he said he was coming up to Garrison to present her with a check for a million dollars. I said, 'Okay . . . see you soon.' "

"Barbra was cordial to him," said Berg. "Then she and I went back to looking at the artwork. We got to discussing the collage of photos on the inside spread of the album. She wanted something changed, and I disagreed. We'd had these differences before. Barbra has a good eye, but it's not always objective, and if you present your side as strong and impartial as possible she'll say, 'Yeah, okay. You're right. Let's go with it.' This time she wanted the photos in the color collage changed around. It didn't look right to me, so I said no. Then all of a sudden this other voice piped in, and it's Clive. He said, 'John, Barbra is right, change it.' He's standing there, preening, asserting himself, but not knowing what the fuck he's talking about. I was furious. Later I said to him, *'Don't!* Don't ever do that to me again in front of an artist.' Clive was slick in that department, ingratiating himself with the talent—but Barbra had his number. After he gave her the check he got back in his limo, and she turned to me. 'Here, John,' she said. 'You take this. What in hell am I going to do with a million dollars?' And she gave me the check."

With the graphics of the album realigned (and the check returned to Erlichman), editing on the soundtrack tapes was supervised by CBS A&R manager, Warren Vincent.

"I inherited the project," said Warren. "I went to Hollywood and got all the tapes from the movie. I had to take the music off the seventy-millimeter film. Then the sound was balanced and cleaned up. After that I made up a master acetate and sent it to Barbra for her approval."

Only *one* acetate?

"[Laughter] Would you believe ten? After I sent her the first one she called me up, real salty like, and said, 'Warren, when people speak, don't they breathe?' I said, 'Yes, of course.' And she said, 'Why did you cut my breathing on the duet with Omar Sharif?' And I knew what she was talking about. Her breathing had been cut from the soundtrack. It was chopped, and badly done, and I said to her, 'Wasn't that your idea, Barbra?' She said, 'Hell no, didn't you do it?' I said, 'Hell, no.'

"It turned out the guys who edited the film cut it. So she got on the horn and laid them out. Eventually I got new tapes with the breathing put back in, and I made a new reference record. I went to her house in Beverly Hills with it and she greeted me in the downstairs foyer. She said, 'Go up to the bedroom and I'll be with you in a second.' And I looked at her. 'The bedroom?' She explained: 'My stereo is there.' I thought, *What a funny place to have a stereo,* but I went up and found Elliott lying in bed, reading a script. He said hi, then went back to reading, like he was used to people walking in and out of his bedroom."

Streisand did not approve reference number two and Warren kept spinning out others for her okay. "There was always something wrong," he said. "She didn't like the balance; the orchestra was too loud; her voice was too soft. I kept making them until eventually it was perfect. I sent the record out to her from New York, by Air Express. The following evening I get a call from her. 'Warren,' she says, 'what in hell is wrong with this record, it won't track?'

"I said, 'Look, Barbra, that thing was cut so damn deep—I listened to it on all kinds of equipment—you could play it with a three-inch nail!'

" 'Do you think I'm lying?' she said in a low voice.

" 'No,' I replied.

" 'Okay, then, it's best you come out here with a new reference right away.' And she hung up.

"I didn't want to go, but Clive, or somebody, said, 'Hey, we have to take care of her. So fly out there with a new cut.' And that's what I did. I flew to L.A. with a new reference in my lap. From the airport I drove to Fox, where she was finishing *Hello, Dolly!* I found her trailer and she's all smiles when I walk in. I take out the acetate and ask her where the stereo is. She points to this machine in the corner. I look at it. It's lopsided. It's off balance. No wonder the record skipped. So I prop it up with a pack of cigarettes. And I play the acetate. It plays perfectly. She loves it. 'Warren,' she says, 'you're a genius.' I tell her, 'Thanks,' and fly straight back to New York."

Throughout July of 1968 Streisand continued to superintend each aspect of the Columbia soundtrack LP, until all components were approved—with the exception of the cover art. "She was sitting on the cover," said Warren, "and I heard somewhere that Capitol was reissuing their *Funny Girl* show album, with the same illustration or the same logo. I knew Barbra hated the show album for some reason, so I called her up. Neither John Berg nor Jack Gold knew I was doing this; they'd have a fit. But I wanted to get her going. I also wanted her to release the cover so we could get the damn albums pressed. When I mentioned Capitol to her she started screaming. '*What! What!* Where did you hear that? Those bastards! They can't do that.' And in twenty-four hours she had the cover approved and released."

On August second, with finished jackets, sleeves, and labels in place, Columbia proceeded to press the *Funny Girl* album at their three manufacturing plants. The initial order was for a half a million, and four hundred thousand of these had been pressed when an urgent message came over the telex machine at all three plants. Production on the *Funny Girl* album was to cease immediately, due to defective parts.

"What happened," said a Columbia executive, "is that Barbra somehow got an advance copy of the LP. She played it and noticed something different. It was small, but she heard it. Some of the clicks in the roller-skate number on the album did not match those in the movie. So she got on the phone to New York and gave orders that it be fixed. So the presses stopped immediately."

The clicks of the roller skates were corrected, new records were pressed, and on August 8 the first copies of the *Funny Girl* LP were shipped to stores—a full month before the premiere of the movie.

THE *FUNNY GIRL* PREMIERE

For over a year producer Ray Stark had prepared for the opening of his $12-million musical. He placed the first full-page ad for the film in *The New York Times* in July of 1967 *before* production commenced. That ad and two subsequent offers drew a $2 million advance. The movie was shown to theater-party ladies, to group-ticket sellers, to corporations, and department-store owners. The latter would help in the merchandising of *Funny Girl* dresses, pocket books, bridal gowns, wristwatches, and rainwear (*"for those 'Don't Rain on My Parade' fun days"*).

Knowing her worth, for publicity and premieres, Stark also made amends with his leading lady. He dropped his lawsuit against Barbra and began sprinkling platitudes about her to the press. "She's warmer, gentler, more considerate and mature," he told the *New York Post,* "and she doesn't keep people waiting anymore." To perk her punctuality he also gave her a cut of his net profits. "We got some points," said Erlichman, "but they weren't enormous."

"She made more from her new deal with Columbia Records," said a former staffer. "The album sold over two million copies and she got close to seventy cents for each one."

"The funny thing about the album," said Tommy Noonan, then merchandising manager of the label, "is that Ray Stark and Columbia Pictures didn't want to have anything to do with it, or us. They weren't getting a cut of the record, and they didn't realize how important it was in selling the movie. They wouldn't even give us a screening, or tickets to the opening. So what I did was rent the theater the weekend before the opening. I got the place for a Saturday night, from midnight on. I invited the disc jockeys and promotion people from New York, Boston, and Philadelphia. We put them up in hotels, with their wives or girlfriends, and invited them to this special showing. It was tremendous. The theater went wild when she closed with 'My Man.' Later we had this big party in the Presidential Suite of the Americana. Marty showed, but Barbra didn't. That didn't matter, because her performance was still on everyone's mind. She was a giant that night."

On the morning of the official premiere, Columbia Pictures built a pedestrian ramp over Times Square, connecting the Criterion Theater to a parking lot across the street where a special tent was being erected to house the postpremiere party. "I heard about the cross-ramp," said Noonan, "and it suddenly struck me: Why not put a long banner on each side of it, publicizing our soundtrack album? No one would see it, except the millions of people going north and south of Times Square. Marty loved the idea, so we did it. We had the banners in place a half hour before the festivities began, and they showed up on national TV."

The premiere, a benefit for Mayor Lindsay's Youth and Physical Fitness Program ("I was always up for charity myself," said Streisand. "I could have used some help"), attracted fifteen hundred swells; among them the Biddle Dukes, Nan Kempner and escort, Rocky and Dr. John Converse, and Ray and Fran Stark. Streisand, accompanied by Elliott, arrived last. Her dress, she explained, an Arnold Scaasi original ("Scaasi—that's Isaacs spelled backwards"), had almost been defaced with crayons by son Jason.

The movie, at 155 minutes, seemed long, but Streisand's performance kept everyone riveted to his seat. "I don't know where Fanny ends and Barbra begins," said Ray Stark. "I was so close to the picture for a while, I couldn't look at it objectively," said wife Fran, "but tonight I found it very moving."

"Barbra was bursting with delight," said a production assistant. "People at the party were coming over to her and practically falling at her feet. She deserved every bit of it, too, because she was wonderful in the picture. But at one point I felt someone was missing. I said to her, 'Is Willie here?' She looked at me with a blank stare. I said, 'Willie, William Wyler, your director?' And she answered, 'I dunno. Why should he be here?' Like he had nothing to do with the picture or her performance."

Radiant! Electric! Hypnotic! Uproarious! Magnificent! Sublime! Those were some of the superlatives bestowed by the press on Barbra's film debut. "She is an actress, now, who uses her versatile singing voice as a poet uses verse, to intensify and heighten experience," said Joseph Morgenstern of *Newsweek.* "The 'message' of Barbra Streisand is that talent is beauty," said Pauline Kael in *The New Yorker.* And Rex Reed, too, was captivated: ". . . she has turned into an orchard harvest of ripening womanhood—warm, moving, soft, sensual, and mature."

"He's trying to make up with me," said Streisand, upon reading Rex's review, "but he can go fuck himself. I had more respect for him when he didn't like me."

A HAPPENING IN CENTRAL PARK

In tandem with the release of *Funny Girl* CBS TV availed themselves of the pomp and hoopla to announce their showing of *A Happening in Central Park,* the concert they had taped a year earlier.

"I'm not sure why CBS waited so long to show the special," said producer-director Robert Scheerer. "There was no problem with the editing. Barbra saw all the tapes, and then I put it together. I edited it in New York very soon after the concert. It took eight or ten days and was a very pleasant experience. There was no one looking over my shoulder. Then I flew out to California and showed it to Barbra. She, to the best of my knowledge, loved it. She asked for some songs to be flipflopped, to be reversed. They were songs that Marty had asked to be put in the other direction, and I had done that. Barbra asked for them to be put back in the original order, which I did. And then I showed it to Perry Lassiter at CBS and he loved it."

"CBS was not behind the show," an advertising executive recalled. "Rheingold Beer had some kind of a sponsorship deal with them, but I believe the money wasn't anything close to what Monsanto had paid for the first two specials. I was handling a cosmetics account and I asked to see the show. They told me it was still being edited. I knew this wasn't so. Then CBS said there were problems with the sound, and that Streisand's singing wasn't too good."

"The sound was lousy," said Warren Vincent. "I had to edit the tapes for the album, and when I heard them I knew we were in trouble."

"Columbia Records wanted to record from their own feed at the concert," said Scheerer, "but that was impossible with the limited time and the huge crowds. They had to go with the mikes the TV crew were using."

"We picked up a lot of noise, of people talking and yelling," said Vincent.

"When you see something on TV or in concert you accept a good deal more than when you're only listening on records," said Scheerer, "so we didn't have the same problem they had."

Early in August the soundtrack album of the Central Park concert was scheduled, then canceled from Columbia's schedule. The word had come down from Goddard: The tracks were inferior; not suitable for release. A week later his order was countermanded. CBS, and Barbra, had lost money the previous year from the aborted *Belle of 14th Street* album. This loss could *not* be repeated. Someone, somehow, had to salvage the concert tapes. That mission was delegated to West Coast A&R director Jack Gold.

"I'm not sure *whose* idea it was," said Jack, "but I was told to splice material from the Hollywood Bowl concert [recorded two weeks after the New York concert] with the Central Park tapes. It was all kept very quiet; few people in the company knew about it."

"I didn't know," said the New York editing manager, Warren Vincent, "but in those days we were working under the 'mushroom' theory. You know, keep 'em in the dark and feed them a lot of horseshit."

"We're talking the bottom line here . . . *money,*" said a music reviewer, "for Barbra and for Columbia. They had lost out on *The Belle of 14th Street* LP, and they weren't going to give up a second soundtrack. Streisand herself stood to make at least a hundred thousand dollars from the album. Which is okay. Making records is a business like any other."*

---

* In a statement issued after the release of the hardcover version of this book, Streisand's personal manager, Marty Erlichman, called the allegation of splicing on the Central Park album "ridiculous and preposterous." "Every note she sang in Central Park is on this album," said Erlichman, "including the wrong lyric at the beginning of 'Natural Sounds.' One can also hear the orchestra out of tune, especially on 'People,' because of the hot, humid air. If CBS, in the interest of brevity, substituted a few of her monologues from a second concert—what's the big deal?"

Chapter 15

In January of 1969 Streisand flew to Paris to attend the European premiere of *Funny Girl*. Originally the score for the European version was to be dubbed in French, Italian, and German, by Streisand herself. This, it was thought, would boost the foreign box office and add to Barbra's reputation as the compleat artiste.

Ettore Stratta, Columbia's linguist specialist, was called to do the coaching and producing. "Barbra was working on *Hello, Dolly!* at the time," he said, "and she had weekends free. Marty Erlichman thought it would be an easy thing to do. I told him, 'Do you have any idea of what is involved? Do you know how long this would take?' And Marty says, 'A coupla weeks.' I told him, 'Months! Six months at least.' There are thirteen songs in *Funny Girl*. She had to learn each one, first in Italian, then French, then German. Multiply that by thirteen, and then we would have to do separate recording sessions for each language. 'You're crazy. She's crazy,' I told him. And he says, 'Does that mean you won't do the job?' So he called my boss, Harvey Schein. I explained the situation to Harvey and that's the last I heard of that insane idea."

In February the Oscar nominations were released in Hollywood. Streisand was nominated for *Funny Girl*, along with Joanne Woodward for *Rachel, Rachel*, Vanessa Redgrave for *Isadora*, Patricia Neal for *The Subject Was Roses*, and Katharine Hepburn for *The*

Lion in Winter. In Vegas the odds were in favor of Woodward, who had already won the New York Critics' Award. Second favorite was Hepburn, who had won the year before for *Guess Who's Coming to Dinner.* Third was Streisand. Her performance was there, but not her popularity; nor did she try to improve her chances. During the voting season, while Ray Stark and Columbia Pictures were outdoing each other with self-congratulatory missives in *Daily Variety* and the *Hollywood Reporter,* Streisand remained reclusive. "We had screenings and elaborate supper parties every night," said a Columbia publicist. "It was an opportunity for her to meet some of the voters. Finally she decided to show, but only after she called me to check out what was on the dinner menu. We had three different entrées—chicken cordon bleu, prime ribs, and quiche with salad. She would have none of that. Barbra ordered her own menu, for a party of five, and then she never showed."

On the day of the awards Barbra spent six hours preparing for her appearance at the ceremonies. She couldn't decide between two outfits: a formal, elegant Christian Dior gown or black, spangled see-through pajamas, with white cuffs and a Peter Pan collar, by Arnold Scaasi, who later designed her hooker outfit for *The Owl and the Pussycat.* "She kept changing back and forth," said Fred Glaser. "When she asked my advice I said, 'Wear the Dior.' So naturally she chose the Scaasi number."

Her hair drew similar agonizing attention. She could wear it short, with a cluster of polyester curls on top; or she could wear her blond Afro. But she had shocked them with that one at the previous year's Oscars; so she decided to wear one of the seventeen wigs Fred Glaser had created for her new movie *On a Clear Day You Can See Forever.* Called "the Daisy Gamble look," it had bangs, with a side part. Barbra insisted that Glaser make the top of the wig fuller. She wanted it teased and raised as high as possible. "I kept telling her it looked overdone, phony," said Glaser, "and she said, 'Good! The whole town is phony, and if I lose they'll know I don't give a damn.'

"She didn't really think she was going to win," said Glaser. "She said, 'Next year I'll get it, for *Hello, Dolly!*' She actually believed that."

Before she left for the ceremonies another vital accessory had to be added. Her escort. She and Elliott Gould—after a prolonged period of fights and estrangements, and a few publicized tantrums wherein Elliott had belted a photographer, and was cited for ninety-eight illegal parking tickets in New York City—became officially separated. The news of their parting came the same week as the nominations and with it the usual celebrity bromide: "We are separating not to destroy but to save our marriage," said Barbra. "The only difficulty with the split," said a more candid Gould, "was with the legal bullshit."

Gould's career took off almost immediately. He was signed to play Ted in *Bob & Carol & Ted & Alice* and was in Los Angeles, staying with Barbra the night of the awards. When she asked him to accompany her to the show, he, being a good guest and fair sport, agreed.

Sitting one seat in from the aisle, Barbra joined the audience ovation for Ingrid Bergman when she appeared on stage to present the Best Actress award. Bergman announced the nominees—enunciating each syllable of their names and respective pictures. She opened the envelope, then gasped. "It is . . . it's a tie. . . ."

"I heard one name," Streisand later recalled, "then another. I wasn't sure if it was mine until Elly turned to me and said, 'It's you!' "

On the way up to the stage Streisand's heel got caught in the hem of her pajamas ("For two thousand dollars they can't sew the goddamn thing," she swore). Steadying herself, she leaned over on the steps to the stage and flashed a generous expanse of rear cleavage to the audience and to America. At the podium she composed herself, held up the statuette, and began her speech. "Hello, gorgeous!"

After graciously acknowledging "the magnificent company of Katharine Hepburn," she gave way to an unprepared-for emotion. Standing on stage, looking down at the audience of three thousand faces, all of whom were smiling back at *her*, Barbra began to cry.

"I was amazed," said a member of the audience. "We expected her to be bold and brash as always, but when she began to cry I thought 'Well, she's not so tough after all; she does have feelings.' "

"No, Melinda. Don't misuse your talents. Please. Or God knows in how many lifetimes you'll be paying for it."

Irene Handl to Streisand in
On a Clear Day You Can See Forever

On the day after the Oscars filming resumed on *On a Clear Day You Can See Forever* at the Hollywood Paramount lot. The musical, one of three big-budget films in production (along with *Darling Lili* and *Paint Your Wagon),* was the story of a New York girl who, under hypnosis for a bad smoking habit, discovers she lived a previous life as an English noblewoman. The role was originally offered to Audrey Hepburn, who had declined after *My Fair Lady.* Streisand had seen the play on Broadway and thought it "was heaven, just heaven. The two parts are close to my schizophrenic personality," she declared. "They appeal to the frightened girl and the strong woman in me."

To kick off the production Paramount staged an extravagant Come-as-the-person-you-would-like-to-have-been Reincarnation Ball at the Beverly Hilton Hotel. Most of Hollywood's leading citizens chose to play Topper that night. They were invisible at the ball. Only a scattering of celebrities bothered to show. Phyllis Diller came as Kim Novak, Polly Bergen as Queen Elizabeth I, Barbara Parkins as Eliza Doolittle, Omar Sharif as Che Guevara (his latest screen role); and Tony Curtis arrived as himself. Another guest, seated at the main table, was Alfred Bloomingdale. His date for the night, a luscious blond starlet dressed in a leaf-bikini as Eve, was placed farther back, with her cover date, a Streisand associate.

"Everyone at the party was being so sweet and nice to one another," one columnist reported. "Barbra was kissing her executive producer, Bob Evans; Bob Evans was kissing her director Vincente Minnelli; and Yves Montand, her costar, was telling everyone 'what a real plee-sure' it would be to work with a star of Barbra's magnitude. Somehow you *knew* they had the makings of a real turkey here."

The shooting schedule for *On a Clear Day* was budgeted for eighty-two days. Twelve of these were spent at the Royal Pavilion in Brighton, England, where Streisand—costumed by Cecil Beaton and tutored in elocution and deportment by Deborah Kerr—became the epitome of British gentility. Comparing her favorably with the aristocratic Joan Greenwood, Sir Cecil said that both had that air "of cunning refinement." "She was positively elegant," Peter Reilly agreed. "People said, 'What a good actress she is.' That wasn't acting. That was who she really is. The rest of it—the Jewish shtik—that was acting."

In England, Streisand's noblesse oblige extended itself to the cameras only, and not the natives or the press. In between scenes she sat in her Rolls-Royce, and on weekends she stayed in her suite in the Hotel Metropole. "We would have liked to have seen something of Miss Streisand," said the *Morning Telegraph*, "but she practically barricaded herself in her hotel, and was, so I am reliably informed, something a good deal less than cooperative with the local press. A smattering of graciousness would not have come amiss."

In New York, for the final location scenes, Howard Koch the producer of *On a Clear Day*, learned that his permit to film at Fordham University had been canceled due to fear of student riots. Alternate college backgrounds were sought, but the climate of campus unrest was widespread, and the producer found he was in danger of losing his star also. During the delay Streisand's contract ran out. "We didn't want to pay her more money," said Koch, "so we made a deal with her. One of the things she wanted was a trailer that we owned. All the furniture. All the wardrobe she wore, and some stained-glass windows on the set.* I think she probably took seventy to eighty thousand dollars' worth of stuff to her home. It was good for us, because those things are expendable anyway."

Eventually the campus scenes were filmed at UCLA, where Streisand had the opportunity to talk with some of the students. In an attempt to raise her political consciousness she asked the reason behind their rebellion. "What are you fighting for," she enquired earnestly, "longer vacations?"

"I know nothing about the Vietnam war, or about black power, or what's happening in the world today," said Barbra. "I've got this backlog of magazines to read and catch up on, but I have no time. It's not easy being me, y'know?"

"Comes the Revolution Columbia's already there. Haydn failed math. Bach had soul. Mozart was blind. Gabriel grooved. Speed kills."

Columbia Record advertisement, 1969

---

* "I made some real money on those windows," said Barbra. "The studio rented them back from me for five hundred dollars, to use in *The Great White Hope.*"

If her cognizance of current events in 1969 was slim, Streisand's record output was equally remote from the contemporary scene. While she was cloistered on Hollywood's sound stages—four-walled by her own superstar existence—an entire revolution had swept across America's musical landscape. The record business had changed radically, and most of those changes could now be heard and seen on her own label.

By the late sixties, having captured a large chunk of the soft-core rock market, Columbia Records went after the hard-core contingent. Oddly enough, one of their most dazzling and lucrative acquisitions came on the same day that Streisand gave her free concert in New York. Almost to the hour, while Barbra was adjusting her nerves and psyching herself to face her Central Park audience, another female performer was making an awesome debut three thousand miles away in northern California. On that Saturday, June 17, 1967, Janis Joplin, along with Big Brother and the Holding Company, appeared at the Monterey Pop Festival. "She bounced out," said writer Myra Friedman, "all gleaming in a sil-ver-white pants suit made of sleek lamé . . . and let loose the first outstanding note of a performance that shook with more energy than the rest of the entire festival. The roar that followed could have been a fissure opening in the earth."

In the audience watching Joplin's performance were Clive Davis and Goddard Lieberson. Shortly thereafter they bought her contract for $250,000, and she soon replaced Streisand as Columbia's first lady of sales. Other rock acquisitions included Blood, Sweat and Tears, the Chambers Brothers, the Electric Flag, Moby Grape, Spirit, Johnny Winter, and Sly and the Family Stone—all successfully launched via Columbia's multimillion dollar "Rock Machine" media campaign.

The rock revolution was not embraced by all within the record company. There were those, staff and performers, who still clung to Columbia's bedrock image of good music and conventional decorum. Oldtime employees frowned upon the new "rock trainees" and dippy secretaries who spoke of "love" and "vibes" and "karma," and who burned incense to cover up the sweet smell of marijuana that drifted out of certain offices.

"If the squares at Columbia were uptight, the CBS television people got real agitated," said a record employee. "We had the east side of the CBS building, and the TV guys occupied the west side.

They always looked upon record people as dirt. Then, when these rock freaks started to come into the building and got into *their* elevators, their Brooks Brothers shorts started riding up their heinies. One day Sly Stone came into the CBS lobby riding a tricycle, and he almost knocked down the vice president of corporate affairs. Paley and Stanton were told about it; they spoke to Lieberson, but nothing could be done. Columbia Records *and* CBS were making a hundred million dollars a year from these freaks. So everyone was told to *smile* and to flash the peace sign, with *two* fingers."

"You either went with the flow or got out," said another staffer. "Bill Gallagher had to quit, and others followed him. Those that stayed let their hair grow long and began wearing bell-bottom slacks and leather-fringed vests, and everything was 'groovy' or 'cool' or 'outa sight.' "

Barbra Streisand was also not pleased with what she saw and heard on the new musical front. "She hated rock music," said Peter Matz. "She thought it was shit—all of it."

Her CBS albums still sold, but she had not had a hit single since "People" in 1964. Anxious to keep her popularity in full flame, she told Columbia she would do some current songs, but only those with "lyrical value."

On January 23, 1968, she recorded three sides at Studio E on East Fifty-second Street in New York. The session was produced by Jack Gold, and the songs covered were "Our Corner Of The Night," "He Could Show Me" (by Gretchen Cryer and Nancy Ford), and "Frank Mills," from the forthcoming Broadway musical *Hair*. "I brought her 'Frank Mills,' " said publisher Nat Shapiro. "I gave her first crack at it. The show was off-Broadway at the time, and I was sure it would be a hit. Barbra listened to the song. She liked it. The lyrics were cute, and she decided to do it. I was there at the session. She did a delightful job, but then for some reason she was reluctant to release the record."

In March *Hair* opened on Broadway. The reviews were evenly divided between praise and disdain.

"It's cheap, vulgar, foul-mouthed, and tasteless," said the *Daily News*.

"So new, so free, and so unassuming in its pretentions," said *The New York Times*.

"It became the most talked-about show in the country," said Nat. "The box office sold out for months, yet Barbra refused to let Columbia release 'Frank Mills.' I don't know why." "I think she was in culture shock," said the wife of a composer. "In those days Barbra was something of a prude. Oh, I know she was from Brooklyn and she had a tough mouth at times, but underneath she was very rigid, very proper. She didn't smoke cigarettes, let alone drink or take drugs. She found it distasteful to even dance in the arms of a man who wasn't her husband. And when she heard about *Hair*, that the cast took their clothes off onstage, she almost died. 'You mean they actually show their *things* to the audience?' " she asked.

"Frank Mills" was scheduled twice for release by Columbia, then eventually postponed until further notice. In March of 1968, Streisand told the label that she was giving the contemporary route another try. She was recording two new songs—"What About Today?" and "The Morning After"—which were relevant to important current issues. "The titles sounded great!" said a former Columbia executive. "Everybody waited to hear the tapes. When we heard them our faces fell. The first song—'What About Today?'—had nothing to do with sociopolitical issues. It was about a girl who lost her guy the night before and wonders *how* she'll ever get through the day ahead."

The second song—"The Morning After"—had a quasi-protest theme. The lyrics referred obliquely to racial unjustice and urban violence, but the orchestrations belonged at the Hollywood Palace. "Here she was singing about brother beating up brother—and while she's wailing away, the brass and the drums in the background are doing their tribute to Wayne Newton. Not only was the record a stiff, it was obvious that she was pandering to the market. To aggravate the exploitation, the record was rushed out right after Martin Luther King was assassinated. *Barbra Streisand—The Morning After—A Song with a Message* was the advertisement Columbia took out in the trades. America's cities were burning and they're saying, 'Be cool, people, and maybe we'll get a hit single out of this.' "

"The Morning After," backed with "What About Today?" did not become a hit, but the songs from *Hair* did—without Barbra. "Aquarius," "Let the Sun Shine In," and "Good Morning Starshine"—all became hit records by other artists. And "Frank Mills"? In January of 1969, a full year after she had recorded it,

Barbra finally agreed to release the single. "It didn't take," Nat Shapiro said sadly. "It was too late; the momentum had passed."

Streisand, now *challenged,* perused the pop charts for current hit songs to cover. In the studio she recorded "Alfie," "Until It's Time For You To Go," and two songs from the group she once loved to hate: the Beatles. On February 8, 1969, she recorded "Goodnight" and "With A Little Help From My Friends." Her interpretation of the last song took a staggering seventeen takes. "With the passing of each year Barbra had become more demanding of herself," said the arranger-conductor, Michel Legrand. "She became harder on herself in each instance, and more difficult to handle because of her entourage. The woman was not as flexible anymore."

She was, however, satisfied with her new pop sound and decided to forge ahead with an entire album of contemporary material. Entitled *What About Today?* it was recorded in New York with a new producer, Wally Gold.

Wally had begun as a singer with the Four Esquires ("Love Me Forever"). He later wrote "It's My Party" for Leslie Gore (produced by Quincy Jones) and "It's Now Or Never" for Elvis—sterling credits of which Streisand apparently was not aware. "I'm not sure if Barbra was aware of my background," he said. "It never came up in conversation. When I was offered the job to produce her, I jumped at it. We met first at the Plaza Hotel. I think she was separated from Elliott at the time and she had a big suite there, with a piano. Peter Matz was arranging and conducting for her, and I felt good about that. Peter is not only one of the best talents around, he's a gentleman. I had never met Barbra before, but I certainly heard about her, and I was nervous. When I arrived, there was sheet music and arrangements scattered all over the floor. She was sitting with Peter at the piano and she said, 'Hi, Wally, how are you? I hear we're gonna work together.' Very straight ahead and friendly. I didn't expect that. I thought maybe I'd sit in a corner and say, 'Yes, ma'am' and 'No, ma'am.' Not that I'd do that, but . . ."

Their first session together was at Columbia's Thirtieth Street studio on May 24, 1969. "All I remember about that day is that Marty Erlichman was there, checking me out," said Gold. "I treated the date like any other. When she did something wrong, I stopped her in the middle of a take. Marty said, 'What are you doing! *You* don't stop her, *she* stops you.' I didn't *know.* I did it out of instinct. And Barbra said, 'Why?'—from her screen. She always worked with a screen around her. She hated people looking at her and it isolated her in terms of sound. When she asked how come I stopped her, I told her. It had to do with the score, which I could read and she couldn't. And she said, 'Okay, let's do it from the top again.' "

Working with Streisand was one of the highlights of his career, Wally confessed. "It was a shining encounter. I enjoyed her tremendously, as an artist, *and* as a person. She wanted things right, but she wasn't tough about it. She had enormous outside commitments to take care of. I remember there were interruptions during the sessions. People would come in with sketches of costume designs for *Clear Day* for her approval. She dealt with everyone calmly. She never lost her concentration. The only drawback was her lateness. She was always late. That was Barbra, and no one really resented it, except maybe the musicians. I'd try to get her there on time by telling her the session was an hour earlier. But that didn't work. She'd come in late anyway, very bright and apologetic. But when she was there, she was prepared to give more than all the musicians could deliver. That instrument of hers—her voice—was amazing. At that first date she hadn't sung for a couple of months. She never took lessons or warmed up, and those first notes out of her mouth were as pure and true and clear as ever. You know how they say the camera loves certain actresses, well the microphones loved Barbra. She has a rare gift."

At the same time he was recording Barbra, Wally was also producing an album with Tony Bennett. "Talk about staying up nights late on the phone," he recalled. "It was interesting to compare the two. With Tony, in a session at playback, we'd listen to the tape. I'd hear a chord out of tune, little imperfections, and I'd say, 'Did you hear that?' And Tony would go, 'No, baby. That felt *good!*' He'd say, 'Print it, it feels good. That's the take. That's it!' Whereas with Barbra every note, every breath, has to be perfect. With Tony we never edited from one take to the other. We always went with a live, complete take. With Barbra we edited from everything. From take four to forty-four. No, it never went *that* far, but there was considerable splicing, compared to Bennett."

Throughout the postproduction of the LP Streisand was gracious and cooperative, said Gold. "If there's one word to describe her it's *curious*. She has a tremendous amount of curiosity about everything—the studio, the sound, the technical aspects. For example, I sent her a reference dub and she called me. She wanted to know, 'Why is it when I sing loud in the studio, why isn't it as loud on the record?' I told her we use what is called 'limiters,' 'compressors.' They cut down on the loud part and bring up the soft parts. It's called 'riding the level.' And Barbra had such an enormous dynamic range—meaning she could sing in a whisper, then go up to this incredible eighty-five-thousand decibel with that *geshrey* of hers. We had to limit that. I tried to explain it over the phone to her. But she didn't understand. So, with a little bit of trepidation, I said, 'Barbra, can you come down to Fifty-third Street to the studio where we're mixing right now, and I'll show you what I mean?' So she came down in a limo, and we're in the studio, with all these secretaries standing outside the glass windows, looking in 'cause Streisand is there. I showed her how we use the meters, and the levels. The state of the art wasn't as sophisticated back then as it is today, but she understood. That was the way it had to be, for *now*. She said, 'Fine,' then left."

BARBRA IN LAS VEGAS

With the recording and the cover approved on schedule, Columbia Records were eager to preview the album at their annual sales convention in Los Angeles. Barbra was again invited to attend but declined. She had a previous engagement to fill in Las Vegas. This would be her first nightclub appearance in six years. It was to bring her yet another million dollars for ten weeks' work—spread out over a year. It would also terminate her six-year friendship and professional relationship with Fred Glaser.

Her agents and manager had suggested the booking. It was time she appeared before an audience again. She had the choice of doing a national open-air concert tour, which would have helped promote her forthcoming album; or she could play Las Vegas. The latter offered more money, plus a tighter security. Concerts meant travel, repeated sound checks and rehearsals, and the vagaries of the weather and local reviewers. In Las Vegas she could do three weeks, pick up her money, then leave.

The Nevada outing was not to be that simple. Las Vegas, Streisand soon learned, was a town where performers took second billing to the main attraction—gambling. To attract and hold that audience's attention a special act was needed. Just being a star, and singing a medley of greatest hits, was not good enough. Mama Cass Elliott had learned that the previous October. For forty thousand dollars a week she floated herself and her band on a helium-inflated set above the stage, and proceeded to perform a straight hour of pop-rock favorites. Her show was canceled after opening night and replaced with Bengal tigers and dancing bears.

Streisand was not prepared for Las Vegas, and Vegas was not prepared for her. The hotel, newly constructed, was not completed when she arrived. "There's an old show-business axiom," said Peter Matz, who conducted the orchestra: "Don't be the first to open a room. It's true. You're the guinea pig for the sound system and for the lights. Nothing was working when we arrived. The pool was leaking, the kitchen wasn't in operation, and the waiters didn't know the floor. It was tough for Barbra. She doesn't like to work live to begin with."

"She was terrified," said Wally Gold who was there for the opening. "She was afraid she'd get weak walking out in front of people, so she asked that a chaise lounge be placed onstage. She wanted to be lying on the chaise when the curtain went up. That way they wouldn't see her knees trembling."

"Barbra was in trouble, and per usual Marty called me in Chicago," said hair stylist, Fred Glaser. " 'You know how to handle her,' Marty told me, and like a fool I dropped everything and flew to Vegas. I always took off when they called me, and I don't know why. I guess I did love her. It had to be that, because I wasn't getting paid. That's the truth. They owed me a lot of money for previous dates. Whenever I brought it up to Marty he'd say, 'Don't worry, Fred, soon we're gonna do a deal and make you very rich.' Barbra's agent, Sue Mengers, was the same way. One night out of nowhere she started in on me. She said I should be happy working for Barbra for free. 'Well,' she said, 'Kenneth will come out from New York and do it for the prestige.' I said, 'Good. Call Kenneth. I'm leaving.' But Barbra wouldn't have it."

Arriving at the hotel in Vegas, Glaser went directly to Streisand's dressing room. "I walked in and she's sitting at the makeup table, staring at herself in the mirror, looking like a lost child. She sees me and doesn't say hello. Instead she turns to Marty and says, 'What the hell is he doing here?' I said nothing to her. She pointed to a clump of hair lying on the table. I don't know where she got it, but I was told to fix it. I took it and made it into something presentable. I got her fixed up and listened to her abuse. Nothing had changed with her. She had her Oscar, her money, all the success in the world, but she was still as miserable as ever. Finally she was dressed and ready to go on. We walked through these corridors, through this godawful catacomb with these terrible cupids stuck on the walls. We got to the stage wings and again she had to be pushed to go on." "It wasn't stage fright," Streisand said later. "It was a thing called *death*. While I stood in the wings my whole life passed before me."

Some celebrities in the audience that night had been flown in by special charter from L.A. that afternoon. They included Cary Grant, Rita Hayworth, Natalie Wood, Rudolf Nureyev, Andy Williams and Claudine Longet, Phil Harris and Alice Faye, and George Raft and Peggy Lee. Opening with "I Got Plenty Of Nothin' "—a jocular jibe at her salary and the working conditions —Streisand rapidly segued to "People," "Happy Days," and songs from *Funny Girl* and *Hello, Dolly!* Despite the familiarity of the numbers the audience was unmoved. Streisand spoke briefly, throwing casual asides to friends and agents seated ringside, but her humor was forced, almost frosty, and finally, after fifty minutes, she bowed off.

"Barbra Streisand is very fortunate indeed to be making a reputed $100,000 a week at the posh new International Hotel," said the *Hollywood Reporter*. "Now she can afford to get someone to write an act for her. It would be money well spent. Her voice, a remarkable instrument about which enough has been said . . . comes through fine. But never does she warm up to the people nor they to her. The sameness of arrangements, the sameness of the treatment that she gives each song, makes for such monotony, you can't believe. A real live 'Barbie Doll.' "

"She overestimated her appeal," said a musician. "Vegas wanted to see a warmup act, a comedian, special lights, costumes, and choreography. Vegas wanted Ann-Margret, who is not only considered a pro in that town, but she *likes* her audiences. Streisand could barely tolerate talking to them."

During the second week of the Vegas booking Ed Sullivan and his CBS-TV crew came to town to present an award to Barbra while taping a portion of her act for his Sunday-night show. Barbra was cooperative until she learned that special lights were needed for Sullivan's TV cameras. "She became very agitated," said Wally Gold. "He had lights in the audience and onstage. She didn't want to walk out and see the audience."

"They'll be *looking* at me," she whined to Fred Glaser, who replied, "Of course they will. They're paying one hundred dollars apiece for that privilege."

Barbra performed for Ed Sullivan, but the footage was useless. She then restaged the act for him, at two in the morning, without an audience.

"She made life hard for everyone," said Glaser. "Marty, God love him, was immune to her abuse. He went off and gambled. One night he won fifty thousand dollars playing chemin de fer. I remember exactly what I said to him—'My God, Marty, now you can pay me.' But he didn't. There was no gold in them thar hills. I was foolish. I had it coming. I let them take advantage of me." Until one evening Barbra pushed Glaser's tolerance to its limit. A half hour before showtime the star was in her dressing room, surrounded by her coterie of friends and advisors. One of them casually mentioned Elliott Gould, and the nerve he had in speaking ill of Barbra. *"What? Where? When?"* Streisand asked. In the current issue of *The Ladies' Home Journal,* she was informed, Elliott had told an interviewer that his estranged wife was a self-centered fourteen-year-old, that she was cheap, and disdainful of men. "Barbra knew nothing about the article," said Fred Glaser, "and I'm thinking: *Please, let her be, I have to get her ready for tonight's show.* But they kept it going, until she sent five people running in different directions to get the magazine. When she read it she cleared everyone from the room. She proceeded to tear the place apart. I tried to calm her down. I had to get her ready. She had these elaborate hairpieces I had to fix on her head. It was impossible. She wouldn't stand still. It was like trying to stick a noodle on a wildcat's ass. I know, I could have left the room, but that is not my style. I was there to do a job, and I did it."

Later that night Fred Glaser sat alone in his hotel room, nursing a severe headache. "I remember thinking, Where is the fun here? I loved Barbra. We spent six years together. We were friends. Where did that go? And why am I hanging around for more of her abuse? I am my own person. My work is respected elsewhere. So why not pick up and leave? And that's what I did. I packed that instant. I checked out of the hotel and took a cab to the airport. Suddenly I felt happy. My headache started to go, the fever blisters on my lips went down. I was the last of the old guard to leave, but I did it. I was free! Free of all the horrible sham, and the lies. I took the next available flight to Chicago, and I never saw Barbra again."*

Although the first weeks in Las Vegas were a disaster, "Barbra turned it around eventually," said Peter Matz, "and made the show something of a triumph." When the engagement ended, she went back to L.A. to await the reaction to her first "contemporary" album, *What About Today?* She was pleased with the finished pressing and the packaging. On her own she wrote the liner notes, dedicating the album to "All the young people who push against indifference, shout down mediocrity, demand a better future, and who write and sing the songs of today." But when it was suggested that these songwriters be identified by listing their names under their songs on the back of the album, Barbra said no. "Why clutter it up?" she asked.

Another spurious element was the album's artwork. The photos, by Richard Avedon, had little to do with the counterculture images of the day. The front cover showed the singer in a frozen pose, her pores airbrushed out, wearing a curly wig, rings, and feathers. The inspiration, she said, came from her longtime fascination with Colette and Sarah Bernhardt.

"I don't know if the packaging hurt the album," said Wally Gold. "Certainly Barbra looked great, and the arrangements may have been too sophisticated, but in the final analysis the album was released at a very hectic period in music history. The rock festival at Woodstock broke around that time, and the disc jockeys did not want to hear from anyone who was not at the concert. Grace Slick, Janis Joplin, and the Who—those were the ones that got all the airplay. No one wanted to hear from Tony Bennett, Jerry Vale, or Barbra Streisand. *What About Today?* did make the charts, but it didn't stay around too long. It may have been a highlight of my career, but not Barbra's."

---

* Three years later, in May of 1972, Fred Glaser filed suit against Streisand in the State Supreme Court in Manhattan. He sued for $9,519.41, for services rendered between July 1, 1966, and July 29, 1969, as well as travel, hotel, and food expenses. The case was settled out of court. "It ended badly," said Glaser, "but I never forgot her. Because underneath the star stuff, when you dig deep enough, you'll find a very special human being."

"I used to prefer fantasy to reality. . . . Real life is more important to me than performing. I get a pleasure you wouldn't believe from scrubbing my pantry."

Barbra Streisand, 1969

Eschewing the superficialities of Hollywood, and the authentic fear engendered by the recent Manson murders, Streisand flew to New York in early September with son Jason. She intended to buy a house and put down roots in Manhattan, where she would continue to record and make films.

With her contract dispute with Ray Stark settled, and her salary adjusted (to $1 million plus stock and seven percent of the profits), Streisand agreed to star in *The Owl and the Pussycat.* Principal filming began on Manhattan's West Side on October tenth. The scenario—twenty-four hours in the life of a New York hooker—originated with the Broadway play starring black actress Diana Sands and Alan Alda. The interracial theme was considered for the movie, with Streisand's friend and business partner Sidney Poitier mentioned as a possible co-star.* "Originally Ray wanted to use Sidney for Nick Arnstein in *Funny Girl,*" Barbra joked, "but we decided he looks too Jewish. So we went in another direction."

Stark at the outset described Streisand's character as "a folkhooker," implying that she would strum the guitar and sing—presumably between tricks. Barbra sent out a fast correction. She would not sing, hum, whistle, or deliver the remotest of musical sounds in Mr. Stark's new movie. She would carry the movie on her acting talent alone. Furthermore, due perhaps to the defection of Fred Glaser, she would appear without the cosmetic assist of "wigs, hairpieces, and dyes. This is going to be the real me . . . the me that is very natural and today."

The "new Barbra" would also send a note of correction to columnist Earl Wilson, when he reported that she'd shown up wearing a curly wig at a New York party. "I never wear anything *false,*" said the girl who had single-headedly kept the women of Northern Italy in crew cuts for the past five years.

---

* Poitier was one of four stars in First Artists, a film company founded the previous spring with Streisand, Paul Newman, and Steve McQueen.

Meanwhile, between takes, and her first topless scene, Barbra kept herself occupied on the set with a new hobby—creative painting. Wearing plastic gloves (to protect the manicure), she worked on two canvases; one set up in her dressing room, and another on the set. She was very much into abstract art, she announced to Charlotte Ford Niarchos over lunch at Charles Evans's Park Avenue apartment. She already owned a Matisse, and pointing to a Vasarely hanging in Evans's living room, Streisand declared it was not worth the money. "I could do it myself," she said humbly. Barbra and Charlotte were together to discuss the benefit performance of *Hello, Dolly!*, her long-awaited second film, which was finally opening. The evening was to be a benefit for the Police Athletic League, and after going over the menu, the guest list, and a reasonable ticket price, the two women got down to discussing serious business—clothes. Making the best-dressed list meant more to her than winning the Oscar, Barbra confessed. But she hated shopping during the day. She did it all at night, from the backseat of her Bentley. "I look in all the store windows and then I call back the next day and order," she explained. "The other day I called Bendel's and ordered everything in the left window. It included a paisley wool dress, but there wasn't enough fabric for a hat, so I managed to get it out of the hem and inside the sleeves."

On December 12, 1969, the first of two gala premieres for *Hello, Dolly!* was held at the Rivoli Theatre in New York City. The chill of the evening dictated that furs be worn, and happy to oblige were Charlotte Ford Niarchos in a nine-foot narrow sable stole "edged with fox tails"; Gloria Vanderbilt in a floor-length Russian mink; and Jerry Zipskin was in black sealskin. Joan Rivers, then relatively poor and unknown, wore a cloth coat, and she arrived seconds before the star of the evening pulled up in her limousine. "Barbra was dressed in white fox and leather," the *Daily News* reported. "She sat for what seemed like hours in the back of her car, looking out in horror at the crowds, who were attempting to break down the barricades to reach their idol."

"It was like *Day of the Locust*," said another publication. "The mob began rocking the car until the police cleared a path and got the door opened. They then formed a wedge to get her into the theater, and she lost her manager, who was being punched by some little old lady because he stood in the way of her Instamatic. 'Marty! Marty!' Barbra cried. 'Are you all right?' "

"Eventually they got her through the lobby and into the theater, and there were all these swells standing in the aisles of the orchestra section trying to get a better look at Barbra. It was unbelievable! You could have lit up the Midwest with the electricity that was flying around the place. Then, unfortunately, they lowered the lights and the movie began."

According to the *Hollywood Reporter* the second opening in Los Angeles was even grander. Tickets to benefit the Women's Guild of Cedars-Sinai Medical Center went for $250 apiece. In attendance were Mr. and Mrs. Ray Stark, Mr. and Mrs. Kirk Douglas, Gus and Goldie Hawn Trikonis, Jack and Mitzi Gaynor Bean, Joan Collins Newley, Jill St. John and George Raft, and the governor of California, Ronald Reagan, and his wife, Nancy. In the spirit of the evening, for charity, former foe Walter Matthau kissed his costar on the cheek. After the movie the festive group moved en masse to the tent erected at the back of the theater. Unfortunately, the orchestra leader did not see Streisand enter, and she was already at her seat, digging into the fruit cocktail, before they struck up the *Hello, Dolly!* theme.

The early reviews for Barbra and the movie were raves. *Variety* called the picture "a dilly of a Dolly." *Women's Wear Daily* said "The kid's a winner, the whole thing is a triumph." And critic Pauline Kael included the star on her Best Performances of the Year honor roll.

On New Year's Eve, Streisand invited a small, select group to her penthouse to help her welcome in the New Year. The star was serene, happy, and just a trifle smug. The sixties were coming to a close, and in spite of the odds, and the skeptics, she had emerged as its leading female star, in every medium. *Hello, Dolly!* in its first week of release was a smashing box-office triumph. And Woodstock be damned, *she* had two new albums on the best-seller charts —the soundtrack on Fox and a *Greatest Hits* collection on CBS. Her position in the mainstream was secured once more. Her ship, she was certain, would set forth in the seventies to conquer new horizons and claim richer, brighter spoils.

On this night she had no way of knowing that within a very short time the winds would change again, that a second mass counterculture force would sweep in, knocking the wind right out of her sails. Other, smaller vessels would topple and sink, but not Streisand's. She would survive; she would drift; she would deliberate. Then, with a few adjustments to her music course, and to her riggings, she would move out to join the enemy—then to lead them.

Part 2

Poor but resourceful during her early days in Manhattan, Streisand slept in various apartments and depended upon the kindness of the press for free meals and mentions.
(Photo: *Daily News* [New York])

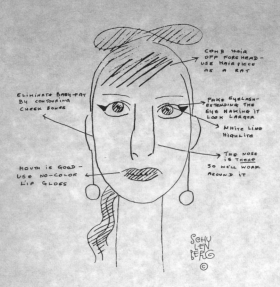

COMB HAIR OFF FOREHEAD - USE HAIR PIECE AS A RAT

ELIMINATE BABY-FAT BY CONTOURING CHEEK BONES

FAKE EYELASH - EXTENDING THE EYE MAKING IT LOOK LARGER

WHITE LINE HIGHLITE

MOUTH IS GOOD - USE NO-COLOR LIP GLOSS

THE NOSE IS THERE SO WE'LL WORK AROUND IT

SCHU LEN BERG ©

Before-and-after sketches, *above and right,* of Barbra by illustrator-best friend Bob Schulenberg, who created her first professional facial makeover. (Hairstylist Frederick Glaser worked on Streisand's hair for seven years and later sued for nonpayment of fees.)

SCHU LEN BERG ©

President John F. Kennedy gives Barbra an unusual salutation with his autograph at the White House correspondents' dinner.

August 1963: Barbra with Natalie Wood at the Cocoanut Grove in Los Angeles during Streisand's first visit to Hollywood. Natalie would later provide camera tips for Barbra's movie debut.

Barbra backstage at the Winter Garden with the Burtons. It was rumored she had an affair with Richard, but others claimed that Elizabeth never let him out of her sight that long. ▶

Barbra with Frank Sinatra: For "a saloon singer" she thought he was okay, but she declined to costar with him in a TV special. ◀

January 16, 1965: *Above,* with Johnny Carson and Ann-Margret at President Johnson's Inaugural Ball. Barbra was cordial to Lady Bird Johnson, but not to the French Ambassador's wife. ▲

(Photo: *Daily News* [New York])

Elliott Gould greets his seven-month-old son, Jason, and Barbra at Newark Airport prior to the commencement of filming on *Funny Girl* at the Hoboken railroad station.▲

When Elliott decided to concentrate on his film career, Barbra fell into the arms of *Funny Girl* costar Omar Shariff.▶

(Photo: Courtesy of Joseph Goodwin)

September 1968: *Radiant! Electric! Hypnotic!* were some of the superlatives bestowed on Barbra's film debut in *Funny Girl.*(Photo: Columbia Pictures)

Advised to become more social in Hollywood, Barbra appeared on the annual Academy Awards show, presenting the Best Song award to Sammy Davis, Jr., for "Talk to the Animals."

(Photo: AP/Wide World)

Barbra ponders her Oscar acceptance speech as director Anthony Harvey accepts the award for co-winner Katharine Hepburn. (Ingrid Bergman is on the right.)

August 1969: Barbra receives $1 million to appear in Las Vegas. Within the year she would eschew the elaborate hairpieces and makeup for the guise of a hippie queen singing "Stoney End."

At age thirty Barbra faces the cameras in Central Park for her first "serious" role in *Up the Sandbox.*
(Photo: Shaun Considine)

(Photo: Courtesy Warner Bros.)

Ryan O'Neal helped Barbra loosen her image both off and on the screen in *What's Up Doc?*

Another of her "flings" was with Warren Beatty, who used Barbra to headline one of his political concerts. She, however, had the last laugh, all the way to the bank.

The Way We Were brought a second Oscar nomination and her first number-one song. Her co-star, Robert Redford, however, resisted meeting with Barbra alone. (Photo: Columbia Pictures)

Jon Peters, a pivotal force in Barbra's life and career, is shown after his 1967 Las Vegas marriage to actress Lesley Ann Warren. ▶

Barbra and Jon attend the Frazier-Ali fight at Madison Square Garden. Later that night Jon got angry and put his fist through a closet door. "I'm so afraid he's going to hurt himself," Barbra worried.◀

(Photos: *Daily News* [New York])

"If I want some —— out of you, I'll squeeze your head," Kris Kristofferson told Jon Peters during the filming of *A Star Is Born*. ◄

In the bathtub scenes Kris wound his legs around Barbra "and got her all hot and bothered," a grip reported. ▼

On the day of the open-air rock concert Barbra huddles with her director Frank Pierson and explains how she wants the crowds photographed. Pierson would later tell all in *New York* magazine. ▲

(All photos: Shaun Considine)

With Paul Newman, Barbra holds her Golden Globe Awards for Best Director and Best Movie for *Yentl*. She was subsequently snubbed in all major categories for the Oscars.▼

(Photo: Steven Miny, courtesy of Randy Emerian)

(Photos: Globe Photos)

Although early in her career Barbra had her mother barred from the Winter Garden Theatre, by the late seventies the two had become close and supportive. ▲

Barbra and new beau, Richard Baskin, eluding the press in Los Angeles, 1985.▶

(Photo: © 1985 ABC)

After two years of relative obscurity, Barbra appears on national TV with Barbara Walters...▲

(Photo: Shaun Considine)

...and at the Oscars, *above right*, arriving at the festivities in a motor home...

...and at the Grammys, *right*, with a new hairdo.

(Photo: Shaun Considine)

"**N**o one listens. No one really cares,"
said the most popular female recording
artist of the twentieth century—who
would rather be known for her acting
than her music.
(Photo: Shaun Considine)

TRANSITIONS

Early in January of 1970 Streisand elected to forgo work and to take some time out for romance. Her separation from Elliott Gould had been finalized and filed in the courts, when Barbra declared she was ready to meet some single, educated, wealthy men of power. One eligible suitor was Pierre Trudeau, the Prime Minister of Canada, who had been introduced to Streisand at the London premiere of *Funny Girl* the previous year. Trudeau, a dapper intellectual who drove a motorcycle to work and was partial to sliding down the banisters of the Parliament Building appealed to Barbra's sense of power and fun. The pair dated in New York in November of 1969, and in January, Trudeau invited Streisand to the opening of the Manitoba Centennial in Ottawa. She arrived in the capital accompanied by three trunks of clothes, two of which were crammed with minks, foxes, a sable—practically every fur she owned. "Barbra enjoyed putting on the dog with Trudeau," said one source. "In Canada he gave her the full visiting-dignitary treatment—the limos, the police escort. She went to hear him speak in Parliament, and to the ballet." Every morning she tore through the newspapers and cut out the photographs of them together. She wanted to be sure that her mother and her relatives back home got to see every printed item.

With Trudeau, Barbra went so far as to fantasize about becoming first lady of the land. "I thought it would be fantastic," she said. "I'd have to learn how to speak French. I would do only movies made in Canada. I had it all figured out."

When asked what ended the dream, the actress replied, "Certain realities." It was *cold* in Canada, and the pay for the Prime Minister's job was paltry (compared to her wages). There was also the matter of official protocol. As a politician's wife she was expected to walk in his shadow and to keep her mouth closed, on diplomatic alert at all times. Phooey! She was from Brooklyn. When she had an opinion to offer, she gave it.

On February 14, 1970, the Oscar nominations were released in Hollywood. *Hello, Dolly!* was nominated for five, including Best Picture, but Streisand was not cited. "She acted like she was very upset," said a publicist, "which was ridiculous. The movie by then had clearly bombed out, and the album [on Fox] was selling for ninety-nine cents in record stores."

Having won as Best Actress the year before, Barbra followed the tradition of presenting the Best Actor award at this year's ceremonies. It went to John Wayne for *True Grit,* and backstage, as the photographers yelled at Barbra to kiss the actor, she pulled a Grace Kelly and said, "He should kiss me." The Duke obliged, wrapping one of his massive arms around her shoulders and bussing her on the cheek. "The big ox almost broke my ribs," she claimed as she exited the press room.

Returning to New York, Streisand picked up the title deed for her new townhouse at 49 East 80th Street. The house, with 18 rooms and six baths, had been purchased after the actress had been denied ownership of a twenty-room coop at Park Avenue and 86th Street. The coop board had voted her "a flamboyant type," to which Barbra cried "discrimination." She was turned down not because she was an actress but because she was Jewish. "It's disgraceful," she said. "I'm a *perfect* citizen. I have references from very important people—from a banker, a doctor, and a well-known government figure [Governor Rockefeller]."

Buying the townhouse eased her angst considerably, she told a reporter. But it needed a lot of work. The library and den actually had walls paneled in *walnut.* "They're ugly," she said. "I'm going to paint over them. They should be lacquered a nice rose color."

On June eighth Barbra gave the first and last party at her new house.* The occasion was a fund raiser for Bella Abzug, who was running for the House of Representatives. The two had met earlier, in a restaurant, during Bella's campaign. "She came up to me," said Bella, "and said she had a young son and wanted to do something for peace." Streisand would also go public for Bella, riding on the back of an open truck down Mulberry Street. " 'Ya better win,' she used to tell me," Abzug recalled. "She was great, and I really feel indebted to her."

During this period another branch of the family appeared in print. Barbra's mother and her half-sister Rosalind, now called Roslyn, age twenty, were interviewed in the *The New York Times* and *The Washington Post*. Each, it seemed, was extolling the other's talent. "Mother has a fantastic soprano," said Roslyn. "At age sixty she would like to go onstage herself, but the minute she gets in front of a crowd she breaks up laughing."

Roslyn, recently signed to RCA Records, was a future star, Mrs. Kind pronounced. Like Barbra, she had a four-octave voice, a deviated septum, and her mother's talent. "As a child Rozie gave me the best pleasure," she said. "She was a terrific eater. She had a lot of baby fat and dieted from a hundred eighty pounds to a hundred thirty after she started singing. But I never noticed those things because I was so happy she was an eater."

"Take One Fat Girl and Make Her a Star," was the headline of a magazine article on the aspiring performer. In the absence of direct quotes they zeroed in on her diet and the rivalry with her sister. "In effect, their relationship amounts to occasional polite dinners," said the publication. "Their separate careers are never discussed. Advice is neither offered nor desired."

"People would love to think that Barbra and I hate each other," said Roslyn, "that there's some kind of rivalry or that I'm completely dependent upon her, but it's not true. Barbra as a sister is just like having anyone else for a sister. No more, no less."

"May I add something?" said publicist Pat Kelly. "It was easy back then to make Barbra the heavy when it came to her sister's struggling career. It was said she turned her back on her, that she never helped her. Anyone who looked at the initial direction of Roslyn's career would know better. Barbra was very loyal to Roslyn and to Mrs. Kind. She *supported* them, for heaven's sake. So

---

* She sold the house at a fifty-thousand-dollar loss the following year.

they fought? What family didn't? Roslyn had a nice little talent. And Barbra made sure she got help from the right people. Ted Brooks, the guy that managed Roslyn, once worked for Barbra. David Shire and Richard Maltby wrote for Barbra and then staged an act for Roslyn. The first dates that Roslyn had were in clubs that Barbra appeared in. . . . Bill Hahn's in Connecticut, the Eden Roc in Miami, the Hungry i in San Francisco. Who do you think arranged those bookings? The only problem Roslyn had was she patterned herself too closely on Barbra. She sang like Barbra, she talked like Barbra, and so the critics naturally compared her to Barbra—and at that age she didn't measure up."

By late spring of 1970 Streisand's own career was slipping into low gear. Following the financial washout of *Hello, Dolly!* her next film —*On a Clear Day You Can See Forever*—was pulled back by the studio for "reevaluation." Paramount Pictures, already saddled with two musical dinosaurs—*Paint Your Wagon* and *Darling Lili*— sought to cover their losses by cutting *On a Clear Day* from three hours to two, then throwing it into wide distribution. "What the public saw was not the picture we envisioned," said Streisand, "and I learned a very important lesson about final control."

Columbia Records shared Paramount's pessimism. They delayed releasing the *Clear Day* soundtrack LP for a month after the film was released (it never made the Top 100 charts), and a single from the score ("What Did I Have?" backed with "He Isn't You") was canceled.

The feeling at Columbia was that they would be throwing good money after bad. The record market had changed. Their customers were no longer interested in Hollywood period musicals. They were buying the assorted rock tracks of *Easy Rider* and *Woodstock*. Streisand was asked once more to update her material. She was indignant, to her ears rock music still sounded like "----." The contemporary market, she told CBS, would have to adapt to her. Furthermore, for her next album she was going back in time. She intended to record a collection of vintage blues, of songs made famous by the legendary Bessie Smith. And the man at the controls would be Bessie's original producer, John Hammond. "I had gotten to know Barbra pretty well," said John. "She came to one of the sessions I did with Helen Humes. Then, after Columbia reissued all of Bessie's songs, Barbra heard 'Gimme a Pig Foot.' She loved it, and spoke to me about doing a complete album of Bessie. But I dissuaded her. I felt she didn't have the background, the knowledge, or the soul to do Bessie's material. She accepted my judgment and we still remained friendly."

Into early summer Streisand worked on another mainstream album. It was to be called *The Singer* and would feature what she called "good music." Three songs planned for inclusion were by Michel Legrand, and lyricists Marilyn and Alan Bergman, who had become close friends to the star. One of the tunes was the ballad "What Are You Doing The Rest Of Your Life?"

"Barbra was the first to record that song," said Marilyn Bergman over the phone from her home in Beverly Hills. "She wanted to sing it in the picture *The Happy Ending* [with Jean Simmons]. But the director, Richard Brooks, said it had to be done by an anonymous voice." ("I'll sing it anonymously," said Barbra.) "And furthermore it had to be a male anonymous voice. The scene in the film needed that. Otherwise it would have distracted from the story. There would have been two stars on the screen and the song would have taken the audience *out* of the picture."

The second and third Bergman-Legrand compositions recorded for *The Singer* LP were "Pieces of Dreams" and "Summer Me, Winter Me." The latter was chosen by Barbra as her next single, but on the B side, at Columbia's suggestion. She needed a stronger hit ballad to kick off the album, they declared. Their candidate was "The Best Thing You've Ever Done," (written by Martin Charnin the previous year for *The Owl and the Pussycat* but never used). On the day she recorded the Charnin tune, due to a technical breakdown with her earphones, Barbra added some dialogue not meant for public airing. In attendance were the Bergmans, producer Wally Gold, engineer Al Schmitt, and Michel Legrand. "Barbra could be easily angered in those days," Legrand told another writer. "If something went wrong, or if someone unnecessary showed up at the session, she could go from this wonderful charming lady to a person I didn't recognize." "I recall *nothing* of that session," Marilyn Bergman announced.

"That was a mixed session," said Wally Gold. "Dave Grusin arranged and conducted "The Best Thing You've Ever Done," and Michel did some of the other songs. Dave had a trio and Michel liked to work with a big orchestra. So while we were changing the setup Barbra stayed in the control room, schmoozing with the Bergmans. When we were ready and she's on the floor, something went wrong with her earphones. 'Wally, these phones I have on—the sound is going in and out. My voice, I don't hear myself.' So I turned to one of the engineers and said, 'Can you fix it?' He put on a duplicate set in the booth and said, 'She's fine,' not knowing that the problem was not in the connection but with what she's hearing locally. So we started the first take, and she's having problems, but as a trouper she tries to get through it. I could tell from the control booth that she's getting more and more distressed, until finally she stopped in the middle of the song, tore the phones off her head, and flew into this fury."

"Christ! These fucking phones. They're off . . . dead . . . Jesus Christ!" Barbra raged.

"She was capable of the most foul vocabulary," a musician recalled. "It was unbelievable," said Wally, "to hear that incredible pure voice singing one moment and then it's effing this and that. But, of course, she was right. The phones were dead. The guys at the controls didn't do their job."

The single of "The Best Thing," backed with "Summer Me, Winter Me," was released on April 7, 1970. Again, sales were tepid. The top play of the day went to "Mama Told Me (Not To Come)" by Three Dog Night, and "I Want to Take You Higher" by Sly and the Family Stone.

Stubborn to the end, Streisand insisted on going through with her mainstream album *The Singer*. She finalized the selections and approved the cover artwork. Then Clive Davis requested a meeting. "I was aware of her resistance to change," said Clive. "She was against the composers of the day because she did not understand their music. I also knew that sometimes the concept is more scary than the reality, so I said to her manager Marty Erlichman: 'Look, I'll come up with specifics.' "

Clive recruited Richard Perry, who had recently produced an album of Ella Fitzgerald singing the songs of Smokey Robinson and the Beatles. "Richard and I cherry-picked some songs for Barbra," said Davis. "They included recent material by Randy Newman, Nilsson, and Laura Nyro. Richard put them together and the two of us worked on a presentation to make to Barbra. All that I wanted Marty to do was to arrange an introduction."

Perry met with Streisand at her home in Holmby Hills. She listened to the tape, and his ideas, and agreed to do one recording session, with one option. If she didn't like her performance she could have the tapes destroyed.

On July 30, 1970, while CBS Records was opening its convention in Freeport, the Bahamas, Streisand was cutting her first rock 'n' roll tracks in Los Angeles. The session, the longest in the history of the Los Angeles American Federation of Musicians, went from seven in the evening to five in the morning. "To keep string players until that time is some feat, let me tell you," said Perry, "probably anywhere in the world, because they like to get home at ten at the latest; but we recorded half the album during that session —five tracks."

The titles included were: "I Don't Know Where I Stand," by Joni Mitchell (suggested to Streisand by the Bergmans); "Maybe" by Harry Nilsson; "I'll Be Home" by Randy Newman; "Just A Little Lovin'," by Barry Mann and Cynthia Weill; and "Stoney End."

After the first take of "Stoney End" Streisand went into the control room to hear the playback and to whisper something in Richard Perry's ear. "I will never forget it for the rest of my life," he said, "especially coming from her, because the night before she had almost threatened to cancel the sessions, and was very nervous, and I said: 'Relax, we've got to go through with it, and I promise you it will be fabulous.' She whispered to me, 'You were right, and I was wrong, but it's nice to be wrong.'"

To add a funkier, more soulful sound to Barbra's maiden rock session, Richard Perry overdubbed background vocals by three of Tina Turner's original Ikettes—Clydie King, Vanetta Fields, Merry Clayton—and by Toni Wine.

In mid-August, in New York, Clive Davis heard the edited tapes of "Stoney End" and instructed that *The Singer* mainstream LP, which had already been advertised and solicited for orders at the sales convention, be canceled. "Stoney End," he prophesied, would be Barbra's next smash hit record.

Streisand still harbored doubts about going in this new direction. She worried about the reaction from her East Coast contingent of intellectuals. What would Leonard Bernstein and Richard Rodgers say when they heard her singing rock 'n' roll? What would Goddard say? What *did* Goddard say? "No comment," the diplomatic

Mr. L. answered, "I haven't heard the tapes yet." Later, when cornered, he listened to one cut of "Stoney End," stroked his brow, and said, "Ummm, bouncy, isn't it?"

At the end of the month Streisand, knowing she had to revitalize her popularity, told CBS to release the record, but she would not participate in its promotion. "We never expected her to get directly involved," said Ron Alexenburg, director of CBS promotion. "Barbra was too big a star to go on the road, calling on disc jockeys. I was all for the change in her music. After I heard the tapes in Clive's office I made up something like eighty to a hundred acetates, seven-inch lacquers, and personally mailed them out to the Top Forty radio stations. Barbra always had a difficult time with Top Forty—they played "People," and some of her other records —but only after they became huge hits on MOR stations. Everything in those days was categorized. Rock music was played only on rock stations; black records were played on black stations; and country on country stations. Barbra and Janis and Elton John helped break down those restrictions."

The transition was not easy. The opposition to Barbra the Rocker was extensive. It began within CBS. "When they played the record at the weekly singles meeting," said Jim Brown, "everyone thought it was Laura Nyro. When they said it was Streisand, people began laughing. Someone suggested we have a radio contest where they could play the record and invite listeners to 'Guess who this singer is?' "

In mid-September, when the single was released, Marty Erlichman went on the road with two of CBS's promotional staff to promote it. "We hit seven cities in ten days," said Ron Alexenburg. "We covered all of the key radio stations and the big record accounts. We also went to a Sears department store. Marty had the idea of using a life-sized cardboard blowup of Barbra, with a telephone. When you picked up the phone it activated a cassette recording. You got to hear Barbra talk and sing a little of 'Stoney End.' "

Even with the special promotion "Stoney End" failed to get airplay. That October the record failed to make one major playlist. "The disc jockeys either ignored or dismissed the song," said Ron Alexenburg. "So we reserviced the record, we sent additional copies to every station in the country, and we concentrated on breaking it in New York, Boston, and San Francisco." This second time out Barbra got personally involved. She wrote letters to disc jockeys, made a few direct calls, and hosted a luncheon at the Fairmont Hotel in San Francisco. "She was a wonderful hostess," said Alexenburg. "She met with the local programmers and disc jockeys." Including Tom Donahue—the Godfather of FM radio—who was also a close friend of producer Richard Perry. Streisand turned on the charm for Donahue. They spoke in her hotel suite, where a record player and copies of "Stoney End" were casually stashed in a corner. "She had all the right moves," said Donahue. "She didn't push. *I* suggested hearing the single. It was like 'Oh, no, do you *really* want to hear it?' "

Later that week Donahue began to play "Stoney End" on his radio program. The song was scheduled every five hours, then moved up gradually until by the end of the week it was featured two and three times within the program. Soon it was picked up in Los Angeles, Kansas City, St. Louis, Chicago, Minneapolis, Detroit, Boston, and New York. On November seventeenth the record finally appeared in the number-73 position on *Billboard*'s bestseller charts. It fell back to number-93 the following week until CBS and Streisand gave it one more personal push.

"She opened in Vegas," said Ron Alexenburg, "and we invited the programmers and their wives to see her do the song in her act. They fell apart. They were in awe of her, and I went to each one and said; 'How can you keep her record off the radio; then? You see her here. She's the greatest. She can sing anything, so why are you stopping her?' And it worked. They went home and within weeks the record went Top Ten."

THE CONTROVERSY

Record reviewers, conservative fans, and old friends became exfriends when they criticized "Stoney End" to Barbra. "It wasn't her style," said Jule Styne. "Those contemporary songs were done better by the original singers, and I told her that. She was very disturbed and we didn't talk for years." "She stole Laura Nyro's arrangements and sang the song note for note, breath for breath, like Laura—what kind of originality is that?" said actor-producer Michael Douglas. "Rock is a gut thing," said Elly Stone. "Barbra doesn't understand that and doesn't feel it."

Toni Wine disagreed. A singer/songwriter ("To Sir With Love" and "Candida") who later became known as the first lady of background vocals for Willie Nelson ("Always on My Mind"), she worked on Streisand's "Stoney End" sessions. She also knew Laura Nyro, the writer of the song. "Laura, Janis Ian, and I went to the same high school," said Toni. "We used to do a lot of street singing in the bathroom. I don't know Laura's reaction to Barbra's interpretation of her song, but I'm sure she was thrilled. If you hear someone singing your songs and it's garbage, it's very depressing. But with 'Stoney End' the combination was perfect. I was always a Streisand fan, and you probably can't print this, but when I first heard her do Laura's song my first reaction was 'My God, she sang the shit out of it.' "

Chapter 17

BARBRA MEETS *ROLLING STONE*

After the success of the single, CBS and Marty Erlichman went after the larger money, which came with an album.

At three o'clock on the afternoon of December 12, 1970, Streisand recorded the last vocals for the LP—"Time and Love" and "No Easy Way Down"—at the United Recording Studio in Las Vegas, with Richard Perry producing.

Perry also supervised the concept for the album's artwork. Richard Avedon and all airbrushed images were *out*. Streisand had to get *down*, be gritty, for the cover. She was willing, and a young contemporary team from Los Angeles—Tom Wilkes and Barry Feinstein of Camouflage Productions—were summoned to Las Vegas. "We had done a lot of album covers prior to that," said Wilkes. "Who? You want credits? Let's see. There was George Harrison, for the *Bangladesh* cover, or maybe that was later. And Crosby, Stills and Nash. And right before Barbra, we shot the album cover for Janis Joplin's last album, *Pearl*."*

Inspired by the title song, it was suggested that Streisand be photographed driving a pickup truck on the road to Stoney End. That exact location—like the yellow brick road—was nebulous,

---

* The day after they photographed Janis, she was found dead of a heroin overdose in an L.A. motel room.

and open to exploration. "We found this spot, outside Vegas," said Wilkes. "It was a dirt road in the desert, surrounded by mountains. Someone—probably Barbra—suggested we have antique furniture placed on the truck. So we rented a red velvet couch and some chairs. Jay York, a friend of ours, went out and rounded up the stuff for us. We went out to the desert early in the morning and set everything up. That afternoon Barbra arrived in a limo. I remember it was winter, and very cold. She put up with a lot of different shootings—in the cab of the truck, on back of the truck, and on the road. She was a real trouper. She kept jumping up and down, and putting her hands under her arms, because it was cold, real cold. She never complained; there was no star stuff. Afterwards she invited us all back to her house. She had this rented house in Vegas, and we hung out there for two or three hours. She fed us and gave us drinks, and made sure we were comfortable. Later, Barry and I picked the shot for the cover, and both Barbra and Richard Perry agreed on it. There were no problems whatsoever. It was a great experience."

> *"Barbra's only twenty-eight, you know. People have the impression she's much older. But that's not old, do you think . . . twenty-eight? Why, that's two years younger than Dylan."*
>
> *A press agent, 1970*

To launch Barbra's first authentic rock album, CBS President Clive Davis authorized the expenditure of a hundred thousand dollars for advertisements in underground newspapers, rock magazines, and on all major FM stations. The media message, he instructed, should emphasize her age, her youth.

A NEW ALBUM BY A YOUNG SINGER [the ad copy read]. "She was the kid with the boom voice and wild gestures. The kook who wore thrift shop clothes when they weren't in vogue, and smothered her steaks in sugar for everyone who watched to see if stars ate like real people." And lest the connection be missed, the correlation with contemporary music was accentuated by listing the names of the composers in the ads (and this time on the back of the album): "Today's most talented composers. Which isn't surprising . . . because Barbra's just as young as they are."

Close to the release date the CBS publicity office sent out special advance copies of the *Stoney End* LP to contemporary reviewers. "There was still some skepticism," said Billie Wallington. "The single was a hit, but no one was sure how an entire album of rock songs would be accepted. She could have been slaughtered." The first review came from Don Heckscher of *The New York Times,* who dubbed Barbra "the First Lady of Contemporary Camp" and called the LP a poor imitation of the originals.

A second assessment came from the rock bible, *Rolling Stone.* "I haven't listened to Barbra Streisand since about 1963, when I lived at home and we had a couple of her albums," said Alec Dubro. "All I remember about her was that she screamed a lot; supposedly had more talent than anybody; made more money than the Pentagon; and everybody loved her in spite of her nose." Dubro went on to say he liked the "Stoney End" single, and "the classy picture of Barbra in a funky old pickup in the middle of the Mojave, or somewhere," so he bought the album. "I'm a little disappointed," he confessed upon playing it, "but it could have been worse. It's like running into an old friend who voted for Humphrey. Now he has long hair and a peace symbol, but still wears a tie. Not a radical change, but one for the better."

Encouraged by the semibenign tone of this review, Streisand's personal press representative, Lee Solters, felt it was time for some alternate exposure for his client. He already had a backlog of interview requests from *Life* and *Look* and the *Ladies' Home Journal,* but that market had been safely corraled for years. What Barbra needed was the attention of the younger free-living, free-spending readers of *Rolling Stone.*

Jann Wenner, the founder and publisher of *Rolling Stone,* was a "pal" of Clive Davis, who subsidized the ailing magazine with CBS ads during its first years of publication. It was this friendship with Wenner that led Lee Solters to believe that a glowingly positive cover story was forthcoming from the rock journal. Solters was further encouraged when he learned that Grover Lewis, a first-class West Coast journalist, had been assigned to do the profile.

Lewis recently recalled how that assignment came about. "We were at a staff meeting," he said, "and the Streisand idea was tossed out on the table with a certain amount of contempt. I was interested because I went beyond rock 'n' roll music. I was interested in the general phenomenon of people in Streisand's position

—powerful, a superstar, all of that. I had no preconceptions of her. I had bought her first two LPs and played them for many years. I was a great fan of popular music. It didn't make any difference to me if it was rock 'n' roll, as long as it had quality."

The journalist and his photographer were promised open access to Streisand. "There was this young rep, in Solters's L.A. office, and his plans were somewhat grandiose. He told us that Streisand was willing to spend upwards of a full day or maybe more with us. That we'd go shopping with her on Rodeo Drive, go to lunch, a recording session, the full superstar scene. But when we arrived at her house her mood had changed."

Making her entrance, dressed head to heels in a biodegradable denim sombrero and "matching denim jacket and flares with that unmistakable de rigeur patina of garments washed precisely once," Streisand whipped into the sun-room of her Holmby Hills mansion, sized up the intruders, complained about the hired help, "and to top everything," she moaned, "I've got this shitty cold. I have to *record* tonight."

"It was obvious we were being patronized," said Grover Lewis. "The interview was obviously initiated on her part, and she was quite blatant in the way she attempted to manipulate the situation."

Item, her image: "Look. I'm considered this kind of . . . institution thing. I'm labeled, pigeonholed. I play for middle-class audiences in Vegas. I made those definitely Establishment pictures— *Dolly, On a Clear Day, Funny Girl.* All of which tags me as 'a veteran performer.' But I ask you. Twenty-eight, is that old? Is twenty-eight all that old?"

Item, her fame: "I don't think of myself as a star; my *friends* don't think of me as a star. The fact is, a large part of me is pure nebbish—plain, dull, uninteresting. . . . I'm still surprised, even embarrassed, when people recognize me in public. People will crowd into your booth in a restaurant, stop you on the street, all that crap. Well, I'm not a person who needs people—not *those* goddamn pushy people, anyway."

Item: smoking grass on stage in Las Vegas: "I'd take out a joint and light it. First, just faking it. Then I started lighting live joints, passing them around to the band—you know. It was *great,* it relieved all my tensions. And I ended up with the greatest supply of grass ever. Other acts up and down the Strip heard about what I was doing—Little Anthony and the Imperials, people like that—and started sending me the best dope in the world. I never ran out. Hmmm . . . I wonder if I should tell that story."

"It was clear we were being *hustled,*" Grover Lewis laughed in recall. "Streisand was trying to make this connection with the youth market, the counterculture, which I considered uproarious. Her act had no limit. The wardrobe, the posture, the false bonhomie and down-home attitude—it was all affected. We were being conned. And that pseudopromise of seeing her interacting with the public was a setup. It was dangled in front of us, and then quickly withdrawn. I wrote what I saw before me, a flighty, temperamental, shallow, ambitious, avaricious person. That was my attitude toward her. But it had nothing to do with the way she sang. She sang quite marvelously."

The photographer assigned to the story, Annie Leibovitz, who would later excel at getting subjects to wallow in mud or pose in their underwear, was not as successful in capturing Streisand's capriciousness. "Annie was very much a child and an amateur at that time. She was quite cowed by the whole situation. Streisand stipulated that she had to okay any pictures that were taken. So, with great trepidation, Annie sent her the proof sheets, and they came back gratuitously marked up. Out of a hundred photographs she had approved two or three. And she delayed sending those back."

After Lewis had written and filed his story, *Rolling Stone* considered upgrading its placement. "Originally, when the piece was assigned, Wenner and the staff had nothing but contempt for Streisand," he said. "As a rock singer they felt she was a joke. Then I don't know what transpired. Perhaps Clive Davis called Wenner. We were at an editorial meeting—a lunch-out—all the editors and in-house writers were there, and out of nowhere Wenner suggested putting Streisand on the cover of the next issue. I objected. I pointed out that the piece was too short. I would have written it longer, but I knew, because of their down-the-nose attitude, it would never have made the magazine. Now it was cover material, and it truly didn't bear the weight of that scrutiny. It would have hurt Streisand because the readers would feel alienated if she were the main focus. I don't know what Wenner promised—and the man was wily, capable of treachery—but I stuck to my original premise."

On June 24, 1972, the issue of *Rolling Stone* appeared. The Streisand profile took up all of page sixteen, but the cover was of bride-to-be Tricia Nixon, smiling under the headline "A White House Romance (The Making of the President's Daughter)." The absence of Streisand on the cover, and the slant of the Grover Lewis piece, caused serious repercussions within the star's PR staff. The Solters press agent who had arranged the interview was fired from his job. And recanting on her admission of smoking grass, Barbra asked for a retraction. "That item was picked up by *Time* and *Newsweek*," said Lewis. "I was literally besieged by movie magazines and the foreign press, anxious to buy more material. Out of a sense of ethics I didn't feel I should do it. Also, to me, it wasn't any big deal. So she got high now and then. Who was it hurting?"

The professional freeze on Grover Lewis lasted for months. "I was off limits to everyone that Lee Solters handled. One or two interviews were canceled, including one with Sonny and Cher. But I didn't care one way or the other. I had done what I considered a straight job. I'm not a grudge writer. I try to put an edge on everything I do, but I had no bias against Barbra as a performer. Her talent was genuine. But in person, face to face, she was playing a phony. I wrote what I saw. The piece was honest." Did he ever see her again? "No! [Laughter] And I'm quite grateful. The word that got back to me was that she or her minions would have been quite happy to have me bumped off."

Stoney End, with or without the help of *Rolling Stone,* became a hit album and went gold within two months. A second contemporary LP was requested, and recording on *Barbra Joan Streisand* commenced in L.A. in early June, again with Richard Perry producing. Eager to win back her conservative audience, Streisand included two easy-listening songs on the album. One of these was "One Less Bell To Answer"—coupled with "A House Is Not A Home" by Burt Bacharach, which featured Streisand singing with herself. This autogenous duet prompted Stephen Holden to anoint Streisand "the singer best suited to record the complete Burt Bacharach–Hal David songbook." Ranked, with a demerit, was the performer's frenzied rendition of John Lennon's "Mother," in which the reviewer felt "she belts out the primal scream—a mechanized shriek, that has all the humanity of a police siren."

Encased in a double fold-out jacket, all of the album's photographs were done by Ed Thrasher. "That was a fluke," he said. "I had no assignment to shoot Barbra. I was head of the Art Department at Warner Bros. Records at the time and one of our groups, an all-female band called Fanny, was recording as backup for her. I went into the studio to shoot them. I wasn't going to go near Barbra because I had heard how tough she was. But I found her totally delightful. She was on her own; no entourage. She was wearing a batik T-shirt and a fluffy engineer's cap, and at one point we were in the control room and I became fascinated with her hands. She has lovely, incredible hands, and I started photographing them. I had a micro lens on the camera and I was right down on top of her hands. She had these long, incredible, snakelike fingers, spread out, holding onto her jeans. She said to me, 'What are you doing? You're shooting my hands. Nobody's shot my hands before.' I said, 'Well, you know—whatever happens to you when you start shooting—it's like instinct.' And that broke the ice. We got along famously. She trusted me, without question. There wasn't a lot of light in the studio, so I had to push the film. I kept shooting for about four hours and took maybe two hundred to three hundred pictures. There was nothing said about an album cover, or her using them at all. Then later that week she called Roy Silver, who managed Fanny, and she asked if she could see the contacts. I sent her a set, and one or two shots blown up, and the next thing I heard she wanted to use them for the album. There was another cover in the works, I believe, but Barbra stopped it and used my material. She made the choice and the layout was created by the gal up at Columbia, Virginia Team."

Employed by CBS Records since 1967, Virginia had been a Streisand fan "forever," she recalled. "When I first joined the company in New York, I told my boss, John Berg, that I was absolutely star struck when it came to Streisand. 'If she ever calls you, can I listen in?' I asked him. And by a strange coincidence he was going up to her apartment that afternoon and he insisted I go along with him. She had just come back from doing *Funny Girl* in London, and she was pregnant. So when we walked into her apartment, she was kinda in a state. She was throwing things around the place, just being a star—doing one of her numbers. I was so dumbfounded I just looked on. I don't believe she even noticed I was there."

Cut to Barbra Joan in 1971. At this time Team was in charge of the CBS Art Department in Los Angeles. "I had a few conversations with her secretary about the album cover, and then I was summoned to her home in Bel Air. I was terrified, but I had a job to do and I walked in, dressed like the country hippie I was, and she said, 'Oh, I didn't know you were going to be so young.' Actually, we're the same age. I just tried to hold myself together and deal with this star . . . person. Streisand always had an attitude, and I was kind of servicing her. She wanted prints made up, and we had to do a little retouching on her nose, flatten that little lump. I put a collage together. And I remember she didn't want any titles or text on the front or the back of the album. Just her first name, spelled the old and the new way, with and without the two *a*'s at the end. Somebody objected to the absence of the song titles on the cover, and suggested I talk to her. But I wouldn't—I couldn't. I still loved listening to her records, but I didn't want to *deal* with her. She made me too nervous."

Ed Thrasher's subsequent encounters with Streisand remained memorable. "We had friends in common," the photographer said, "so we met on a few occasions and it was always pleasant. My ex-wife (Linda Gray, of *Dallas)* and I went skiing to Aspen one winter with our kids and we joined up with Barbra and Jon [Peters] and their boys. She took to the slopes—not often, but she was game. Then recently I bumped into her at a party, with her mother. I finally got her to sign one of the Barbra Joan photos, ten years later.

> *"Women? What do I find attractive in women? Well . . . their muscles, and their fuzzy moustaches . . . and what's-her-name—Barbra Streisand. I found her very sexy . . . a terrific girl . . . but I think she used me."*
>
> Ryan O'Neal

Sometime in November of 1970, while Barbra was preparing her *Stoney End* album, a potential hit ballad came her way and was vetoed. It was then recorded in tandem by Andy Williams, Tony Bennett, and Ray Conniff, all affiliated with CBS Records, and all anxious for a number-one hit. The song was the theme from *Love Story,* and though Streisand declined the melody, she did not let the leading man, Ryan O'Neal, pass her by.

Ryan and Barbra were represented by the same agent, Sue Mengers. Once described as "a cross between Mama Cass and Mack the Knife," Mengers pursued new clients relentlessly. With stars like Streisand, Ali McGraw, Candice Bergen, and Gene Hackman on her roster, she reportedly landed Ryan when she cornered him at a party and asked, "When are you going to get rid of that ---hole of an agent who represents you?" Under Sue's expert guidance O'Neal moved from *Peyton Place* and forgotten B movies into the big league with *Love Story*. Along the way he acquired a formidable reputation with the ladies. "He is an incredible lover, totally devoted to giving a woman pleasure," said his first wife, actress Joanna Moore. Other luscious women he dated were Barbara Parkins, Lana Wood, and Joan Collins, which led some to question Streisand's unlikely presence on his arm. "A publicity arrangement" was how the pairing was snidely referred to.

Columnist Liz Smith disagreed. She recalled Streisand's allure at that time: "Barbra has always been appealing to men," said Liz. "And why not? She has the most beautiful arms and breasts and shoulders. She's really quite a girl. I'm sure she has a warm, realistic sex life, as she very well should have. She obviously likes guys, and they find her to be a very juicy person."

Ryan was good for Barbra, many believed. "He certainly helped her image in this town," said a female Hollywood executive. "She once asked me what I thought of them going together. I told her, 'It's terrific! Think of all those girls back in Brooklyn who envy you.' And she was pleased with that. 'Yeah, he's great looking,' she said, and then added: 'But he's no Einstein.' But that was the whole point, I told her. Ryan was not one for serious discussions, or for looking into the deep dark side of things. He was gorgeous, and physical, and playful. He got her to loosen up, to have some fun, to start acting her age in public."

Not quite in public. Ryan at the start of his dalliance with Streisand was still married to actress Leigh Taylor-Young. He was also in the running for an Oscar for *Love Story* and upon the advice of his press agent he was told not to alienate the older, more conservative Academy voters by appearing in public with any woman who was not his wife or his mother.

Early in January of 1971, while the nominations were still being solicited, Ryan and Barbra were semi-discreet about their romance. They dined and dipped at private parties. They were seen with a group of ten at the opening of James Taylor at The Troubadour. A week later, accompanied by a cover date, Ryan's brother Kevin, they attended a rock concert at the Civic Stadium in Santa Monica, but in the parking lot the trio ran into a roving pack of freelance photographers. A scuffle ensued, and as fists and flashes flew, Barbra and Ryan were captured in action by a photographer for *The National Enquirer.* Following the Oscars, which Ryan attended with his wife (and which he lost to George C. Scott for *Patton),* he and Barbra went public with their romance. She accompanied him to a screening of *Wild Rovers* and he showed up at her recording session for *Barbra Joan.* That same month agent Sue Mengers burbled the happy news that she had found the perfect film project for her "two golden bubbies" (Barbra was now also blond and bronzed from her days at Malibu Beach, playing with Ryan, sons Jason and Griffin, and eight-year-old Tatum O'Neal, not yet a movie star). The pair were set to star in a major feature for Warner Bros., entitled *What's Up Doc?*

The genesis for this new movie had come inadvertently from Elliott Gould, who, following his breakup with Barbra, had emerged as the hottest new male star of the seventies. After *M*A*S*H* he made five movies in a row, then "freaked out" on the set of *A Glimpse of Tiger* in New York. Wearing a New York Giants football helmet, with a New York Yankees baseball cap over that, he harassed his director, Anthony Harvey, by blowing a whistle while other actors were doing their scenes. He also shook up his costar, Kim Darby, and fired, then rehired, his producer-partner, Jack Brodsky, who tried to get Barbra to intervene.

"Barbra was getting all this news on the phone in L.A.," said Ryan O'Neal. "She spoke to Elliott for thirty minutes and got him to apologize. Then Brodsky would call back ten minutes later with some new item."

"Someday the world will know how bad the situation was," said Anthony Harvey, "but Barbra was very loyal. She tried very hard to talk some sense into him."

"Barbra was still very attached to Elliott," said Arthur Laurents. "When they separated, he lived in a house across from me on St. Luke's Place. From time to time they would come through the fence to visit me, with Jason. When he began dating the girl he eventually married, Barbra was very curious. She would call me and ask, 'Is she pretty? Is she smart? What is she like?' "

Elliott also remained mesmerized by Barbra for years after. Reporter Arthur Bell recalled a 1974 interview in his apartment when Elliott still had Barbra very much on his mind. "He was behaving very strange with me," said Bell. "One minute he'd be talking about acting with George Segal in *California Split,* and then he'd suddenly start singing 'Who's Afraid Of The Big Bad Wolf?' which was Barbra's song. He'd talk, then sing her songs, then stop. It was so bizarre. I asked him if he still heard from her, and he'd say, 'Barbra Streisand. Barbra Streisand. Oh, yes, Barbra Streisand.' And then he'd go, *'Who's afraid of the big bad wolf, e-i-e-i-o!'* "

When production closed down permanently on *A Glimpse of Tiger,* to avoid further bad publicity and extensive litigation against Elliott, Streisand agreed to replace him in the movie.* She then found a new director, Peter Bogdanovich, who had recently completed *The Last Picture Show.* But Bogdanovich did not want to make *A Glimpse of Tiger.* "I don't want to do a drama with you," he told Barbra, "I want to do a screwball comedy." That's how he saw her, "as sort of a Carole Lombard." So he sketched an idea. Barbra would play an eccentric, wacky girl who gets involved with a stuffy musicologist at an academic convention in San Francisco. Adding her input to the script, Barbra suggested that her character possess a near-genius IQ. The writers agreed, then balanced the beam by having her thrown out of thirty colleges for irrational curiosity.

To support his stars Bogdanovich hired a first-rate ensemble of actors, including Madeline Kahn as Ryan's shrill, befuddled fiancée; Liam Dunn as the Judge; Mabel Albertson as Mrs. Hoskins; and Kenneth Mars as the acerbic, smarmy Hugh Simon, who was a caricature of real-life critic John Simon. It was Simon (the critic) who had once compared Streisand's profile to that of "an amiable anteater," and who had written of *The Owl and the Pussycat* that "it took, apparently, no less than two color cinematographers to make Miss Streisand look her unfortunate best. What she cannot accomplish by mere physical repulsiveness, she achieves through the ultimate in aggressive yentaishness. The fact that playing opposite her, George Segal can occasionally look sexually aroused, should be reckoned as a major acting triumph." "Mean! Make him

---

* Gould and Streisand officially divorced the following July in the Dominican Republic.

meaner," Barbra urged the writers of *What's Up Doc?* in retaliation.

During rehearsals Bogdanovich shot tests of Streisand and O'Neal. He showed the tests to director Howard Hawks, whose *Bringing Up Baby*, with Cary Grant and Katharine Hepburn, was the admitted plot from which he'd stolen *What's Up Doc?* ("You made a mistake telling 'em where you stole it from," Hawks told the young director. "I never said who *I* stole it from.") Hawks, upon viewing the Streisand-O'Neal footage, stated that Barbra had the same problem as Hepburn. She was trying too hard to be funny. "Tell them to just read the lines," he instructed. "They've got to play off each other and get the laughs from their attitudes."

In production Streisand worried about the lighting, the sets, and the wardrobe. "She doesn't work from a confidence base," said Ryan. "She likes to go into a project thinking it's the worst, and she builds from there."

Bogdanovich recalled: "All through the picture Barbra kept telling Ryan: 'Ryan, we're in a piece of ----. I mean, we're really in trouble.' She also tried to direct, but I put a stop to that real fast."

"Peter used to scold Barbra because she didn't do what he said," said O'Neal. "Barbra can do a scene twenty different ways and they all sound right to me. She'd say, 'Pick one.' But Peter always wanted one she hadn't done. He tried to condense her and pull her back. He made her cut her nails. He wouldn't let her wear makeup, hairpieces, or all the things she's used to doing, because all her movies have been vehicles."

In August, after six weeks of location filming in San Francisco, the unit returned to the Warner Bros. lot in Burbank where the interiors of the hotel complex were constructed. To accommodate their female star the studio furnished a dressing trailer with velvet couches and a crystal chandelier. "I didn't ask for it and it makes me uncomfortable," Barbra told the *Los Angeles Times.* "It's not good for morale on the set." "What's she gonna do in a situation like this?" added Ryan, who commiserated with the star over a private lunch in her trailer. "If she requests another dressing room, the studio knocks her for being hard to please. And if she doesn't, everybody here on the set figures she's strutting. She can't win."

Barbra's concern for morale on the set was applauded, albeit softly, by her supporting cast. According to the veteran pros Mabel Albertson and Liam Dunn, she was both "pleasant" and "professional" to work with, but on the cool, forced side of being friendly. Actress Madeline Kahn, who made her film debut in *What's Up Doc?* and who later romped home with most of the attention and the accolades for her scenes, recalled her expectations. "I was a little apprehensive about Barbra. I had heard that a lot of performers wound up on the cutting-room floor in her movies. But I knew Peter had control. I was looking forward to working with her. We're both Jewish; we're both from New York; I sing and she sings —I thought we'd have a lot to talk about. But Barbra wasn't having any of that. Ryan was wonderful. Very funny, and helpful. But Barbra preferred to keep a polite distance."

Filming was completed on *What's Up Doc?* in October, and the first cut of the movie was shown to Barbra, Sue Mengers, and John Calley of Warner Brothers. The executive and the agent were ecstatic in their appraisal, but Streisand was displeased. She was still not amused by the comedy. "I know from funny," she said, "and this is *not* funny." She bet Calley $10,000 that the movie would not gross $5 million. Calley refused the bet because "I knew that Barbra would never pay me." Streisand did agree, however, to sing over the opening credits, and she recorded Cole Porter's "You're the Top" as a duet with Ryan O'Neal.

When the film opened in March to rave reviews and an eventual $50 million gross, CBS Records approached the star about releasing a soundtrack album. The LP would include her duet with Ryan and a full version of "As Time Goes By," plus some snappy dialogue and incidental music. The star vetoed the idea. There would be no soundtrack released. Streisand the *serious artist* was at the forefront once more. She was putting *What's Up Doc?* and Ryan O'Neal (who had returned to his wife) behind her. She was about to turn thirty; time, she felt, was running out. "My father died when he was only thirty-five," she said. "Perhaps I'll die young also. And what will I leave behind? Some record albums, a few lightweight films? That's not enough. I would like to do some important work."

Chapter 18

NEW YORK—Patience is a virtue, but it can also cause cramps. After four weeks of being ignored, dissuaded, and then told to sit tight by the telephone, the call to visit the Up the Sandbox set, assembled around Barbra Streisand, finally comes through. However, with the call comes a set of PR Commandments, the weight of which would send Moses crashing down the Mount.

Thou shalt not speak (to Barbra) unless spoken to.

Thou shalt not talk of ex-husband Elliott Gould, of ex-friend Ryan O'Neal, or any incumbent attachments.

Thou shalt not photograph her from above, below, or from her right.

Thou shalt not ask her to assume any candid poses.

Thou shalt not click while she is concentrating.

Thou shall observe all of the above or be promptly bounced from the set.

Shaun Considine—a story, 1972

UP THE SANDBOX

Up the Sandbox, Streisand's first production for the autonomous First Artists Company, was to be a serious statement about housewives "too old for an identity crisis, but not past the age of uncertainty." In April, after the interior scenes had been shot in Hollywood, the Sandbox troupe went to New York. Exterior scenes were scheduled for Central Park and an interview request from this writer went to Streisand's publicity office.

Barbra was not talking "directly" to the press, the reply came. But with persistance, and compromise, a "pass privilege" was granted to observe and photograph the star (at a discreet distance) at work. The setting was to be the carousel, near the Sheep Meadow.

Day one—the star had premenstrual symptoms and could not work.

Day two—it rained.

Days three and four—a weekend.

Day five—the Lord decreed, "Let there be sun, and let *her* appear."

It was ten A.M., and the crew and cast (costar David Selby and two six-month-old identical twins, who would be switched throughout the day, playing Barbra's baby) were waiting inside the carousel. At ten-ten A.M. the doors of a mobile dressing-van, parked fifty yards away, swung open, and Barbra stepped out, followed by director Irvin Kershner, her hairdresser, makeup man, costumer, one assistant, and her son Jason, who was to make his movie debut this day—riding the merry-go-round. Barbra, humming to herself, failed to notice a cable lying on the ground and she tripped the light fantastic. Her retinue pulled up short, all but Jason, who was more interested in getting on the carousel. "Hey!" Barbra yelled after him. "Don't I get a good-bye, a kiss, anything?" Jason shook his head and kept running for the merry-go-round.

Barbra inspected the set while this reporter inspected Barbra. She looked surprisingly young and vulnerable; her hair, long and casually streaked, was sans the falls, pieces, and lacquer of yore. Her face, very lightly made up for the camera, was also free of the mandatory layers of Max Factor. In total, her appearance from head to toe (plum-colored, no-bra-look sweater; beige-colored double-knit slacks, and sensible brown shoes) was one of organic composition—except for the chewing gum cracking against her right jaw.

Introductions were made, Barbra smiled cursorily, sweeping her gray-green-eyed radar over this intruder. And in that swift scan one could immediately sense the power and insulation that fame and fortune provided. One false move or trespass and this frail flower could call to have both your arms broken, or quite possibly do it herself.

She said it was a "swell" day; the script of the movie was "terrific" and she thought her role was "fantastic." Why? Because she knew and understood Margaret, the heroine of *Sandbox*. (Margaret was described as a restless housewife who took off on such fantasies as blowing up the George Washington Bridge and bedding down with Fidel Castro, who, beneath the beard and army-green fatigues, was a *woman.*) One question was asked: Where and when has Barbra *known* such a housewife? No answer was forthcoming. Barbra excused herself and walked away.

"It's true," said director Irvin Kershner. "Barbra does know Margaret. Maybe not directly, but she can identify with the frustrations and hidden terrors that housewives are subject to." Streisand was a brilliant and intuitive actress, Kershner added. "She is not difficult to work with, but she is wary of amateurs. She detests mediocrity. She's been screwed so many times by bad judgment that she feels until she can trust you, she'll make her own decisions. Watch her work, you'll be surprised."

Inside the carousel cinematographer Gordon Willis *(The Godfather)* showed the camera setup to Streisand. She peered through the viewfinder, then asked about the lighting. Willis explained that he'd shoot her with half-lights, to balance her face against the bright sunlight outside. Barbra did not take his word for it. She walked over to her taped mark, asked for a mirror, checked her reflection from the camera angles, then nodded, "Yeah, I like it."

"Okay, let's rehearse," shouted the director.

As the carousel turned, young Jason sat on one of the painted ponies, and as he rode past his mother, he waved to her. "No, Jason," Barbra admonished. "The lady next to you is playing your mommy. This is a movie, darling, so please be careful." The rehearsal was repeated four times; the scene was filmed five times. Both Barbra and Kershner were satisfied. Three hours' work for the crew, one hour for the star; final footage approximately three minutes.

Throughout the afternoon, after lunch, and after Barbra had sent a technician to her dentist (with an infected tooth), the crowd around the carousel trebled. Schoolgirls, sanitation workers, strolling nuns, joggers, and cyclists congregated and watched Streisand toil. At one point, as the Central Park police tried to keep the crowds behind the barricades, two young boys slowly inched their way inside the set until they found themselves standing next to Streisand. One boy pointed to his Instamatic camera and asked the star if she would pose with his friend. Barbra inhaled, helpless, and the kids went to work. One stood next to her as the other took the picture. Then they reversed roles; but Barbra looked far removed from their scene. The second lens-kid then asked if she would mind looking happy—smile or something. The terror from Flatbush went one better—she laughed out loud.

"Barbra has a lot of patience," said Shirley Strom, costumer with Barbra since *On a Clear Day.* "Especially with kids. She would never hurt their feelings. She's also very considerate of those who work with her. This is my third film with her. We start another in the fall. Last year I worked with Sandy Duncan on her TV series. I love Sandy, and she wants me to return for the new season, but Barbra needs me here. After this we leave for Africa."

> *"There are animal droppings all around. The people have dirt on their hands, maybe from the time they were born. They don't have any soap. I gave some women a few Wash 'n Dris yesterday. But, you know, they probably didn't like it. They probably don't like the smell of eau de cologne."*
>
> *Barbra Streisand in Africa*

She was scared to go, she later told the *Los Angeles Times.* She was afraid of wild animals. "I'm not a zoo person. After a while here, though, you are less frightened. Then you are blasé. Then you realize how beautiful it is. You walk to work in the morning and see a giraffe, and realize that it's *his* land."

The Samburu women natives also fascinated Streisand. They did not know she was a movie star and treated her accordingly. They dressed her up in yards of bright-colored fabric; they put her fine hair in corn rows; and one of them spit on a twig, rolled it in blue caked mud, and applied the twig to Barbra's eyelids. "That's how I now apply my eye makeup," the star said proudly.

"I shot a lot of photos of Barbra with the women," said still photographer Steve Schapiro, "but every time we met with a new group, Barbra insisted that we ask their permission before taking a picture. 'They might not like the idea,' she said. 'I know I don't like having my picture taken.' "

The warrior males were also taken with Barbra's nose. They

considered large, flat noses sexy. One day a member of a visiting tribe kept circling Barbra and pointing to her nose. Through an interpreter he asked if he could touch her face. She said, "Sure." He spread his palm out and flattened her nose against her face. "It must have excited him," said a reporter, "because he and his pals took off for the bushes, whooping and hollering, like it was uptown Saturday night."

Back home in California after *Up the Sandbox* was completed, Streisand took a four-month break between pictures. She also acquired a new lover—Warren Beatty.

"One of my flings," she later categorized him to *Playboy*.

"Barbra has such good taste," purred Joan Collins, referring to ex-beaus Warren, Ryan O'Neal, and ex-husband Anthony Newley (an earlier Streisand fling). "All my castoffs," said Joan.*

Warren—the star of *Bonnie and Clyde* and *McCabe and Mrs. Miller*—was attracted to successful, accomplished women, and if they had won an Oscar, or had been merely nominated, they would, actress Leslie Caron once stated, soon find him tapping on their door. Miss Caron, Natalie Wood, and Julie Christie were long-term Beatty liaisons, with scores of other beautiful conquests in between.

"Warren would proposition a chair if it looked at him sideways," said Jackie Collins, the author of *Hollywood Wives*.

"He was insatiable," sister Joan agreed. "Three, four, five times a day—every day—was not unusual for him, and he was also able to accept phone calls at the same time."

Warren and Barbra knew each other socially, especially at the time she was dating his good friend Ryan O'Neal. These two pals frequently shared the same ladies (not at the same time, it should be noted), and Barbra was not a part of the traffic.

Actually she was staying at home a lot that spring, being tutored on political history by a UCLA professor of history. This was in preparation for her next movie, *The Way We Were,* in which she

* When Collins's autobiography, *Past Imperfect,* was released, Barbra read one passage aloud to friends, wherein Joan described Ryan O'Neal as the best lover she'd ever had. *"Wh-a-a-t!"* said Barbra, wounded. "Ryan? The *best* she ever had. *I* went with Ryan."

"It was like she felt cheated, that Ryan had been holding out on her," said a source who had heard the exchange.

was to play a political activist. "I don't know who won the Civil War," Barbra lamented, explaining her homework.

Then one day during recess the telephone rang. It was agent Sue Mengers again, calling to say she had thought of the perfect leading man to play Hubbell Gardiner—the all-American smile in *The Way We Were.* Her suggestion: Warren Beatty. He had not read the script, Sue explained, but was hot for the idea and he wanted to meet with Barbra as soon as possible.

"Warren wasn't remotely interested in doing *The Way We Were,"* said another source. "The script, the actual movie at that time, favored Barbra, and Warren was not about to hold up the scenery for anyone."

Warren *was* interested in Barbra's name as a live performer. Attracted to politics since Bobby Kennedy's campaign in 1968, he was then organizing a series of fund-raising concerts for the Democratic candidate, George McGovern. He needed a big name, a huge headliner, for the show in Los Angeles. He needed Barbra Streisand.

And so it came to pass the two icons of the "New" Hollywood met, to discuss their mutual goals. "Both Warren and Barbra, when they wanted something, could be very seductive," said a studio production executive. "So the games went on and soon they were in bed. It went on for weeks. They'd meet at her house, or at El Escondido, his hideaway suite at the Beverly Wilshire. Warren was relentless. He worked on her head. And on her hands, feet, and shoulders. Barbra matched him, stroke for stroke. He'd get her into bed and he'd turn on the famous Beatty charm, and then he'd slip in a plug for the concert. He'd whisper, 'Barbra, you *should* do it. You *have* to do it. It's your civic duty. For me, baby, come on, come on.' And Barbra would moan and sigh and say, 'Oh, I know, Warren. I know. I *am* considering it. Now let's read some more of the script.' And he'd say, 'Okay, Barbra. You want to take it from the top or the bottom this time?' "

Early in April the posters and advertisements for the McGovern concert went up in L.A. The show was called *Four for McGovern,* featuring Carole King, James Taylor, Quincy Jones, and, making her first live concert appearance in five years, Barbra Streisand. Other friends recruited as ushers by Warren were Jack Nicholson, Ryan O'Neal, Goldie Hawn, Jon Voight, Sally Kellerman, Burt

Lancaster, Cass Elliott, Gene Hackman, and Carly Simon (who would later pen a hymn to Warren, entitled "You're So Vain").

On April fourteenth, the day before the concert, Barbra was her usual bundle of nerves. Her old fears and insecurities had resurfaced. She threatened to cancel; then she wanted the order of the show changed. She was scheduled to close the first half. She had to close the second half, because she was the bigger star. Warren was called and the switch was made. Then Streisand changed her mind again. "Those people at the Forum," she said, "they're going to hear James Taylor and Carole King. They won't stay and listen to me."

"They'll stay," Warren assured her. "You're the star. You're the show. They'll love you."

The following afternoon Streisand put her conductor, David Schire, the thirty-one-piece orchestra, and the sound and lighting crew through four grueling hours of rehearsal. Which meant that James Taylor and Carole King had approximately thirty minutes left to run through their act and combine their cues and lighting.

That evening Taylor and King opened the concert with "Song Of Long Ago" and "Close Your Eyes." The squeals and shouts of approval from the audience—eighteen thousand strong—could be heard backstage by Barbra as she practiced deep breathing in her dressing room. "They're gonna boo me," she swore; "they're gonna boo and hiss and walk out when I come on."

Following an intermission Quincy Jones was introduced and led his band and Clydie King and her Sweet Things through Marvin Gaye's "What's Going On?" and "Oh Happy Day." The follow-up was Quincy's theme from the TV show *Ironside,* and some jazz variations, which prompted a dissatisfied voice from the cheaper seats to bellow, "Let's rock 'n' roll!"

"They are gonna kill me," Streisand kept chanting in the wings.

And then her name was announced. She walked onstage, wearing a red halter and black satin pants suit. Her right hand shook slightly as she raised the microphone and began to sing: "Sing, sing a song . . . make it simple . . . make it strong."

"It was amazing," said Gui Landen, a backstage witness. "Streisand went on singing this simple, childlike song, and you could hear the rustlings in the audience—of people who came to boogie —and here she's doing *Sesame Street.* And then she went into "Make Your Own Kind of Music," picking up the rhythm, beat by beat, and you could *tell* that Streisand was slowly taking over the place. There were stars backstage, like Goldie Hawn and Jack Nicholson and Shirley MacLaine, who had been talking by themselves before this, and gradually they became quiet and started moving towards the wings, and they stood there, *awestruck*, staring at this incredible phenomenon in the spotlight—center stage."

Barbra's act ran forty-one minutes. She sang the old ("Happy Days Are Here Again," "On A Clear Day"), the almost new ("Didn't We?" and "Stoney End"); she did a cutesy monologue wherein she faked lighting up a joint ("It's illegal? [Toke-toke] We should face our problems head on.") and she closed with her anthem, "People." "They gave her a standing ovation," said Landen, "and then another strange thing happened. Beatty came out with this guy in a suit and tie who was waving his arms in the air. You could sense people saying, 'Who is this person? And what is he doing in Barbra's spotlight?' And then the realization struck home. It was George McGovern, the presidential candidate. Streisand had made the audience forget that *this* show was for him."

The McGovern concert in L.A. grossed three hundred thousand dollars, and Warren Beatty's traveling campaign show moved on to San Francisco, Cleveland, and New York—but without Streisand. She had agreed to do the one show only; and furthermore, Warren already had a traveling companion, his steady girlfriend, Julie Christie. "Julie had been out of town when Warren and Barbra were making whoopee," one insider claimed. "She had been in England visiting her family, but once she was back in L.A., and the Forum concert was over, Warren resumed with Julie and bid adieu to Barbra."

He also declined the role of Hubbard in *The Way We Were,* but Barbra had the last chuckle. The concert at the Forum, when all expenses were paid, netted a slim eighteen thousand dollars. Barbra, however, had her performance taped by CBS Records and released as a live album the following November—after the elections. It became an immediate best seller. She got the gold, and a new leading man, Robert Redford, and also an unsolicited honor she treasured for years. Because of her participation at the concert, the newly appointed President of the United States, Richard M. Nixon, put Barbra on his political enemies list.

Chapter 19

"It didn't take long, not long enough for her, and he only kissed her on the neck. For a few moments he was still. She knew he was going to move, didn't want him to, but he did. A leg straddled her, his head rested on her shoulder. Before tears filled her eyes and her throat, she had to find out. 'Hubbell?' she whispered. 'It's Katie.' He turned his head; his profile was to her. 'You do know it's Katie?'"

from The Way We Were, written by Arthur Laurents*

THE WAY WE WERE

The impetus came from producer Ray Stark, who asked Arthur Laurents "to write something for Barbra." Laurents wrote a hundred pages, almost a novel (which it later became) about this clangorous, dowdy student activist in the 1930s who pursues and marries the all-American campus hero. "The character was not based on Barbra," said Laurents, "but on two different women I knew. Barbra may have been involved in politics, but she was not as sophisticated or as smart as Katie—though she had the passion and energy, certainly."

Streisand loved the finished script. She recognized other similarities. Katie never smoked or drank or used foul language until she went to Hollywood. "Yes, that was rather like Barbra," Laurents claimed. "In the early days, in *Wholesale,* she was very puritanical. Basically she still is, but after she went to Hollywood, she put on a

---

* ©1972 Harper and Row (used by permission.)

façade. If you remain in that town for any length of time and you want to protect yourself, you adopt an attitude."

For the golden WASP hero Laurents wanted Ryan O'Neal, "but Ray Stark said they had already done a picture together, and he wanted someone new, someone stronger." Actor Ken Howard was briefly considered. The tall blond star of the Broadway musical hit *1776* was auditioned for the part over a game of tennis doubles with Barbra, Arthur Laurents, and Nora Kaye, the wife of director Herb Ross. "You've never seen bad tennis until you've watched Barbra on the court," Laurents told Rene Alpert. "Humor her, she's the star," Nora joked. Laurents insisted on playing to win. He and Nora were wiping Barbra and Ken out, but Streisand's spirit prevailed. "At one time the ball hit one of her breasts," said Laurents, "and she quipped, 'Don't worry, I have another one.' " Everything was fine until a beautiful girl arrived to pick up Ken Howard. "Barbra froze," said Laurents. "Next day she told me there was no sex appeal between them, that nothing would happen up there on the screen, and that we needed that for this kind of story. I agreed with her one hundred percent and Howard was out."

Robert Redford was the first choice of director Sydney Pollack. But Redford hated the script. Katie Morosky had the stronger role. Hubbell Gardiner was dumb, shallow, passive, a sex object, the actor claimed, insisting on extensive script rewrites. "Redford had no desire to *act,* but to be a movie star," Arthur Laurents said, defending his script. *"The Way We Were* was Katie's movie, and no amount of changes would take it away from her."

Exit Arthur Laurents.

Ten additional writers, including Francis Ford Coppola, were brought in to add dimension to the male role, until Robert Redford was happy. "They made the character less perfect," said Redford. "They showed the darker side of his golden-boy character. They showed the chinks in his armor, and made him less sure of himself."

Barbra meanwhile continued with her history lessons and became fastidiously involved with the wardrobe and makeup tests for *The Way We Were.* "You want to talk clothes and wigs here?" said a production assistant. "She went *bananas.* She was trying on outfits and posing for test shots for weeks. For one scene she wanted to wear jeans and a custom-fitted T-shirt. She was told that women in the forties did not wear T-shirts or blue jeans. 'But I look so cute in the outfit,' she argued. Then she picked up a line in the script where her character went to Harlem each week to have her hair straightened. Now, *that* was character development for Barbra. She drove her hair stylists *crazy.* She had them burning wigs by the mile to get the look she wanted. And her nails; that was another story. In the opening scenes she was supposed to be playing a dowdy college activist, but she wore these long red fingernails, like a Revlon model. She refused to cut them. Robert Redford wouldn't cut his hair either. *He* was playing a naval officer during World War II. They had regulation haircuts then, but not according to Bobby. He had to have that boyish, tousled look. He was a star, she was a star, so hooray for Hollywood."

When Redford was signed to be her leading man, Streisand got a print of his latest film, *Jeremiah Johnson,* and screened it at home. This was directed by Sydney Pollack, and she wanted to gauge his expertise also. "She was watching this story about a bearded mountain man stuck in the wilderness, who seldom spoke or seldom moved unless he was on top of a horse," a friend reported. "It was all very slow and moody, until Redford pulled out a knife and scalped an Indian, and Barbra went, 'Holy ----, what have I gotten myself into here? These are the guys I'll be working with?' "

Producer Ray Stark, anxious to placate his star, then limoed over a wet print of *The Candidate,* Redford's next movie, to Barbra's house. Sitting in the dark, munching on homemade popcorn, she watched the film and soon found she was experiencing the same basic emotion of millions of red-blooded women. She was falling *in love* with the world's leading blond male sex symbol. "Barbra was rather intimidated by Redford," said Arthur Laurents. "She had enormous respect for him as an actor. She was also mesmerized by his looks. She thought he was gorgeous, but contrary to what gossip writers said, there was no romance there."

It was not for her lack of trying, others claimed. "She used all of her wiles to get to him," said one agent. "She became obsessed with him. Night and day it was Redford this, Redford that." She couldn't wait to get him alone. She called Sue Mengers, she called Sydney Pollack. Redford was going to be her leading man and she *had* to prepare. She had to meet with him—privately. The fact that he was married, or not interested in being alone with her, never crossed her mind. After all, she was Barbra Streisand—men, beautiful men by the numbers, came when she beckoned. Hadn't Ryan? Hadn't Warren? And then when Redford would not respond, she began to get angry. "Who is this Redford character anyway?" she began to say. And she started picking out flaws . . . was he tall enough for her . . . and what about those lumps on his skin? What if they had no "chemistry" together?

"Finally it got destructive," said Sydney Pollack. "I said to Bob, 'You've got to see her because she's taking it personally.' So he agreed to meet with her, but only if I went along. So the three of us sat down to dinner at her house and talked, and we had about three meetings before the picture began—that's all."

The lack of familiarity helped the opening scenes of the picture, Pollack believed. These scenes were filmed on the campus at Union College in Schenectady. It was here that Hubbell first saw Katie—proselytizing from her soapbox. Streisand appeared combative, defensive, but evidently adoring; Redford was breezy, confident, and not entirely unaware of her romantic interest in him. *His* method worked.

The two stars became friends in due time. Throughout the filming Streisand was persistent and professional, and Redford was patient and charming. "He was ever so pleasant," said Arthur Laurents, "because he thought he was stealing the movie away from her."

Streisand also became a staunch supporter of Redford's work and family-man reputation. When she heard they were previewing *The Sting* at Harvard, she organized a group to go and see it; and later, when a jocular remark about Redford and Paul Newman passed her ears, she leapt to her costar's defense. "Listen, he's *straight,*" she admonished in very serious tones, "and so is Newman. Furthermore they're both happily married and *faithful* to their wives. How many actors can you say that about?"

In late November the closing scenes of *The Way We Were* were filmed outside the Plaza Hotel in New York. On weekends Barbra indulged in her second favorite pastime—shopping. On a jaunt to Saks Fifth Avenue she and her secretary stopped off in the luggage department. The star pointed to five pieces of Vuitton luggage and said to the saleslady, "I don't pay sales tax, y'know." The saleslady, Sandra Morbeck, replied, "No problem, ma'am. We will ship the merchandise to you in California." "No!" said Barbra defiantly. "I want to take the pieces with me and I am *not* paying the tax. I'm Barbra Streisand; I usually get what I want."

From time to time Streisand's secretary, Natalie Wilner, stopped in at a store, Past and Present on Madison Avenue. Eventually she introduced herself to the shop's assistant, Fred Fowler, and inquired as to the availability of phrenology heads for her boss. "She told me that Barbra wanted to give one as a gift to Vincente Minnelli," said Fred Fowler. "I volunteered to run all over the city looking for the right heads. I put them all in a shopping bag and went up to her Central Park West apartment, where I was told Miss Streisand was not in residence. She had this team of frenzied decorators *gutting* the place. The red flock wallpaper, the medieval bed, were *out;* and the Louies, the pastel Monet, that whole color scheme was in, because Barbra was about to be featured in *House Beautiful.*"

Fowler, with his shopping bag of phrenology heads, was redirected to the Plaza Hotel, where Barbra was staying, registered under the name of Katie Morosky. He knocked on the door to her suite, whereupon a black maid—"a dead ringer for the one she had in *Funny Girl!*"—opened the door, ushered him into the room, and announced that Miss Streisand was taking a bath; all visitors were asked to wait. Fowler recalled: "The maid left and I'm sitting there when the doorbell rings. I open it and there's another black maid there, except it all happened so fast I was confused and thought it was the first one. So I said, 'Forget your keys, hon?' And she says 'Huh?' And I try to help her out by saying 'Your key, did you get locked out?' Stepping past me she said, 'I'm from Bergdorf's and I'm here to pick up the clothes that Miss Streisand was trying on.' So I said, 'Sure.' And I simply went to the bedroom, opened the door, and shouted, 'Barbra, where are the dresses from Bergdorf's? The woman is here to pick them up.' And she's in the tub and yells back, 'They're hanging on the bedroom door. Will you give them to her?' And I said, 'Okey-doke,' and I got the dresses—handed them to the gal—and I went back to the living room, where I remained seated for almost an hour."

The door to the bedroom eventually opened and Barbra appeared, looking very soignée. "She was all in taupe—that kind of mushroomy gray-beige color—sweater, slacks, and a turban. She was very subdued and elegant. And I began taking the wooden heads out of my shopping bag, and she looked at them, very quietly, still very subdued. Then she asked the prices and all of a sudden right there before my eyes she turned into the biggest, loudest Jewish fishwife I had ever seen. She began to *haggle*. 'Whadya mean, five hundred dollars? For this crap?' I was flabbergasted; I was unprepared. She went from this veddy elegant lady to this . . . shrew. She'd look at one of the heads and shriek, 'At this price? For *what*? It's a piece of wood.' And I said, 'Yes, but it's one-hundred-year-old wood.' She wanted to bargain, but I couldn't because I collected the heads from different places and they had fixed prices. I was actually doing her a favor, and I must say I agreed with her, because, except for one or two pieces, they were garbage. But I did my best, and then the doorbell rang.

"A visitor arrived. This guy. This tall, handsome, gorgeous guy came in and sat on the couch in front of the fireplace. I don't know *who* he was. It obviously wasn't business, from the way she looked at him, and the way she now behaved. When he walked in, she immediately went back to her gracious lady-self. She said to me, 'Well I'll think about these, sir, and if there's any one I want, I'll give you a ring at the shop. And thank you for coming to my gracious chateau.' I left and never heard another word from her."

In mid-December, while the decorators continued to gut and refurbish her New York showplace, Streisand returned to New York and checked into the Sherry Netherland. She was back in town to publicize the release of *Up the Sandbox*, the advance reviews of which did not meet her high expectations. "A multi-radiant performance in a mess of a movie," said arch-admirer Pauline Kael.

This film was supposed to be Streisand's "little art movie," and to get the message to a serious audience, she needed the support of *The New York Times*, with whom she had been feuding. "Her press agent called and set up the interview," said Guy Flatley, The *Times* movie editor. "We agreed to give her what we never gave anybody—we would show her the quotes—we didn't say we would take them out or anything—but if we got it wrong she'd be able to say how."

When Flatley met with Streisand in her suite, she jumped first on the paper, then on Rex Reed, who had slaughtered her in print in 1966 by depicting her as "a rude, gum-snapping, banana-eating egomaniac." "She wanted it to go on record that she had been violated, by Rex, The *Times*, and other publications," said Guy.

"And now a truce had been called. She insisted that I write down everything she said. She was determined that I get it right. Then she started on Rex again. She called him dishonest. 'He's not a nice man, and I think you know the kind of man I mean,' she said. 'He doesn't like children and I know you do because you have two of your own.' It was as if she had checked me out."

Purged, Barbra moved on to other topics—to Nixon ("I don't understand the Nixon landslide. Maybe people are afraid of change; it's as if they've grown comfortable with corruption") to going to the moon ("I don't know why we've gone to the moon, do you? Spending all that money to go there and saying *screw you* to the people who need to be fed here") to old-fashioned ideals ("I believe in marriage. A husband and children—that's happiness").

Over lunch, as Barbra cut and tasted her son's steak ("I want to be sure the meat is good, that's the Jewish mother in me"), and munched on a chicken salad on toast, she eventually brought up the merits of *Sandbox,* of housewife liberation, and the stupidity of censors who had given the movie an R Rating. "Why? Because a woman's breast is shown. *There is nothing dirty about breasts!* What kind of morality do you have when people would rather have children see blood and gore than a woman's breast?"

When the piece had been written by Flatley and was ready to go to press, as promised he extracted the quotes and sent them over to Streisand. Her agent, Sheldon Roskin, called back and requested changes. "They wanted all the stuff about Rex Reed dropped. He had given *Up the Sandbox* a nice review, so she wanted to let bygones be bygones. But she had hammered away so much at poor Rex that if we dropped that section the piece would have fallen apart. So we took out her quotes and left blank spaces where her dialogue about him would have appeared. I didn't renege on our agreement; I was fair to her. I didn't write about her adorable kid who had been running around the suite wrecking the hotel furniture. I didn't mention her being phony. I even called her sexy, which was stretching it—although I did find her surprisingly attractive, since what's inside of her is becoming more visible on her face."

The article with the blank quotes, ran on the front page of the Sunday *Times* "Arts and Leisure" section. Barbra was still not pleased. "She didn't like what I wrote," said Flatley, "although later I heard she changed her mind because her friends told her I made her sound intelligent. Which she is—sort of. But she's also paranoid. I'm not sure if the article helped *Up the Sandbox*. It certainly had a short life, but she couldn't blame that on The *Times.* Or could she?"

Chapter 20

"A ROSE AMONG THORNS"

Disappointed by the failure of *Up the Sandbox,* Streisand returned to recording in March of 1973. With the exception of one session ("If I Close My Eyes," the *Sandbox* theme), it had been close to two years since she had been in a recording studio. To make up for the slack she began work on two separate albums.

The first was an album of classical music, lieder by Schumann and Handel. It was recorded with the Columbia Symphony Orchestra in Los Angeles during April and May, and was then pulled from release, for reasons unexplained at that time. The second LP was a concept album entitled *Life Cycles of a Woman,* with music by Michel Legrand and lyrics by Alan and Marilyn Bergman.

Legrand, who had been responsible for Barbra's first cultural foray onto vinyl, the French album, had suggested this second project the year previous. "It had always been my idea to write a concept album for Barbra," he said. "I wanted to use a story, a scenario, something like *The Umbrellas of Cherbourg,* but for a record only. I got the idea of taking the life of a woman from birth to death. So Alan and Marilyn Bergman and I started to write songs. We wrote twelve."

"No, we never wrote twelve. Wrong," said Marilyn Bergman.

"We wrote ten," said Alan.

"No, we didn't write ten, honey. I think we wrote six."

"No, no. We wrote ten. But only three or four were recorded."

"We played them for Barbra," Legrand continued, "and she loved them. She said, 'Now we must do the album.' And we recorded a few. They were 'Mother And Child,' 'Can You Tell The Moment?', and 'Between Yesterday And Tomorrow.' And then suddenly we stopped. Barbra would not continue. She gave me no reason. She said, 'Michel, I cannot finish this. I know you will understand.' But I didn't. We had worked for many months and now it was cut off. So I picked up my things and I went home to France. Later, I understood. She got scared. She was becoming more vulnerable with age. She began to feel so many things: about life and people. She would become upset if she heard of a child being hurt, or when a friend died tragically. She felt she didn't know enough about life and death, and so the album was stopped."*

Early in May the possibility of a third Streisand LP materialized. It featured songs she had sung at a defense fund-raising party for Daniel Ellsberg, held at the home of Jennings Lang, in Beverly Hills. For pledges of one hundred dollars to one thousand dollars Barbra sang requests. "She did it in person or over the phone," a guest recalled. "If you called in and pledged such and such a sum, she'd sing it in your ear. It was terrific fun. She did a duet of 'Twinkle, Twinkle, Little Star' with Carl Reiner. She also sang 'Long Ago And Far Away,' 'Someone To Watch Over Me,' 'You're The Top,' and 'Happy Birthday' to Ellsberg. It was also his birthday. She made something like fifty thousand dollars for the guy's defense."

The musical phone-a-thon was taped by Streisand, and to raise more money for Ellsberg's defense, she requested that CBS Records release an album. This notion, however, was quickly killed at CBS headquarters in New York. The powers of the network wanted no further alienation or trouble from Washington. The previous year they had telecast *The Selling of the President,* followed

---

* Twelve years later, in the spring of 1985, work resumed on the *Life Cycles* album. "Barbra came across the tapes one day and listened to them," said Marilyn Bergman. "She begged us to go back and write some more songs." "It is a dream I never gave up," said Michel Legrand. "I feel this album can be something special."

by two national reports by Walter Cronkite on the brewing Watergate break-in scandal. The second of these reports, shown after the election—trimmed from fourteen minutes to eight minutes by corporate orders,—nevertheless drew the ire of Chuck Colson, the chief White House aide. After the program, Colson called CBS vice-chairman Frank Stanton and swore the Nixon-Agnew administration "was going to bring CBS to its knees on Madison Avenue and Wall Street. The CBS stock was going to collapse."*

It was under this climate that Streisand's Ellsberg LP, and other delicate record projects were put on sudden hold. On the morning of May 29, 1973, Clive Davis, president of the CBS Group and president of Columbia Records, was relieved of his twin positions and was told to pack his belongings and leave the CBS building immediately.

The trouble for Clive had purportedly begun the previous February with the bust of a major international drug ring in Montreal. Indicted in the affair was one Pasquale Falcone, who was described as a member of the Genovese "family." He was also identified as the manager of various record acts, and among his papers the federal agents found the name of David Wynshaw. Wynshaw was Clive's director of artist relations. Rumors of drug trafficking and drug payola within CBS Records soon abounded, and Wynshaw was fired.

"Drugs? That was never proven, and they were certainly never a part of Columbia's business dealing," said a CBS spokesman. "Dope? You talking grass? Smoking hashish? Sure, that went on at Columbia," said a studio engineer. "Pills, uppers, downers, at recording sessions and before and after gigs; some recording artists, sometimes got wired. But heroin? I never saw it or heard about it. I know that Janis was into it, but she was never supplied by anyone from Columbia."

Clive was fired because it was his time to go, some record executives believed. The Feds, as warned by Colson, were circling the CBS building, crying for blood, and Clive was thrown out as the sacrificial lamb. Excuses—"alleged misappropriation of company funds"—were given as a reason for his dismissal, among them $53,700 for alterations to his apartment, $20,000 for his son's bar

---

* As reported by David Halberstam in *The Powers That Be.*

mitzvah, and $20,000 used by the ex-president to rent a Beverly Hills house.

"They were talking at the most a hundred thousand dollars," said one industry leader in *Rolling Stone,* "and for that they busted the man who brought in millions for the record company. Clive was responsible for every major act on CBS."

"He was the Barbra Streisand of record executives," said producer Wally Gold. "Clive knew what was good for his artists and for the audiences."

"He knew absolutely nothing about music," said editor Warren Vincent. "Once, after Janis died, he wanted me to splice two of her songs together. It didn't work, I told him, because she was singing in two different keys."

"He had the Midas touch," said Elton John. "Clive Davis *was* Columbia."

"Clive *thought* he was Columbia, past and present," said CBS art director John Berg. "He acted as if the record label *began* when he took over. He was hooked on seeing his name and his face in the papers. But the real brains and the class of the label was Goddard [Lieberson]. Clive behaved as if Goddard didn't exist, but he was still Clive's boss. It wasn't bar mitzvah money that got Clive thrown out. It was his ego, and the way he had taken over."

Goddard Lieberson could have saved his protégé, other colleagues claimed. Goddard had called in his key Columbia executives months before the firing to ask their opinion of Clive. "I laid my employee's badge on his desk," said John Berg, "and I told him, 'In the area of shows, classical music, pop music, even rock music . . . *you* were there . . . but Clive is taking all the credit.' " In London, after a convention concert, Lieberson asked David Wynshaw to walk him back to his hotel. "What am I going to do about Clive?" he asked. "I made a big mistake; he's gotten too big for the company. They're complaining upstairs."

"Sure, it was politics," said Wynshaw years later, employed now by a cable TV company in Florida. "The strings are always pulled by the hands of the guys at the top. If they wanted you out, nothing could save you. I miss those times, those years at Columbia Records. Those were very important years in the music business. I believed then, and now, that Clive was a very important part of that history. And I still stand by the work I did. The artists never complained. I booked them into the White House, on *The Tonight*

Show. I got Simon and Garfunkel their first major TV appearance. I knew everybody. But once I was out, no one remembered me. Except Steve and Eydie, and Johnny Mathis. And, of course, Barbra.

"I'll tell you a story about that lady. It was after I was terminated at CBS. I went to the opening of Tony Bennett at the Waldorf. I was sitting ringside, and she came in with an entourage. As she walked through the room, she kept her eyes straight forward, acknowledging no one. As she passed in front of me, she must have seen me out of the corner of her eye, because she stopped dead. 'Dave?' she said. And I said, 'Yeah . . .' She comes over and kisses me and says, 'How the hell are you?' I said, 'I'm fine, Barbra.' She says, 'Anything you need? Are you all right?' I assured her twice that I was okay. 'That's great,' she says, and gives me another kiss, and took off for her table. I felt such loyalty from her. I appreciated it so much. She was really a rose among thorns."

Chapter 21

"I wanted Barbra to work with Frank Sinatra. I told her, 'It's a part of history.' But she didn't want to actively pursue it."

Marty Erlichman

THE SUMMER OF '73

"Will I ever be free of contractual obligations?" Streisand lamented to manager Marty Erlichman.

She was supposed to be a star—free to say yes or no on all matters pertaining to her life and career. Yet she was still under bondage to producer Ray Stark, and to CBS television. She had signed a contract with CBS in 1965 for five TV specials. She had done four—the last in 1967—but each year after that the network kept honking her for the last show. "It wasn't that we were above doing television," said Erlichman. "We just couldn't agree on the type of show to do, or whom she should appear with."

Erlichman came close to arranging the perfect match. He wanted to pair her with her male counterpart in popular music, Frank Sinatra. Sinatra was a big Streisand fan. He had sent her red roses and a note saying *You're the best,* when she was on Broadway in *Funny Girl.* Streisand thought Frank was okay too—for a saloon singer.

Sinatra had been considered for *Funny Girl,* the movie, but producer Ray Stark thought he was too old. Then songwriter Sammy Cahn had a dream. He wanted Frank to play the Broderick Crawford role in a musical version of *Born Yesterday,* with Barbra in the Judy Holliday role, playing Billie Dawn. "Frank was supposed to do *Pink Tights* with Marilyn Monroe," said Cahn. "Then Marilyn ran off and married Joe DiMaggio, and the movie was scrapped. Then I thought of *Born Yesterday* for them, but unfortunately Marilyn died. Then when Barbra came along, I thought she and Frank would be spectacular together. They're both originals, both perfectionists. When you buy a Frank Sinatra record you get the best. Both he and Barbra always surround themselves with the greatest arrangers and musicians. For a movie I'm not sure if the screen could contain these two. But can you imagine them meeting head on in song? I made phone calls. They were also approached by Garson Kanin, who owned *Born Yesterday*. But it was the kind of idea that was so good it never happened."

The best mating ground for Streisand and Sinatra was on television, Marty Erlichman felt, and he initiated talks with Sinatra's lawyer, Mickey Rudin. "I proposed that since Barbra had a commitment to a network and no sponsor, and Sinatra had a sponsor and no network, that we should have them team up. No guests— just these two—singing. We could do two shows, back to back. That way we'd own one and he'd own the other. One would be on CBS, the other of his choice. We'd split everything down the middle—two specials, two record albums. Mickey got back to me and said Frank would do one, not two. One became too much of a problem for us. Also Frank's sponsor was a beer company and that didn't seem right for Barbra. I told her, 'There are things you should have as part of your lifetime. When you get older, you can sit back and look at it and say you have played with all of the best.' There would have been nothing wrong for her to work with Sinatra. When you're as big as he is, it's a part of history. But she didn't want to actively pursue it. She was more interested in going it alone. So the deal fell apart."

For her final CBS TV special, after the network insisted that Streisand feature guest stars, the singer offered her candidates: Pablo Casals, Andrés Segovia, and four other classical musicians. She would title the show *The Music Masters*. *

"CBS didn't go for that idea," said Ken Welch. "They wanted conventional stars. They had actual guest lists. She could pick one from column A, or two from column B. *A* featured names like Fred

---

* Retitled *Barbra Streisand and Other Musical Instruments*.

Astaire and Paul McCartney. It also had Ray Charles, and we all jumped for him."

Streisand liked the idea of featuring classical musical instruments, and she asked for augmentation. With the traditional symphonic sound she added bagpipes, bouzoukis, a glockenspiel, a Swanee whistle, a cimbalom, electronic synthesizers, ring modulators, and for one special scene, she wanted to add such household appliances as a vacuum cleaner, a blender, a washing machine, and a sewing machine—to appease her sponsor, Singer. In a further spoof, when the CBS brass insisted that she include a medley of her greatest hits in the show, Barbra gave them "Second Hand Rose" with flamenco, "Don't Rain On My Parade" with deer-horn rattles and Indian tom-toms, and "People" was accompanied by Turkish tambourines, a kanoon, and darabukka.

Rehearsals for the specials were held in Los Angeles and New York. The actual filming was done at Lew Grade's TV studios in London. "It was an extremely expensive special," said Ken Welch, who, with his wife Mitzi wrote special material for the show. "Everybody lost money. It was the first time that we ever recorded on thirty-two tracks. Pye Recording had a special truck on the premises. Everyone knocked themselves out. We went further with Barbra than anyone; she inspires that."

The duet with guest star Ray Charles began with "Cryin' Time." It took five hours and twelve takes before Streisand was pleased. "An eyelash batted out of place, and they sang it again," the London *Times* reported. "Look. If you close in on my nose, I look cross eyed," Streisand admonished the cameraman. "If you close in on my eyes, my nose looks too big. How many times do I have to say it? That camera is nearly in my teeth."

Ray Charles sucked on a cigarette and Barbra chewed gum in the sixth hour as the lights were changed for "Sweet Inspiration," their second song. She argued with the director, Dwight Hemion, over her costume and the camera angles for the song. "Dwight!" she admonished in curt, twangy Brooklynese. *"You* are going to have to adjust to me. I am not going to adjust to you. I'm *not* going to screw up my whole performance over this."

At eight P.M. they tackled "Sweet Inspiration" for the twelfth time, until the star and director pronounced themselves satisfied. Ray Charles, relieved, played a few bars of "Jingle Bells" on the organ. By nine P.M. Streisand was being limoed home. "I don't know how she does it," said Grace Davidson, her personal companion. "She's worked the whole day, and when we get back I just close the door and say good-night. But she's on the telephone, calling home for hours. She only gets five hours' sleep."

While in London, Barbra made one rare public appearance. The story of that evening was told by Jim Brown, a Columbia promotion executive. "CBS Records called up this guy in London and told him to make Barbra comfortable. He invited her out to dinner. She said she would rather catch the Elton John concert. He got the tickets and called her back, and asked her what she was wearing. 'Something casual,' she replied. So he went out and bought one of those tacky, polyester leisure suits. When he showed up at her place, she opened the door, took one look at him, and said, 'Christ! I'm not going out with you in that piece of shit.' He told her, 'I spent almost three hundred dollars on this suit.' So anyway, they left. They were late and the concert was already on when they got there. The people in their aisle had to get up to let them into their seats. And as Barbra settled in, this guy behind her said, 'I don't care if you're Barbra Streisand—but you're late, and furthermore, I can't see through you—so settle down, girl.' And that pissed her off because after about six songs she said, 'Let's get out of here.' "

From there, hoping to resuscitate the evening, her escort took her to a posh restaurant. "When they were seated, Barbra asked, 'What are we here for? I'm not hungry.' He replied, 'I am, and I'm having dinner.' So he ordered and she watched him eat. Then when the dessert tray came around, Barbra picked up her fork and took a bite out of each dessert that was on the tray. And when she was finished, she put her fork down, smiled, and said, 'See, I told you I wasn't hungry.' The poor guy had it up to here at that point, and he said, 'You know, Barbra, you can take the Jew out of Brooklyn, but you can't take the kike out of the Jew.' With that she started to laugh, and they became great friends."

"Just the nature of being interviewed disturbs me, therefore what I say comes out hostile or negative or defensive. When I try to put something into words

somehow the whole meaning of what I feel is altered. Anyway, interviews stick but I change."

Barbra Streisand, 1973

In England, Streisand gave what she called her last interview, to Peter Evans of the London *Times*. During the talk she confessed she was in love with a businessman, and she liked to travel with him. "It's a terrible thing," she said, "but I actually enjoy being subjugated to him." This man of no name was married, another publication reported; and, as it transpired, was not about to leave his wife or family for Barbra. When she returned to New York early in June she appraised the situation and decided to terminate the relationship.

A short time later, to get away from the pressure and the New York City heat, Barbra took a one-day excursion by car to upstate New York with son Jason and two friends. They stopped for lunch at a Howard Johnson's restaurant near Tarrytown, where she encountered an admirer, writer-poet Marcy Sheiner.

Sheiner had been a devout Streisand fan since the age of sixteen. "Barbra represented an important symbol for me and millions of young Jewish girls," she said. "Her image on screen, the notion that her nose and her mannerisms were not only acceptable to but adored by the American public, was a form of validation for girls who'd never gotten any from the faces of Debbie Reynolds, Doris Day, or even Annette Funicello." Marcy had all of Barbra's records, she knew the words to every song, and had seen all of her movies several times. She could act out *Funny Girl* from start to finish and was often told she resembled her idol. "In 1965 that wasn't always meant as a compliment, but by 1973 it was."

That summer evening in Tarrytown, Marcy was waiting for a male friend outside Howard Johnson's when a woman closely resembling Streisand passed by. Curious, she followed. "I think I went into a kind of trance," she recalled, "because when I came face to face with Barbra, all I could do was grab her arm and exclaim idiotically, 'You are!' She shrugged free of my fervent grip and headed for the dining room. I followed. 'Look,' I babbled, 'I don't want to bother you, but . . .' She then put her hand on her hip, looked me up and down and spat out, 'Why don't you cool it.'

Icicles emanated from her body; there was no response for me but to leave."

Marcy spent the entire next day crying and blaming herself for the way she had behaved. "But in retrospect there was no way to approach her; she was unavailable to her fans. Certainly I do understand the need to protect herself. Through my work, over the years I've experienced limited 'fame' and the annoyances of strangers' intrusions. But I also think celebrities have some responsibility to their fans, and I've met others who are much more accessible."

Chapter 22

"I think The Way We Were *was a good movie, and it was successful. How often do we get to see a movie in which a Jewish woman communist is the hero and a tight-lipped, anal-retentive WASP loses? And the film makes $30 million!"*

Jane Fonda, Cineaste, 1974

HER FIRST NUMBER 1 SINGLE

In Los Angeles in late July of 1973 Streisand's spirits were lifted considerably when she was apprised of the rave reactions being generated from studio screenings of the almost-completed *The Way We Were*. At this time she also agreed to sing a theme song over the credits. The song would become her first number-one single and it would also bring her two gold albums.

The melody for "The Way We Were" was written by Marvin Hamlisch and used to underscore a scene in the film, the one at El Morocco, where Katie, now chic, meets Hubbell, dressed in his officer whites. Barbra at first resisted singing any song in the movie. "She did not want it to detract from her impact as an actress," said Hamlisch. Six months later, however, according to another source, when Barbra viewed the partially edited film and saw that Robert Redford was stealing the movie away from her, she had a change of heart. To balance her star impact she agreed to sing a theme song, *twice*—over the opening and closing credits. But by then she had grown tired of the original composition. "It's already six months old," she argued, "and it's too simple." To please her, a second, more complex song, with artier lyrics by Marilyn and Alan Bergman, was written. Later entitled "The Way We Weren't" (by Streisand), one listener said the second song was "boring, a real dirge." But Barbra loved it! "I wouldn't know a hit song if it walked right up to me," she admitted. "We recorded both versions with a piano accompaniment," said Marvin Hamlisch. "Then we took the cassette player into the projection room and played each song against the film. It was clear the first song worked; Barbra agreed, so we went with the original."

"Marvin always thought I disliked his melody for 'The Way We Were,' " said Barbra, "because I changed two of the notes when we scored the film. I don't think he'll ever forgive me."

"Barbra can change any of my notes," Marvin answered. "Her musical instincts are pure and astounding."

When "The Way We Were" was recorded for CBS Records, a different arrangement was used. "The song as performed by Barbra in the movie did not work for a pop record," said Marty Paich, who arranged and produced the hit single. " 'The Way We Were' in the movie was very laid back. It worked fine with the picture, with the visuals, but for radio, for the ears only, it kind of put you to sleep. So they called me in, and Marvin and I went over to see Barbra, to her house on Carolwood, in Beverly Hills. They played the song for me and asked if I'd do something with it, to make it more commercial. So I took it home and worked on an arrangement. I rewrote it with a much hipper rhythm section."

A week later Paich conducted and produced the session. "Marvin was there. He had the movie arrangement with him and wanted me to use it, but I told him I couldn't. Barbra was perfect. I have nothing but praise for her. She always listens very carefully to what you write for an orchestra. Therefore, when she sings it doesn't seem like a singer in front of an orchestra, it sounds like a singer *with* an orchestra. Also at the end of the song, I asked her if she wouldn't mind humming a close. She thought about it. Tried it to herself. And said, 'That's a good idea.' And that's how she did it, humming the opening and the closing."

The single was mixed that same night. "It was a rush job. Columbia Records wanted it out to coincide with the opening of the picture. So Barbra stayed on to repair a few lines, and we worked straight through the night. I think it was four hours for the recording, and four hours for the mixing, which goes to show if you have the right artist and the right orchestra, you can make a hit record in one night."

It didn't become a hit overnight. "I couldn't get anywhere with the disc jockeys at first," said Hamlisch. "They wouldn't play it because it wasn't rock. Then when the picture began to take off, the record began to make it big." So big that Columbia Records rushed out *two* Streisand albums entitled *The Way We Were*. One was a skimpy soundtrack, the other an uneven collection of songs. "We had a gold record from *The Graduate* soundtrack a few years before," said Bruce Lundvall, "so we figured, why not try it again with some incidental music and Barbra's voice on the one song? Sure enough, it worked. It went gold in a very short time."

For the second album Columbia dipped into the vaults for some old unreleased Streisand material (from the canceled *The Singer* sessions), and Barbra supplemented these with another rush session in Hollywood. That album struck gold also, much to the chagrin of producer Ray Stark. "Stark wasn't getting a cut of the second LP, so he threatened to sue," said Lundvall. "We had to drop the title of the movie from the album cover." But there's more than one way to skin a cat—or sell a record album, as the CBS pros knew. To avoid litigation, they agreed to strip out the title of the movie from the album cover; as a substitute they designed a sticker featuring the name of the song (and one other) and they slapped that on the plastic wrap of the album. It sold two million copies.

The year 1973, which had begun in failure, closed in triumph for Streisand. She had a new hit movie, two hit albums, a hit single, and her love life was flourishing also. She was seeing a man who would shortly change her life, and her career. He referred to himself as "a businessman, an entrepreneur." But in Bel-Air and other L.A. boroughs he was known as "the hairdresser."

Chapter 23

"I think for a woman, getting your hair done is a very
personal thing. I hate for just anyone to fool with my
hair."

Barbra Streisand to Women's Wear Daily, **1974**

"In the last five years I've made a lotta lotta lotta money. I
hate actresses, though. I used to do Streisand and all the
big stars and they drive me nuts! I'm not anybody's
slave."

Jon Peters to TV Guide, **1970**

JON PETERS

He was a loudmouthed slum kid from L.A., the magazine
said, the son of an Italian mother and a Cherokee Indian
father. Another publication had him born in Brooklyn, and
his parents' nationalities were reversed.

At the age of nine Jon Peters (né Pagano) got hooked on celebrity. In Cecil B. De Mille's *Ten Commandments* he was one of
10,000 extras, riding a donkey in the parting-of-the-Red-Sea episode. He never got to meet Moses, but he was close to his costars.
"I fell in love with Debra Paget and John Derek," said Jon. "I fell
in love with having my hair done, and with wearing makeup. I
didn't wash the makeup off for six years."

Not long after this Jon saw his father die before his eyes. He
soon hit the L.A. streets, got into trouble with the law, and was put
into a reformatory. At thirteen he ran away to New York and

stayed for a while with two hairdressers, friends of his mother's. "She didn't know they were gay," he said. "I lived in their house until one night I heard them trying to carve me up in the other room. I went out the window. I hit the road, went on the street. I figured anything is better than that."

Through other connections Jon got a job at the Larry Mathews beauty salon in the Great Northern Hotel on Fifty-seventh Street. He worked the night shift, catering to prostitutes and poodles. At fourteen he moved to Philadelphia, where he married an older girl of fifteen. "Her name was Marie Zambatelli," he said. "We lived on Twelfth and Shunk Street in South Philly." The marriage lasted three years; then Jon returned to Los Angeles where his mother got him a job with Gene Shacove, the hairstylist who is said to have inspired Warren Beatty's movie *Shampoo*. Jon was a quick study. Within a year he could clip and rap with the best of them. "All you gotta do," he said, "is smile a little bit and dance around and tell them they look good and they'll drop a hundred bucks just like that."

At the age of twenty-one he borrowed a hundred thousand dollars and set up his own salon. Within two years he had one location in Encino, another in Newport Beach, with two fashion boutiques and a dress-manufacturing business. He also fell in love and acquired a celebrity wife—former Walt Disney starlet Lesley Ann Warren—who would provide Jon with his official entree into the entertainment business.

"When I met Jon, I had just come to Hollywood, crazed with insecurity," said the talented Lesley Ann. "I was scared and thinking I was dependent on him in every way. He liked and encouraged that feeling." "Forget Cinderella," Peters told the ingenue, and proceeded to change her image and career. He lopped off her long hair and the second half of her first name. When Lesley was hired to replace Barbara Bain in the TV series *Mission: Impossible*, Jon made himself notably visible during filming. When he showed up at a network gathering and proceeded aggressively to express his views on his wife and her show, the CBS-TV brass showed him the door. "Jon turns a lot of people off," said Lesley. "It's because he's so strong and positive and knows what he wants." When *Mission: Impossible* and Lesley Warren failed to attract the public's continued interest, she retired to raise their three-year-old son, and Jon returned to his mini beauty empire. He opened two more stores and purchased a wig factory in Hong Kong. But each morning as he wheeled his silver Porsche along Sunset Boulevard, he kept his eyes raised to the HOLLYWOOD sign. He *had* to be a mogul, he declared, "I really wanted to be what Mike Todd was—a showman." But for that he needed a hot property—a hot, ready-made star. It was easier to start at the top, he figured, and work his way down. It was time for him to meet another older woman—Barbra Streisand.

She had *that* problem again. In her new movie, *For Pete's Sake*, Barbra was to ride a water buffalo, pop in and out of manholes, and get chased through the streets of Brooklyn by the Mafia. With all that, who had time to fuss with the hair? She needed another wig—a short, natural-looking wig, and she saw the perfect specimen sitting on top of a woman's head at a Hollywood party. She made discreet inquiries and found out that the creator of the wig was Jon Peters. She sort of knew who he was.

Jon knew Barbra too. He'd had her photo—the cover of *Newsweek*—stuck up on the wall of his office since 1970. And though he "put her down" to *TV Guide* that same year, he was aching to get his hands on her head.

When the call came in from the *For Pete's Sake* production office, Jon was out of town. When he returned she was in London, making her final TV special. When she came back in August, a meeting was arranged. Jon Peters showed on time, wearing a white Indian cotton shirt, genuine hand-tooled cowboy boots, faded blue jeans, and no underwear. Barbra kept him waiting an hour ("That gave you a chance to look over my house," she told him later), and when she appeared she imperiously announced that she wanted him to do a wig for her.

First off, he told her she was rude in being late; secondly, he didn't do wigs; and thirdly, as she walked away, he added, "You've got a great ass."

"I couldn't *believe* it," Barbra chirped happily to friends. "He treated me like a *woman,* and not like some star thing."

Jon, of course, did the wig—for free. There was a catch, however. There would be no consultations or further house calls. He'd style the wig, but she had to pick it up.

"The way *I* heard the story," said one trusted source, "is that Jon called Barbra and said, 'The wig is ready, come pick it up.' She had to drive to Malibu—to his ranch. When she got there he was working, hauling timber or something, and she sat on the grass and watched him. Then he showed her his spread—the trees, the hot tub, the fenced-in corral with the Tennessee walking horse. Barbra, being a Taurus and a latent earth mother, loved all of this.

"In the house that he built from old wood and stucco (with no furniture), Jon showed Barbra the wig he had fashioned for her. She tried it on and looked adorable. She looked, at the most, seventeen. So they celebrated. Jon opened a bottle of wine and rolled a joint. You've heard of Hawaiian Gold? Well, he had Peruvian Platinum. Five hundred dollars an ounce. With just one toke, Barbra could feel her toes talking to her. She sat on the floor and looked at Jon, who, straight, without the influence of *anything,* looked hot. Stoned, he looked like a god, an Aztec god, an Aztec god that *moved.* Towards Barbra. He took her shirt off, then her slacks. He *carried* her out to the hot tub, and they made love, for hours—in the tub, on the ground, in the house. When she couldn't move for happiness, he drove her home. He deposited her at her front door, kissed her good-night, and then didn't call her for a week!"

Barbra was in love and did the pursuing, the gossips said. Jon Peters—like the others before him—was "attached," so the courtship began in private. He would sometimes drive to her home after work; and more often than not Barbra made the long trek to Malibu to visit him. Arriving one evening she found another car parked side by side with his in the dirt driveway. It belonged to his wife, Lesley, so Barbra put her Jaguar in reverse and drove back to L.A. in tears.

"Lesley had no idea that Jon was seeing Barbra," said reporter Arthur Bell, who interviewed the actress for *Cosmopolitan.* "She really believed they were having a professional relationship." "Barbra called the house one day and my stomach dropped," said Lesley. "I believe in intuition and immediately felt some anxiety. But Barbra was not the reason we split. Jon and I had some severe problems."

There were two sides to Jon Peters, Barbra soon learned. He could be as soft and smooth as silk one minute, then as sharp and cutting as barbed wire the next.

"Jon was very charming and seductive when he wanted you to do something for him," said a co-worker. "He came across as very sexual, with great charisma, to both men and women. He was secure enough, like most Italians, to kiss another man on the mouth. But then if you displeased him he'd go from Doctor Jekyll to Mr. Hyde. If you didn't do what he wanted he'd start screaming 'You ----ing ----sucker! I'm gonna bury you.' And he loved macho games. He liked to 'butt heads,' to arm-wrestle, and show off. One night at the ranch he and Barbra were in bed, asleep, when he heard some raccoons outside, going through the garbage cans. He got out of bed, went to the closet, took out these six-guns and strapped them on. He was like John Wayne, nude, with these six-guns tied around his waist, and he started shooting at the raccoons. Barbra woke up. He scared the hell out of her, but she loved it."

Jon was not intimidated by her celebrity, Streisand believed; but some felt his indifference was studied. Although he couldn't spell or write too well, in the use of power and manipulation he had a Ph.D. If Barbra was late one hour, he stalled her for two or three the next time—and sometimes never showed.

Early in December, when she was recording the album for *The Way We Were*, Jon was at the studio for two sessions. On the third night, after a lover's tiff, he stayed away. Barbra, in the midst of recording a song, could not continue. "She began to cry," said a musician; "she got on the phone, begging Jon to forgive her. She couldn't sing if he wasn't there. She pleaded with him to come to her. And meanwhile we're sitting around, something like forty musicians, listening to all this. Barbra usually was *tough* in the studio, but this guy got to her, and eventually he appeared. The songs she sang that night were 'Make The Man Love Me,' 'Being At War With Each Other,' and 'All In Love Is Fair.' Appropriate titles, I felt."

Two days before Christmas, when Barbra showed up at Jon's salon for an employees' Christmas party, Peters felt it was time to tell his wife that he wouldn't be around much for the holidays. He had "fallen in energy" with Barbra, he said. "Lesley was shocked," said Arthur Bell. "She took it very badly. She didn't blame Barbra, though. She said that Jon was the bastard in this case, because they had this little boy."

After the New Year, when Lesley and Peters announced their official separation, Barbra was eager to show off her new love to the press. She agreed to be interviewed and photographed at home, with her new lover, for the fashion-gossip publication *Women's Wear Daily*. Wearing faded patched jeans and a black floral blouse, "with burnt-sugar hair cascading down her shoulders," she pointed out to Jean Cox, the reporter, that "it's Barbra without an *a* and Jon without an *h.*" Then, as Peters reclined on her luxurious chintz sofa (his right foot was in a cast, broken from a badly aimed kick at a photographer a short time before), Barbra shuffled between chores in the kitchen and the living room. After serving shrimp, with a guacamole dip, and champagne, Barbra snuggled next to Jon and confided that although she washed and blow-dried *his* hair, he wouldn't touch hers. "She wants me to back-comb it, I won't back-comb," he said. Jon introduced her to health foods, Barbra confessed ("Now all the hot dogs have all-wheat buns"), and to porno movies. The night before, in her lipstick-red and gray art-deco screening room, surrounded by her gold records and her million-dollar collection of Erté sketches, the couple watched *Deep Throat*. "It was terrible," said Barbra; "we fell asleep in the middle."

FUNNY LADY

In the third week of February 1974, "The Way We Were" became Streisand's first number-one single, and her performance in the movie brought her a second Academy Award nomination. When asked to sing the song on the Oscar show, she refused. "I'm being honored for my acting," she explained, "not for my singing."

During the ceremonies she sat in the audience, holding on tight to Jon Peters's hand. She wanted to win. She *believed* she should win. "I deserved it," she said. "Of the five performances that year I felt mine was the best." The voters nevertheless chose Glenda Jackson for *A Touch of Class.*

"It's a popularity contest," Barbra explained to Jon, riding home in her limousine after the show, "and in Hollywood you know where that leaves me."

"That'll change, baby," Jon assured her, "that'll change."

The following month filming on part two of the life of Fanny Brice began in Hollywood. "He's gonna have to drag me into court to do this one," Streisand said when Ray Stark sent her the script. She hated sequels. She did not want to play Stark's aging mother-in-law. "She did not want to play a thirty-five-year-old [she was thirty-two] . . . and eventually an older woman," said the screenwriter, Jay Presson Allen. "She was, figuratively speaking, escorted to the set every day by a team of lawyers."

It was Jon Peters, anxious for some on-the-job training as a producer, who managed to pacify the star and get her to look upon the role as "growth experience." Barbra agreed. "The script is about really learning to accept yourself," she said, "and that's what I've been starting to do in my own personal life."

At her request Jon was unofficially involved in the picture as a "style consultant." ("It was like the old days at MGM with Lana Turner," said Arthur Bell. "When Barbra got tired or tense Jon took her to the dressing room and gave her a little -----.") He offered "creative input" on the costumes (by Bob Mackie and Ray Aghayan), the hairstyles, and the makeup. For the later-day scenes, to play Fanny at fifty, Jon supervised the dusting of Barbra's hair and the placement of age lines on her face. "---!" said the star, looking at herself in the mirror. "Is that how I'll look when I'm old? Take them off! Take them off!"

Vlimos Zsigmond, who later won an Academy Award for *Close Encounters of the Third Kind,* was hired to photograph *Funny Lady.* He shot for two and a half days and was fired for "artistic differences." Word on his dismissal spread through the town and the story grew to monster proportions. "Did you hear the latest on Streisand's movie?" *Interview Magazine* reported. "She came to work this morning, pointed to the left side of the set, and said, 'Everybody standing over there is fired today.'"

"There were only the usual differences," said Peter Matz, who did the arrangements and scoring.

Vlimos Zsigmond was fired because he wanted "realism," he stated. "I spent six weeks researching the film, I wanted the movie to look less like *Funny Girl* and more like *Cabaret.* Realistically a theater is dark when a performance begins. When the curtain rises you do not see the audience. And that's how I lit the scene. But they said it was too dark. They wanted *Funny Girl* or *Hello Dolly!* They wanted the old concept of musicals. They were not interested in art, but in making it safe."

One exterior scene for the film was shot at the Olympic swimming pool in L.A. Stadium. Dressed as a clown, Barbra was supposed to frolic in the water with twenty-five female synchronized swimmers. "It took her fifteen minutes to wriggle her big toe in the water," said *Newsweek*. "She wouldn't go in until Ray Stark had heated the pool to ninety-two degrees."

Another day, another scene was shot outdoors, half a mile up, in the sky over Santa Monica Airport. Barbra as Fanny was persuaded to fly in a 1937 open-cockpit, double-seater plane, while lip-synching "Let's Hear It For Me." She objected at first. The number could be done just as well in the studio in a mock plane set against a process shot. But Ray Stark had rented a plane and a pilot, and as Barbra was already shooting scenes at the airport in Santa Monica, why not take one short five-minute spin? "It would look authentic," Stark told her. "And think of the adventure," the director, Herb Ross, added. And so the game lady took off. "The scene was shot rather quickly," said a unit publicist, "but coming down they got caught in sky traffic. The pilot had to circle the airport for thirty minutes. Then they got caught in headwinds, and as the fragile plane bounced around, Barbra, now nauseous, could see Ray Stark on the ground, propped against a truck, calmly smoking a cigar. She began yelling and cursing at him, and Stark kept smiling and waving back."

Fortunately her relationship with her costar, James Caan, was more harmonious. Originally candidates under six feet—Robert De Niro, Dustin Hoffman, and Robert Blake—were considered for the part of theatrical impresario Billy Rose. Barbra wanted a tall, handsome leading man, and Caan was a good friend of her ex-husband Elliott Gould. He was also a fellow New Yorker. "We're very compatible," said Streisand. "We both talk very fast and understand each other." "She's a terrific, sweet girl," said Caan. "People in Hollywood don't really know her."

Caan lived a few hills over from Barbra, and on her way to work each morning she began to drop by his house to chat with his mother, Sophie, who was visiting from Sunnyside, New York. Also at the house was Fred Fowler, who had not seen Streisand since their phrenology-head encounter at the Plaza a few years before. Fowler was a friend of Caan's secretary, Ronnie. "One night we went out and really tied one on," he said. "The following morning I was crawling down the back stairs when I heard voices in the kitchen. One belonged to Jimmy's mother, Sophie, and the other I recognized as Barbra. The two of them were sitting in the kitchen nook, reading the racing forms, picking out horses for that day's race."

When Caan's sister came to visit, with two small daughters who were close to Jason's age, Barbra began to leave her son at the house to play and swim in the pool. "Talk about *Le Petit Prince,*" said Fowler. "He was a little terror. The first day at lunch Ronnie asked, 'What do you kids want to eat? Peanut-butter sandwiches or what?' And Jason said, 'I'll have peanut butter on toast, not too brown, not too light, with all the edges trimmed off, sliced and triangled.' And Ronnie replied, 'You'll get it the way *I* make it or you won't get anything.' "

Another day while Fred and Ronnie were on the job, practicing pool in the living room, they heard the two little girls screaming outside. "Ronnie and I ran outside, and there was Jason, standing on one of the steps of the pool, with his bathing suit pulled down, and his little ding-dong exposed to the girls. Well, Ronnie grabbed him, smacked him on the bottom, and told him, 'You don't do that in front of little girls!' "

Later that same night when Streisand arrived to pick up Jason, Caan's secretary asked to have a word with her. "He told her what happened," said Fred. "Barbra stood there looking at him and listening, then she shook her head and said, 'Well—do you happen to know of any seven-year-old hookers?' "

Toward the end of filming a request came from the staff of a Very Prominent Person who desired to visit the *Funny Lady* set and meet Barbra. The VPP was Prince Charles of Britain, who was visiting Los Angeles while on naval duty, and when asked what Hollywood star he would most like to meet, he deliberated. "I'm sure they thought I'd say Raquel Welch," he told his valet, Stephen Barry, "but I said Barbra Streisand. I wanted to meet the woman behind the voice."

Barbra, when told of the request, said, "Huh? What for?"

"She got very nervous," said a publicist. "Everyone else at Columbia, Ray Stark and the studio heads, were very honored and ready to avail themselves of the publicity, but Barbra was tormented. 'What'll I say to him? What will we talk about? I am real lousy meeting royalty,' she said. We told her to just be herself, and that made it twice as bad. 'Yeah, yeah, be myself,' she groaned. 'He'll never buy another record.' "

The meeting was arranged on a Columbia soundstage where Streisand was dubbing dialogue. The singer and the future King of England shook hands, drank some coffee, and made small talk. It was very informal, very relaxed and private, except for the two hundred reporters, photographers, studio chiefs, and crew, who stood behind a yellow rope twenty feet away. "I think I caught her on a bad day," the Prince told his valet that night. "She had very little time and appeared very busy."

At a party on the last day of shooting Ray Stark praised Jon Peters to reporters. "He got her to work on time. He said to her, 'Look, you're in business. I'm in business. We have to be on time.' And sometimes it worked." For a parting gift, for this their final movie, Barbra gave Stark an antique mirror. Across its face she wrote in lipstick PAID IN FULL.

James Caan's gift to Streisand had also been carefully chosen. "He wanted something special for Barbra," said Fred Fowler, "so he sent Ronnie and me out to buy something. 'Spend up to three thousand dollars,' he told us. We got her this beautiful jade pendant and on the day of the party, he gave the gift to Barbra."

That night Caan came home, shouting at the top of his lungs. "He came into the kitchen and threw this package on the counter. 'That bitch,' he said, 'that cheap bitch.' Her gift to him was two record albums—the soundtrack of *The Way We Were* and the one with the vocals. With it she enclosed a note that said, *Lovely working with you, Babs.* Jimmy was furious, but at the same time he was laughing. He said he told her he wanted his gift back, but she wouldn't part with it."

> *"My youth was about getting laid and big tits and all those physical attributes of women. I learned about real women from Barbra. I learned about power."*
>
> **Jon Peters**

BUTTERFLY

By the summer of 1974 Barbra and Jon had been together for almost a year and their relationship was now considered "serious" by Hollywood standards. They were seeing the same psychoanalyst, and Barbra had forsaken her *"tsatskes"* and art treasures in Holmby Hills to rough it with Jon on the ranch in Malibu. "Jon put Barbra more in touch with the mainstream of life," said one columnist. "He said to her, 'Hey, baby, this is what happens— people take drugs and this is what drugs are like. People get it on and this is what that's like.' I'm sure Barbra did her little experiments—nothing drastic, of course, because she's too smart for that —and Jon, by telling her she could be loose and still be great and powerful, made himself indispensable to her."

Peters at the same time advanced himself further into Streisand's career. When CBS Records in New York inquired about her recording plans, she told the label that Jon was creating, producing, and designing her next album.

"Peters knew diddley-squat about producing an album," said a musician. "When Barbra told him she had to record an album for CBS he said, 'Good luck and good-bye.' He was off to Acapulco or Hong Kong. He had too much energy to hang around watching her sing and overdub. Then Barbra got upset. She needed him *there.* So she said to him, 'How about if you design the album cover?' And Jon replied, 'How about if I produce the whole thing?' And she agreed."

"Do they think I would let Jon produce a record if I wasn't absolutely sure he could do it?" said Barbra. "I believe in instinct. I believe in imagination. I believe in taste. These are the important ingredients, and they're all the things he has."

Among the songs Jon Peters chose for their first recording session were "You Light Up My Life," "Everything Must Change," and a ditty called "Type Thang." On a second date they recorded "There Won't Be Trumpets" and "God Bless The Child." But none of these songs would ever reach the public.

"They were atrocious," said a West Coast engineer. "We got the tapes to make a dub for New York and no one believed that Barbra could sound so bad. It was as if she were singing off key in a garage somewhere."

"What I recall wasn't good," said Bruce Lundvall, the new president of CBS Records. "So I asked Charles Koppelman, who was head of our A&R department, to look into the matter." Koppelman assigned Gary Klein, a young and talented staff producer, to go to L.A. and talk with Jon and Barbra. That was a difficult task,

the producer admitted. With Peters by her side Klein had to criti-
cize their work, cut by cut. "I was very specific about what I
thought was wrong with it, and they knew that I knew what I was
talking about, so I gained their respect."

Kathy Kasper, a professional music contractor, was brought in
to rescore some songs; Al Schmitt, a skillful engineer, was hired to
remix the sessions. After three days Schmitt quit, claiming that Jon
Peters wanted all the credit and money, while he was doing all the
work.

"Obviously he was upset because Jon was going to be on the
gravy train," Charles Koppelman told Joyce Haber. "Schmitt told
Peters, 'I've been in this business twenty-five years, and you've
been in it twenty-five minutes.' It just sometimes happens that
twenty-five minutes produces genius," said Koppelman. "The album is not only one of the best; it'll be one of the biggest Barbra's
ever made."

In July, while the new sessions were being arranged and conducted
by writer-producer Tom Scott, the packaging for the album was
being created by Jon. The title came from their courtship. When
they'd first met, Jon had told Barbra she reminded him of a butterfly—which happened to be her favorite insect. He also gifted her
with a hundred-year-old pendant, in the shape of a butterfly. Thus
the title of the LP: *Butterfly*.

Peters then commissioned an artist to paint a portrait of his
ladylove, looking serenely heavenward, while the strands of her
golden hair were being held aloft by a thousand butterflies. "We
gagged when we saw the painting," said a former CBS designer.
"But everyone said, 'Great cover, Jon.' Then he pointed out that
this was *not* the cover—it was for the back of the album. The *real*
fun began when he explained his concept for the cover."

"*Butter—fly*—you get it," Jon explained patiently. "I want to
show a stick of butter, and a fly perched on the edge. That's the
cover. No photos of Barbra—no last name—just her first name, the
title, the fly, and the butter. And it has to be *sweet* butter. Salt is a
no-no."

To effect the concept top advertising photographer Carl Furuta
was hired. He met with Jon and Barbra in Malibu. "I went out to
the house and they explained the idea to me. It was a cut-and-dried
situation. There was no problem. She was real nice; I enjoyed the

visit, except for this pet lion, who was running around the living room, jumping up on everyone."

In the studio the bulk of Furuta's time and energy was spent in getting the proper fly. "It had to be a dead fly," he explained, "so we had to go to a garbage can and put a bag over a fly and let him suffocate to death. Then you had to spread out his wings and his feet with a tweezers. We went through a *lot* of flies. And maybe the butter melted under the lights. But to me it was just another job."

"Barbra takes you on the floating wings of song, as only she can," the full-page ads proclaimed as they featured Jon Peters as producer. And if the sweeping eye missed the credit, Jon was shown in twenty of thirty photos, with Barbra sitting in his lap, in the album's inner spread.

Columnists, disc jockeys, and industry executives mocked and ridiculed the Svengali-like production, but a few critics were kind. In a review for *The New York Times,* this writer found her vocals "softer, more human; clear and shining." Lester Bangs in *The Village Voice* said the album "ain't half bad." Singling out Barbra's feverish rendition of "Guava Jelly," he added, "Streisand was not born to sing reggae, even if she is feeling horny these days."

Butterfly rose to number thirteen on *Billboard*'s charts and was certified gold in January of 1975. At a presentation ceremony in New York that March, Jon Peters accepted a special gold record for producing the album. Holding the award he posed for photographs with Bruce Lundvall, Irwin Siegelstein (the president of the CBS Group), A&R head Charles Koppelman, and Gary Klein, who salvaged the project. When asked about his next professional collaboration with Streisand, Peters aggressively replied: "I've had it with producing records. I made my mark. Barbra and I are now going on to bigger stuff, like doing big concerts and movies."

Chapter 24

Barbra Streisand: *"It's a drag, a real pain. I can't go to a supermarket to buy a loaf of bread without someone bothering me. It's very difficult for me to even shop for food."*

Arthur Bell: *"Well . . . couldn't you call up and have the stuff delivered?"*

An Interview for The Village Voice, 1975

FUNNY LADY: THE GRAND TOUR

No! She was *not* moving. She was adamant about this. Since the completion of *Funny Lady* eight months earlier, Barbra was on sabbatical. She had made five movies in four years —plus a TV special and seven albums. She needed a break. She was happy loafing, hanging out at Jon's ranch, planting flowers, making meals, being a housewife. "I played all the roles he expected of me," she said. "I did the laundry, the cooking, and baked bread."

Jon Peters, however, was not as inclined toward leisure. While continuing to oversee the operation of his beauty empire, he was still hustling to produce a movie. He had become good buddies with producer Ray Stark, who owed him one for getting Barbra to the set on time. Stark and Peters were now going to do a picture together—*Suppose They Met?*, the story of a millionaire male chauvinist and a women's-lib leader. Jon was angling for Steve Mc-Queen and, of course, Barbra. The script was in development and Stark had other collaborative ideas—but first, he needed another favor. *Funny Lady* was ready to open in March, and Ray wanted Barbra to publicize it. Nothing much—just hit a few cities, do a few interviews. Maybe Jon could put in a good word? "No!" said Barbra emphatically. "No publicity, no premieres. Stark got his pound of flesh. I'm retired. I'm not moving."

"Selfish bitch!" Jon yelled back. "So we go to a few parties. You do a few interviews. It helps *me*. It helps *us*."

"I don't care. I won't do it."

"You will."

"I won't!"

"You will! Come here. *Now!*

"Oh, Jon."

WASHINGTON

On Sunday evening, March ninth, the world premiere of *Funny Lady* was held at the Eisenhower Theater at Kennedy Center with President Ford, daughter Susan, and other Washington politicos attending. The evening was described by *The Washington Post* as "the most cleverly engineered movie plug in history."

It was supposed to be a benefit for the Special Olympics, headed by Eunice Shriver. Barbra was a Kennedy advocate from way back, and she agreed to meet the clan that weekend, including Teddy and matriarch Rose (whom Barbra had cut in on at a dance at the Iranian embassy the night before).

What Streisand didn't agree to was to perform, onstage, at the premiere. Ray Stark, it seemed, had arranged with ABC-TV to televise the proceedings. It was to be a special—entitled *From Funny Girl to Funny Lady*—and interspersed with it would be live footage of the opening in Washington. Special Olympics medals would be presented onstage to various youngsters, and Barbra would be getting one too. Then it was suggested that while she was up there, and the guests were paying a hundred dollars per seat, why not give them a song or two?

"They told her this the day of the premiere," said a publicist, "and Barbra just smiled and said, 'Gee, I'd love to, but I don't have my music with me.' Then Stark or Jon Peters replied, 'Your *music?* You mean you don't know the words to "People" by now?' "

"There was a champagne party in the foyer before the show,"

said Michael Homa, a Streisand fan, "and Barbra was supposed to attend. She was the main attraction for selling the tickets. But while everyone was milling about the lobby, she was upstairs rehearsing. She put the orchestra through hours of rehearsal for two or three songs. They gave everyone the story that things were running late because her music went on to New York. She kept rehearsing until minutes before the live show went on. And when everyone found out she was inside singing, they left the lobby and went into the theater. So when President Ford arrived, there was no one there to greet him. They asked everyone to go out and shake his hand for the TV cameras, but who needed that? The fans wanted Barbra."

Introduced by Dick Cavett, Streisand came onstage to a standing ovation. She sang a medley, a duet of "It's Only A Paper Moon" with James Caan, and she spoke to the audience. A staunch Democrat, she congratulated the largely Republican crowd: "I thought you'd be real stuffy, you Washington people—but you're not."

At the party afterward Barbra, Jon, the Starks, and Columbia Pictures chairman Leo Jaffe sat in a corner surrounded by bodyguards. "They don't work the crowd the way we do," said House Minority Leader John Rhodes. "At first I thought they didn't give a damn, and then I thought, 'Well, maybe they don't know what to do.' "

"No one got near Streisand," said Michael Homa. "I tried to get some pictures of her, but the bodyguards weren't letting anyone near her. Then Barbara Walters took my camera and started snapping pictures of everyone. She was fantastic. There were other celebrities there doing gymnastics, and Walters took off her high heels and did somersaults in her evening gown. That lady really knew how to have a good time."

NEW YORK

The morning after the Washington premiere Barbra and Jon traveled to New York by train. Writer Chris Chase was sitting in the parlor car when the couple made their entrance. "I looked up and saw this pair. The woman was wearing a yellow fox coat and hat and I thought *My God, that's Barbra Streisand.* What they were doing on a train, I could not imagine. But they looked around and she seemed to be *stunned* to see other people there. Maybe she thought it was going to be a private car or something—but then they *vanished*. They were there one minute, and the next they were gone. It seemed so strange."

At noon on Tuesday a luncheon for the New York media was held at the Hotel Pierre. Attending was *Village Voice* reporter and columnist Arthur Bell. Arthur had been a Streisand fan from the early sixties. "I saw her at the Bon Soir night after night. I loved her voice, her hair, her little sailor-suit. She was like Ella Cinders. She was also extremely cute and Jewish and Brooklyn. I loved that too. She mopped up in *Wholesale*. She was sensational in *Funny Girl*. I played her records all the time, the early ones. I still do. As a singer there is really no one *close* to Barbra."

In person, at the luncheon, Arthur lost some of his ardor for his favorite. "She started to complain how hard it was for a star of her stature to go to a supermarket without having people bothering her. 'They're always coming over and asking me for things,' she whined. I could see right off she was playing Little Girl Lost. It was really phony. She was pretending that all she wanted to be was one of the crowd, and extremely humble. I remember firing away questions at her, and she didn't like it. 'Couldn't you wear glasses or something?' I asked. 'It's very hard for me,' she said. I didn't like that. Had she been a *mensch,* she would have come into the press luncheon and sat down and talked about the movie, like a normal superstar.

"Then that night I went to the premiere in Times Square, and she was literally mobbed. They had fifty policemen and bodyguards on the street trying to get her from her limo into the theater. And I got a look at her face. She looked scared; *but* she was also reveling in it. She was playing both sides of the fence. 'Oh, I'm so frightened; I'm scared. Why do I have to do this?'—but she was also *thrilled.*"

The New York evening was also for charity, a benefit for the Hospital for Special Surgery. Tickets were two hundred dollars, and for that the guests wanted their money's worth. Society columnist Suzy reported: "As the fans stampeded Barbra (maybe they were after her fur shako), the guests stampeded the food." "It was an incredibly dreadful cocktail buffet, at which several hundred guests converged like hungry vultures on the food and drinks," said Eugenia Sheppard.

At midnight, after the movie, a more civilized sit-down supper was given at El Morocco. Ray and Fran Stark—dressed "in a sexy waterfall of gold beads"—received the guests. Barbra arrived in a new outfit—a silver fox jacket, a Jean Muir burgundy jersey dress with matching turban ("Did she change in the car?" one guest asked), and Jon Peters wore a tuxedo, no tie, and sunglasses.

"Barbra sat in a corner banquette surrounded by her entourage," Suzy wrote, "and kept saying that she wished they'd stop playing Barbra Streisand records on the hi-fi. 'I don't even do that at home,' quoth our superstar."

Then someone spilled a glass of water on Barbra. "But she was adorable about it. Besides, when she leaped up to dry herself off with a napkin, it gave everyone a chance to see what she was wearing."

LONDON

For the next stop of the *Funny Lady* tour Barbra and Jon had a choice. They could go back to L.A. (where two gold-sprayed elephants and five thousand helium balloons were on hand for the hoopla) or they could cross the ocean to London for the Royal Film Performance. Jon opted for London. He'd been to L.A., and furthermore he wanted to meet the Queen.

"She caused a stink, an absolute stink," said Pamela Gorman, who was at the London opening. "Everything had been arranged. Ray Stark and the Columbia staff were the best at details and precision. They orchestrated everything with Buckingham Palace and the theater. The evening was planned to perfection, until Barbra caused trouble.

"Queen Elizabeth and Prince Philip arrived, saw the film, then moved backstage to greet the performers. Well, Barbra had arrived earlier, looking breathtakingly beautiful in a velvet cape and hood, but as she listened to the protocol instructions for the presentation she turned sour. There was to be a front line of people to be presented to the Queen including James Stewart, Lee Remick, James Caan, and Barbra. In a second row, cordoned off with a red rope, were the wives, husbands, and lovers—including Jon Peters. Barbra got in a snit over that. She wanted Jon in the front row by her side. The Queen *had* to meet him, she said. But that couldn't be. Unless you were in the show, or directly connected, you were supposed to be in the second row. Barbra didn't like that one bit, and just to be contrary, she subjected the Queen to that terrible question.

" 'Your Majesty,' said Barbra, 'why do women have to wear gloves and the men don't?'

"The Queen, startled, replied: 'Well, I don't really know. It's just tradition, I suppose.'

"Turning around to Jon in row two, Barbra said aloud: 'Well, I guess I still don't know.' "

Chapter 25

"I was watching Marvin Hamlisch on television, playing the piano for Ethel Merman. And I'm thinking to myself, and I said to Jon: 'Boy! Look at that Marvin Hamlisch. That kid played for me in the pit during Funny Girl. And look at him now. He's playing for Ethel Merman.' And Jon said to me: 'Who's Ethel Merman?'"

Barbra Streisand, 1975

LAZY AFTERNOON

Even though the soundtrack album of *Funny Lady* sold close to a million copies (and the movie grossed $40 million), CBS Records did not partake of the windfall. The LP rights had gone to another label, Arista Records (under the helm of ousted CBS chief Clive Davis). That summer, however, Barbra began recording a new Columbia LP entitled *Lazy Afternoon*, coproduced, composed, and arranged, and conducted by Rupert Holmes. A thin, bearded, bespectacled writer and singer of cinema-inspired songs, Holmes had a recent album on CBS called *Widescreen*. It was a limited success, yet one copy found its way onto the turntable of Streisand's twenty-five-thousand-dollar stereo system in Malibu. She loved the sweep of the melodies and found the lyrics compelling; so she asked to meet the singer-songwriter-producer.

"The greatest thrill that I've ever experienced," said Holmes, "was the day I went to her home and she put the *Widescreen* album on. She sang most of the tunes, and she didn't have lyrics in front of her—she had memorized them. I couldn't believe it."

When Barbra asked Rupert to stay in California and work on her new album, he was hesitant. He was a New Yorker, he didn't drive, and he hated living in hotels. "She took care of everything," he said. "She put me up in her Beverly Hills house for six months. She was my chauffeur. She drove me to the recording studio, to the ranch in Malibu where I stayed in her guesthouse. It was a wonderful time."

The *Lazy Afternoon* LP was recorded in only three sessions, Holmes told an interviewer, neglecting to add that those sessions were spread over a three-month period.

The first session was at Capitol Studios on April eleventh.

"Rupert could not believe the reality of the situation," said Normand Kurtz, his lawyer and partner. "Here he was, this young kid. He arranged for the forty-piece orchestra. And on the first day, when he got there, Barbra went over to him and said, 'Before we start I want you to have this.' It was a note and a gift. The note said, 'I love you, You're the best. Barbra.'"

Barbra's relations with the CBS Records executive staff also went through some benign changes during this period. The previous year she had become friends with product manager Tony Lawrence, her liaison with the company. "There was a problem on her last album, *Butterfly,*" Lawrence recalled. "The cover was supposed to be peach colored and it turned out white. She hit the ceiling. I was recommended to deal with her. I had been told how tough she could be, but I was willing to give the job my best shot. Jon called me and asked if I could straighten things out with her. I said that I'd try. He told me to call Barbra at the ranch and arrange an appointment. I called her and went out there and said, 'What's wrong? My job is to make it right. So tell me.' And she showed me the album. We went over it carefully; she showed me the changes she wanted. I took it back to the Art Department and they reproofed it. I showed it to her again. It was as she requested. She was happy, and that was the beginning of a very good relationship for both of us."

There was no trick or secret formula in working with Streisand, he claimed. "I was myself. I never catered to her. If I didn't know what she wanted, I asked her to explain it. I also was not in awe of her. I had been raised in show business. My father was an actor and announcer. I had been around stars all my life. I didn't want to

◄ 266 ►

be a fan of Barbra or ask her for her autograph. I didn't want to be her best friend. If we got along, that was the icing on the cake. And I was lucky, I got more than the icing. We had a lot of lunches, at the ranch and on Carolwood Drive. We went shopping to a nursery. We'd talk and listen to music. I brought her new Columbia releases that I thought she'd like—albums by Billy Joel and Dan Fogelberg, who hadn't broken loose yet. I played her Billy Joel's 'Piano Man' in her living room. She was busy doing things, but she listened and we talked. The same with Dan Fogelberg. She listened to his music, and said, 'Uh-huh.' It didn't lead to anything; she didn't go, 'Hey, where can I get that song?' And Rupert Holmes. He didn't come from me, but she put a lot of work into the *Lazy Afternoon* album. She picked most of the material, and she wrote the liner notes herself. And that was a big deal. She went over every line. She was very funny about it too. 'Should we put a colon or a semicolon here?' She was indecisive about everything. Where a plant or a pot of flowers should be placed. She was always busy. Busy and very quick witted. She appreciated the absurdity of things. Sometimes she could laugh at herself, and be very self-deprecating—about her music, about her life, about her son, and her point of view about everything."

Photographer Steve Schapiro shot the *Lazy Afternoon* cover under the same relaxed circumstances. "I went out to the ranch. She already had the clothes picked—the gypsy dress and headscarf—with no shoes. We shot indoors with afternoon light. We did the session in twenty minutes."

"There was a funny incident with the cover," said Tony Lawrence. "We were on a deadline because CBS wanted to present the album at their convention. We were both caught for time, so I arranged to meet Barbra halfway between L.A. and Malibu, in a supermarket parking lot. Well she couldn't make it and she tried to reach me. She didn't want to stand me up. She somehow got ahold of my mother's house, where I was not living, but she called, maybe thinking I was there. My mother tells the story to this day. She answered the phone: 'Hello, who is this?' 'This is Barbra.' 'Barbra?' 'Yes, Barbra Streisand.' 'Oh, hi, Barbra.' My mother was unruffled because she knew we were working together."

To publicize *Lazy Afternoon* and the release of the first single from the LP, Barbra was asked to make a rare TV appearance with

Johnny Carson on *The Tonight Show*. She agreed to appear only if Johnny were hosting, and if she could rehearse her two songs with a full orchestra the afternoon of the show. Furthermore, she had to check the lighting; she was to be the first guest; and she would talk to Johnny *after* her second song. Then immediately following their chat, they would segue to a commercial, but when the show came back she would be gone.

Carson agreed to all her requests. After all, this would be Streisand's first talk-show appearance in twelve years. NBC were also thrilled, and they hastened to solicit more lucrative sponsors, and to arrange saturation advertising and publicity. On the afternoon of July ninth, with the full orchestra standing by for the rehearsal, the call came in from Streisand's secretary. Barbra would not be appearing. "No explanation or excuse was given," an NBC spokesman informed the press.

The following night Carson announced to his audience that due to unforseen circumstances, Barbra had not shown the previous evening. But she was indeed there tonight, and ready to perform. The audience went berserk, screaming and applauding, and as the curtains parted, there she was. She stood perfectly still, holding a hand microphone, her famous profile lifted slightly at the proper angle to the left camera. The orchestra began and she started to sing the familiar lines "Pee-*pull!* . . . Peepull who need pee*pull,*" when Carson got up from his desk shouting, "No! No! Off! Off! You're terrible."

The band stopped; everyone was shocked, and Carson began to laugh as Barbra tore off her wig. Then the audience got the joke. It was not Barbra Streisand. It was a female impersonator. Johnny, like Barbra, was clearly not a host to cross; nor one to forget.

"Once you finish a book you can look forward to it being published. Once you finish a movie script, the ---- starts."

John Gregory Dunne

"This movie, I gotta tell you, was the worst thing I've been through since Ranger school. I thought it was going to be the one regret I'd carry with me to the grave. I think that in the back of my mind, I

knew it would either be something real good or we'd end up killing each other."

Kris Kristofferson

A STAR IS BORN

In his book *Quintana and Friends,* John Gregory Dunne recalled the exact time and place when *A Star Is Born* number four was conceived. It was eleven-thirty P.M. on July 1, 1973, and he and his wife, novelist Joan Didion, were passing the Aloha Tower in downtown Honolulu on their way to the airport. He turned to his wife and said sixteen words: "James Taylor and Carly Simon in a rock 'n' roll version of *A Star Is Born.*"

Dunne later claimed he had never seen any of the other versions of *A Star Is Born,* but he knew the premise—one star rises while the other falls. And he and Didion were mainly interested in a movie about the rock 'n' roll business. That's where the big money was, and if they somehow got the conventional theme to fit, the profits could be enormous.

In six months the Dunnes had a first script; a producer, John Foreman; a studio, Warner Bros. (who owned the original movie); a director, Jerry Schatzberg; and a musical consultant, Richard Perry.

Perry was the one who had converted Barbra to rock 'n' roll. He'd produced three albums for her and was a close friend, so the natural progression of events would have him giving the script to Barbra. But no. After Carly Simon and James Taylor passed on the story as being too close to their own situation, other star couples were considered. Among them were Liza Minnelli and Elvis Presley; Mick and Bianca Jagger; and Sonny and Cher Bono.

But then the script passed to Barbra Streisand and the course and control of the project changed considerably. *"I* discovered this project for Barbra," said Jon Peters. "I was the one who found it for her and convinced her to do it." Barbra needed a change "from playing Ray Stark's mother-in-law," Jon felt. He wanted the world to see her as the young, warm, sexy, open, soft woman he knew.

— Barbra did not want the world to see her at all. She was quite content to play Garbo in the valley. But Jon persisted. This was the story of *their* life, he told Barbra, of two people trapped by their money and success. They meet and fall in love and together they rise above the hype and the hucksters in show business. The leading male character, like Jon, learns how to trade "macho" for "feelings." The woman learns how to trust and really *love* someone. And together they live in joy and harmony, up until the last ten minutes of the movie when he has an accident and dies. *"No* suicide," said Jon, referring to the original ending. "Suicide is a downer. No guy with real balls would walk out on the woman he loves by taking his life."

When Streisand agreed to do *A Star Is Born*, Peters proposed a long list of changes to Joan Didion and John Gregory Dunne. The writers exited shortly thereafter (with two hundred thousand dollars and ten percent of the net), followed by the producer and the director. No sweat, Jon told Warner Bros., he would produce, and direct, and *costar* with Barbra in the picture. "That was a joke," Jon said later. "Barbra and I were kidding around at home reading the script, and I said, 'Hey! I can do this part. I got the looks and the energy.' And Barbra said, 'You can do *anything,* Jon.' And somehow that got picked up by some shmuck who printed it.

"Listen," Peters told another reporter, "if the president of General Motors were asked to appear in a picture with Barbra Streisand, he'd jump at the chance. So why shouldn't I?"

Other leading men were sought. Barbra wanted Marlon Brando, who had not done a musical since *Guys and Dolls.* "He was here!" Jon exclaimed. "He was cute! The son of a bitch, he wanted to screw Barbra—I was ready to kill him! I take him off and I kiss him! He's beautiful!"

Brando was not into singing rock music, however, and the next choice was Elvis Presley, a singer Barbra never liked as a kid. "I preferred to listen to Johnny Mathis," she said. As a grown-up she was still not a fan, and vice versa, it seemed. Elvis knew Barbra, slightly. In 1969 she had preceded him in Las Vegas with her nightclub act at the International Hotel. Elvis slipped in one night to watch her. He noticed the half-empty room and made faces when Barbra used her Yiddish expressions. When her act was over, he turned to his bodyguard, Lamar Fike, and said, "She sucks."

By 1975 Elvis was still the number one attraction in Las Vegas, but he was fat, his voice was shot, and he had not made a movie in eight years. All of that worked in his favor, Jon Peters said, when he and Barbra met with the singer in his hotel suite that summer.

The guy in their movie was a wreck, on the skids, said Jon. But it was a *great* part, he hastily added. Two of the actors who had played the role before were nominated for an Academy Award. Now Elvis could get the Oscar he deserved. "This could be a whole rebirth for you," Barbra told the King of Rock 'n' Roll.

"Elvis listened," said his associate Bob Denney. "Elvis was a gentleman, through and through. He was also fascinated with Streisand. 'She's a star, a big movie star. What's she got?' He kept trying to figure it out. And the Peters guy, he kept shoveling it on. They tried to make his part sound like the Second Coming. Elvis would get the best lines, the best songs; they'd shoot the movie in Vegas or Memphis, wherever he was comfortable."

Elvis was not persuaded. It was *her* movie. In his film career he let only one female take over his show: that was Ann-Margret, in *Viva Las Vegas*. That was okay; she was a friend, a good friend (and the only star to show at his funeral). "Elvis kind of knew he wouldn't be making another movie," said Denney, "and he didn't want his fans to remember him for this one. When Peters and Barbra left he called George Parkhill and the Colonel and told them, 'No more talk about pictures.' " The final casting for the male role came down to Mick Jagger or Kris Kristofferson. Jon Peters suggested Jagger. In rock 'n' roll he was the bigger draw. But Mick, who was all strut and swagger, and who could spit bullets on stage, did not project that same force in his acting. "It didn't look right esthetically—me and him together," Streisand stated. She wanted Kris Kristofferson. "He's an actor. He's beautiful to look at. He can sing and play the guitar. And he's gentile, which seems to work with me—the Jew and the gentile."

With the leading man cast, Jon Peters turned his attention to directing. Warner Bros. was not convinced of his qualifications. "Directing is a thing I've done my whole life!" he yelled to journalist Marie Brenner. "It's getting people to do what I want them to do!"

Certainly he had Barbra's vote. She campaigned for him, calling up her old friends, Herb Ross and Sydney Pollack, hoping they would give him some pointers. Another director solicited was Robert Altman.

Altman had directed Elliott Gould in *M*A*S*H*, and again in *The Long Goodbye*. Barbra took son Jason to see his dad in a private screening of *The Long Goodbye*. After one particularly violent scene in which one of the actors broke a bottle in a girl's face, Barbra grabbed Jason and swept him out of the room. She sent a note to Altman, explaining the circumstances, and she was forgiven.

In June of 1975 Altman invited Barbra to another of his films, to a preview of *Nashville*. She arrived with Jon, and immediately after the movie she began pitching him to Altman. "She never mentioned the film," Altman later complained to Sally Quinn. "She just wanted to talk about *her*. I said, 'You're a rude bitch; get out of my office. You're only here for a reason—to take something.' "

While Warner Bros. continued to balk at having Jon Peters produce and direct *A Star Is Born,* a new writer—number seven—was asked to come in and punch up the script. Frank Pierson, a former *Life* reporter, had written the scripts for *The Anderson Tapes* and *Dog Day Afternoon*. He had also directed a passable film called *The Looking Glass War,* and "in a moment of mad ambition" he told Warner's that he would work on the *Star Is Born* dialogue, but only if he could direct. Warner's said that was Barbra's decision, and to their surprise, she agreed. "It was the perfect solution to all their problems," said an agent. "Jon got himself another writer, and Barbra got a director *she* could direct." "I need you as a buffer between me and Jon," she told him. "I couldn't really let him direct. Can you imagine Jon Peters directing?" "How could I direct her," Peters asked separately, "and keep our relationship? I had to decide which was more important, our love or the movie. You and Barbra make the picture. I'm here to expedite. You need something; I'll kick ass to get it."

Rewriting the script, Pierson received constant input from Barbra, who changed the name of her character from Esther McQueen to Esther Hoffman ("I don't look like Steve McQueen's sister," she explained, "so I took the name of another friend, Dustin Hoffman"); and from Jon Peters, who was anxious to bare the intimate details of life with Barbra—on how they loved, fought, and made up. "The lines go in, and come out again when Barbra objects to their public laundering," said Pierson.

Musicians, songwriters, soundmen, a set designer, and a cinematographer, Robert Surtees, were hired. Surtees had photographed some of MGM's most beautiful women: Ava Gardner, Grace

Kelly, Liz Taylor, and Deborah Kerr. His age—seventy-two. "He's old," said Barbra. "We should have someone young on this picture. What does he know about backlighting?"*

In November, Jon and Barbra went to New York to attend the Ali-Frazier fight. Wearing matching black Stetsons, gold and jade bracelets, and jeans, they arrived at Madison Square Garden and found their seats taken. The occupants refused to move, and one of them heckled Barbra. This being her hometown, and being a lady, she told the gentleman to go fuck himself. "Pow!" said Peters, "I let him have it. He's gonna hit my woman. I go crazy! They're pullin' me off him."

Rolling Stone saw the brawl from another angle. Putting up his dukes, Jon Peters broke his wrist, they said. Not accurate, said Barbra; that had happened at home. "Jon got so mad at something I said, he put his fist through a closet door. I'm so afraid he's going to hurt himself."

By mid-December, away from distractions, Frank Pierson finished the script of *A Star Is Born* and sent the pages (colored pink —to set it apart from the previous blue, green, and yellow rewrites) to Barbara's Place, a typing and duplicating office on Sunset Boulevard. Streisand read the script and invited the director to lunch— serving lobster soufflé, his favorite dish. She had to be guided in this picture, she told him, but not bullied. "Ray Stark always used to bully me, the son of a bitch. I made him, and he made millions from me, millions!"

---

* In 1979, for an article on cinematographers for *The New York Times,* this reporter asked Surtees how he had made Streisand look so good in *A Star Is Born.* "I treat all actresses like the woman I love," he replied. "I highlight their best features and keep the bad ones in the dark. Barbra is cross eyed in one eye, so you have to put a shadow near her nose to minimize that."

Chapter 26

BUT FIRST—A LITTLE CULTURE

In January of 1976, when CBS Records learned that their star female vocalist would be devoting most of the coming year to acting in, scoring, and editing *A Star Is Born* without giving them any new product, they reluctantly agreed to release the album of classical songs she had recorded two years ago.

Producer Wally Gold claimed it was he who gave Barbra the idea for the album. "Barbra was always stretching, wanting to do different things, and when she mentioned the desire to do an album of lieder, I encouraged her. I introduced her to Claus Ogerman, who did the arrangements. I said to Barbra, 'You got to include a lyric sheet in the album. That way people can follow the words, and you can call the album *Follow the Lieder.*' "

Claus Ogerman had previously produced Connie Francis, and he had worked on some arrangements for Barbra's *Stoney End* album. In the early 1970s he quit the music business and bought a castle and farm in Germany. He would not come back, he said, unless he had an interesting project. When Barbra suggested the idea of her classical album, he agreed to do it, if he owned the copyright to some of the songs. She agreed.

The album, as stated previously, was recorded in Los Angeles in the spring of 1973. The tapes were then shelved, though from time to time Barbra ordered copies for friends, who urged her to share this experience with her fans. She was willing, she claimed, but her record label had no confidence in the material.

"That is not true," said a CBS Records employee, "None of us heard the album for over a year because she wouldn't let go of the tapes."

"They were a mess," said a West Coast engineer. "Barbra was way out of her depth with this classical stuff, and she knew it. But, like her French album, she became obsessed with trying to prove she was right. She almost strangled herself with the mass of tracks she laid down."

To the rescue came Frank Laico, the master engineer in New York who had supervised the sound on her first seven albums. Frank had not seen or heard from Barbra since she relocated to Los Angeles in 1969. "No, let me correct that," said Frank. "In all fairness to the lady, I had been in a bad car accident in 1972, in a head-on collision, and she called. So did Marty. They said if there was anything I needed, to let them know. And for years after when anyone was coming to New York, she told them, 'Be sure and say hello to Frank.' I appreciated that."

The symphonic tracks, according to Frank, were laid down first in Los Angeles. "They were beautiful, because Claus is so talented. But Barbra had changed since she went to Los Angeles. She got very lazy, especially on this album. She'd come into the studio, put a wild track down over the orchestra, and fake it. Then she'd go on to something else, come back, and overdub again at a different studio. She eventually overdubbed herself at nine different studios in L.A. There wasn't anything left on the twenty-four tracks, she had them all. Her voice was on everything. Claus didn't know where to begin to edit. He called me in New York and said, 'Hi, I'm coming in; I've got a truckload of Barbra.' I asked him why he was bringing the stuff to me. He said Barbra suggested I mix the album. And I said, 'Gee, thanks a whole lot.'"

There were over two dozen reels of tape carried into the studio, Frank recalled. "We did it at Thirtieth Street. We took those two dozen reels down to fourteen or twelve. Then we began to go through them. Each song had about nine different versions, nine different vocals. Claus and I had to go through each one over and over again. We had to draw a map. We'd take a word, a phrase, from take two, then go on to the next bar, then onto the next take. It was done piece by piece, splice by splice. And the sound on the good ones we picked had to be equalized, because they had been done with different microphones and different engineers. We'd work three or four hours at a shift, then Claus would look at me and I'd look at him, and he'd say, 'Time?' And I'd say yes, and we'd go out to a bar on Second Avenue for a few drinks. I'm not a drinker, but boy we needed those breaks. The job went on for close to eight months. We spliced the entire album by hand. There wasn't a complete continuous Streisand vocal in the lot. I said to Claus, 'Now, mark my words, this lady is going to get the finished tape and she's going to forget the work that was involved. She's going to be convinced that this was *her* work, her original performance.' And I'm sure that was the case. I know I never heard a word from her about our contribution. But that's okay. She was never big on acknowledging what was finished. It was always on to the next thing. But I'll tell you, if they ever gave out awards that year for the Best Patch Job on an album, Claus and I would have won it hands down for *Classical Barbra*."*

To validate her entrée into the classical field, Barbra had Leonard Bernstein pen a few words on her proficiency with lieder. She also commissioned *Cosmopolitan* photographer Francesco Scavullo to shoot the cover. "She okayed the proofs for the cover while she was rehearsing for *A Star Is Born*," said Tony Lawrence. "I was about to leave the company for Warner Brothers when she called. She wanted some slight changes. I went to the sound stage where she was performing, and when she saw me she stopped. She came over and we began looking at proofs. There were photographers around, I guess, because about two months later, after I left CBS, a package came to me by special delivery at Warner Bros. I opened it and it was a picture of Barbra and me looking at the album cover. She enclosed a note that said, 'Dear Tony, Well, here we go again. Love, Barbra.' I'll never forget that. For her to take the time out, especially while filming, to do that. Well, what can I say?"

CBS Records had to be careful with the ad placements, and the reviewers, for *Classical Barbra*. They did not want the album as-

---

* On January 10, 1986, in a two-page statement, Claus Ogerman claimed that the classical album was mixed entirely—without overdubs or splicing—in Los Angeles. Frank Laico, when questioned on this, confirmed all of his original quotes. According to Laico, the remixing was done in New York, where his time was documented by his union; furthermore, he is credited on the album's inner sleeve as the final recording engineer.

sessed by pop critics. The solicitation was confined to serious publications such as *The New Yorker* and *The New York Times.* The reviews in turn were far from somber. *"Classical Barbra* is just about the most potent album I've heard since Margaret Truman hit upon opera as a way to express herself," said Don Heckscher of the *Times. Opera News* commented, "This record produces the strange but distinct impression of total lack of rapport between the singer and the rest of the orchestra." Joseph McLean of *The Washington Post* compared Streisand to Florence Foster Jenkins, "the New York lady with more money than talent, who used to hire Carnegie Hall for an annual song recital, which the critics would review in deadpan double entendres." And in defense, John Rockwell, in *Rolling Stone,* said, "It's not as bad as it could have been . . . this is an acceptable album."

But it was a fellow CBS recording artist who bolstered her pride and the blurbs for the ads. Classical piano virtuoso Glenn Gould opened his review in *Opera World* with "I'm a Streisand freak and make no bones about it. With the possible exception of Elisabeth Schwarzkopf, no vocalist brought me greater pleasure or more insight into the interpreter's art." Her voice, he claimed, was one of the natural wonders of the age, an instrument of infinite diversity and timbral resource. In popular music she could make the torchiest lyric an intimate memoir, "and it would never occur to her to employ the 'I'll meet you precisely fifty-one percent of the way' piquancy of say, Helen Reddy, much less the 'I won't bother to speak up because you're already spellbound, aren't you?' routine of Peggy Lee."

Classical Barbra sold well, "for its form," CBS Records stated. Streisand put the figure at two hundred thousand copies the first month. CBS put the figure at two hundred thousand in five years.

Chapter 27

THE FILMING OF *A STAR IS BORN*

Throughout January and February location scenes were filmed at a revamped nightclub in Pasadena, on the streets of L.A., and at Bernie Cornfeld's empty mansion in Beverly Hills. As Jon kicked ass, Pierson became exhausted, Barbra judgmental, and Kris Kristofferson managed to sail above everything by drinking tequila with beer chasers for breakfast each morning.

In an intimate bathtub scene, lit by a thousand tiny candles, Barbra slipped into the tub wearing a flesh-colored bathing suit and found Kris nude. "For God's sake, get him to put something on," she cried to her director. "If Jon finds out he's naked he'll kill him." But Kris was content to stay in the tub and play Pearl Harbor with his torpedo, and with Barbra. "He wound his legs around her, and got her all hot and bothered," a grip reported.

On another day the pair posed for publicity stills. These were taken by Scavullo in Malibu, with Jon Peters absent by request. For the first roll of film Barbra was static, not projecting. A break was called and while she was out of the room Kristofferson told the photographer of a recent *Playboy* session he had done with actress Sarah Miles. They'd posed nude, on top of one another, in bed, and when the steamy shots were featured in the magazine they almost broke up his marriage. But art was art, Kris insisted, and maybe that's what they needed to warm up Barbra. They should both strip and pose in the buff. "Then I could put a bag over her head and ---- her," the Rhodes scholar quipped. "I *heard* that," said Barbra, entering the room.

SCENES FROM LOCATION

The idea came from Jon Peters. He envisioned publicity—vast, global publicity—for the picture and for himself. To capture the ambience of the rock 'n' roll circuit he wanted to stage a massive outdoor concert in Phoenix, Arizona. Barbra and Kris, and other heavy acts, would perform live. The audience would act as unpaid extras, and the filmed footage would be used in the movie and for a network television special. The following is a report of how this writer came to attend the concert.

March 12: New York
Virginia Lord, a publicist for Warner Bros. calls to talk about Streisand and the forthcoming concert in Phoenix. She wonders if I— i.e., *The New York Times,* for whom I free-lanced—would be interested in going to Phoenix to meet Barbra and see the concert— first-class passage, with all expenses paid.

I've met Barbra before, I tell Virginia. She has beautiful blue eyes, and an exquisite singing voice, but with the press she's Johnny Belinda. As for Phoenix, on a freebie, *The New York Times* has a firm policy on junkets. The policy is no-can-do.

Virginia, a direct, no-nonsense redhead, is prepared. "But, kiddo," she says, "the no-junket rule applies to reporters on assignment for the paper. We're not asking you to get one—or to guarantee you'll write anything. However, when you're there, and if you see something that interests you, and you want to write about it six months from now, when the movie is released, be our guest."

"No work?" I think, "No hustling for scoops, or hanging around, waiting until the star deigns to talk to you."

"And it's *warm* in Phoenix," Virginia presses on, "ninety degrees and sunny. Just think, you'll have to miss the snowstorm that's due here on Thursday."

I don't say yes. I don't say no. I say, "I'll think about it." Which I do, instantly. Phoenix *could* be fun. All play and no work. And God knows a break from the winter cold would be welcomed. But then those old cronies of mine, Mr. Ethics and Mr. Righteousness, speak up. A junket? A paid PR trip? What if we bump into Andy Warhol or Sylvia Miles? And what if they talk? Think integrity and reputation here, not swimming pools and unlimited room service.

And then the telephone rings once again.

It is Arthur Bell—a good friend and loyal colleague. "You got a second?" he asks. "I've got something I want to share with you. Guess where I'm off to next week? [Pause] A hint. [Another pause] It's the set of a million-dollar movie, a musical remake, and it stars—"

"Barbra Streisand; Phoenix, Arizona; *A Star Is Born*," I interrupt.

"What!" Arthur sputters. "Did they invite *you* too?"

"Yup."

"Well," my good friend and loyal colleague concludes, "they're really dragging the bottom of the barrel for this one, aren't they?"

March 18: Phoenix, Arizona

Awaiting members of the press in their hotel rooms is a large basket of fruit, a press kit, a record album *(Classical Barbra)*, a production T-shirt, and a full-size art deco poster-sketch of Barbra and Kris, advertising the rock concert, to be held two days hence. Also with the package is a schedule of events for each day, and a personal letter of greeting from Jon Peters. It begins: "Dear Friend."

According to the schedule there are no plans for this evening. Various guests assemble in Room 314, the press room, where fifteen publicity coordinators are poised to feed tidbits and nuggets of useless production information to those who will listen. "The movie is right on schedule," they chorus. "It looks like a smash! Kris is wonderful, and Barbra—consummate professional that she is—has cut her nails! Right hand only. So she can play the guitar for a scene in the movie."

"Where is Barbra? *Where* is Kris?" Arthur Bell asks as he rumbles into the room. "I flew three thousand miles, and I want to see them both—as soon as possible!"

"And they want to see you too," a publicist answers, "but they are not here. They're staying at the Ramada Inn miles out near the stadium, where the concert will be filmed. It is more convenient. They have to concentrate; they have to learn their lines; they're artists, you know."

"Bullshit!" said Arthur, as we sit at a window table in the revolving Penthouse Bar of the Hyatt Regency. "She has her nerve. She knows we're here. I swear I won't write one word about her or her movie. I'll write about cowboys. I will! Did you bring your camera?"

March 19: Sun Devil Stadium, Noon

Lunch is to be served on the 20-yard line. Ten tables, decorated with red roses, spotless white linen tablecloths, and sparkling hotel silver, are set up in the field to accommodate the hundred reporters, photographers, and TV crews from Atlanta, Chicago, Dallas, New Orleans, Cleveland, Vancouver, London, Tokyo, and Munich. "Starving stringers and free-lance freeloaders," Bell Tell calls them, as he proceeds to sop up the strawberries, prosciutto, and champagne.

Also at our table are Aaron Gold of the Chicago *Tribune,* Patrick Pacheco of *After Dark,* and Shirley Eder of the Detroit *Free Press.* Shirley is an old friend of Barbra's. Once in an emergency she arranged to have twenty pounds of kosher hot dogs flown (from her husband's meat-packing company) to Barbra in London, for her closing night party of *Funny Girl.* Barbra was eternally grateful. "She never forgets a favor, that one," says Shirley.

Downfield, on the concert stage, there is a scene being filmed in which Kris Kristofferson rides a motorbike off the stage, onto the football field. Jon Peters intended to hire Evel Knievel to do the stunt, but Evel set too high a fee for his services. "He couldn't get Kris to do it either," I remark, noticing through a long lens that a double is doing the daring work.

"Where are the stars, we want stars," Arthur begins to chant, as the waiters pour more champagne, using a public relations ploy of getting the press soused so they will ask "nice" questions only.

Everyone has a buzz, everyone is cool, until the stars are spotted coming through a side gate of the arena. As the trio of Barbra and Jon and Kris Kristofferson approach, linking arms, the photographers and the TV crew jump to their feet to record their arrival (oblivious to the fact that they, the media, are being photographed by the movie company, and will appear without permission in the final film).

"Order please!" fifteen press aides cry out in unison. "Stay at your tables. The stars will come to *you* in circular order."

Barbra, perhaps drawn by magnetism, comes to our table first. Arthur, who has rearranged the seating while others rushed for the field, beams when she takes the empty chair beside him. She says hi to everyone, then gaily flutters her fingers in the direction of Aaron Gold. "Aaron?" she asks. "Did you curl your hair?" He did, "Me too," she says. "I always wanted curly hair."

Arthur begins. For the warm-up he tells her she looks "shining, like a brand-new penny." Barbra glows, looks at Arthur as if to say, "Who is this adorable munchkin?" and she wonders if they've met before. "Barbra," Arthur continues, "you're a unique, original, one-in-a-million artist. So tell me. Why *A Star Is Born?* Why a remake?"

Barbra is prepared. "Because there is a change in women's roles every twenty years," she announces. "I am making this character very personal, very meaningful to me. I think this film will have a lot to say about the changing roles of men and women. Women are no longer afraid to confront the male society. Which is why, in the wedding scene in this movie, I'm wearing a man's suit. Now, I think that has a lot to say about the changing roles in today's society."

"Right on!" says a hovering female press agent.

"Oh," says Arthur, ever alert for the sound of humbug.

"Stop!" I want to say. I want to lean over and whisper, "Put a lid on it, Barbra, or some of this group will eat you up."

But she bravely marches on. She talks about feminism and machismo, about love and hate, and yin and yang. "It's all point and counterpoint," she says. "This balance of things will be shown visually in the movie when I sing. In one take I'll be wearing a lacy dress. In the next I'll be wearing men's pants. There are no roles anymore. There's no time for them."

"Did you *believe* a single word that came out of her mouth?" Arthur asks when she's left the table. "Who was that free-floating flower-child? That fashionable hippie? Her women's consciousness must have been raised by Ann Miller."

The master plan for the press conference is to move the stars, one by one, from table to table, at twenty-minute intervals. All goes well for the first two sets. Barbra leaves, then Kris comes by. When he leaves, Jon Peters and Frank Pierson take his place. And the press act semiprofessional. They are polite, they ask relevant questions, but even as the producer and the director are giving their answers, collective inquisitive heads are turning elsewhere—to the table where Barbra or Kris is now sitting. And in time all civility melts in the ninety-two degree heat. The press—bar none—leave Jon and Pierson in midsentence to follow the stars.

March 20
It is the morning of the following day and we are bused out to the stadium once more to witness the concert and the filming. The stadium is packed tight. The kids begin arriving at five A.M. and by nine A.M. the gates are shut. Sixty thousand fans, on festival seating (the ground) are primed to drink, smoke, and boogie to the sights and sounds of Peter Frampton, Santana, and Graham Central Station. But first the scenes for the film have to be shot, and as the temperature pushes up to ninety-eight degrees, the multitudes grow restless. They paid $3.50 to come in, and are now being used as extras, *without* permission or entertainment. The rumble begins, and Jon Peters declares he will go onstage to soothe the audience. He will tell them his name and his function as producer "and they'll ----ing stone you to death with beer cans and bottles," he is told as a stage hand pulls him back. Barbra volunteers to pacify the mob. Normally she is terrified of standing up live in front of anyone, but it is *her* picture, and *her* $3 million. So dressed in clogs, jeans, a long white woolen dress-coat, and matching hat (in ninety-eight degree heat) she totters out to face the audience.

A roar of recognition goes up from the crowd. They get to their feet whistling and cheering her appearance. Some of these kids were still in diapers when she made her first record, but they dig her today.

"Hey, you motherfuckers," she yells into the microphone, "are you having a good time?" "Did she really say that?" Shirley Eder asks. This is clearly Barbra the rocker, Barbra the profane, Barbra the strategist and crowd pleaser. She explains the situation to the audience. She points to stage left. There is a motorcycle there. For the scene in the film Kris drives his motorcycle off the stage and into the crowd. "But we did that scene yesterday, so we need your reaction today. So, everybody, when I point left, I want you all to look left. What? You wanna look at me? Fuck you."

"Look at her directing the crowds," Jon marvels to Arthur Bell, who is now standing on the stage next to the producer. "She's got balls. She's telling them, 'I give to you, you give to me.' "

They give, and give, and Barbra rewards their cooperation with a few songs. She sings such heavy rock favorites as "People" and "The Way We Were" over a prerecorded orchestral track. "It's just like a scene from a Jane Powell movie," Arthur writes, "with the heroine bursting into song in a meadowfield, and out of the blue comes an orchestra."

As the day continues and the concert roars on, the media—those who manage to tear themselves away from the free bar in the air-conditioned press box—are given open access to the backstage area. It is here that director Pierson later reports that Streisand ran around screaming and sulking about some of the shots he'd laid down. Funny. For most of the morning and afternoon I see none of that. Barbra, unshackled from press agents and bodyguards, wanders around greeting friends from L.A., holding and kissing their babies, and changing her outfits four times (for four impromptu stage appearances, which does upset the concert's promoter, Bill Graham, who has synchronized the acts carefully).

At midafternoon Barbra meets rock star Peter Frampton. He, "The Face," is all smiles as he is introduced to Streisand, who does not know him from a hole in the ground. "Peter," a functionary at her elbow whispers. "Peter *Frampton*. He's headlining the concert."

"Oh, yeah," says Barbra, the name dimly registering. "I got your new album last week. I would have played it, but I left it on the backseat of my car and it melted in the heat. Y'know?"

As for Jon Peters, Kris Kristofferson, and Frank Pierson, all three move in different directions throughout the day and never seem to connect. At one point Barbra is sitting alone in the back of an ambulance; Frank Pierson whizzes by. "Frank!" she calls as he passes with his head down, not hearing her. *"Frank!"* she calls, louder. He stops and looks at her. "Hello," she says. "I've got an idea." He scrambles into the back of the ambulance and she delivers her idea, which has to do with a wide-angle shot she envisions of the concert audience. He grunts and jumps out of the van, leaving Barbra looking wounded and forlorn. "No one listens," she says, "no one really cares."

At six P.M. the concert is winding to a close. The remaining audience lie sprawled half naked across the football field. Those who OD'ed from the heat, drugs, and liquor are being revived in the open showers at both sides of the arena. Frank Pierson and Kris Kristofferson have already retired to their air-conditioned trailers, but Barbra remains onstage. She is not leaving until she's exhausted every possible take from this event. She suggests a pan of the casualties on the field. It's too depressing, she is told. "But it's real," she argues. "It's rock 'n' roll."

March 21: the Hyatt Regency

It is Sunday—checkout time. Some of the press departed the night before. Shirley Eder is going on to L.A. to visit a longtime friend, Barbara Stanwyck. I tell her that's one Brooklyn star I would give up good sense for. Shirley replies, "Good taste."

At breakfast Arthur Bell announces he's staying on in Phoenix for one more day and night. He has been promised a private audience with Barbra and Jon. I wish him luck. Arthur asks if I am going to write about this junket. "What's to write?" I answer. "We all got the same stuff, and most of it will be printed before we get home."

"I *know,*" says Arthur. "That is why I must get an *exclusive.* They owe me this."

Back in New York I go through the out of town newspapers and national magazines. With the exception of a short mention in *The Washington Post,* and a longer piece in the *Arizona Republic,* there is nothing on the press conference or the concert in the press. Could it be that Streisand is no longer news? I allow three days to pass, then call Dick Burgheim, the managing editor of *People* magazine. He has nothing on the event. "No photos? No items for 'Chatter'?" I ask. "Nothing," says Dick. "This is the first time I'm hearing about this thing. [A pause] What you got?"

"Bits and pieces, with some photos."

"Anything on Streisand?"

"Lots."

"Heck, we've been trying to do something on her since we started the magazine," said Dick. "Let's talk."

To fill out the piece I place a call to Barbra. She's in the desert—filming scenes, I am told. She cannot be reached by phone, but Jon Peters is available.

Jon is a "gentleman." He is cooperative and concerned that the truth be told about his movie and his relationship with Barbra. "Some people think because I'm giving it to her that she let me take over this movie. I'm a bright guy. I know how to do business. She's a genius. She's got the talent, and I do the deals."

I ask him to confirm a quote she gave in Phoenix about how, when they fight, they spit at one another. "Did she say that? Well, yeah, it's true. She likes to fight. Once she threw something at me. It was heavy and I couldn't throw it back. So I went over and spit at her. She spit back. Turns you on, right?"

In closing, Jon asks about the cover planned by *People* magazine. Will he be featured? "Do you want to be featured?" I ask. "No," he replies, "I'd like to give a fair shake to Kris. Try and get him and Barbra together on the cover. Okay?"

On April nineteenth *People* goes on sale—with Streisand alone on the cover. The headline reads: "BARBRA STREISAND For the First Time, She Talks about Her Lover, Her Power, Her Future." According to editor Dick Burgheim the magazine is on the stands Monday and is sold out by Wednesday. On Thursday Warner Bros. calls. They are grateful for the publicity. Barbra, I am told, has not read the article. But Jon Peters has. And he is not happy. One of the photos shows him (dressed in a white T-shirt, white shorts, and hiking boots) holding hands and walking off into the sunset with Barbra. The shot displeases him. "It makes me look like I have a fat ass," he says.

A week later Arthur Bell's article appears in *The Village Voice*. It is a witty, rollicking, corrosive tale. His headline reads: "BARBRA STREISAND Doesn't Get Ulcers. She Gives Them." Barbra reads Arthur's story and weeps. And Jon threatens legal action. It's all lies and fabrications, he says, especially one passage about a fight with Kris Kristofferson: Barbra was on stage directing Kris, Arthur reported: "Look," she says in front of 200 people, "you're not doing what I tell you to do." Kris isn't listening. "Listen to me when I talk to you, goddamn it," she shrieks. Kris is now listening. He tells her to go fuck herself. Jon Peters sees what's going on and jumps in. "You owe my old lady an apology," he says to Kris. All this is being boomed over the sound system. Kris retorts, "If I want some shit out of you, I'll squeeze your head."

"That has got to be one of the all-time great lines," Kristofferson tells *Rolling Stone* magazine the following year.

POSTPRODUCTION

Filming on *A Star Is Born* was completed on April twenty-fourth. There was no party, except for Barbra. It was her thirty-fourth birthday, and she and Jon took over a Beverly Hills restaurant to celebrate. Everyone appeared with gifts and "she plunged into the huge pile like a delighted child," said Frank Pierson.

The following morning the director would receive a note, telling him that his cut of the picture was due in less than four weeks. He delivered in six. It was shown against Barbra's wishes to Warner Bros. They deemed it "a huge hit," whereas Barbra took the film to Malibu and proceeded to recdit it to her specifications.

"We've turned the pool house at the ranch into an editing room," said Peters (at a cost of five hundred thousand dollars) "And the tennis house has been converted into a sound-and-music studio, with twenty-four-track recording equipment. Barbra is working on the sound with a guy called Phil Ramone. He's a genius. He did the Paul Simon album and it won an Oscar [sic]."

Over the summer no one saw the reworked film except her round-the-clock editing staff of twenty-four and her agent Sue Mengers, who every day after work drove to Malibu, where she watched the new cuts until three in the morning. In July, Barbra took a break to host a fund-raising party for Bella Abzug. Wearing a white Victorian-lace dress, she greeted the guests at her Holmby Hills mansion, and when asked about the progress of *A Star Is Born,* she replied, "Don't ask."

Early in August she also dropped in on the CBS Records convention at the Century Plaza. Wearing sandals, a housedress, and a red bandana tied around her head, she arrived at the morning meeting to screen some footage for the distributors and employees who would be selling the soundtrack album. Pitching the movie and Kris Kristofferson, a fellow CBS artist, she told the assemblage: "This is only a rough cut, but we are very excited. We feel the movie is going to be a huge hit and Kris is going to win an Academy Award. He's that good."

She then proceeded to show the 8-minute finale of the film where she appeared alone with multitudinous close-ups. "Kris is dead, you see," she said, "and I'm singing a rock 'n' roll tribute to him."

"The guys applauded like crazy," said one conventioneer, "but when the movie was over, everyone *ran* for the nearest bar. What we saw was abominable."

In September, Jon Peters flew to New York to talk to the CBS executives about the merchandising of the album. "We had a meeting—Jon, Bruce, Jack Craigo, and myself," said Jim Brown. "There was also a lady there from Warner Brothers. I was the product manager for all Barbra's albums and I felt we should have the album out at least three weeks before the movie was released. That way we'd have it in place; we'd get some airplay, and the disc jockeys could talk about the music as being from the forthcoming film. But Jon Peters argued this. 'Oh, no,' he said, 'I want the album out a month *after* the movie comes out. If people hear the music first, they'll get tired of it and won't go to see the film.' He really didn't know how the business worked. Also I was the one who told him not to call the main song just "Evergreen," but to identify it as the theme from *A Star Is Born.* That way when disc jockeys announced the song, they'd also get the title of the movie in there. Jon said he'd have to think about that one. Afterwards, in the corridor outside, I spoke to the lady from Warner Brothers. I said, 'I don't know about that guy. What does Barbra see in him?' And she laughed. 'Have you ever seen him with his pants down?' she asked."

On November tenth Suzy reported in her column that Barbra, Jon, Kris Kristofferson, and Mac Davis had left L.A. at ten-forty A.M. for Scottsdale, Arizona, to attend two sneak previews of the movie, sans the press and the Hollywood insiders. Also missing from the preview junket was the director, Frank Pierson, who was barred from the plane. The reason for this action would be explained five days later, in a provocative twelve-page story entitled "My Battles with Barbra and Jon."

Barbra and Jon had been prepared for the *New York* article. It had been sent to them weeks before by one of their network of friends. They tried to stop it from being published. "Don't hurt this film, Frank," she pleaded. Warner Bros. also offered a cash settlement not to publish. But Pierson the former journalist felt he had a good story to tell. And he told all: about the infighting, the upstaging, the power machinations, and the rampant paranoia that is inherent to most big-budget Hollywood films.

As a result of his confessions Pierson was castigated by some in the film industry for betraying the confidentiality of the relationship between a director and an actor. Others agreed he "got screwed." "But when you walk onto a battlefield you don't expect to be handed cookies and milk," one director observed. "Frank Pierson will never work in this town again," said agent Sue Mengers. (But he would. After *A Star Is Born* he was employed by none other than Ray Stark. He also wrote and directed the unsuccessful *King of the Gypsies* for Dino De Laurentiis.)

To help repair the damage and reverse the bad publicity of the Pierson article, Barbra and Jon held a press conference at the Writers Guild Theater in West Hollywood. "As Jon Peters spoke, Barbra listened intently, and stroked his hair," said *The Washington Post.* The following week she drafted a personal letter to the theater owners of America, giving detailed instructions on how to run the forthcoming film in their theaters. "In setting your usual level of sound," she told them, "please make sure that Reel 1 and Reel 2 are allowed to play as *loud as possible.* They were intentionally mixed this way and provide exactly the right amount of energy for the film. If for any reason you must play them lower, it is imperative that the sound level be raised for Reel 3 and remain the same for the balance of the film. The color is also at its best at 14½ footcandle power. Thanking you in advance—and you should please take good care of my kid. . . . [Signed] Barbra Streisand."

On Saturday night, December eighteenth, the world premiere of *A Star Is Born*, complete with klieg lights, marching bands, and baton twirlers, was held at the Westwood Theater in Hollywood. The evening, at a hundred dollars a ticket, was a benefit for Filmex, and guests were asked to wear white, black, or gray. "There was a huge limo traffic jam as minor names no one ever heard of were announced as they deplaned from their rented cars," Bob Weiner of *The Soho Weekly News* reported. "It did not look like a hundred-dollar-ticket crowd. It was a very gay, tacky hairdresser crowd, and there was talk that lots of seats were given away to fill the theater."

Following the movie the audience walked four blocks on a red carpet to Dillon's discotheque, where they were served one complimentary glass of Christian Brothers wine. Those with special blue passes were granted access to the fourth floor, where such celebrities as Ed McMahon, Rona Barrett, and Helmut Berger were gathered, and where a Solters and Roskin press assistant was posted outside another private dining room with a clipboard pressed to her chest. If your name was on the clipboard, you got to enter the room and personally greet Barbra, Jon, and Kris.

"I was sitting outside, dining on egg rolls and sweet-and-sour pork chunks," said one guest, "and across the table from me were these two sweet old ladies. Not old-old, but to the north of middle age, and they were chatting away, very friendly, asking questions about the movie. I assumed they hadn't seen it, but one of them said to me, 'Oh, yes. We've seen it—a few times. At the house.' And I'm thinking, The house? What house? Sing Sing? Who are these two women? Ex-jailbirds? But it turns out one of them is Barbra's *mother*. And the other one is Jon's mother. And here they are in Siberia, left out of the private do. But they didn't care. They were chirping away, having a grand old time."

From Los Angeles the star contingent moved on to New York. The West Coast reviewers in L.A. had been kind, respectful, and they were hoping for the same from the major magazine and newspaper critics in Manhattan. One factor was in their favor: It was Christmas week and they felt that the holiday season would soften the reviewers' hearts, *and* the lead in their pencils.

But Warner Bros. added an edge. They announced there would be no advance screenings for the press. The media could see the film the day before the opening, and not before. Therefore the fourth estate braced themselves to do full justice to the movie which critic Frank Rich described as "riding into town on the largest wave of negative advance publicity since *Cleopatra.*"

Barbra, in tune with her new liberated image, wore a tuxedo to the opening at the Ziegfeld. She posed happily for photos with Jon and Kris (who was on the wagon and "thankful to Barbra" for having saved his life). Later, at the party for seven hundred guests at Tavern on the Green, all was festive until columnist Arthur Bell arrived. "I was not invited," said he, "but I had a friend, I won't mention her name, Marjorie Rosen, and I knew she was going, so I went as her date. Then the minute I entered the room I saw Barbra sitting in a corner with Jon and Sue Mengers. Sue came clomping across the room like a baby elephant and said, 'Don't go near Barbra. She hates you. She hates you. This is her night of triumph, so leave her alone.' Then Jon came over. 'I thought you were a friend,' he said. 'I took you up to that stage in Phoenix and *confided* in you, and then you sold me out.' I told him, 'Jon, I took down your words *exactly.* What did you think I was doing? Writing a letter to mother?' Jon went on: 'You said I was *fat.* That I had *pulkes.* You made me lose thirty pounds.' He opened his jacket to reveal this Scarlett O'Hara waistline. I *liked* Jon. I still do. He's very straightforward. But he was doing *her* number, playing Little Boy Lost. On this night he was really concerned about what I had written nine months *before.* And already I knew what some of the morning reviews were going to be like. Rex Reed was reading his over the phone to friends. So as Jon left I said, 'Well, good luck with the reviews tomorrow.' He turned back and said, *'Reviews?* We're talking *major* awards here.' "

"A Star Is Born: dead on arrival," said *Rolling Stone.*

"What the hell does Barbra Streisand know about directing or editing a movie?" said Rex Reed. "Every aspect of the story has been trashed along with the dialogue."

"Hearing her light into a rock song is like listening to Al Jolson sing Leadbelly," said *Time.* "A concert sequence, where the debuting Barbra brings a hostile audience to their feet with the wonder of her funkiness, is a milestone of piquant absurdity, equivalent perhaps to having Kate Smith conquer Woodstock."

"Streisand's constant upstaging of Kristofferson often goes beyond the bounds of run-of-the-mill narcissism; the camera spends a great deal of time watching her watching him talk," said *Newsweek.*

"The only interest the movie provides is its documentation of all Streisand's assorted power plays," said Andrew Sarris in the *Village Voice.* "As she rises and Kristofferson falls, she still does most of the nagging. In the end he drives his red sports car off into the mountains with *her* revered cassette blaring on the soundtrack."

"I wept when I read the reviews," said Barbra. "I was devastated. . . . I was in shock. . . . It was like: Who's crazy? Can people call the movie brilliant, and can the same movie be called a piece of trash? Well, the audience is the only one who knows, the only one who can't be bought."

And the audience bought the tickets. Through Christmas and New Year's, through January, February, and March, *A Star Is Born* sold some sixty million dollars' worth of tickets. The soundtrack LP became her largest seller ever, with 5 million copies snapped up by her fans. And "Evergreen," the theme from the movie, went to number one—not only in the United States but in fourteen other countries—selling in excess of 7 million singles. The worldwide popularity of the song was especially pleasing to the singer, because she had written the melody. "I couldn't believe it when people actually *liked* it," said Barbra. "It was such a simple melody, just a little something I wrote."

"A little something? She's telling the truth there. All she composed of 'Evergreen' were a few lines of the melody," said a music publisher who co-produced the recording of "Ma Première Chanson," an earlier disputed Streisand composition.

Barbra had always been envious of songwriters such as Joni Mitchell and Carole King. She told *Playboy:* "I felt so inadequate singing other people's songs, not being able to write." "Evergreen" (not unlike "Ma Première Chanson," her first copyrighted composition) came from beginning chords in her head. Product manager Tony Lawrence was one of the first people to hear those chords. He recalled being at the ranch in Malibu one day. "It was a Friday afternoon and I was going over some *Lazy Afternoon* cover proofs with her. Jon had just come home; he was outside reading a script. After we went over the proofs Barbra said to me, 'Hey, I want to play you something.' She played the first two lines of the melody for 'Evergreen.' That's all she had."

Referring to "Evergreen," Holmes's lawyer and manager, Normand Kurtz later said: "Obviously we never claimed that it was part of Rupert's work, but there was some collaboration on it."*

"Rupert Holmes had something to do with writing that song, or co-writing it," said CBS Records President Bruce Lundvall. "But he never got any credit."

Holmes had worked on the primary score of *A Star Is Born.* He told a reporter for *Barbra* magazine (a "fanzine" approved by the star) that he "certainly did write an honest dozen tunes for the film," including one called "Love Out of Time," "which had it been used, would have been the equivalent of 'Evergreen' in the movie." His ties with the film were severed after he was profiled in

---

* Author's note: At the time Normand Kurtz made this statement (taped), he agreed that I should talk to Rupert Holmes directly. Over a period of six months I tried repeatedly to arrange a meeting with the composer. On one occasion Holmes came to the phone and consented to be interviewed at a later date (which never materialized). When the hardcover edition of this book was released, the composer, in a statement written for Miss Streisand, denied any involvement in the writing of "Evergreen." He also denied any recollection of having been contacted by this writer.

Interview magazine—where he expressed his admiration for Barbra, but described her as "the devil's advocate." "Rupert is frightened by Jon's temper," director Frank Pierson wrote in his journal, telling how the sensitive young composer flew to New York after one argument and never returned.

Chapter 28

"*I can't ever disturb my daughter, she's so busy, y'know? She'll send me flowers. If I call her and she's busy, she says, 'Mom, I'm too busy, but when I have a chance I'll call you back.' And the next day I get flowers.*"

Diana Streisand Kind

STREISAND SUPERMAN

With the abundant flow of new riches coming in from *A Star Is Born,* Streisand began to spend freely on her family, her friends, and on herself. Each week truckloads of new clothes, furniture, flowers, food, and delicacies arrived at the front gates of the ranch. Already protected from the outside world by a six-foot electrical fence, a TV-monitored patrol system, and three guard dogs, the affluent celebrity couple decided to enhance their privacy further by building three new homes on their fourteen acres of property. The new houses would be for Barbra's exclusive use, each one designed to accommodate a different persona. "If I feel like being in an art-deco mood, I'll go to the art-deco house," she said, "and if I'm in a Victorian frame of mind, I'll go to that house."

A coop apartment in Los Angeles was also purchased for Barbra's mother, who had moved to California permanently—to be closer to her older daughter, and to continue nudging her younger daughter Roslyn's acting and singing career. Roslyn, Mrs. Kind believed, still had the makings to be a star, a bigger star than Barbra. At a "Salute to Israel" concert TV writer-producer Kenny

Solms recalled talking to Mrs. Kind after Barbra had performed her rousing rendition of "The Impossible Dream." He said to Mrs. Kind, "Well, Diana, how did you like *that?*" And she answered, "Oh, but you should hear *Roslyn* sing." "It was as if she felt that Roslyn could have done it better."

"Roslyn has her own wonderful voice," Barbra said to *Playboy* interviewer Lawrence Grobel, after she had arranged a recording contract for her sister at CBS Records. Roslyn cut two singles with producer Jack Gold, and was then dropped by the label. "But there is just so much a record company will do to promote you," Barbra stated. "Before *A Star Is Born* I never heard my last few records on the radio. I never heard—not one—a song from *Butterfly,* or *Lazy Afternoon,* or *Classical Barbra.* So what is there to do? I was able to get her a record contract, but I can't make them play the record."

During the summer of 1977 another important member of Streisand's family, her ten-year-old son Jason, spent part of his vacation at the ranch in Malibu. By then he had become friends with Jon Peters's nine-year-old son Chris. "At the beginning it was interesting because they were opposites," said Jon. "My son is gregarious, kind of a street kid. Jason was kind of protected by Barbra. But I like kids being thrown into the mix of things; to know what's going on. They taught each other. They fight, like most kids; but they're friends."

> *"I can't stand to fire people. My manager has been with me seventeen years, my agents sixteen years, my press representative sixteen years . . . yet the press says I fire people. That's the joke."*
>
> **Barbra Streisand, 1977**

In the fall of 1977 Streisand and CBS Records were scheduled to celebrate their fifteenth year of musical togetherness. To mark the occasion a special five-LP set was scheduled for release at an affordable price, as a thank-you gesture to her million of fans.

The package was to contain previously unrecorded material—starting off with a demo Barbra made at age fourteen, singing "Zing Went The Strings Of My Heart." Also to be featured were the live performances from the Bon Soir in 1962; from the Hungry i in San Francisco in 1963; the duet with Judy Garland from Judy's TV show; the TV soundtrack of *The Belle of 14th Street;* dialogue from the Friars Club roast in 1969; medleys from the American embassy concert in London, and one from the International Hotel in Vegas; and the duet of "You're The Top," with Ryan O'Neal, from *What's Up Doc?*

The coordinator of the anthology was Jim Brown. "It was Marty Erlichman's idea," said Brown. "Most of us at CBS weren't even aware this material existed. I went through the vaults and we kept finding boxes of tapes. It was fascinating. For example, the demo that Barbra made of 'Zing Went The Strings Of My Heart', —on the 'zing' part you could still hear her Brooklyn accent. On the Hungry i tapes she spoke to the audience. You could hear her say, 'Ohmigod! There's Paul Newman sitting out there.' It was great material and the fans were going to love it. We spent months putting the stuff together, until one day I got the word from Marty that the project was being killed. Not too long after that I heard he was no longer with Barbra either."

Talk of the breakup had begun the previous year. Marty Erlichman, Barbra's personal manager for sixteen years, was being gradually ousted by boyfriend-cum producer Jon Peters. Peters, it was said, wanted total control of Barbra's career. During the making of *A Star Is Born* his role as producer enabled him to circumvent Erlichman by dealing directly with the executives of Warner Bros. and CBS Records. When he began to question Marty about former contracts and percentages, the sparks flew. Heated arguments erupted between the two men at the studio and at the ranch; and Barbra was torn. She was grateful to Marty for his long-term support and guidance, but she was "in love with Jon." He was, she believed, directly responsible for her greatest success and financial fortune from *A Star Is Born.* For the future she needed younger, more aggressive management. And who was better qualified than Jon to serve her best interests, day and night?

Still Streisand could not do the deed directly. She could never bring herself personally to fire people. "Barbra always had a hatchet man to do the dirty work. When she was married to Elliott she made him do some unpleasant things," said Bob Schulenberg. "Sis Corman and Sue Mengers also played the heavy for her," said Fred Glaser. But it was Erlichman himself who provided the out this time, ending the professional relationship. He was not willing to engage in any unpleasantness or legal battles with Barbra. "She was family," he said. "We had been together since 1961. During those years I was a terrific manager. I was giving her twenty-four hours of my day. And I couldn't do that anymore. I was single then, and she was my child. Now I'm married. I have my own family. I stayed with her through *A Star Is Born*. Maybe she needed new direction. Barbra and I are still close. We speak on the phone once a week. As for Jon Peters? Even before I left he was calling himself her manager. My thoughts on what he does and how he does it, well, they're not for publication."

> *"Barbra Streisand fascinates me. Even though our styles are different, we've been compared as having the best ears in the business."*

> Karen Carpenter

> *"When Barbra recorded my song 'New York State of Mind,' my mother said to me: 'At last; you're a success.'"*

> Billy Joel

As her personal manager, the first order of new business for Jon Peters was to put Barbra in the recording studio with a new production team. The person chosen as executive producer of her next album was Charles Koppelman.

Koppelman, a man of bland features and disarming manners, began his record career in the mid-sixties promoting or coproducing such rock and roll acts as The Critters, The Lovin' Spoonful, and The Turtles. A virtuoso at making contacts and massaging egos, Koppelman's actual musical expertise and foresight were questioned by more than a few. "He's a wheeler-dealer, very ambitious," said composer Mickey Leonard. "He's got one of the great musical brains of the eleventh century; he wouldn't know a good piece of music from a bad one." "Mister Koppelman," said songwriter Paul Jabara, "is a man that gets ideas. He has wonderful musical hindsight. He can spot a hit when it's already on the charts."

In the early 1970s Koppelman joined CBS Records as head of

their pop A&R department. He was hired by President Clive Davis to keep the artists on schedule and the product flowing. "Koppelman and his staff were a very strange crew," said Jim Brown. "They were very close mouthed. You could never walk into their offices and say, 'I think we've got a hit here.' They kept themselves huddled behind closed doors, doing all these deals between themselves."

Koppelman and Jon Peters met in 1974 during the production of Jon's almost-aborted album debut, *Butterfly*. When Koppelman helped to rescue Jon, the two, as the story goes, became "instant pals; thicker than thieves in an open flea market."

Bruce Lundvall recalled one episode of Koppelman-Peters dealing. "I had become head of the CBS label, and I knew Charles was very tight with Jon. Charles was very good with Streisand. She was prone not to deliver records, and he was excellent at getting her to move. We were in London at this time. I had to go over to deal with a Pink Floyd situation, and Charles came along. We were sitting in his room at Claridge's having a drink before going out to dinner, and Charlie gets this phone call. And he's going, 'Yeah, Jon; yeah, Jon.' He's talking and talking and I realize it's Jon Peters. And Charlie says to him, 'Look! If you can deliver her album by, like, October, you got it. A Corniche.' And I'm thinking, 'What is this? A Corniche?' So when he gets off the phone I say, 'Charlie, what are you doing?' And he says, 'I'm giving Jon Peters a Rolls-Royce and he'll deliver the album to us by October. If he doesn't—no car.'

" 'We can't do that,' I said, 'we're CBS.' This was something that a private record company would do. But Charlie was insistent. 'If he gets Barbra to record, we get the billing this year. And Jon gets the Rolls.' I stopped it, of course, and not long afterwards Charlie was transferred over to April-Blackwood, the CBS music publishing division."*

When Koppelman was relocated to April-Blackwood, Jon Peters, sensing the loss of an important ally, tried to intervene through Streisand. "Barbra has different personalities," said Lundvall. "She can be very funny or very shy, very elegant or very crude. I saw a little bit of the latter at her house one night. Irwin Siegelstein, who was the president of the CBS Group, and I, and

---

* Jon would get his Rolls that Christmas, as a gift from Barbra.

Don Ellis, the new head of A&R, had been invited for dinner at her house in Malibu. When we got there we had drinks, and she had prepared this dinner herself. It was laid out very nicely, a beautiful meal, and just as we were sitting at the table, ready to eat, Barbra said, 'Let me ask you a question. Charlie Koppelman is our best friend. Was he fired from A&R or did he leave?' And we're sitting there, looking at each other. Marty Erlichman was also at the table, silent. So we said, 'Barbra, you know this is a company thing. He's still with the publishing division.' And she said, 'No! I want to know. I do not want to be lied to.' And she started this loud angry scene at the table. It went on for ten minutes. The food was getting cold as she was yelling, 'I wanna know! I wanna know!' And Irwin,—the brunt of it was on him—he was the president of the group, I was the president of the label. He kept trying to calm her down by saying that we still think very highly of Charlie, that he was in this other division, and so on. And Barbra said, 'Is that a demotion? Tell me now. He's our friend.' Jon joined in also. You could see this caustic nasty edge to both of them. Until finally we ate the meal in silence, and I sort of broke the silence by talking about some new songs.''

Not too long after this Charlie Koppelman left CBS to join forces with Sam Lefrak, the realty millionaire who was interested in getting into the music business, and whose number-one idol was Barbra Streisand. "She used to live in one of my buildings; she put money in my oil companies," the magnate boasted to *New York Post* reporter Stephen Silverman. Lefrak met Koppelman through his son-in-law Martin Bandier. When Koppelman mentioned he was thinking of leaving CBS Records to independently produce Barbra's next album, Lefrak jumped to with interest, offering financing. Koppelman held out for a producing and publishing deal. So it came to pass that The Entertainment Company (soon to become one of the largest music publishing houses) was born—with Koppelman as president and Martin Bandier as vice-president. Sam the Fan, who supplied the bankroll, was presented with a life-size cardboard cutout of Barbra which stands today to the left of the realtor's office desk.

As promised, Charles Koppelman delivered Streisand as the first major client to the new production house. Beyond the guarantee of autonomous control and aggressive independent promotion, another lure was the pledge of extra income from publishing royalties, which in time would add extensive riches to Barbra's already enormous holdings.

Getting a cut of the song-publishing royalties was nothing new to Streisand, or to the multitudes of recording stars, past or present. Owning the copyright to one or more songs on a hit album could mean extra income of fifty thousand to two hundred thousand dollars a year. Every time a record was sold or was played on the radio or TV, the publishing holder got paid. "That's the name of the game," said publisher Nat Shapiro. "Many artists in the twenties and thirties—Bing Crosby, Paul Whiteman, Rudy Vallee—put names on copyrights even if they never wrote the songs. They wanted a piece of the action. Al Jolson used to arrive in town and he'd be met at the train by these young composers who'd greet him with 'Al! Wait'll you hear these new songs you wrote.' Barbra, in all fairness, never overdid it. At certain times she added creative input, so when she felt she had credit due, she took it."

"Silent Night," Gounod's "Ave Maria," and "Jingle Bells" were published by Streisand's company, Emanuel Music. Other companies owned by the star were Kiki Music, Diana Music (named for her mother), Primus Music, and First Artists Music, which co-owned the copyrights for *A Star Is Born*. Publishing on the new album—*Streisand Superman*—would be split equally. The copyright for six of the nine songs chosen by Koppelman for recording went to Emanuel or Kiki Music, and to Koppelman-Bandier. (When the album sold over a million copies the publishing pot swelled to over $500,000.)

In April of 1977 the first tracks for the LP were done in Los Angeles with Gary Klein producing. The purpose of the album, Klein said, was to keep Barbra on the pop charts, and not have people think of her as just middle of the road. He would also call the performer "brilliant . . . a perfectionist . . . driven . . . unconventional . . . and as close to perfect as she can be. She can hear one violin out of twenty that's out of tune."

The tastiest aspect of the new LP was not the music (there was not a hit single in the lot) but the visuals for the package. In full-length photos—front and back—Streisand posed wearing short shorts, tube socks, and a white T-shirt with the Superman emblem emblazoned across her firm, ample chest.

The photographs were the work of a seasoned Streisand professional, Steve Schapiro. Schapiro, a photographer for *Life,* had done the publicity stills for *Funny Girl* in 1968. Later, in between photographing Robert Redford for *The Great Gatsby* and Warren Beatty in *Shampoo,* he worked with Streisand on *The Owl and the Pussycat, Up the Sandbox,* along with shooting the covers and inside photos for the albums of *The Way We Were, Live at the Forum, Butterfly,* and *Lazy Afternoon.*

"There was always a reason," said Schapiro, "for my photographing Barbra. It was either for a magazine or an album cover, or for publicity stills. Being photographed was always 'work' to her. She never did it just for vanity or for the fun of it, although we did have fun at times. Since *Funny Girl* I knew she would never compromise a situation. She was very persistent and right about the lights. She instinctively knew they had to be in a particular place and that was that."

The *Superman* shots were done in two sessions. "Barbra had a photo of herself from *A Star Is Born* that she liked. It was a backview. She had her arm up—like a women's liberation pose. So the *Superman* cover was supposed to be a front view of that. But when we started to shoot at her home in Holmby Hills, it didn't look like it was going to be that terrific an image. So we fooled around and the one we eventually picked was only one of many pictures. Then she decided she needed a side view for a cutout, for the back of the album. So we did a matching session at Malibu. It was done with lights and seamless paper, and it took about an hour. It went fast because she looked great and felt great. Of course, she had final approval. Barbra owns most of the shots I've taken of her. She's got boxes of them on file in her home. She can pick out one and tell you when and where it was taken. The cover for *The Way We Were* was from a fashion layout we did for *Harper's Bazaar* a few years previous. She remembered the shot and knew it fit that album. Most everything she chooses I also go for. What I look for in a picture is what she wants—to look strong and terrific."

Streisand Superman was released in June of 1977. When it went platinum by August, Barbra agreed to accept the award at the CBS convention in Los Angeles. She also consented to perform for the distributors who sold the record.

"It was the final dinner show of the convention," said Jim Brown. "There was supposed to be a cocktail party from six o'clock to seven-thirty, and then the dinner. But no one could get into the main room because Barbra was still rehearsing. So the cocktails went on for three hours, until nine o'clock, and everyone was sloshed. By the time she let us into the room the guys were bumping into each other, falling down, trying to find their tables. Then she came out and sang her standard stuff. At that point she could have stood on her hands and waved her legs in the air, and the guys would have applauded."

THE NEW RECORD CONTRACT

With Marty Erlichman removed as personal manager, the negotiations for her new recording contract with CBS Records were handled by Jon Peters. Always shrewd and fast on his toes in business deals, he was still a parvenu in music circles; but good friend Charles Koppelman briefed him extensively as to the workings within the CBS bureaucracy. "Jon learned fast," said President Bruce Lundvall. "He was very smart and had a good street sense. I never found him to be an adversary. When he found out about marketing and promotion campaigns, he got involved. He rode high on everything we were doing with Barbra."

Streisand did not get involved directly in the negotiations for her third successive contract. "I'm sure she had a lot to say about it—behind the scenes," said Lundvall. "My sense of it was that she wanted to stay at CBS. Her whole catalogue was there, and we were prepared to make a very big deal with her. Certainly there were other record companies interested, but I don't believe Jon shopped them. It became one of those things where she said, 'Hey, this is family.' She knew people like John Berg since she started with the company. There was a lot of loyalty on her part—absolutely."

The CBS executives met with Streisand and Peters on the West Coast, and later there was a further meeting over dinner at David K's on Third Avenue in Manhattan. "There were four of us at that dinner," said Lundvall, "—Barbra, Jon, Walter Yetnikoff, and myself. It was a wonderful meal. Barbra was very curious to find out what was going on in the business. She asked about Billy Joel and Bruce Springsteen, what they were doing and what they were like. We also talked about the old days at Columbia. I had worked on the *Wholesale* album, her first show. I remember telling her that

Mike Berniker, who was my roommate in college, produced her first album; and he was then head of A&R for RCA Records. Barbra got real excited when I told her that. 'Ah! he did great,' she said, 'and you did great. And John Berg too.' She was happy that all of the people she knew and had lost track of were still doing pretty well."

The meal at David K's was eventually disrupted by Barbra's fans. "We had a private table in a corner and then people started seeing Barbra. They began to come over for autographs. Barbra was very gracious about it, but after a while it became impossible. The word must have spread throughout the restaurant, because she was besieged. We couldn't eat, so after a while we all decided it was best to just leave."

Not long afterward the deal with CBS Records was closed. The terms were five albums over five years, plus a "greatest hits" package. The advance guarantee was $1.5 million for each LP. "I think there was a specific completion date for each studio LP," said Lundvall. "There was a bonus given if she delivered within a certain time. That way we'd hopefully get an album every year. The producer and the material was also up to her, but we had a consultation clause. If she wanted to use Charles Koppelman and the Entertainment Company, they would budget the album and we'd pay them. The average budget came to two hundred fifty thousand dollars. The publishing arrangements were also controlled by Barbra. But CBS got a good deal. We were sure she'd continue to sell."

On the night of December twenty-second, to celebrate her re-signing with the label, CBS Records threw a party at La Première, a restaurant on the East Side of Manhattan. The party was Streisand's idea. She planned to take care of two groups at the same time—the CBS Records staff, most of whom she had never met before, and her relatives in Brooklyn, who had been complaining to her mother that they had not seen the star in some time. She arrived early, wearing a blue satin and silk dress and a very friendly disposition. "Usually in crowds she gets tense," said Jim Brown, "but this night she was relaxed and very pleasant to everyone. Bruce Lundvall and Jack Craigo brought her around from table to table. She wanted to know everyone's name and what they did. And it wasn't condescending or phony. She was really interested."

Reporters Janet Maslin of *The New York Times,* Stephen Silverman of the *New York Post,* and Arthur Bell of *The Village Voice* were also invited to the party. "When I got the call to come, I asked, 'Does Barbra know I'm invited?' " said Bell. "The press lady said, 'Yes, Arthur. And if you're not nice to her, *I'll* slap your face, Christmas or not.' I laughed at that and decided to go. Barbra was great. This was the first time I ever saw her behave like a normal human being. She had all of her Brooklyn relatives there and she was touching them and feeding them. It wasn't a time to bother her or ask her any questions. We spoke a little, friendly stuff. I also remember seeing these two huge cakes on a table in the center of the floor. One of them was decorated to resemble her CBS contract, and the other had a likeness of Barbra and Jon together. And then I made the connection, or the lack of it: Jon Peters was *not* at the party, and maybe that's why she was being so nice."

"Jon has the flu," columnist Earl Wilson said to Streisand. "Is he running a temperature?"

"You used to ask Jon about *me,*" Barbra replied. "Now you ask me about him. He must be making out very good."

After celebrities Billy Joel and Shirley MacLaine arrived, the party got out of control. "It was the holiday season," said Sheila Schandler, a CBS promotion executive, "and the restaurant was too narrow. Barbra had picked the place herself. It was a renovated tenement building and the rooms downstairs were only about twenty-five feet wide. Later, after the fact, a lot of people said Barbra was snobbish and didn't want to mix, but that wasn't the case. She had already elbowed her way to the back of the room, and when she knew she didn't have a chance of meeting everyone, it was decided to bring the people to her, in a larger room upstairs. So they managed to get her up the stairs, and into the room. She was very gracious. She posed for photographs with everyone—not only with Billy Joel and Shirley—but with the CBS staff, with everyone. Furthermore, her pocketbook was stolen. We never knew if it was a fan or someone who was after her cash and valuables. But Barbra didn't cause a scene. She just sort of shrugged her shoulders as if to say, 'Oh, well, Merry Christmas.' "

Chapter 29

"When I went into this business all I read was that I was a pimp and a conniver and a 'nobody' latching on to a star's wings."

Jon Peters

"Jon is very creative. He knows a lot about hair, clothes, and design. But he's also very macho. He has the scars on his hands to prove it."

Barbra Streisand

HITS AND MISSES

On Sunday morning, January 29, 1977, Jon Peters realized one of his loftier ambitions when he turned to the "Arts and Leisure" section of the New York Sunday *Times* and found himself the main focus of an interview written by Janet Maslin. The fulcrum for the piece was *Eyes of Laura Mars,* his first feature film without Barbra.

For the title role, that of a quasi–sado-masochistic-inspired fashion photographer, Faye Dunaway was recruited by Jon (and Barbra) at breakfast at the Polo Lounge on the morning after she won the Oscar for *Network.* The package, with Irvin Kershner *(Up the Sandbox)* as director, was financed by Columbia Pictures, but it ran into trouble during preproduction. The executive in charge at Columbia Pictures, the man who gave the green light to *Laura Mars,* was none other than David Begelman, who was about to be exposed in a company scandal concerning a ten-thousand-dollar check he had autographed with actor Cliff Robertson's name.

David Begelman had been Barbra's agent in the sixties. He'd negotiated her contracts for *Funny Girl,* the play and the movie; and after the fact had managed to persuade the producer, Ray Stark, to let his client share in the profits. He also cut himself in on the action from time to time. When Blackglama mink wanted to feature Streisand in its *What Becomes a Legend Most?* campaign, Begelman promised to deliver her, and another client, Judy Garland, if he received a free mink for his time and trouble.

When Begelman left the agency business to become a film producer he and Streisand remained close, both socially and professionally. He and his wife Gladyce accompanied Barbra and Jon on the publicity tour for *Funny Lady,* and they in turn were his special guests at Columbia's Gala Fiftieth-anniversary party in 1977. That fall, when Begelman's forgery problems began to surface, Streisand was one of the first stars to come to his defense. Her name was listed on telegrams sent by Sue Mengers to the Columbia board of directors, pleading that his job be saved.

Over Thanksgiving, at the peak of the Begelman investigation, Barbra, accompanied by Jon and son Jason, limoed from Manhattan to Scarsdale to the home of Alan Hirschfield, the president and chief executive of Columbia Pictures. It was assumed they were there to plead on Begelman's behalf. But it turned out that Jon wanted to talk about his Columbia movie, *Laura Mars,* and Barbra needed financial advice. She had lost considerable sums on bad investments, she told Hirschfield, and she needed the name of a good investment broker.

Eyes of Laura Mars survived the Begelman scandal, and shooting commenced on the East Coast in early 1978. Jon Peters, however, was not happy with filming in New York City. He told one interviewer that he disliked the weather and "the dogs going poo-poo in the street." On Eighth Avenue late one night filming was disrupted by a street gang. The crew tried to placate them, "but they didn't want money," said Jon, "they wanted to fight. So we gave it to them. We whipped them with our fists."

Laura Mars completed shooting in Los Angeles by March. During the editing Peters had another brawl, this time with the law.

The rains had come to Malibu. A creek that ran through the ranch began to overflow and was in danger of destroying his house and property. Jon, assisted by his son Chris, went to town to get sandbags. On their way back, Jon drove through a roadblock. The police gave chase. He was pulled from his car, hit with a nightstick, and a gun was put to his head. "We cursed a little bit, and then I stopped," said Jon. "I was appalled by this. I couldn't understand it. I kept saying, 'Hey, I live here.' I was a block from my house when it happened. But the cops had their story, and I had another, so you kind of let it go."

When *Laura Mars* was edited, Barbra agreed to sing over the credits. A theme song, written by Karen Lawrence, a protégée of Charles Koppelman, was recorded and released as a single by CBS in July. A soundtrack LP followed, and Peters predicted it would outsell *A Star Is Born*. It sold less, considerably less, and was soon dropped from the Columbia catalogue. The movie, according to Jon, "made a bundle."

> *"There's only one thing I can't do. I can't wink. Whenever I try, my eyes just squeeze."*
>
> *Barbra Streisand*

Whatever losses CBS Records incurred with the *Laura Mars* music, the ledger was wiped clean in the second half of the year. "You Don't Bring Me Flowers," Streisand's duet with Neil Diamond, added millions to the CBS coffers, and the background of how the duet came about was in itself a relay of interrupted starts and finishes, ending in a contest of bruised egos and a lawsuit.

"You Don't Bring Me Flowers" was written by Neil Diamond and Marilyn and Alan Bergman as a forty-five second theme for a 1976 Norman Lear TV series, *All That Glitters*. When the series was abruptly canceled, the song was forgotten until 1977 when Diamond rediscovered it while rehearsing for a TV special. "Neil called us," said Marilyn Bergman, "and said the song felt real good. 'But it's not a song yet,' we told him. 'It's still only forty-five seconds long.' But he still wanted to do it, so we said, 'All right, but let us write the second half of the song.' The title was there, and we wrote the second half."

In September of 1977 Diamond sang the completed song on his

NBC-TV special. Watching the show that night was Gary Le Mel, who managed Barbra's publishing at First Artists Music. The following morning he called Diamond's publisher, David Rosner, for a demo and a lead sheet. He also called the Bergmans. "I told them that the song would be perfect for Barbra. And the Bergman's said, 'You're right, but we don't like to push our songs to Barbra.'"

"That's absolutely true," said Marilyn Bergman. "There are many songs of ours she has never heard. Once she was in an exercise class and a song was played. She had it checked out and it was one of ours. The assumption that she sees everything we write is far from correct, and I'd like to straighten it out."

Gary Le Mel called Streisand in New York to tell her about the "Flowers" song. She was not too thrilled about the song or the title. She felt the premise was just a tad too whiny and solicitous.

Five months passed and Streisand was finishing the recording of her new album, *Songbird*. On February seventh she recorded a tune called "Looking Out For #1," a title implicit in its message. The self-serving song, however, did not fit the *Songbird* concept, the images of which showed a softer, homelier Barbra, dressed in old clothes, with her seven dogs. So "Looking Out for #1" got axed, and the sensitive, more tender "You Don't Bring Me Flowers" was substituted as the last song for the album.

The scene then moved to Louisville, Kentucky—approximately one month later—where a disc jockey named Gary Guthrie lived. Guthrie's wife loved the Neil Diamond version of "Flowers" and he had gone to great lengths to persuade CBS Records to release the song as a single. They did not. When the Streisand version came along (again, not as a single, but on the album), Guthrie decided to mix his own duet. "My wife and I were just breaking up at this point," he said, "and we were still great friends, so I wanted to give her something as a going-away present. When I got the test pressing of Barbra's new album and I heard the song, a light bulb went on in my head. I decided to match Neil's version with Barbra's. I know about recording, so I taped both songs, and varied the speed on Barbra's version. I laid her voice over his instrumentals, and vice versa; and eventually I had a dynamite duet going."

Guthrie played the taped duet of Barbra and Neil over the radio for his about-to-be ex-wife. The phones at the radio station rang nonstop. The following day he played the tape again and the switchboard lit up. "I got a little braver as the day went on," he said, "and I stuck the duet into pop rotation playing it every two hours and fifteen minutes. The record stores started calling up, saying, 'What are you doing to us? People are coming in every five minutes wanting to buy this record and there's no such animal.'"

Guthrie sent a copy of the tape to Sheila Schandler at CBS Records in New York. Sheila said, "That's hot," and passed the tape on to the company president, Bruce Lundvall. "When I heard it, I said, 'This is a great idea,' " said Bruce, 'but the first thing we have to do is put a cease and desist on the record because every other radio station across the country will be playing the duet, and it's illegal.' "

The order went out, and Lundvall then called Jon Peters. "I told him about the song, that Neil and Barbra should go into a studio and cut it for real. I also called Jerry Weintraub, Neil's manager, and said the same thing. It could be a smash. I sent them both copies of the tape, but I never heard from them."

The month of May passed, then June and July. "I was in Los Angeles for a convention," Lundvall recalled, "and I had a meeting with Neil. He was talking about his new fall album—that he was going to have a two-record set. It was going to be a major event. 'Two records?' I told him, 'There's no event for two records —it's a more expensive item.' But he said, 'Two albums of Neil Diamond. Think of it.' And I laughed. I said, 'Look—Neil—an event is you and Barbra Streisand doing "You Don't Bring Me Flowers." ' He asked why. I explained, 'You're both major stars, and to do a record together that is going to be an enormous hit makes great sense.' 'Well,' he said, 'you really think so?' I said yes. 'Forget the two-record set. Barry Manilow had a two-record set and it wasn't a success.' Then he thought further and said, 'You know, you're right. I'll do it.' "

Getting to Jon Peters to get to Streisand was a snap. For quite some time Peters had wanted Barbra to sing a duet with a male recording star. Stevie Wonder was once a prime candidate. He even wrote a song specifically for Barbra. She turned it down because "it didn't have a beginning, a middle, and an end." A second Motown star, the late Marvin Gaye, was also considered. Marvin met with Jon and Barbra over dinner. He responded enthusiastically to the idea of a duet ("I wanted that hit ballad"). Peters told him to have his lawyer call them the following day at noon. The lawyer called at two P.M., and Jon announced the deal was off. Calling late was an indication he "had no respect for Barbra Streisand." So when the concept of a duet with Neil Diamond presented itself, Jon was ready. "She'll do it," Peters told Bruce Lundvall. "Tell me the date and the time and she'll be there."

On October 17, 1978, Streisand drove herself to the Cherokee Studios on Fairfax Avenue in Los Angeles. "It was like she was running an errand," an associate recalled. "She had been in script meetings at the ranch all morning and at noon she said, 'Well, excuse me; I gotta go out for a while. But I'll be back soon.' Later I found out she had recorded the song in something like an hour. I mentioned this to her and she went, 'Well, it wasn't any big deal, you know. I already knew all the words.' "

"You Don't Bring Me Flowers" became the fastest-selling single in the history of Columbia Records. It also spurred a nationwide stampede on flower stores by husbands, boyfriends, and others heeding the call of the song. But lost in the gold rush was Gary Guthrie, the originator of the duet. "I'd been kept informed as to the recording and stuff," he said, "and there was some subsequent publicity. Rona Barrett came on one morning and said that Jon Peters recognized my part in it. But I felt I should have gotten paid."

"We gave him a finder's fee," said Bruce Lundvall, "but it was modest. Maybe it was five thousand dollars, and the guy got insulted. My position after talking to our legal people was that this could be construed as payola if we gave him a huge amount."

"CBS sold something like thirty-seven million dollars' worth of records between the single and the two LPs," said Guthrie. "All I got from Neil was some flowers. And Barbra sent me a telegram. So when CBS made their paltry offer I said, 'Let me think about this.' They wanted me to fly to New York and hold a press conference with Neil and Barbra. I decided to pass, and I called a lawyer."

Guthrie's case was settled out of court. "It was a traditional David and Goliath situation," he said. "The small guy against the big New York corporation. Heck, CBS must have wheeled twenty-two lawyers down to Memphis to defend themselves. We also tried to get a deposition from Barbra. I wasn't suing her, or Neil, but we needed that deposition. We got it from Neil, but Barbra was tough. No one could get near her. We hired a guy to sleep outside her house in Los Angeles. We followed Jon Peters to work in the hope that she might be in his truck. She was tough to track down, and when we did she was surrounded by bodyguards."

Streisand, Neil Diamond felt, had the larger success with the duet. Although they shared royalties on the sales of the single, she sold more albums on her own. "That happened by chance," said Lundvall. "Neil was already working on his album when the single broke. And Barbra had nothing in the works. And she was concerned. So I said to Jon Peters when he called, 'Look, we'll put out a *Greatest Hits, Volume II* package with the song on it. We've got enough new hits, including "Evergreen"; she doesn't have to record a note.' Jon said, 'Great idea, she'll love it!' "

Both superstars were happy, believing they would share the album market equally. Then Streisand's album came out *before* Neil's. "His was a studio album and it took more time," said Bruce. "Neil was seething. 'Barbra got all the sales on her album,' he told me. Soon his came out and went gold also. Neil, however, remained upset, because about six months later I was talking to him about his next single, and he was having some doubts about it. I reminded him of the phenomenal reception for 'You Don't Bring Me Flowers.' And he said, 'Well, Barbra was more successful than I.' And I said, 'But, Neil, you *wrote* the song.' He smiled, and nodded, then said, 'Thank you.' I was taken aback and said, 'What do you mean?' He repeated, 'Thank you. You're the first person that ever recognized me for writing the song. There would not be a hit song if I hadn't written it.' And I said, 'Exactly.' "

Playboy: *"How innovative are you sexually?"*
Streisand: *"What? Well . . . I do have some*
               erotic art books."
Playboy: *"Do you learn from them?"*
Streisand: *"Absolutely."*
Playboy: *"How often are you the one to initiate*
               sexual activities?"
Streisand: *"We're equal, honey, we're equal."*

In August of 1978, to fulfill her contract to First Artist Films, Barbra Streisand agreed to start production in September on a new film entitled *The Main Event,* costarring Ryan O'Neal, with Jon Peters as producer. *"The Main Event* was my partner's idea," said Howard Rosenman, the executive producer of the project. "Renee Missell, my partner, wanted to do a comedy about a woman who owned somebody, a man, a boxer. Through Sherry Lansing we got a deal at MGM and we hired Gail Parent (author of *Sheila Levine Is Dead and Living in New York)* and Andrew Smith to write the script.

The idea grew to a story line, which was pitched to Sherry Lansing at MGM, who agreed to finance the project.

"I gave the script to Sue Mengers," said Rosenman. "We were developing it for Diana Ross, and we wanted Sue to get Ryan O'Neal interested—to costar with Diana. Then Sue saw the potential of getting Barbra involved *with* Ryan. She had packaged *What's Up Doc?,* which made millions for the agency, so she decided to try for that combination again."

Gail Parent, meanwhile, had slipped a copy of the script to Jon Peters, through her manager. "Jon liked the script, but Barbra didn't," said Rosenman. "So Sue Mengers arranged for me to meet them at this very important dinner party in her home. She said to me, 'Jon likes stylish people, so look great.' I was broke but I bought a gray Calvin Klein jacket, and white painter pants, and a Nudie silver belt. I looked great and when I arrived at the party, the Dunnes—John Dunne and Joan Didion—were there, along with Marty Scorsese and Julia Cameron—very heavy types. I didn't tell my partner, Renee, about the dinner; she didn't believe in that kind of socializing—she's a true artist—but *I* would have killed to do a Streisand movie. After dinner Sue directed traffic so that Jon and Barbra and I were cordoned off from the others. Barbra was sitting in a chair and Jon was sitting on the arm of it. He was saying how hip I looked. I started a conversation with Barbra, about her music, her records. I told her she was in danger of losing her audience and that she should do a duet with Stevie Wonder. She looked at me and said, 'Sue told me you were smart, but I didn't think you were that smart.' And we chitchatted some more until Jon had to show how assertive he was by saying to Barbra, 'Get me a glass of water.' And she said, 'You get it.'

Did she get it?

"Yes. And I knew there would be trouble getting a director to work with her—as more than a few wouldn't go near her—so I said to her, 'Barbra, you should direct this movie.' And she replied, 'No way!' "

When Streisand gave a definite maybe to doing *The Main Event,* it was up to Rosenman to get the script away from MGM (who were unaware of Streisand's interest) and over to Warner Bros. (her studio). "There was an executive at MGM holding on to the script," said Rosenman. "I had asked him to get it to Barbra and he didn't. So now I wanted it back, to give it to Warner and First Artists. So I set up this meeting. And prior to going in, I got some inside information on this guy, something I could use to make him give it up—without letting him know it was going to Barbra. And at the meeting he called me an amateur, and said the script was too vulgar. I used the information I had gotten. It wasn't against him, but it was very personal. And he was shocked. He said, 'Don't talk to me like that, young man.' And I said, 'Don't patronize me about age and don't tell me what you know about movies.' My whole point was to get him enraged, out of control. If he had been a real man like Barry Diller or Ned Tannen, he would have taken me by the scruff of the neck and thrown me out of there. But this one got so huffy and puffy that he gave the script back to me without a struggle."

THE DEAL

With the script secured and accepted by John Calley of Warner Bros., and with Barbra and Ryan definitely committed, the final contract negotiations among the stars, writers, and producers were held at First Artists. "There were twenty lawyers there, with just as many agents," said Howard Rosenman. "At the meeting Jon Peters began to renege on the deal set up with Sue Mengers. He and Barbra decided they would only give us half of what had been originally promised. When my agent, Michael Black, heard this he lost his tan. He got on the phone to me at Universal Studios, where I was preparing *The Resurrection* with Ellen Burstyn. 'They want to give you less, half your percentage points,' he whispered, and I yelled back, 'You tell Mister Jon Peters, in front of that assembly, to take his new deal and shove it up his ————.' And Michael said quietly, 'Howard, you don't have any money—you can't do this.' And that was true—I was broke. But at that point I was ready to take a job hanging wallpaper in West Covina, and Renee was ready to be a cocktail waitress—or maybe it was the other way around—but I wasn't going to give in. I knew I owned that material. I also knew that Jon had put a million and a half of his own money into the project—signing Ryan and other expenses. He got on the phone. 'You self-destructive ----sucker,' he began, 'I'm offering you the chance of a lifetime. Your whole career is gonna be made with a Streisand credit. She made Ray Stark; she can do the same for you. You're ---ing insane; you belong in Camario [an expensive sanitarium].'

"And I replied, very calmly, 'Jon, when you can pronounce *Camario,* I will have a conversation with you. But since I graduated from Columbia magna cum laude and Phi Beta Kappa, and since you graduated from the Valley School of Hair Design, I don't deign to speak to you. Now, here are the *new* terms I'm giving you and your greedy girlfriend.' And I added another fifty-thousand dollars and another percentage point, and I said, 'At the close of business today, if the check isn't in my lawyer's hands, then *we* will go to Diane Keaton, to Jill Clayburgh, and to Diana Ross, because I own this piece of material, and you, Jon, have made it *hot.* Good day!' "

Rosenman got his points, but was told to stay far away from the filming of his movie. "I knew that going in. Sue Mengers told me, 'Darling, good news! You are *now* the executive producer. You'll get two hundred fifty thousand dollars. So take your tuxedo to the Hollywood Cleaners. Pick it up, put it in your closet. One year from now take off the plastic bag, put the tux on, and when you arrive at the premiere of the movie, and you see Barbra, and she forgets your name . . . *smile!'* "

As full-line producer, Jon Peters drew up the budget, scouted locations, and designed Barbra's new look. Her hair was dyed red by a stylist at Sunset Plaza, and her body was trimmed and firmed by Gilda. He also hired the production staff, including the director, Howard Zieff, whose agreement *forbade* him to write about, or talk ill of, Barbra or Jon after the picture had been made.

Zieff's major problem was not with the star or her producer, but with Ryan O'Neal. "Zieff went to New York to talk to Ryan," said Rosenman, "and Ryan kept him cooling his heels for three or four days. The picture almost fell through at this point, because it was really contingent on Ryan. Barbra would only do the movie with him."

Ryan, whose career had been hot and cold—mostly cold—since *What's Up Doc?*, had been set for two other boxing pictures, *Flesh and Blood* and *The Champ*. In the latter remake he wanted his son Griffin to play the Jackie Coogan role, but the director, Franco Zeffirelli, wanted Rickey Schroeder. So Ryan turned down the movie. *Flesh and Blood* also fell through, and Ryan went through an identity crisis. He announced he was quitting pictures and he took to his bed. He would not do *The Main Event*. Sue Mengers called. Barbra Streisand called. But Ryan would not pick up the phone. Sue drove out to the beach and she and Tatum pulled up chairs and sat by his bedside. "Ryan . . . Daddy . . ." they pleaded, "you've got to get out of bed and do this movie." Ryan kept his eyes closed with the covers pulled up to his chin. Then Sue called Barbra and held the receiver to Ryan's ear. "Ryan! Honey!" Barbra cooed. "You need a hit picture. This is it. I'll protect you."

"I'll do the picture," said Ryan finally, "but only if Jon Peters cuts my hair."

"That was kind of like throwing the gauntlet in his face," said scriptwriter Andrew Smith. "Jon was jealous of Barbra's leading men—especially of Ryan, who was her old boyfriend. And Barbra liked to get things going between the two men. She had this quilt, this embroidered quilt that Ryan had given her after *What's Up Doc?* and she slept under it. When Jon came along he used to kick the thing off the bed onto the floor, but Barbra would retrieve it and put it on her side of the bed. Then when they had rehearsals for the love scenes in *The Main Event*, Ryan would always put a little 'something extra' in the scene if he knew Jon was watching. He'd tweak her ass or bite her earlobe. It drove Jon crazy. He stopped coming around when they did love scenes. He told Ryan that when the movie was over, he was going to get into the ring and beat the hell out of him. It never happened. But Jon did give him a haircut. Ryan insisted upon it; that was the deal maker. And on the first day of rehearsals at Warner Brothers, Jon showed up with his scissors and his barber's cloth, and he clipped Ryan's curls."

Despite her assurance of protection, the strength of *The Main Event* shifted to Streisand. "It became the story of Barbra finding this boxer and her experiences with him as seen through her own eyes," said Howard Zieff.

"Every entrance, exit, composition, and quip favors her," said one critic. "Even in the fight scenes, when Ryan is getting pummeled, the camera picked up *her* reaction to the beating."

"I got paid a million dollars to do *The Main Event*," said Ryan. "With a Barbra Streisand movie if you show up, it's a hit. I haven't had one in a long time. I don't care if I'm riding on her coattails."

"Ryan was very dependent on Barbra," said Andrew Smith. "He trusted her so much he wouldn't do a scene alone, without her. She was there. He was professional. He was on time. He knew his lines, and he never questioned a line. He never said, 'What is this crap I'm supposed to say?' He knew that Barbra was working so hard on the script, that if she brought in a scene, it was fine—no discussion."

For the duration of the production writers Smith and Gail Parent were kept on the payroll. "*The Main Event* wasn't *art* and wasn't supposed to be," said Andrew. "Whatever original conceptions we had for the movie went right out the window when we knew Barbra would be involved. Once we decided it was going to be *her* picture, that we were writing for her and with her, that she was the boss, then we adjusted to the situation. Screenwriters are not authors. We get paid a lot of money to write for hire . . . to write at somebody's whim . . . those are the rules of the TV and movie game. We're there as secretaries, highly paid creative secretaries. It's her picture and you do whatever she wants. But in her favor—correction: in *our* favor—she never changed a line, a word, without consulting us."

The script consultations and rewrites continued up to the moment of filming on each scene. "We were with her day and night," said Smith. "We met at her house in Holmby Hills or we went out to the ranch on weekends. She'd stay up till eleven or twelve o'clock the night before she had to be on the set. Our heads would be dropping, but she would not let go of the scene until she felt it was perfect. 'It has to be smart,' she'd say. 'It has to be smart and sharp, like a forties comedy.' The revisions and rewrites were endless. I used to bring my typewriter onto the set and out to the ranch. I didn't mind. She was working with us. She wasn't just lounging around like some old-time movie star saying, 'Write me something clever.' She was *there* with us, improvising, suggesting, doing our lines. Jon would come in for a three- or four-minute spritz session. She'd ask for his reaction, but his attention span was not the same as hers. He couldn't bear down on one thing for a six-hour stretch like Barbra."

Between writing bouts Barbra fed her guests lavishly. "God, she loved food," said Smith, "preparing it, looking at it, eating it . . ."

"The first day I went to the set," said Parent, "she got out of the car and when she saw me she was concerned that we were there and she didn't have enough for lunch. It's like arriving unexpectedly at your sister's house and she's checking to see if there's enough food for everyone."

"One night we went to Mousso and Franks's," said Smith. "It's a restaurant in Hollywood. We sat at a corner table and Barbra said to the waiter, 'Now, all I want to eat is every potato you have on the menu.' The waiter said, 'What?' And she repeated, 'Bring me every kind of potato you've got.' So he brought her *eight* varieties and she ate them all." "She also loved juicy hamburgers, jumbo dill pickles, and gallons of ice cream," said a publicity assistant who visited her one day to show her some photo proofs. "It was hilarious to watch her," he recalled. "She sat at a table with a Big Mac in one hand and a red marking pencil in the other. Then, while one hand was putting the food in her mouth, the other was taking the weight off from the photographs, with the red pencil. 'Nah, nah,' she'd say, 'My belly is too big, or my ass is too fat here,' and she'd fix up her body with the pencil, while gorging herself. She had no pretense—she was priceless."

Barbra had no vanity off camera, said Gail Parent. "She was never concerned with clothes. She never wore movie-star 'outfits.' At the ranch the clothes she wore to dinner were usually the clothes she had on for breakfast—casual ranch clothes. And she didn't seem to be at all concerned about 'the world out there.' One night when we were working the phone rang. She picked it up and said, 'No. You have the wrong number.' And I said, 'Why didn't you say, "You have the wrong number but guess who you got." ' And she said, 'Yeah! And then I could have sung "People." ' "

"Barbra could get really *great,*" said Andrew. "She'd be like sitting on a back stoop telling stories. Jon and I would talk 'man talk'—like about chicks and guns and cars—and Barbra and Gail would get real 'girly.' "

"Girly?" said Ms. Parent. "I resent that description. Barbra and I never talked about hair or makeup. We spoke like grown-up women, fantasizing about whom we would like to *date*. I told her I thought John Updike was very good looking, and she should go out with him."

On a date Barbra and Jon seemed to be the perfect high-school couple. "Yes, it seemed as if they were going steady at times," said Gail. "One night we doubled in Jon's pickup truck. We went out for Mexican food—and I thought this was great. It was very basic *except* on this double date, Jon and Andrew were in the front of the truck, and Barbra and I sat in the back—on the floor."

"She was really like a nineteen-year-old girl with a high-school guy," said Andrew. "He was her crush, and he treated her like a hot girlfriend. He was very sexy and physical with her. He would grab her like a woman. He never gave her that movie-star treatment, saying 'Oh, Barbra, you're the greatest.' He treated her like a woman. In bed he took her off her pedestal. He had a raw passion, but he was never abusive to her."

Jon, the producer, used some of the same passion to get his way in business. "The guy was very sexy, very charismatic," said Andrew. "He gives you an excitement and an energy. Intellectually you may say, 'What am I doing with this guy? He's a record kind of person—a swinger, very pushy.' And he's very bad with people, with staff. He goes through people very fast. He considers making a movie like waging a war. He used to say to me, 'Hey! We're in a battle here—you're not going home.' And he demands more than one hundred percent. But when he turns on the charm to you face to face, for three or four minutes, in those few minutes you *believe* —you say, 'Yes, I will follow you to the end of the world.' You are his best friend. And whereas Barbra is cooler, more distant, she is also more even and truthful. She is very dear. Once you are her friend, she is loyal, very warm. Long after the movie was finished and released, for years she sent me invitations to screenings, or to her birthday parties. She kept in touch, she remembers people. But Jon, who had this great pretense of 'Hey, you and me are pals, we're lifelong buddies,' once the picture is over, he doesn't remember your name or return your calls."

On December 15, 1978, filming on *The Main Event* was completed. Although her director, Howard Zieff, had a "first cut" clause in his contract, Barbra took over the film and edited it at the ranch in Malibu. (Zieff would rebound with Goldie Hawn and *Private Benjamin.*) Meanwhile the producer, Jon Peters, auditioned composers for the movie's soundtrack. Barbra's first choice for the music was David Shire, with Marilyn and Alan Bergman as lyricists. The job was eventually given to Paul Jabara.

Jabara was also from Brooklyn. When he was twelve he'd auditioned for *The Sound of Music* and met a seventeen-year-old Barbra in the casting office. They'd gone to Howard Johnson's for fried clams, split the check, and a few years later while she was starring on Broadway in *Funny Girl*, he was taking his clothes off in *Hair*. Their paths had crossed again in Elaine's restaurant when he got down on his knees in front of her table and said, " 'I love you very much.' I was with some very important people and so was she. But I didn't care, because this was my girl. I told her I had all her records; I saw her TV shows; that I stood in the rain and the snow outside the Winter Garden Theater just to see her enter and exit. And she said, 'So?' "

In his twenties, Jabara continued to act, then compose. He wrote an off-Broadway musical entitled *My Name Is Rachel Lily Rosenbloom and Don't You Ever Forget It*, about a Jewish girl from Brooklyn who idolized Barbra Streisand. In 1977 he wrote "Last Dance" for Donna Summer. This song would bring him an Oscar and a writing contract with First Artists Music. "The reason I joined First Artists," he said, "was because I knew Barbra owned the company. Donna Summer and I were in *Hair* together with Diane Keaton—but they were my peers. I wanted to work with Barbra. She was the reason I got out of Brooklyn. There were things she was fighting for that I was fighting for also. I had this fantasy that when we met and worked together I'd be embraced."

Jabara wrote one song for *The Main Event*, and Streisand rejected it. "Barbra hated that song," said Gary Le Mel, the music publisher at First Artists. "So she had David Shire and the Bergmans compose a second."

Jabara, though crushed by this rejection, would not give up his dream of writing for Streisand. "I went to Jon Peters. I wanted to prove myself to him, to show him how talented I was. I played him a lot of stuff and he was very wiped out. I also told him how much I felt for Barbra. The next thing I know they gave me a map to their house, and I was invited to their ranch for the weekend to play around with the song."

Streisand met him in the driveway, with his collaborators Bob Esty and Bruce Roberts. "I wasn't cool," Jabara recalled. "It was difficult for me. I didn't know what to say to her. She wanted changes made. She had to have her input, which is okay. Everyone does that in this business. But some of her suggestions weren't good. I felt blocked. I couldn't speak up. She intimidated me. It's like when you're trying to go home with someone and you want them so bad you just happen to say all the wrong things."

Away from Streisand, Jabara went back to his first instincts for his song. "I had not seen the movie. I read part of the script. My image for the title—*The Main Event*—was that it was the Main Thing—a celebration. I wasn't thinking of the fighting part—I started with the words *Extra! Extra!*—I heard her voice enunciating those two words—and I felt they would draw immediate attention to her. I followed those words with *Hurry! Hurry!*—which I knew she'd do something sensational with. Then I used other expressions I felt were associated with her—like 'I've got to thank my lucky stars' was from *Hello, Dolly!*—but I avoided the word *people*. And then I got stuck and brought in Bruce Roberts."

The Bergmans, meanwhile, and David Shire, had written their *Main Event* theme, but Gary Le Mel took the Jabara song and had it laid against the scene in the film. The images jumped out with the help of the disco tune. The clip with music was shown to Barbra, who said, "I hate the song. I especially hate the 'Extra! Extra!' lyrics, but it works. I'll make a demo, *but* if I still dislike the thing, we won't use it."

The demo was made at Studio 55 with Bob Esty producing, arranging, and conducting. "Barbra came in and knocked it off and it was great," said Gary Le Mel. "She loved it, and said so; then she split. The guys in the band were told to be cool while she was performing. Everyone, the crew and engineers, were told, 'Don't be crazy with Barbra, don't act like fans'—and they didn't, they were professionals. But after we left she found out she had left her handbag behind. We came back to the studio and the guys were cheering. They were so excited that they had done this song with her, and it worked, that they finally had to let it out."

"The Main Event," coupled with "Fight" (by Jabara and Esty), was chosen as the film's principal theme, and was recorded at Studio 55 over a period of two weeks. Missing from the sessions was Barbra's premiere fan, Paul Jabara. "They had me banned from the studio," he said. "Initially it was Bruce Roberts who was locked out. They said he was interfering, but I told them you can't victimize one person. Then *I* was locked out. I couldn't understand it. I had just won the Academy Award for Best Song [for "Last Dance"]. Barbra never called—never mentioned that, and then I was banned from the recording of my own songs. I don't believe for one minute that she or Jon had anything to do with that. It was my good friends, the guys *I* brought in, Bruce and Bob, who did it. It was like what happens at school. Jealousy, Jealousy and greed. Everyone wanted to get close to Barbra, so they pushed everyone else aside."

"Paul was too enthusiastic," said Gary Le Mel. "He was too much of a fan. And the thing with Barbra, if you show too much of that, it turns her off. So she spoke to Jon, I guess, and he took care of it."

"Of course, I *cared,*" said Jabara. "I ran to a dance studio. Then I went to a health farm. I cried for a week. I was very naive. Then I pulled myself together and went back to writing hit songs."

During the first week of April, Barbra, Jon, Gail Parent, and Andrew Smith flew down to San Diego to attend two sneak previews of *The Main Event.*

"We stayed at the Del Coronado Hotel," said Parent, "and went to both previews that night. I remember riding to the theater with Barbra and thinking, The fans are going to mob her. But they didn't. Maybe they didn't know she was there. And she wasn't. I mean, she *was* there—but not as a star. She didn't wear a wardrobe. There was no big change in her—she was one of *us.* And the picture started slow. A writer could die of a heart attack in the first twenty minutes. But then it picked up, and people laughed. The preview cards were fabulous. We read them at dinner and we were . . . happy."

Because of the positive reaction from other screenings, Streisand elected not to do any personal publicity for the film. She felt the good reviews and the possible popular airplay from the soundtrack record would pull in the audiences. In mid-April CBS Records in

New York received the artwork and tapes of *The Main Event* album. The record executives were not overjoyed. This was not a Streisand collection. She sang one song, repeated twice, on the album. The rest of the material was by Frankie Valli, Loggins and Messina, and by a dubious duo named Michalski and Oosterveen, who were managed and published by Jon Peters and Charles Koppelman. "They were giving us another *Laura Mars,*" said a CBS spokeman. "The package was a dud."

Not quite. Jon Peters—now wise to the ways of the record biz—had a clever marketing campaign up his stylish sleeve. He announced to the CBS brass that Barbra was going the disco route. Two singles of "The Main Event" were to be released a month before the film came out. One of them—a seven-inch version of the main theme—would be shipped to Top 40 stations and record stores. The second single—an elongated twelve-inch version of the same theme (eleven minutes timing) to disc jockeys and to the gay disco circuit. "The gays love Barbra," said Jon. "They'll eat up the longer version; but they won't be able to get it in the stores." That was the scheme. If her fans wanted the longer version of the disco song they would have to buy the album, at full price—$8.98 list.

On May 31, 1979, the two versions of "The Main Event" single shipped to DJs and disco programmers. The song went Top 40 by mid-June, concurrent with the release of the movie and the album. Each component boosted the other. All were pleased, except the Streisand purists, who did not care to hear their favorite singing disco. One reviewer of the film wanted "to throttle" the actress, whose primary goal was "to be all things to all people . . . the feminist heroine who treats her man like a sex object and the adorable goofus who confirms every male-supremacist fantasy."*

Along with her acting and vocal performance in *The Main Event,* close critical attention was paid to another Streisand liability—her derrière. "When she's not chattering like a hypertensive chipmunk, she's fanny waggling," said the Akron *Beacon Journal.* "Although her rear end seems reasonably decorative and probably is quite comfortable to sit on, it does little to advance the plot and may slow it down a bit," said the Detroit *Free Press.* The scenes in question were shot in Gilda's gym. Streisand was at her peak physically and would never have a better chance to show off her body, a

_____
* *Newsweek* magazine

friend believed. So wearing leotards, a bikini bottom, and a tight T-shirt, she "paraded her proud tush" to the beat of the disco music. Viewing the rushes of the close-up shots—where she "sodomistically bent over for the camera" (quotes from critic James Wolcott), Barbra felt her feminist friends would be offended. Producer Jon Peters overruled her concern. The shots were done in good taste, he assured her. Furthermore, her new sexual image would add another few million to the box office.

Peters' prophecy was correct. *The Main Event* grossed close to $60 million. Physical fitness buffs, along with plain, ordinary voyeurs, applauded Barbra's body and exercise-gymnastics. One staunch supporter was Jane Fonda, who two years later, with the proliferation of video recorders, taped *her* workout to music and quadrupled her fortune. "Damn it!" said Barbra, reportedly vexed at the loss of that market. "Once more I was *before* my time."

Chapter 30

"Mister Koppelman is a very clever, very bright man. His closeness with Barbra gives him enormous power. No one gets close to her with a song unless he says so. She is not aware of this. I swear to you. Barbra doesn't know. He rules the empire, and no one is spared the wrath of the tiny rod."

Songwriter Paul Jabara

THE DUELING DIVAS

Paul Jabara, the exiled composer of *The Main Event,* worked with his idol again. In June of 1979 Jon Peters sent out the word that Barbra was recording "a concept album." The concept in one word was—*Wet.*

"It was a silly theme," a CBS executive said, "but being an ex-hairdresser, Jon felt the wet look was going to be an important cultural movement—or whatever. And Barbra could sell anything at that point, so everyone said, 'Great idea, Jon—way to go.'"

Among the composers commissioned for *Wet* were Michel Legrand, Marvin Hamlisch, and Paul Jabara, who would supply the only million-selling single on the album. "When they called me for a wet theme I said to Bruce Roberts, 'Why don't we take "I'm Gonna Wash That Man Right Out Of My Hair"—traditional Broadway—and merge it with a contemporary song?' And I already had a title, 'Enough Is Enough.' This came from a line I was using at the Ashram, another health farm. I had a key phrase there

—enough is enough—meaning of overeating, of exercising, et cetera."

Jabara presented his song concept to Charles Koppelman, who turned it down. "Mister Koppelman did not like 'I'm Gonna Wash That Man Right Out Of My Hair,' because he did not own the copyright to *South Pacific,*" said Jabara. "And he didn't like 'Enough Is Enough.' He said it wasn't 'wet.' So I went back to Bruce and we rewrote part of it, and for opening lines we said, 'It's raining, it's pouring, my love life is boring.' And then we went into a studio and did a demo. But I still had to get to Barbra. She knew nothing about the song. I decided to call her directly. By a stroke of luck she answered the phone. I said, 'Barbra, they asked me to write this song. I've been working for two days—you've got to hear it.'"

Barbra replied, "I don't like to hear songs live, send me a tape."

Jabara pleaded. "Please, take five minutes." He raised his voice. "I was excited. I said, 'If you'll give me five minutes, I'll come out on Saturday and play the tape for you once.'" That was on a Thursday. "The next day my best friend, Donna Summer, came home from tour."

A duet between Summer and Streisand, that was another Jabara fantasy. He had won the Oscar and the Grammy with the help of Donna; he had a current hit single with Barbra—"So why not go for three home runs and put these two divas together?"

While helping Summer unpack, he set the wheels in motion for the pairing. "With my blind ambition I said, 'How would you like to come with me to lunch tomorrow at Barbra Streisand's house?' We were *not* invited for lunch. I was not invited. I don't know why I said lunch. But Donna asked me to call Barbra and see if it was okay. I called and her son Jason answered the phone. Barbra was at a session, so I said to him, 'Would you ask your mother when she gets home if it's all right for me to bring Donna Summer to lunch tomorrow?' And Jason got very excited. It turned out that Donna was *his* favorite singer."

On the road to Malibu the following day Donna drove as Jabara taught her the words to the song. He also briefed her on procedure. "There were so many people at the house—neighbors and friends and everybody was being *heymishe*—which means instead of talking about Barbra and her career, you talk about shoes, about decorating. The Gubers were there, and the Bogarts, and maybe I shouldn't mention names but the truth, on the other hand, is I don't give a ----. Everyone was acting very polite to Donna, but we didn't get a bite to eat—not even a glass of water. It was kind of breaking up at four o'clock or four-thirty, and no one was really talking to me except Jason. And finally I saw Barbra going to the bathroom, and with the last bit of aggression I had left, I cornered her coming out of the bathroom. I said, 'You asked me to write the song, they asked me to write the song, and you have to hear it.' She whined, 'I don't wanna hear songs on weekends.' I said, 'I know! But you've got to hear this!' She said, 'All right! All right!'—because she's a *good* girl basically. She is. Barbra is a very good girl. And I told Donna to watch for the moment I'd get Barbra alone in a room, and she was to follow. So I called to Donna, and I called to Jason, and I got them in the room and slammed the door. And like a dervish I sang the song to them, performing *both* their parts. Then I got on my knees and begged them to do it together, to try the song just once. Donna of course was as excited about doing a duet with Barbra Streisand as I was. And Jason was smiling. And Jon was outside the door, listening, and he was smiling too. I had already told Jon of the idea. He was for it. He wanted Barbra to branch out more. To him it was another growth process. So he was on my team. And right there everyone said yes."

The copyright negotiations for "Enough Is Enough"—who got the publishing, the copublishing, and administration—were handled by Charles Koppelman.

"Mister Koppelman was *not* involved in putting the girls together," said Jabara. "Whatever his resume states, he was not responsible for assembling this duet. He came in *after* it was set up. He called me to a meeting with the Entertainment Company staff. Gary Klein was there. They said they loved my song. And after the meeting Koppelman put his arm around me and said, 'You know something? We're not going to ask you for any of the publishing.' Which was great, except a week later he changed his mind. I refused at first, but then he persisted. I was thrown into a room of people I would never want to see again in my life. Koppelman made me an offer I couldn't refuse. They got my publishing, but not Bruce's. I lost a lot of money on that deal."

On August fourteenth "Enough Is Enough" was recorded at Crimson Studios in Santa Monica. "There were five or six different sessions," said Jabara, "but the girls sang together first. And let me say this—I don't like to talk—no I have to talk, without betraying anybody—but those first vocals were *terrible*. The girls were screaming. Donna sounded horrible and Barbra sounded horrible. And I said so. But one of Barbra's 'power people' said, 'Shut up; it'll sell a million anyway.' Years later I told her about that. She wasn't aware what was going on around her—certainly she needed protection—and I'm not talking Jon here . . . he was always supportive and direct . . . but . . ."

A different day, another session, and Jabara directed "the dueling divas" in private. "I told them, 'This is the same as high school, you have to learn your parts.' " The vocals were recorded again, together. "There was a popular rumor going round Hollywood that Donna and Barbra recorded separately. Not true. The master tracks were done face to face. It was wonderful to watch. Each had done her homework. There was *no* competition."

Well, perhaps a little. That night, hours after the session had wrapped, Barbra returned to the studio to add some improvements to her performance.

"What?" said Jabara. "Who told you that? . . . Maybe so, maybe not. What the hell! Barbra *did* come in on her own. And so did Donna. And then Barbra came back again. Each wanted to be the best—do the best. But only certain lines, and overdubs, were done. And certainly that's normal procedure in recording today."

In the midst of the retakes a technical snafu caused a production delay. During the overdubbing, the tape of the rhythmn section stretched, then broke, due to the Malibu sea air, which affected the tape machine. So the musicians were called back to rerecord the tracks.

"All minor problems," said Jabara, "when you consider, in retrospect, we were making a major hit record, a classic. It was fun. It could have been *more* fun. My fondest memory was driving Barbra and Jason in my two-seater, which I hardly drive because I'm a New Yorker. But as we drove up the Pacific Highway, and as the waves broke, and the sun came down, Barbra stuck the finished tape in the tape deck and she began to sing along with it as Jason ate a Bit-O-Honey bar. It was magnificent, truly one of the most glorious moments in my life. At one point I figured, 'This is it, I'll never be as happy again, so I might as well drive off the cliff.' But then I said, 'No. I'll be better than that. I'll save her life. I'll let her live.' "

Late in August, Streisand called Francesco Scavullo in New York and asked if he would come to Los Angeles to photograph her and Donna Summer for the release of their single. This would be the fifth and final Streisand record cover for Scavullo. "When I got to her house," the photographer said, "Barbra asked, 'What's your idea? What do you wanna do? How do you wanna take pictures?' She and Donna Summer had all these clothes assembled. I turned to my assistant, Sean Byrnes, and said, 'I don't see them with clothes.' Sean said, 'I'll take care of it.' "

Speeding to a store in Hollywood, Byrnes purchased two Merry Widow corsets and brought them back to Streisand's house. She objected at first to wearing one. "They're going to make us look like old-fashioned whores," she said. Scavullo patiently explained that the corsets would not be seen on camera. They would give the girls good posture, and at the same time raise their bosoms. "Yeah!" said Barbra, "I see it. The contrast of skin will look terrific." "Barbra is marvelous," said Francesco. "She is very intelligent. If you give her a good idea she'll grab it fast."

On October fifth two versions of "Enough Is Enough" shipped to disc jockeys and the stores. One belonged to Barbra on CBS Records; the other was on Donna's record label, Casablanca. "That was the deal," said Jabara. "The girls could both release the song as singles and on albums. CBS had the seven-inch version, and Casablanca, which was the big disco label, had the twelve-inch version."

Donna Summer and Casablanca had the fastest hit, however. Their twelve-inch single went platinum, selling 2 million copies within ten days. A week later Streisand's new album, Wet, appeared. Moist tunes included "Come Rain Or Come Shine," "Niagara," the Bobby Darin oldie "Splish Splash," and "No More Tears (Enough Is Enough)." But again Donna Summer's new album, On the Radio, featuring "Enough Is Enough," sold faster and jumped to the number one position on the charts. In a reversal of the sales situation with Neil Diamond and "You Don't Bring Me Flowers," two years before, Streisand was now in second place, and the position did not suit her. "She became very peeved; but it was her own fault," said a CBS marketing executive. "Barbra felt she didn't need Donna to sell her LP. She left off all mention of her and their duet from the cover of her album. Donna, on the other hand, had a full-sized Scavullo photo of herself and Barbra posing back to back on the cover of her twelve-inch single. So the fans were snapping up *her* album. Barbra wanted action. A rush meeting was called at CBS. It was decided to take the Scavullo photo, reduce it in size, and slap it on the front of the *Wet* LP. They made four-by-four photo stickers. They actually had guys going into record-stores, sticking these things on Barbra's albums, posters, the walls, everywhere. Later they released another single from the *Wet* LP, but it couldn't touch the Donna Summer duet. Altogether that song helped to sell close to six million records."

"I remember only the good things. My wallet remembers nothing."

Paul Jabara

"Working with Barbra? Why is everybody so interested? It was, let's say, a different experience."

Donna Summer

"The song with Donna Summer? What song? Oh, yeah, the disco thing. It was cute. My son, Jason, played it a lot; which was unusual. My son likes Donna. He never plays my stuff."

Barbra Streisand

Chapter 31

BAD DAYS AT BLACK ROCK

Eventually the Streisand LP of *Wet* went platinum, and CBS Records was grateful. It had been a bad year for the record label and the industry in general.

After a decade of unbounded growth, in which the record business raked in sales of $3 billion to $4 billion a year, the bottom dropped out and the boom was suddenly over. "Record Industry Profits Plummet," said *Rolling Stone* in June of 1979, adding a subtitle: "CBS Hit the Hardest."

From an all-time high of $94 million in 1978, CBS profits dropped to $51 million in 1979. The losses, a spokesman said, were due to "various ills"—including the competition from Pac-man and other video games; "foreign-exchange losses" (due to the devaluation of the dollar); and a strike at the Columbia pressing plants in the fall of 1978 which, when settled, led to massive orders and record-store overstock (and returns) for the Christmas holiday.

CBS was also criticized for its extravagant financial advances to record stars. A reported $2.5 million per album was guaranteed to Paul McCartney when he joined the label. Walter Yetnikoff, the current president of the CBS Records Group, denied this sum as "absolutely *wrong.*" The figure, others stated, came to $1.9 million (which was $400,000 more per LP than Streisand was receiving).

Defending the advance, Yetnikoff announced that the new McCartney album had sold 1.3 million units, and in terms of comparative chart positions, Columbia was "very hot at the moment," with five out of the Top 10 albums. "We're not in anything *like* a loss," said he, "and that goes for the domestic operation by itself, let alone the foreign operation."

Beyond the positive braying, CBS Records throughout 1979 implemented a strict cycle of cutbacks and cost disciplines. They dropped the price of most catalogue LPs from $7.98 to $5.98. They cut the standard hundred-percent return privileges for record retailers to twenty percent (including defective product). And a retrenchment in the area of artist tours was made. Such luxury staples as chartered Learjets and stretch limos were eliminated and promotional parties, billboard ads, tour jackets, free buttons, and T-shirts were reserved for major artists.

On June 29, 1979, fifty-two employees at CBS were discharged. The dismissals were described as "middle-level administrative and secretarial personnel,"—and no further staff reductions would be made. On August tenth—a day called Black Friday—another 120 employees were fired. "The shock was apparent in the halls and elevators, where conversations were carried on in whispers," said Kurt Loder of *Rolling Stone,* "and in the various offices, where empty desks and floors littered with torn-down posters and other promotional items offered mute testimony to the effects of the mass sackings."

Jim Brown—the former national promotion manager for albums, and then in charge of soundtracks and special products—recalled his dismissal. "I was called in and told, 'We've got some bad news and some good news. The bad news is your job is being eliminated. The good news is there is another opening for you in our office in Paris.' I said, 'Paris? Paris, France? But I don't speak French.' " Brown had been with the company for close to twelve years. "I loved the place. If you cared about music, Columbia was the only place to be. They were the king of record companies. They had the best of everyone—from show music, to pop music, to classical music—I worked with everyone. I started with Streisand—promoting the *Funny Girl* album. I worked with Janis Joplin. In 1968 she performed at the convention in Puerto Rico. I came across her lying on the beach one day and put my towel down next to her. She was wonderful. Totally different from what you saw onstage. We spent the afternoon together. We spoke about everyday things, about home and people. Nothing about rock 'n' roll or the record business. In 1972 I went on tour with Andy Williams. His contract was up for renewal. He was just coming off 'Love Story,' which was a million seller, so Columbia said to be nice to him—to make sure he was happy. They knew he had a movie and recording offer from United Artists. And eventually I told Andy why I was tagging along. He appreciated my honesty and said, 'Jim, I'll be frank with you too. A. I can't act my way out of a paper bag, and B. I'm happy at Columbia, and I don't need another million dollars. So I intend to re-sign, so in the meantime, let's relax and enjoy ourselves.' "

"There are others," said Jim Brown. "Liza Minnelli, Johnny Mathis, and Michael Jackson. All terrific artists. I got Michael Jackson tickets for *Annie*. It was a hard ticket on Broadway at the time, and CBS had access to house tickets. People like Mary Kay Place would call, and what a pleasure it was to get *her* tickets. But Michael, he called and in that quiet soft voice said, 'Oh, Jim can I get two tickets, and can I ask you a favor? Can I really be pushy and get backstage to meet Andrea McArdle?' I said, 'Michael, no problem. I'm sure she'd love to meet *you*. And Sandy the dog also.' Michael was thrilled. Such a sweet kid. Most of them were nice. God, there were great times. [Laughter] And I'm rambling on. Let's see . . . about Streisand . . . She didn't hang around New York too much. Once I had to go up to her apartment on Central Park West. She wanted to have some tape cassette speakers put in. Barbra wasn't there, but her mother was. She didn't say a word. I was with a Columbia engineer and we had to install the speakers in various rooms. Her mother followed us from room to room. Talk about being inhibited. She never spoke. I was very impressed with the place. I thought the decor would be early Korvettes, but it was antiques, Oriental rugs, very well done. In the bedroom you had to walk up three steps to the bed, which had a dark-green velvet canopy over it. It was awful. Off the bedroom she had this one room where she had her Oscar, her Emmy and Grammy, and pictures all over the wall with herself and people like JFK—all autographed by these people to her. She also had an old-fashioned school chair, with the arm on it, and the inkwell. That must have come from her school. When she graduated she probably said, 'Well I sat in it for twelve years so now I'm taking it with me.' "

Brown later got a thank-you note from Streisand for installing the speakers. "It was on her personal stationery. It said, 'Barbra Streisand Gould—Thanks for all the stuff. Love, Barbra.' I don't recall the year—maybe 1978. She and Elliott were long divorced, but she still had the old notepaper. Thrifty as always. But I didn't care. I framed the thing. I've got it hanging in my house with all the other memorabilia. And that's all that's left from Columbia; the memorabilia and the music."

GUILTY

Well into 1980 CBS Records continued to squeeze every available dollar from budget cuts and income revenue. To generate further cash, studio union-personnel were transferred to menial jobs, and the vast Thirtieth Street recording site in Manhattan was put on the auction block. It was here that such Broadway shows as *South Pacific, My Fair Lady,* and *A Chorus Line* had been recorded along with Stravinsky, Casals, Leonard Bernstein; and Streisand, too, made her recording debut at Thirtieth Street. Despite pleas from the cultural community, made directly to Bill Paley and to Thomas Wyman, the president of the network, CBS sold the studio for $1.2 million. It was later razed, and in its place today stands a parking lot.

Artist rosters were carefully revised; marginal performers were dropped; and a concentrated effort was made to get as much product as possible from the remaining major sellers. Among them were Bruce Springsteen, Pink Floyd, the Jacksons, Billy Joel, Boz Scaggs, and Streisand herself, who would soon record *Guilty,* an LP that would replenish the CBS coffers and become the largest-selling work of her career.

"We set out to make the great Streisand LP that she never made. The album represented six months work for me, and two weeks for Barbra."

Barry Gibb on Guilty

The legend of how Barbra Streisand was paired with Barry Gibb varied as told by the principals. It was his idea, Charles Koppelman claimed. He had always been a big Bee Gees fan, he told

Billboard. He remembered their "wonderful songs of years back—'To Love Somebody' and 'Massachusetts.'" (The fact that they were also responsible for the $25-million success of the soundtrack album of *Saturday Night Fever* one year before may have also crossed his mind.)

In October of 1979 Jon Peters and Barbra went to see the Bee Gees in concert at Dodger Stadium in Los Angeles. The following day she requested copies of all their albums, and a meeting was set up with the trio. Songs owned by Koppelman and Streisand were presented to "the boys" and were politely turned down. They performed their own compositions, they explained. Barbra then asked if they'd write some tunes for her. "We jumped at the idea," said Barry Gibb. "She was my favorite singer ever since I heard 'People' in Australia."

The Bee Gees came up with five songs for Barbra. They included "Woman In Love" and "Run Wild," written by Barry and Robin; and "Guilty," written by Barry, Robin, and Maurice. Barbra "fell in love" with the material and asked that they record together as soon as possible. But negotiations had to be made with the Bee Gees' manager, Robert Stigwood, who was headquartered in a pink palace in Bermuda. "Streisand's group spoke to Stigwood, and all was very jolly until they asked him for a cut of the publishing," said one source. "But Stigwood wouldn't give up one lousy E-flat to them. Not this tycoon. In making deals and pulling in money he was a pro; he could outwit the best of them."

Stigwood kept the publishing, and furthermore he asked for three quarters of the CBS advance and royalties from the record. That was only fair, he claimed. Streisand was but one voice; the Bee Gees were *three.* "But they all sound alike," Streisand countered. "How much for just one?"

And hence a deal was struck. Only one Bee Gee would sing with Streisand. Barry Gibb would perform and coproduce the album (with his partners Karl Richardson and Albhy Galuten). For his performance on the duets he would receive half royalties; with a full producer's fee and royalty for each record and tape sold. (Stigwood would later bill Streisand for the use of Barry's face and body on the album's artwork, but the bill was never paid.)

"This project could have been a disaster," said Koppelman. "You're dealing with a lot of egos, mine included."

"I was a nervous wreck at the beginning," said Barry, who had heard that Streisand was a very tough lady. "And she is this *enormous* star. That's got to intimidate anyone. I didn't want to work with her at first, but my wife told me she'd divorce me if I didn't."

Gibb was also apprehensive that Barbra would demand too many changes on his songs (she asked for rewrites on only one—"Woman In Love") and that she would emasculate him in their studio duets by her powerful voice. His amplified vocals, at the best of times, could hardly reach the next room, whereas Barbra at full wail could be heard in the next county.

Gibb's fears were for naught. In February of 1980 the instrumental tracks were laid down at Criteria studios in Miami, and the subsequent vocals were overdubbed in Los Angeles. Barbra was "mellow, laid back, a pussycat." She was not interested in working her lungs out as she had done with Donna Summer.

"She was perfectly nice, a true lady in every sense of the word," said Gibb. "But we did have to lock her up when the food came, because she always wanted to eat. We had to keep her away from the food so she'd keep singing."

Keeping Barbra away from visitors during the *Guilty* recording sessions was a task shared equally by Jon Peters and Charles Koppelman. "They had a guard posted outside the door to the studio," said composer Mickey Leonard ("Why Did I Choose You"). "I ran into Barbra and Koppelman in the parking lot one day. She was wonderful, very friendly. She mentioned a new song of mine that she had heard, but then Koppelman got nervous. She wanted to talk, but he said, 'Oh, Barry's waiting, and he'll be angry.' So he led her away. It was as if he was afraid I'd give her some material without his sanction. To me that kind of behavior is counterproductive, countercreative, counter-everything."

On another day a female executive from CBS Records attended a session with her boyfriend, whom she described as "young, tall, and very good looking." She recalled: "We stood at the back of the recording studio, watching Barbra and Barry overdub. When they took a break, Barbra asked if anyone had some herbal tea. I had some in my bag so I offered it to her. She came over and spoke to us. She was charming, a lot of fun, until the studio doors opened and Jon Peters walked in. He took one look at Barbra talking to my boyfriend and he ordered us both to leave. He was actually jealous, with good reason I suppose. Barbra was looking very attractive in those days—'very foxy,' my boyfriend said—and Jon Peters wasn't about to let anyone near her."

Mario Casilli, one of Hollywood's leading photographers of beautiful women, captured Streisand's "foxy" look during that time. Casilli had photographed Barbra for the cover of *Playboy* in 1977. "That assignment was done in my studio, which was way out near the mountains," he said. "We sent a limo for Barbra, and before she arrived I was very apprehensive. From all the stories I heard I was expecting to meet a monster, a real terror. But she turned out to be a fantastic lady. She told me up front what she would do and wouldn't do. Then she left me alone." The photographer and Barbra "played" during the *Playboy* session. "She got into a bunny outfit and posed, but it wasn't used," said Mario. "Barbra had final approval of all the shots and I guess she felt she didn't look right in it. The shot she chose was one where she was wearing white shorts and a *Playboy* T-shirt. She had her socks on and I asked her to take them off. 'Okay,' she said, 'now you can say I took something off for *Playboy*.'"

The following year Casilli shot the cover for Streisand's *Wet* LP. "She requested me for that, and contrary to what people think, when she calls she never says, 'I have a shot I want you to do.' She always asks if I'm available and if I'd like to do it." Casilli went out to the ranch with his assistant and with CBS art director Tony Lane. "Jon Peters wasn't there. Barbra did her own hair and makeup. We photographed her in three or four different wet settings. One was in the hot tub at the redwood house. Another was in the pool by the art-deco house, which had just been built. We worked fast because there's just so much water the skin can take before it becomes unattractive. Also it was a cold day, so the pool was heated. That added steam to the shots. There was nothing arty or contrived, because she didn't want that. It was a good experience. Each one was better than the one before."

Barbra and Barry Gibb were in the midst of recording the *Guilty* album when Casilli arrived at the studio to take some production shots. "I wasn't hired to shoot the cover," he said. "Tony Lane from Columbia already had an idea for the *Guilty* cover. He wanted to have her photographed in a studio with a saint on one shoulder and a devil on the other. So when I got to the session I took some test shots, with no concept at all in mind. They were just production shots of her with Barry, wearing a white blouse and white slacks. She looked at the shots and said, 'Let's do more of these.' "

"Suddenly this was an *opportunity,*" said Tony Lane. "With Barbra in those days you had to take advantage of whatever time you were given. I figured we better do something. Mario sent out one of his assistants for some white background paper. We decided to set up a part of the recording studio as a photo studio. A messenger was sent over to Barry's hotel to get his white shirt and slacks. It was rather quick and was the most offhand way of trying to do a cover." "There was no pressure from Barbra, from anyone," said Casilli. "When you're shooting for a cover, which we weren't, well, that's a tougher situation. We shot for about an hour. It was fun. Sometimes you're lucky enough to ride on a wave. Something happens and you've got your camera going."

Mario went out to the ranch with the processed slides and his projector to set up a showing. Barbra was delighted. "She said, 'These photographs are so flattering to me. How the hell did you do that?' I told her, 'Barbra, I've got to do something well. I can't sing.' And she broke up."

On March sixteenth Gibb produced Streisand singing two rock 'n' roll classics, "Kansas City" and "Lady Madonna," which were never released. "We never heard those songs," said Bruce Lundvall, who visited the L.A. studio during the recording of Guilty. "The concept was for an album of Bee Gee songs, so I guess the others were discarded."

In all, eleven Gibb compositions were recorded. Two of those, "Secrets" and "Carried Away," were discarded, and a third—"What Kind Of Fool," a duet with Barbra and Barry also came close to being cancelled. "They kept overdubbing on that song and they still had a problem," said an engineer. "Barbra's performance was flawless. Her vocals on "What Kind Of Fool" were so pure, so good—too good, in fact. She made Barry sound like an intrusion. She didn't need his voice or any voice on the song. Her advisors kept telling her, 'Do it alone, drop Barry.' But she wouldn't. It was written as a duet and the guy only had one other song to sing on the album, so she insisted that he stay with her. They must have overdubbed the thing twenty times in Los Angeles, and it was eventually finished at Media Sound in New York."

The editing and remixing on *Guilty* continued through the summer of 1980. On August twenty-ninth the first single, "Woman In

Love," was released. It became an immediate success. The album followed one month later. The reception from the fans and the critics was rapturous. "Streisand, a Jill of all pop-trades, sounded young, renewed, and coquettish," said Richard Harrington of *The Washington Post*. "It's as beautifully crafted a piece of ear candy as I've heard in years," said Stephen Holden, who reviewed the album in tandem for *Rolling Stone* and *The New York Times*. "Gibb is a better partner than either Neil Diamond or Donna Summer, since he never competes with Streisand. Instead, he's like a smart chauffeur, whisking his princess heavenward."

Guilty would spawn three Top 10 singles over the following nine months. The album would also reach number one in fifteen different countries, including Russia. Sales in total came to 8 million (not including the USSR tally) and the profits carried CBS over the recession slump. The company asked for a repeat, a second album. Gibb was willing, as were Charles Koppelman and Jon Peters. But Streisand was not amenable. "Barbra does not like to repeat herself," the label was told. Furthermore, Barbra the "serious" artist had come to the fore. Once again she felt it was time to stop singing and pursue the true legacy of her art—acting, in movies.

Chapter 32

"I wanted to play Juliet . . . in Romeo and Juliet. . . . I saw her as a real horny kid . . . a little animal . . . I would have done it for TV, but the networks said, 'Does she sing in it? Who's playing Romeo?' "

Barbra Streisand

FAVORS AND FREEZES

Throughout the 1970s Streisand frequently expressed dissatisfaction with her acting career. With the exception of *Up the Sandbox,* and most of *The Way We Were,* she felt she had not fulfilled her destiny as a dramatic actress. Producers and studio executives only saw her in flimsy comedies or musicals, she complained. Yet a review of the roles she turned down showed a similar deficiency of foresight. She passed on *They Shoot Horses, Don't They?* and *Klute,* which starred Jane Fonda; and brought her an Academy Award. Barbra said no to *Cabaret* and *Alice Doesn't Live Here Anymore.* Declining the latter role, she stated, "No one would have believed I was a mediocre lounge singer."

After she expressed her willingness to work "in something important" on television, the script of *Playing for Time,* written by playwright Arthur Miller, was sent to her agent. The role of Fania Fanelon, the half-Jewish nightclub singer who was sent to Auschwitz during World War II, seemed perfect for Streisand. Certainly it would have fulfilled her every acting challenge. But her agent turned it down. Mainly because of salary, it was said. Streisand, art or not, was still a star. She had her price (which was double the budget of the TV play) and opted instead to take the well-paid, and well-played, secondary role in *All Night Long*.

All Night Long was originally planned as a low-budget comedy starring Gene Hackman and Dennis Quaid. The director was Jean-Claude Tramont, who was married to Sue Mengers, who represented Gene Hackman *and* Streisand, who came across the script one day, read it, and "laughed her --- off."

The role of Cheryl Gibbons, a dim, dippy bleached blond, who was married to a fireman and aspired to be a country-and-western singer—but sang off key—appealed to Barbra. It could be a welcome respite and a radical departure from her usual high-energy, rapid-talking performances. However, the part had not only been cast with Lisa Eichhorn—the bright new star of *Yanks*—but filming of *All Night Long* was already in its third week.

"Hold the phone," the producer said when told of Barbra's interest. The picture was shut down, Eichhorn was let go ("for artistic differences"), and the small, low-budget comedy now became a major, expensive film, with a large chunk of the new outlay going to Streisand. Her supporting salary, as negotiated by Sue Mengers and Jon Peters, was $4 million, plus fifteen percent of the profits—and lest anyone use the word rapacious, it was announced that the actress agreed to accept second billing after Hackman.

While the negotiations were being finalized Barbra went on a fast diet to lose the weight she had gained since she'd last faced the cameras two years previous. She went to a health spa—the Ashram, in Calabasas, California, described as "a boot camp without food." Streisand skipped the early-morning four-mile hikes, but she did attend yoga and exercise classes. She worked out with weights, played volleyball, and dined twice a day on raw vegetables, fresh fruit, and herbal tea.

In late August, lighter by fifteen pounds, she reported to work on *All Night Long*. In line with her character, her behavior on the set was low-keyed and sweet-tempered, and she offered only the barest amount of direction to the other actors. The following March, after two disastrous previews and some hasty reediting, Universal Pictures slipped the film into release. In a bid to get back some of the huge salary they had paid the star, they featured Streisand, in the poster ads, with her skirts hoisted and her legs wrapped around a fire pole. The critics panned the picture, but some praised Streisand's performance. *Boxoffice* felt she was a victim "of the worst miscasting since John Wayne played Genghis Khan," but she added a giddy feeling of the unexpected to the movie's plot. *Rolling Stone* called her portrayal of the subdued, soft-spoken blonde "her best performance since *The Way We Were.*" Others who commended her work were Arthur Bell and Liz Smith. Arthur went to see the movie twice, and swore he paid for the repeat ticket. Liz thought Barbra "was amazing, quite wonderful, she reminded me of Marilyn Monroe."

The movie itself was a dud. It had a very limited run. It also terminated the relationship between Streisand and Sue Mengers, her agent since 1969. The two had been close friends. In 1973, when Mengers married Jean-Claude Tramont, Barbra booked a full symphony orchestra and spent three days recording French and Jewish love songs. She made one copy of the session and presented it to the couple.

"Barbra believed that Sue talked her into doing *All Night Long,*" said Liz Smith.

"No one talks Barbra into doing *anything,*" said Mengers. "She is a girl who makes up her own mind."

When the movie was shown at a private screening in New York, Streisand attended, wearing white mink, and was "noticeably cool" to Mengers and her husband at the party afterward. The following week *People* carried the news: Mengers had lost her star client. "It was because of *Yentl,*" a studio executive said. "Barbra thought that Sue wasn't crazy about the story and didn't want to push the project." "It was because of her manager, Jon Peters," another source claimed. "He told Barbra she didn't need an agent. He could handle this job also." "It was mainly because of money," said Liz Smith. "Barbra never paid Sue her commission for *All Night Long.* She owed her something like half a million dollars. Streisand said, 'I did the movie as a favor.' She got four million dollars and felt she had a right to keep all of it. Sue didn't pursue it. She dropped Barbra and stuck by her husband. I always thought that was one of Sue's finest hours. She jeopardized the most important business relationship of her life—in order to support her husband's movie."

"'Memory' is a beautifully crafted, meltingly lovely reverie. What happens when larger-than-life

Streisand sails into this ecstatic, heart-pounding material is probably why record vinyl was invented in the first place."

Peter Reilly, Stereo Review

"MEMORY"

Although she had sworn off pop recording, Streisand consented to cut some new songs in September of 1981. She did this as a favor for Charles Koppelman, and for CBS Records, who were still stuck in a recession. When Walter Yetnikoff, the new president of the record label, called and urged her to help them out, Barbra told him she did not have time to do an album, but she would record some singles.

One of these was the Puccini-esque ballad "Memory," from the British hit musical *Cats*. Streisand had seen the play in London that August. Her visit to Britain had been carefully observed by one newspaper, which accused the star of "skulking around London trying to avoid being noticed—thereby making sure everyone realizes she's here." Arriving at the theater "dressed in a stunning gold outfit, with gilt turban," Streisand created as much diversion in the audience as did the actors onstage, the paper reported—"So it was just as well she left at halftime."

Streisand was quite taken with "Memory," but she knew the song had been recorded, and smashingly so, by the London star of the show, Elaine Paige. When she was assured by Charles Koppelman (who had secured the administration for the U.S. publishing of *Cats)* that the Elaine Paige single would be released only in England, she agreed to record her version for the larger and wider American market. Another perk was added when the composer of *Cats,* Andrew Lloyd Webber, agreed to produce the sessions for Barbra. It was also hoped that she would record "Don't Cry For Me, Argentina" from his other hit show, *Evita.* Barbra considered it, then said no. She liked the melody, she told the composer, but she was bored by the show, and furthermore she felt that Evita Peron "was a fascist."

As *Cats* was not scheduled to open in the U.S. until the following year, it was decided that the first single released from the London sessions would be "Comin' In And Out Of Your Life," written by Richard Parker and Bobby Whiteside. It was shipped to disc jockeys on November third and received prompt, wide airplay on Top 40 stations. It was climbing up the best-seller charts when it was stopped by the sudden release of Streisand's "Memory." The reason for the rush release of "Memory" was explained by former CBS President Bruce Lundvall: then president of Elektra Records. "I had seen *Cats* in London the first week it opened. I felt that 'Memory' would be a perfect song for Judy Collins. When she heard it, she agreed. We recorded it and were just about to release it when we heard that Barbra had also cut it. Then the reports got back to me that Charlie Koppelman and his staff were calling all the independent promotion people, telling them to block the Judy Collins record of 'Memory,' because this was going to be Barbra's next big single. CBS rushed their version out, which wasn't a very smart move. They already had a hit going with 'Comin' In And Out Of Your Life,' and they killed it."

"Memory" by Streisand was shipped twice to disc jockeys and reviewers, but neither release made the Top 40. The song, however, helped propel her new album, *Memories,* to platinum status, even though seven of the nine featured songs were old cuts. "They really angered the fans with that repackage," said a CBS publicist. "You should have seen the mail they sent in. Certainly they had cause for anger. Some songs on the LP, like 'Evergreen' and 'The Way We Were,' had already been released two and three times before. But the attitude within the company was 'What the hell, Streisand fans will buy anything.'"

And they did. *Memories,* the album, sold 3.7 million copies. "We needed it," said Walter Yetnikoff. "She needed it too."

In December, while passing through New York, Streisand contributed her name and her presence to a benefit for Women U.S.A.—a hotline organization for women in trouble. The fund raiser, a cocktail party, was to be held in the Fifth Avenue fashion offices of Diane Von Furstenberg. Other names who promised to attend were Bella Abzug, Gloria Steinem, and Marlo Thomas.

Befitting her new image of a struggling producer-director, Barbra dressed down. Her poverty-chic wardrobe included an old black fur coat, with a plain black beret, and six-hundred-dollar suede boots. She rode up to Von Furstenberg's studio in the freight elevator and was swept into the designer's private office. Arriving a short time later was columnist Liz Smith, who was also given the VIP service. "I was yanked into this inner sanctum," said Liz. "I didn't get it. All the other guests were assembled outside. But they told me, 'You don't have to see those people. Come in the back way and say hello to Barbra.' So I'm taken into this private office and there's Barbra, with her good friends Sis Corman and Renee Taylor. These three yentas were sitting there chatting and laughing while Bella and Gloria Steinem were outside working the room, being nice to the crowd. People had paid seventy-five dollars to see Barbra, but she was in hiding with her attendants. Secretly I was so enraged by this that I couldn't think of anything to say to her. Finally I said, 'Well, I don't know about you all, but I'm going outside.' And they all looked at me like I was crazy, because to be by her side was all anyone should ever want from life. And I said to Barbra, 'I think you should go out and mix with your guests.' And she said, 'Oh, I can't do that.' She was acting like she was going to be *fire-bombed.*"

Moments before the official speeches began in the main room, Barbra joined the gathering. "You should have *seen* her entrance," said Liz, cheerfully demonstrating the reluctant star's arrival. "She came into the room with her back up against the wall. She moved along the wall inch by inch until she found a safe spot by a fireplace, and she proceeded to sit down. Bella is standing on her left, and Gloria Steinem is on her right, but she's sitting down. No one could see her. Then after Bella spoke she called upon Barbra to talk. She stood up and said, 'Anything that Bella says is okay by me,' and she sat down again. That was the sole sum of her contribution, and I thought, 'What is this? What is her problem with herself?' She could have come out and let the people talk to her. No one was going to hassle her or ask her for an autograph. And if they did she could have said, 'Hey, this isn't the place for that.' She could have charmed them. Really. The cream of New York was in that room, but she was acting like she was the queen and they had some terrible disease."

Chapter 33

THE *YENTL* YEARS

"Yentl, the Yeshiva Boy," the story of a rabbi's daughter with "the soul of a man and the body of a woman," was written by Isaac Bashevis Singer in 1962. Optioned for film by Valentine Sherry, it was sent to Streisand in 1968. "I had just finished *Funny Girl,*" she said, "and I called David Begelman and said, 'I got my next part.' " But Sherry had also been to Begelman, who turned him down. He did not want his client to follow Fanny Brice with another ethnic role. Still Barbra persisted. She met with the producer and with the director, Ivan Passer, who told her she was "too old, and too famous" to make the story believable.

"Those were wonderful words to hear," said Streisand. "It was like I was a kid again, listening to the experts say I wasn't suitable, that I would never make it in show business. I knew right there I was going to play *Yentl.* I would not be stopped."

In 1972 Streisand picked up the option on her own, and proceeded to commission various scripts, including one by Singer, and another by playwright Leah Napolin, who expanded the story for a 1975 Broadway play starring Tovah Feldshuh. The movie project went through title changes. One was *Sweet Dreams,* another *Leah/Leon,* until Streisand was told that it did not matter what the title of the movie was as long as she starred in it.

By this time Jon Peters had entered Streisand's personal and private life, and *Yentl* was put on a back burner until the pair had completed and launched *A Star Is Born.* "It will be my next film," she said in 1976, "but I'm too old to star, so I'll just direct." But even with the success of *A Star Is Born* there were no takers for Streisand the director. Or for Streisand the straight actress, as *Yentl.* The story was too ethnic, too esoteric, it was decided. If she wanted to do the film she would have to sing—to make it a musical.

Barbra eventually agreed, and Orion Pictures put up the development money for writers, researchers, and a composer and lyricists. But less than a year later, on November 27, 1980, Michael Cimino's $40-million production of *Heaven's Gate,* starring Kris Kristofferson and Isabelle Huppert, opened and closed in one night in New York. "That changed the face of the motion picture industry," said Streisand. "All of a sudden studios didn't want to hear about any movies over ten million dollars." *Yentl,* with a budget of $14 million, was one of the films dropped at Orion Pictures. "The trials and tribulations of Barbra Streisand as a girl rabbi do not strike me as a commercial picture. I don't think the picture would be a hit even in Tel Aviv," said one of the company's executives.

Barbra was devastated, but a temporary reprieve came from boyfriend Jon Peters. He brought the picture to Polydor Pictures, where his business partner, Peter Guber, was in charge of production. Polydor agreed to finance the picture with Peters as producer, but that arrangement ended when he and Barbra "began to butt heads over the way the film would go." Peters reportedly wanted to jazz up the story with jokes and flashy production numbers. "For personal reasons we decided not to work together," Streisand told the *Los Angeles Times,* her eyes narrowing at the word *personal.* "It was a time in my life when I really needed to be independent, both personally and professionally. I thought to myself, I have to make this picture, and I have to also be the producer. Before that I was just going to direct and star."

"She was so brave," said Jon Peters, "so tenacious. I wondered where it came from."

"It came from the opening lines of Singer's story," Barbra later explained: " 'After her father's death Yentl had no reason to remain in Yanev.' "

Barbra's father had left her when she was fifteen months old. She was too young to fathom death, but she felt his loss, and she was angry. "Angry because he left me. My mother used to tell me that after he died, I used to crawl over to the window and look out—like I was still waiting for him to come home."

Growing up, she knew from visits to other kids that they had fathers, and when they came home from work she was told to leave. Adults, she came to feel, were the enemy. They were not to be liked or trusted, but they could be bested, she learned, through schemes of deception and manipulation.

After she became a star, and through therapy, Barbra proceeded to put some of her childhood grievances to rest. She settled and accepted her differences with her mother ("I love my mother," she said. "She's probably responsible for my success. Because I was always trying to prove to her that I was worthwhile, that I wasn't just a skinny little *marink*"). She also began to discover who her father really was. He was not just a high-school teacher. He wrote doctoral dissertations; he was interested in drama; he played chess, and was on the debating team in college. He was also an athlete, played tennis, fenced, and was once a lifeguard. "I look like my father," she said. "I have his build and his features."

Streisand also learned how her father died. It was not from a cerebral hemorrhage, her mother admitted. He suffered from epilepsy, at that time a shameful affliction. In 1979 Barbra finally visited his grave. Her brother took her there and she posed for the only picture of them together, with her arm around his tombstone. "But that night I had a much stranger experience," Barbra said. "My brother Sheldon brought a medium to see me." Her brother, she hastened to add, was not a dreamer or on drugs; he was very structured—he was in real estate. And this nice, ordinary-looking Jewish lady with blond hair sat with them around a table with their hands touching. Soon the table began to bang out letters. It spelled her father's name, and B-A-R-B-R-A (the table knew she had changed the spelling years ago), whereupon Barbra fled to the bathroom and locked the door. When she returned, the medium asked the table for a final message. It rapped out S-O-R-R-Y, and S-I-N-G, and P-R-O-U-D.

"It sounds crazy, but I know it was my father who was telling me to be brave," said Barbra, "to have the courage of my convictions—*to sing proud!* And for that word to come out—*sorry*—was his answer to all that deep anger I felt about his dying."

After that experience her father's spirit grew stronger within her and Barbra began to explore her religious roots. She sought the help of a rabbi, a young South African, Daniel Lapin, in Venice, California. After his counseling she offered him payment; he asked instead if he could prepare her son Jason for his bar mitzvah. Barbra, who three years before had told *Playboy* that she did not believe in the ritual of bar mitzvahs, was very moved by Lapin's offer. She accepted, supported his school, and when she had exhausted his knowledge she moved onto other sources. "Like a peripatetic bee flitting from flower to flower, soaking up a bit of Talmud here, a Torah portion there, she consulted rabbis all over the country in her quest for instant education in Judaism," said reporter Ivor Davies.

Howard Rosenman, the erstwhile producer of *The Main Event,* recalled a different Streisand during this time. "One day Linda and Peter Guber had this big Passover seder. The entire Hollywood hierarchy was there—the David Begelmans, the Ned Tannens, Sue and Jean-Claude Tramont—about eighty people, including Jon and Barbra. I come from this intense Orthodox Jewish background; I'm an Israeli and I know the traditions. I was asked to lead the seder, and I sang Kaddish over the wine. It's a beautiful song, and Barbra, who was already into *Yentl,* and her Jewish roots, loved it. She turned to Jon Peters and said, 'Who is that angelic person singing?' And Jon replied, 'That's your producer, schmuck. That's Howard Rosenman.'"

Howard and Barbra formed a bond that night. He offered to introduce her to rabbis he knew and to lead her to other sources. "She became monomaniacally obsessed with getting as much information as possible, and with getting it right."

Her search also led her to Molly Picon, a respected actress from the Jewish theater. Molly knew Barbra. They had worked together in 1973 on the film *For Pete's Sake.* But that had been the old Barbra, the one who treated her costars like scullery maids. She had humiliated Estelle Parsons, another costar, by refusing to say her lines directly to her on or off the camera. Molly Picon was treated a little better. Barbra simply whittled her part down to one or two words. But she did follow up with a gift. Weeks after the movie was finished a package arrived at Molly's house. It contained a stack of albums and a note which read, "For Molly, You were perfect, Love, Barbra."

Segue to the summer of 1979, when Barbra watched a TV movie about the Holocaust in which Picon appeared. She called the actress. "Molly," she said, "I just saw one of your old movies which was done in Poland. And I'd like to know, is that street you lived on in Warsaw, is it still there?" And Picon became angry. To think that Barbra Streisand did not know that the Nazis had destroyed Warsaw during the war.

"Barbra's knowledge is confused and rudimentary," said Chaim Potok. "Yet she asks questions openly, unselfconsciously, and with no hint of embarrassment."

Rabbi Chaim Potok, author of *The Chosen,* was asked to work on the script of *Yentl.* In exchange, as payment, she would grant him an exclusive interview. He agreed, and taught her about Hillel and Shammai, two talmudic sages; and also about sacred texts and man-woman relations in Jewish orthodoxy. Streisand picked up on the sexual-sociological orientation. "It's not law," she said. "It's bullshit. Men have used these things to put women in their place." Potok's wife was in accord. "The Church did the same thing," Barbra continued. "It's that same struggle we're coming back to, this male-female power struggle. I think it has to do with erections. A man is so capable of feeling impotent that what makes him able to have an erection a lot of the time is the weakness of women."

Chaim Potok got his interview eventually. He described the star as intense and indefatigable. "I sense about her something of the aura of the narcissistic personality: alluring, playing at being charming, centered on one's own self, laboring relentlessly and expecting the same of others, too soon bored with achievement, too quickly disdainful of permanence, grasping at opposites, at times impatient to near ruthlessness with those of smaller mind or lesser vision." The benevolence, the melioration, came, he said, "through her self-effacement, her recently reinforced sense of Jewishness, and her awareness that if you pretend to be something you are not, you are nothing."

In February of 1981 Barbra found a permanent berth for *Yentl* when United Artists agreed to finance the picture. The budget was set at $14.5 million, with any overage coming from her actress salary. Being at UA pleased the actress-director even more when the company merged with MGM, and two old friends came in at the top echelon. They were her former agents—Freddie Fields, and David Begelman, who had survived his forgery scandal.

For the role of Avigdor, the handsome, young, brash yeshiva student with whom Yentl falls in love, several actors were considered. Richard Gere was touted, especially after he and Barbra were seen "necking up a storm" at a Hollywood party. Actor Christopher Walken, who had won an Oscar for *The Deer Hunter,* was also a candidate. At home one night Barbra screened *Pennies from Heaven,* in which the actor costarred with Steve Martin and Bernadette Peters. Bored with the first ten minutes of the movie, Streisand yelled to the projectionist to fast-forward the film to Walken's scenes. And actor John Shea, from the movie *Missing,* was called for an interview. Shea had played Avigdor on Broadway. He met with Streisand in her Central Park West penthouse. "She was very nice," he said. "She had a lot of great ideas for the movie. But we both decided I wasn't right for the role. On the stage I could get away with it, but on the screen—blown up to twenty feet—I didn't look Jewish."

And so, Mandy Patinkin, who had played Che Guevara in *Evita* on Broadway, was chosen to act in *Yentl,* but not sing. This would *not* be a traditional Hollywood musical, with each character bursting into song. Only Barbra would sing, and then the music would come as her inner thoughts. "So the other characters don't have thoughts?" she was asked. "They do," she replied, "but they keep them to themselves."

To write the musical score, Barbra considered using Marvin Hamlisch or Leonard Bernstein, then decided to go with someone in between the pop and the classical—Michel Legrand. The lyricists were the team who had been on call since the project began—the Bergmans. "We started to work officially on July 15, 1980, in Los Angeles," said Michel Legrand. "I had read two or three scripts, and I worked from there."

"We had many discussions with Barbra as to where the songs should appear," said Alan Bergman. "We would work up a scenario or a title for the song, and Michel would come up with five or six melodies . . ."

"Or eight or ten. . . ." said Marilyn Bergman.

"Yes," said the prolific Legrand, "I wrote many, many songs. It could have been twenty, even thirty. I compose, and then I begin to eliminate. I narrowed it down and played the melody for the

Bergmans, and for Barbra. The melody came first with each song, except for "This Is One Of Those Moments." I did that from the lyrics."

The phrase *Papa, can you hear me?* came when Legrand played the musical notes for the Bergmans. "Michel writes such *vocal* music," Marilyn told *Billboard.* "We always say there are words on the tip of his notes."

"It took about three months to write the score," said Alan. "Most of it was done in our home."

"They came to me in Paris once," Legrand stated. "Barbra and the Bergmans. Then for the finish I went back to Los Angeles."

"The numbers were blocked and videotaped in our living room," said Alan. "Also, it was wonderful to be able to call our director and say, 'Can you come over and sing this song for us?' Barbra would come over and we'd go upstairs and she would sing all day long as we worked on the song. And to have the definitive version of your songs done the first time . . ."

". . . was wonderful," Marilyn agreed. "When Barbra does anything, you don't have to wait for the authoritative version, because there it is. It was a dream."

In April of 1982, after fifteen years and twenty different scripts, production on *Yentl* began at Lee International Studios in London. For the duration of filming Barbra rented the four-story house of Rod Stewart's former manager. According to a published schedule she awoke each morning at six-thirty A.M. and immediately went into her specially designed set of stretch exercises. After a light breakfast she was driven in a bright-yellow Mercedes to the studios, where the closed set of *Yentl* was assembled on three huge soundstages. After makeup and wardrobe, filming began at ten A.M. sharp (they were on European hours—ten to seven). Lunch was a working break, and that evening after shooting, she viewed the rushes from the previous day. At nine-thirty P.M. the "exhausted" star was taken straight home, where she had a meal sent in from Wags, one of her favorite restaurants. On weekends she stayed in, going over the script and the production schedule, except on those rare occasions when she dined out with Michael and Shakira Caine, and with Warren Beatty. Warren was there for professional support only, her aide explained.

"I have enormous respect for directors. I found having all that control was very humbling. I am very embarrassed by having power. Zelda, my script girl, would sometimes say to me, 'Gotta speak louder on the set, Barbra. You speak too softly.'"

Barbra Streisand

It was indeed a *new* Streisand. Her fellow actors adored her. As a director "she was demanding, yet flexible and compassionate, with the gentleness of a woman," said Mandy Patinkin. As an actress "I never thought of her as a girl. She was a guy, period."

When they kissed, her costar Amy Irving was "pretty excited. I mean, I'm the first female to have a screen kiss with Barbra Streisand! She refused to rehearse, but after the first take she said, 'It's not so bad. It's like kissing an arm.' I was a little insulted, because I believed so much that she was a boy that I'd sort of fallen in love with her."

The British crew of *Yentl* was also enamored of the producer/director/star. The grips and electricians drafted a letter and sent it to the editors of *Time, Newsweek,* and *The New York Times.* Those publications chose not to print it, but the *Hollywood Reporter* did and it said, in part: "Because she is subjected to so much adverse press, we thought it might interest you to know . . . she has completely captivated us all. Though undoubtedly a perfectionist, in her dealings with everyone . . . she has shared jokes, chats, and pleasantries each and every day. She appears to have no temperament, her voice is scarcely heard on the set but her smile is seen constantly . . . this letter is entirely unsolicited and is the result of a collective affection."

"I became very aware of not being self-serving. Barbra-the-actress could not get her close-ups because Barbra-the-director was otherwise occupied."

Early in the summer, while her mother worried about "communists and machine guns," Barbra and the *Yentl* company flew from London to Czechoslovakia to shoot the exterior scenes. "It was rough; the conditions were primitive at times, but Barbra saw only the good things," said a crew member.

Jon Peters flew from California to visit the location and was revolted by the smell of urine and sewage. "Barbra never noticed," he said. "There were flies as big as beetles but they never bothered her. She just swatted them."

In Prague, Streisand shut down the city traffic for three days to film the old Charles Bridge. Recruiting five hundred extras in period costume, Barbra as Amshel rode in a horse-drawn buggy across the bridge, to the toll of three hundred thousand dollars. The scene came to only two minutes in the film but it was worth every penny, the MGM/UA executives agreed. And in the village of Yanev, for the cemetery scene where Yentl said Kaddish over her father's grave, Barbra the director had the old gravestones uprooted and moved temporarily to a hill "because I like the idea of the dead having a view."

The following spring in Los Angeles, while Streisand worked non-stop on the editing, negative ruminations about *Yentl* bounced across the patios and tennis courts of the movie colony. It was jocularly referred to as "Barbra's Folly," and *Tootsie on the Roof.* The costs had escalated to $20 million, it was said, and the insurance company had seized control of the film. This was inaccurate, the star's publicist maintained. She was only $1 million over budget, and that sum was being withheld from the actress's $3-million salary. As for the seized footage, Barbra was still editing the film, but her time was limited to six weeks. "Please!" she pleaded with the Bond Company. "We're going to ruin this movie. I'm going to die from the pressure. This is supposed to be a joyous experience."

Early in June a special screening, with dinner, was hosted by Barbra for 250 MGM/UA executives and employees. As the film rolled, she stood at the back of the screening room "twiddling with the sound controls." After the film Steven Spielberg greeted her, saying, "This is the greatest directorial debut since *Citizen Kane.*" Three weeks later, with a completely redubbed score, *Yentl* was shown to Walter Yetnikoff and the CBS Records staff in New York. Asked for an assessment the following day, one of the record executives replied, "If you love Barbra Streisand, you will love this movie."

And the music? They loved that too. Her voice was flawless as ever. The dulcimers, zithers, cellos, and wooden flutes were "exquisite"—perfect for an album. For the release of a single, however,

CBS was in big trouble. There wasn't a cut from the score they could push on Top 40.

When Barbra was apprised of the record company's reaction, she was not happy. Nor were MGM/UA, who were depending on the record sales and airplay to promote the film. Then a solution was found. Why not rerecord two of the best songs from the picture with more modern, up-to-date arrangements? These could be released as singles, and also be put on the LP, bringing the number of songs from eleven to thirteen. Certainly the fans, famished for new Streisand product, would be pleased. And for the pleasure of the extra songs the price of the album could be raised to $9.98, a dollar more than usual. ("The higher price was necessary," said a CBS publicist. "The packaging costs were exorbitant. Close to thirty-five thousand dollars was spent on retouching the photographs until Streisand was satisfied.")

Barbra agreed to rerecord, but this time Michel Legrand would not be arranging or conducting. "They had a big fight," said Legrand's manager, Nat Shapiro. "She hated him because after London he wouldn't go back to Los Angeles with her for post-production. She wanted him to mix and edit, but Michel is a composer, not an engineer. He had a James Bond movie to do, and he missed his family in France. He spent eighteen months with her, but Barbra doesn't know when to quit."

"I hate to be there during dubbing time," said Michel. "It's such a waste of time because maybe I'm needed five minutes a day. For that you waste fourteen and a half hours doing nothing. I'm there when I have to do full work."

"She got very demonic," said Shapiro. "She said his name was going to be taken off the producer credits on the album. And they were. Michel went through this with her before and I told him, 'Don't worry. She'll forget. At Academy Award time you'll be close again.'"

The new arrangements for "The Way He Makes Me Feel" were done by Dave Grusin, and the recording session was produced by Phil Ramone. Barbra was apprehensive about the new sides. TV writer and producer Kenny Solms recalled an evening at Burt Bacharach and Carole Bayer Sager's home. A group, including Streisand, Neil Diamond, and Neil Simon, were asked to tape a "good luck" message, for Heartlight, the Bacharach's horse, running that weekend at Belmont. After the taping they listened to music. Richard Perry played his new single of "To All The Girls I've Loved," by Julio Iglesias and Willie Nelson. "And finally someone," said Solms, "I think it was Carole who was gutsy enough to say, 'Barbra, did you bring the cassettes from *Yentl?*' And she said, 'Yeah . . . but,' And then she finally went out to her car and she must have had twenty cassettes with her. She only played one. It was the last song of *Yentl,* where she hits that incredible note. She put it on, and it was such a funny feeling, 'cause on one hand you're listening to this magnificent voice, and on the other hand she's in the room, so its doubly nervous. You're not used to her *being* there, or doing that. Barbra never plays her own music for people. But we all listened, and from time to time I sneaked a look over at her. Her eyes were down. She was very self-conscious. And I'll never forget what happened—right after that last wonderful note Carole said, 'Was that really you, Barbra, or did you loop it?' It was embarrassing, but Barbra laughed, and someone else said, 'Play another one, play another one.' But she wouldn't."

On October twelfth the updated version of "The Way He Makes Me Feel" was released by CBS Records. The release coincided with her first public appearance on behalf of the film. The occasion was the United Jewish Appeal dinner in New York, where Streisand was to receive their annual Man of the Year Award.

This was to be an industry affair, the press were told. Photographers would be allowed in the lobby for five minutes to take pictures, but reporters were not invited unless they paid the tariff of $250 per ticket.

And who had made this ordinance? Streisand? The UJA publicity office? No. It was CBS Records and the other record companies, whose presidents were on the UJA board of directors. "They've been keeping out reporters ever since the Richard Perry affair," said one source.

Richard Perry? The record producer? Barbra's close friend?

"Yes."

But he wasn't press.

"True, but he did something they were ashamed of, and *Rolling Stone* wrote about it."

Flashback to 1973, when Perry had a string of hits, including Streisand's "Stoney End" and "You're So Vain" by Carly Simon. Perry decided to turn his multitrack talents to film. He wanted to produce and direct full-length features. So, for starters, he shot a twenty-minute documentary on the record business. The short was called *Sliced Steak* and focused on the UJA testimonial dinner of that year, when Morris Levy, the president of Roulette Records, was honored as Man of the Year. "The slow death of the record biz . . . one *ugly* movie," said Ben Fong-Torres, describing the short.

It opened with a harpsichord playing the theme from *Love Story* as the camera panned the room of flushed faces, thirteen hundred people eating, drinking, and pressing flesh. Then, one by one, to an off-key brass accompaniment, the record-industry leaders entered the room and paraded to the dais. The toastmaster of the evening, Joe Smith, a former disc jockey and "the much-liked president of Elektra Records," proceeded to introduce the dais, calling the pioneers of the record business "cheats, cutthroats, and pains in the ass." The first industry leader was really there to line up hookers, he said; two others were brothers "who invented the four-bookkeeping system, with four separate sets of books. It took those guys ten years to find out they were screwing *each other!*"

Sliced Steak was not released commercially, and it is not known if Perry was invited to attend another UJA dinner. His name was not on the CBS guest list for 1983, a spokesman stated.

On Friday, October twenty-eighth, the day before the UJA banquet for Streisand, Liz Smith reported in her column that the star was flying in for the fête in a private jet with a load of friends—one of whom was the Prime Minister of Canada, former beau Pierre Trudeau. The announcement certainly added a patina of high class to the event, but Barbra was not pleased with the scoop. She called Liz, who, it should be told, was touting *Yentl* day in, day out, in her column. "I always thought the movie was a wonderful idea, and I wanted it to be good," she said. "So whenever I heard anything positive, I printed it. Then this story came in about Barbra and Trudeau, and I printed that also. Well, she called me. She said, 'Liz, I have to know where you got that story. Nobody knew that.' I said it was just somebody I ran into at a party. She wouldn't accept that. She started. She named one million people we knew in common, including Pat Newcomb (who handled the press for *Yentl).* I told her, 'Surely you know by now that Pat wouldn't tell me anything.' And she wouldn't, not if she felt that Barbra wouldn't want it known. I said, 'Look, Barbra, it was just somebody I ran into; they didn't mean you any harm.' But she had to know. It was her personal life—she didn't say you shouldn't have printed it—she wanted me to give her the source. She named Steve Ross [the chairman of Warner Bros.] and his wife. 'Did Steve and his wife give you that?' she said. I said no. She said, 'Well, they're friends of yours.' They were acquaintances, I told her; I had never been in their home, and they never call me to give me items about themselves and their guests. I later heard she called them, too, and gave them a very hard time. For what? It was a harmless item, and it was accurate. She did arrive with Trudeau, and they posed willingly for photographers."

Two simultaneous premieres were planned for *Yentl* on November sixteenth. One was in Los Angeles, the other in New York. Barbra chose to attend the West Coast bash, which was a benefit for the Women's Guild of Cedars-Sinai Medical Center at two hundred and fifty dollars a ticket. The evening was chaired by Anne (Mrs. Kirk) Douglas. Other committee members were Harriet Deutsch, Fran Stark, and Joanna Carson, who was listed as the Women's Guild chairperson for gifts.

The Los Angeles evening at the Cinerama Dome Theater was described by Mary Louise Oates, a *Los Angeles Times* staff writer. It had "more than a touch of the halcyon days of Tinseltown. There were platoons of red-and-yellow-jacketed valet parkers (looking like the Michigan Marching Band gone astray, said another reporter), traffic coordinators with walkie-talkies, publicists, photographers, and hundreds of fans, who were kept behind ropes across the street." The frenzied crowd got only a glimpse of Streisand, as she and her escort, Jon Peters, bolted from their stretch limo and into the theater. "No down-in-the-polls candidate on the last day of a losing campaign ever waved more perfunctorily," said Oates.

Inside the theater a harried publicist complained that Barbra's entrance had been too rapid for the photographers outside. They needed more arrival photos. And "back she came, just outside the door, where the photographers shot, and she smiled, for about twenty-two seconds."

"Barbra looked as if she had not slept the night before," said Randy Emerian, a fan from Fresno who attended the premiere. "I think she was very nervous about Hollywood's reaction to the film."

At the postpremiere party, as fourteen hundred guests dined on Chinese chicken salad and rack of lamb, Barbra received guests in a trailer parked outside the vast tent in the Dome parking lot. No-shows were Goldie Hawn, and Ray and Fran Stark (who, with the Deutsches, went to New York that day for some shopping). Jane Fonda ("Her well-known, worked-out body encased in what resembled a robe from a wealthy monk," said Mary Louise Oates) and her husband, Tom Hayden, spoke to the *Yentl* star for a half hour in her trailer, but passed on their five-hundred-dollar meal inside the tent.

Leaving the trailer, Streisand continued to play hide-and-seek with the photographers. As they lined up at the front of the tent canopy, being briefed on her imminent arrival by a press aide, Barbra slipped through a side entrance and made straight for the center-stage table. There she accepted congratulations on the film from Gregory Peck, Steven Spielberg, Michael Douglas, Danny Thomas, Roddy McDowall, and any of the other affluent guests who could get past her flank of "spear carriers."

The premiere in New York—a benefit for the Ms. Foundation and the YIVO Institute for Jewish Research—was also festive. On the guest list were Mandy Patinkin, Amy Irving, Liza Minnelli, Gloria Steinem, Marlo Thomas, Phil Donahue, Judy Collins, Alexander Godunov, and Diane Von Furstenberg, with Howard Rosenman, who had already seen the movie at a screening set up especially for him at MGM by Barbra. "I had seen Barbra two weeks before," said Howard. "She stood by my table at the Russian Tea Room for almost an hour, talking about *Yentl*. When she heard I was going to Europe and that I wouldn't see the film in Dolby stereo, she arranged a private screening. Afterwards I went to the opening, with Diane. Barbra called the next day. She said, 'Was the music too loud? What did you think? What was the audience's response?' She was really concerned. I told her at one point, 'You were fabulous as a boy. Anshel was very sexy.' And she said, very cutelike, in that nasal voice, 'Howard! Anshel is taken.'"

On the following Friday *Yentl* officially opened to the public in twelve main theaters. That morning, "thoroughly spooked," anxiously awaiting the reviews, Barbra said, "The hell with it. I ran out and bought all the chocolate-covered marzipan and walnut cookies I could carry and sat there and stuffed myself. That's how scared I was."

Gradually, as the reviews came in over the phone from New York, Los Angeles, and Toronto, the chocolate and cookies were put aside and Barbra found herself *levitating*. The reviews were *raves!*

"*Yentl* is a delicious, sly, profound fable . . . a courageous and heartening achievement," said Jack Kroll in *Newsweek*.

"Barbra Streisand gives *Yentl* a heart that sings and a spirit that soars," said *People* magazine.

"*Yentl* is extraordinarily fine . . . this is no small-scale undertaking. . . . Barbra Streisand is a good director," said David Denby in *New York Magazine*.

There were some pans, naturally. Howard Kissel of *Women's Wear Daily* criticized the feminist tract, and the lack of poverty in turn-of-the-century Poland. "No one in Bel-Air will need to be embarrassed to acknowledge such decorous folk as his forebears," said Kissel. And Janet Maslin of *The New York Times* admired the earnestness of the production, and Barbra's convincing performance as a boy, but faulted the lip-synching, and the *Funny Girl* ending, where Barbra strode through the emigrant boat bound for America, singing at the top of her lungs, "while none of the bleak-looking refugees even bats an eye." Yentl was wearing two different wool hats, and a matching sweater, Maslin commented, and "you'd think her fellow passengers would have noticed the outfit, at the very least."

While few reviewers faulted Streisand's acting, or her singing, many had reservations about the music she had to sing. Richard Corliss of *Time* called the score "the most romantic and sophisticated, original . . . since *Gigi*," but others deemed the music slow, repetitive, and boring. Lyricists Alan and Marilyn Bergman, whose lyrics were widely praised, defended Michel Legrand and his music as follows: "There are no cop-outs with this film. Everything is exactly as we envisioned—or better. This is one case where the reviews didn't mean a thing. We felt for those people who weren't as thrilled as we were. It's not unlike some reviews Stephen Sondheim received for *Sunday in the Park with George*. Some critics commented on the sameness of the music—where he states something in Act One and that reechoes in Act Two. This is structurally deliberate. Someday maybe the people will understand what

Sondheim is doing musically, and they'll better understand what Michel wrote musically in *Yentl.*"

"Standing Ovations for Barbra and Yentl!" was Liz Smith's column headline on November twenty-third, a week after the movie had opened. The gross was $341,769 in three days at twelve theaters, said Liz. The word-of-mouth was runaway, and while Streisand was still at MGM every day "correcting prints of the movie as they come from the lab," the MGM/UA brass were happily projecting the figures for the nationwide release two weeks hence.

Streisand was tactically prepared for the mass release. Her two public relations firms, Rogers and Cowan, and Solters and Roskin, had carefully planned and orchestrated their media blitz.

During the two years of production and postproduction of *Yentl,* the star had imposed a firm blackout on all publicity for herself and the film. There had been no exceptions, not even for *People* magazine, who had voted her one of the twenty-five Most Intriguing People of 1982. For the honor, and their two-page spread, she'd given them a photo, but *no* quotes.

Now *Yentl* was walking and Barbra was talking, nonstop, to the press. She opened the gates to her Holmby Hills castle and one by one the reporters trouped in, to lunch and to listen to her story. Then, one by one, in late November and early December, their cover stories (with approved photos) appeared in *Harper's Bazaar,* the *Ladies' Home Journal, McCall's, People, Life, Billboard,* the Sunday *Daily News Magazine,* the *Los Angeles Times, Vogue,* and *Newsweek.* The proliferation of publicity prompted one reader of *People,* John Ryan of Tarpon Springs, Florida, to respond: "We haven't heard from Streisand in years. She wouldn't consider giving an interview. Now that she has her own money tied up in a movie, she's all over the place plugging it. For the next few weeks, she would probably appear at my house if I could guarantee fifty people."

The medium of television was not overlooked either. On November seventeenth, the eve of *Yentl's* opening, Barbra received a full hour of prime time on ABC's *20/20* program. The interviewer, Geraldo Rivera, had spent a year following the star from Malibu to Prague to Liverpool to London and back to southern California. "This was her first TV interview in seven years. There were no ground rules, and we had almost complete access behind the scenes," said Geraldo, neglecting to add that the access could have been provided by the man who managed both of them, Jon Peters; and that Barbra considered him "safe." Geraldo would not pry or persist with personal questions, she felt. If he did, she could handle him.

Rivera: What about Pierre Trudeau, the Prime Minister of Canada?
Streisand: You mean, you want to know about my love life?
Rivera: I just want to know about that one.
Streisand: You just want to know about that one.
Rivera: I mean, he seems like such a nice man, so—
Streisand: Oh, he's a lovely man.
Rivera: Not that I'm pushing it.
Streisand: Very interesting. I like him.
Rivera: So you think you'll see him again?
Streisand: I'm sure.
Rivera: Would you vote for him, if you lived in Canada?
Streisand: Absolutely.
Hugh Downs: And there's more to come. We'll be right back.

In December a five-part interview with Gene Shalit was aired on the *Today* show. In one segment Barbra took the opportunity to blast *The New York Times,* which had failed to adhere to her carefully planned *Yentl* publicity campaign. The previous month she had given the paper an interview, which they failed to print. That was the third "favorable" piece killed by the august publication— the conspiracy and bias were obvious, or so it seemed to Barbra.

"There is no bias toward Barbra Streisand," said the deputy managing editor of *The New York Times,* Arthur Gelb, who added that he had also been the first critic at the paper to review the star, in 1961. ("I went to the Bon Soir to see a comic and was delighted to find such a wonderful new singer on the bill.") Examining the coverage on Miss Streisand's work since then, Mr. Gelb stated the policy of the paper was to "reflect the state of her progress, or lack thereof, as an artist," and certainly in her day the actress-singer had received many favorable *Times* notices.

"I don't remember good reviews; only the bad," Barbra told Gene Shalit. "But I'll tell you the truth, I'm gonna change my way. I'm gonna do exactly what I said I didn't want the world to do; I'm gonna *not* do what I said I didn't want the world to do. By me remembering a bad review and not a good review—this is me doing exactly what the press do—emphasizing the bad and not the good. I'm as guilty as they are. But from now on I'm not gonna tell you about my bad things. I'm gonna try to remember only the good."

Chapter 34

"I'm sure Barbra has changed. She seems to have a more generous spirit and doesn't seem as threatened by the world in general. Therapy has helped, to a degree. We can all do therapy, but personality transplants are not possible."

Bob Schulenberg

YENTL AND OSCAR

Throughout January of 1984 *Yentl* remained in the number-three and number-four top-grossing position in *Variety*, behind *Sudden Impact, Scarface,* and *Terms of Endearment.* The film was not yet a blockbuster, but that extra push would come when the Oscar nominations were released in February, it was hoped. Winning an Oscar for Best Picture could add as much as $30 million to the gross. Winning for Best Actress could increase ticket sales by $8 million. And for Best Director? Well, to count on all three was pushing the fates, but certainly the odds to win something were in Streisand's favor.

Can you buy an Oscar? That was the question asked in a *Times* cover story during the 1984 Oscar season. Their answer was, probably not, but the Hollywood studios spent millions each year trying, and MGM/UA was no exception. In January and February of 1984 they spent approximately two hundred thousand dollars in trade advertising—for *Yentl* the movie; for Streisand the actress; for Streisand the director; for Streisand the co-writer; plus occasional ads for Mandy Patinkin, Amy Irving, and members of the technical crew.

Streisand on her own agreed to cooperate with some low-keyed Oscar campaigning. Her platform was aimed at two important groups in the film industry—the large Jewish contingent and the women voters. In mid-January she made a special pitch to the latter bloc in an interview with Bob Thomas. "If I fail," she said, "not only would the film fail, I would set back the cause of women." Streisand also socialized a bit, making herself visible at designated luncheons and dinners. She even gave a cocktail party, and made a rare appearance at a press screening for another movie. The picture was *Reckless,* also from MGM/UA, and at the party afterward she happily posed for photographs with the film's young stars. "This kid has a great future," Streisand said of the male lead, Aidan Quinn, neglecting to make any public predictions for his blond costar, Daryl Hannah, standing on her right.

On January twenty-eighth, the Golden Globe Awards were held in Hollywood. Cohosts of the evening were John Forsythe and Julie Walters *(Educating Rita),* who quipped, "I almost lost my knickers" when she saw the legendary Streisand sitting in the audience. Other stars present that night were Paul Newman, Shirley MacLaine, Robert Duvall, Jack Nicholson, Ann-Margret, Jane Wyman ("I'm such a bitch," said Golden Globe winner Miss Wyman, referring to the character she played in *Falcon Crest),* and Cher ("I have no speech prepared," the winner for *Silkwood* announced, "so look at the dress while I think of something").

Barbra was nominated for Best Actress in the musical or comedy field, but the award went to Julie Walters. She was also nominated for Best Director, with James L. Brooks for *Terms of Endearment,* Peter Yates for *The Dresser,* Mike Nichols for *Silkwood,* and Ingmar Bergman for *Fanny and Alexander.* When the winner was announced, Streisand's hands flew to her ears in disbelief. She had won!

The second major award for *Yentl* came when the Foreign Press Association voted it the Best Musical Comedy of the Year. "I feel very grateful to have had the opportunity to make this film, and that to me is its own reward," the star said in acceptance, then moved on to the press room to answer questions about the next big competition—the Oscars. "I am very Jewish, and very pessimistic," she said. "If I say I want to win it, I won't. So I'm saying nothing."

On January twenty-ninth, the morning after the Golden Globes, Streisand's buoyant mood was abruptly lowered. An auto-interview by Isaac Bashevis Singer appeared on the front page of the "Arts and Leisure" section of the Sunday *New York Times*. In it he blasted the movie *Yentl* and its star.

It was no secret that for some time Barbra and Mr. Singer had not exactly been crooning lullabies to each other. The previous fall, when the author was asked to comment on the forthcoming screen adaptation of his work, he had commented, "First I'll see the killing; then I'll perform the autopsy." He had been dissatisfied with Barbra for a long time, he added.

The dispute was over money, his publisher said. "I sold my story to poor producers," Mr. Singer said, referring to the original contract made in 1967. Barbra, when she picked up the option in 1972, paid him a very modest sum, with no percentage of the profits. She had also asked him to write a treatment of the story. He had complied. She had never used it and never paid him for it either.

The author was invited to the New York opening of the film, but sent his wife and his rabbi in his stead. (Mrs. Singer's full comment after viewing the movie was "Barbra has nice skin.") Then in December Mr. Singer agreed to see the movie, and afterward he sat down and composed his auto-interview.

His objections were manifold. He was opposed to the insertion of music. "My story was in no way material for a musical, certainly not the kind Miss Streisand has given us. Let me say: one cannot cover up with songs the shortcomings of the direction and acting." He protested the omnipresence of Streisand the actress to the exclusion of the other actors; and he decried the new ending, in which Yentl leaves for America. "Weren't there enough yeshivas in Poland or in Lithuania where she could continue to study?" the Nobel winner asked. "Was going to America Miss Streisand's idea of a happy ending for *Yentl?* What would Yentl have done in America? Worked in a sweatshop twelve hours a day when there is no time for learning? Would she try to marry a salesman in New York, move to The Bronx or Brooklyn and rent an apartment with an icebox and dumbwaiter?"

The kitsch ending wrapped up all the faults of the adaptation, he concluded. "It was done without any kinship to Yentl's character, her ideals, her sacrifice, her great passion for spirited achievement. As it is, the whole splashy production has nothing but a commercial value."

The Singer article came at an unfortunate time. It would hurt the Oscar campaign, it was thought. But then two weeks later, days before the voting was closed, *The New York Times* printed a full page of letters from readers, rapping the author's complaints. Gallantly leading off the defense for Barbra was the wife of her old *Hello, Dolly!* costar, Mrs. Walter Matthau, who knew a few things about writers, having been twice married to playwright/author William Saroyan. "I was shocked to realize that Mr. Singer is a mean-spirited, ungenerous, and cranky man. I am thrilled that Barbra Streisand lives dangerously and breaks ground," Mrs. Matthau wrote from her home in Pacific Palisades, California. "Why did you sell it to the movies?" she asked the author, and wondered if George Bernard Shaw ever thought that the Eliza Doolittle of his *Pygmalion* would one day sing. "I love Mr. Singer's work," the letter concluded, "but I am dazzled by Barbra Streisand's valor and passion and aspiration. It made my heart burst with pleasure."

> *"The Oscar nominations are out and Barbra Streisand didn't get any. Today she found out the true meaning of* The Big Chill.*"*
>
> *Johnny Carson to his TV audience on the night of February 16, 1984*

At eight o'clock on the morning of February sixteenth, every studio press agent and independent flack in Hollywood gathered in the auditorium of the Samuel Goldwyn Theater on Wilshire Boulevard in Beverly Hills. They were there for the reading of the annual Academy Award nominations.

Seventeen minutes later Barbra got the call at home. *Yentl* had won four nominations: two for songs, one for score, and one for Amy Irving as Best Supporting Actress. But she personally had gotten nothing. The majority of the voters chose to ignore her acting, directing, and the fifteen years she had spent trying to put the film on the screen.

"Barbra was *stunned.* It was like someone hit her on the side of the head with a bag of bricks," said a friend. "It was a very sad, very depressing, day for her. Her friends rallied to her side. They rushed to her house, or called. It was like a wake. She was inconsolable. She couldn't eat or drink. She didn't know whether to cry or be angry. Everyone around her was furious."

"I want a recount," said actress Shelley Winters. "I haven't talked to anybody who didn't vote for her."

"Not nominating her was unconscionable," said Martin Bregman, her former business manager and the producer of *Scarface*.

"It diminishes *my* nomination, I am very saddened," said Shirley MacLaine.

"Barbra has every reason to be bitter and bewildered by what amounts to a flagrant slap in the face from the show-business community," said columnist Marilyn Beck.

The din and the furore over the Oscar snub continued to be discussed and written about in the succeeding weeks. "Fair play or foul?" *People* magazine asked in a three-page story which gave its readers some theories on why she was ignored. Hollywood hated her; Hollywood was jealous; Hollywood was sexist.

Certainly the latter could be substantiated in the category of Best Director. The directors' branch of the Academy (who picked the five nominees for that category) had 256 men on their roster and 1 woman, Elaine May, who worked on the script of *Yentl* but wasn't credited.

"You want to know what I really feel?" said actress-director Lee Grant. "Screw 'em. So what? It's not the only game in town. What's important is that Barbra keeps making films."

As for failing to receive a Best Picture nomination, Streisand's lack of popularity within the movie industry may have been a factor. Certainly in the past she had unsettled a few egos and cut a few fast corners in financial dealings. But she had changed, hadn't she? What about all those recent articles on how friendly and cooperative she had become, and what about her generosity? She had given close to a million dollars to Jewish charities in recent years.

Journalist Arthur Bell had a few words to say on Streisand's new image. "The change was too sudden. She went from Barbra the monster to Barbra the misunderstood, practically overnight. I watched her on the *Today* show with Gene Shalit. She told him she had never been temperamental in her life. Who was that other person? Mary Magdalene?" Columnist Liz Smith also remarked on the dichotomy: "I respect Barbra's talent; I think she is the greatest performer of our time. But as for her not being temperamental, all she has to do is be unselfconsciously forgetful for a moment and she'll lapse into Napoleon or something."

Arthur Bell nevertheless believed that Streisand's philanthropic acts were sincere. "You see, that happened to my father and his friends," he said. "My father is very rich and successful. But when he was young he was very poor. He had no time for religion or other people. Then as he got older he knew he couldn't put all his money into a bank. So he gave it to temples and other worthy Jewish causes. So did his friends. They bought trees in Israel and supported the UJA. And they are people who literally wore torn underwear when they were nine or ten years of age, and who sort of clawed their way to the top of the heap—or the *schmata* trade— or wherever. And it's not that they had to step over so many people—but aggression had a lot to do with it. So when they got there they felt they had to atone for some of their sins, and for some of the stuff they forgot to do on the way up. I know without talking to Barbra that she might say that's the truth in her case also."

"Barbra's generosity *is* authentic," said Howard Rosenman. "I know this, not from her, but from other people. She once asked a rabbi, 'What's the highest form of charity?' And in Judaism there are about twelve gradations of charity. The highest form is that the donor does not know who he or she is giving to, and that the person who receives doesn't know who it comes from. And Barbra saved a lot of yeshivas that way. She would find out from religious people which yeshivas or shtetls—which are communities populated by old men from Eastern Europe—were dying out. And she donated money to save them."

"I have enough money, thank God, and the only reason I want it is to give it away. There's nothing more I need."
Barbra to the Los Angeles Times, *November 1983.*

"Hello? Can I ask a question?" said another objective, reliable Hollywood source. "If she was giving so much away, how come she was still being so thrifty with her staff? As a gift at Christmas she gave her employees a copy of the *Yentl* soundtrack. Furthermore, how come Amy Irving got stiffed on the royalties for that record? Amy's voice was on one of the songs from the soundtrack. Barbra came to her crying poor-mouth. She had put a fortune of her own into the movie, she said, and the only way she was going to get anything back was with the record album. She asked Amy to give up her royalty. Amy agreed and Barbra gave her the gift of a lovely little cocktail ring. Then the album sold three million copies, of which Barbra got a hefty chunk ($4.5 million, not including publishing) and all Amy had was her little ring. So what was that other ancient proverb? One hand giveth and the other taketh away?"

Two down and one Oscar category to go. Why wasn't Streisand nominated in the Best Actress category? The reviews were raves; she delivered a sublime performance; and actors nominated their own, mostly on merit, regardless of popularity or politics. George C. Scott, Marlon Brando, and Vanessa Redgrave were but a few who were nominated—and won—regardless of adversity. "I thought Barbra Streisand's performance was good, very good," said a leading film and stage actress. "She was definitely on my top list. But there were other contenders, besides the obvious ones of Shirley MacLaine and Debra Winger for *Terms of Endearment,* and Meryl Streep for *Silkwood.* I also liked Bonnie Bedelia *[Heart Like a Wheel],* and that English girl, Julie Walters. Certainly I considered Barbra. Hers was a worthy performance. However, in the final consideration, against the others I felt it was more of a Hollywood star performance. She gave herself the best lighting; in certain scenes she had her own spot. She was supposed to be playing a boy, yet she wore mascara, eyeliner, and lip gloss. She wanted to appear glamorous."

And then there was the matter of the hair-cutting scene in *Yentl.* Actresses chopping off their hair in films has always been considered a dandy dramatic turn, and a surefire way to get award attention. Bette Davis and Glenda Jackson both went bald to play Elizabeth I, the Virgin Queen; Meryl Streep lost most of her hair (and twenty pounds) for *Sophie's Choice;* and Vanessa Redgrave had her scalp shaved and nicked to play Fania Fenelon in *Playing for Time.*

When it came time for Streisand to transform herself from a girl to a boy in *Yentl,* she stood in front of a cracked mirror and began to cut off her long brown hair, which was a wig. And underneath that wig was another one. "As a boy she wore a short wig throughout the entire movie," said a makeup artist. "There was no way she was going to part with those Medusa curls of hers. She loved her long hair."

The controversy over Streisand and the Oscars continued up to and including the night of the award ceremonies. A mass demonstration was organized by a group called PEP (Principals, Equality, and Professionalism in Films), who picketed the theater and handed flyers to the fans.

Barbra was on her way to England during the actual ceremonies and did not watch the telecast, but she found out early that Michel Legrand and the Bergmans had won. "There was a message from Barbra waiting when we got home that night," said Marilyn Bergman. "She was very happy for us."

THE EUROPEAN SELLING OF *YENTL*

Without the endorsement of any major Academy Awards, Streisand was obliged personally to publicize the movie in Europe. Reluctantly she agreed to appear in five countries over a three-week period. In London she arrived at the premiere of *Yentl* dressed in a white gown, white coat, with her head wrapped in a white bandage-like turban which prompted one reporter to ask if she had been in a recent motor accident. Inside the theater, after the film was shown and the lights came up, the audience gave the star a standing ovation. Sitting beside her, Princess Alexandra, her patron for the evening, dispensed with royal protocol and insisted that Barbra rise first to acknowledge the acclaim. "She blew the Oscar, but grabbed the world," said reporter Cindy Adams.

In Paris Barbra was awarded the French Art and Literature Officers' Medal and later appeared in the audience at the taping of *Live at the Champs Elysées,* a French variety TV special. Coaxed onstage by Michel Legrand, she spoke a few words in French, then was persuaded to sing "What Are You Doing the Rest of Your Life?" in English, but stopped midway when she forgot the words.

In Paris on the night of the premiere, Barbra was the toast of the town. Thousands of fans line up on the Rue Royale outside Maxim's waiting for the star, who showed up only one hour late for the ten-thirty P.M. postpremiere dinner. Escorted by Pierre Cardin, the designer, who also owned the restaurant, Streisand greeted each guest personally. She threw her arms around another gifted actress-director, Jeanne Moreau; she kissed Charles Aznavour and Placido Domingo; shook hands with Marie-Hélène de Rothschild and Princess Ira Von Furstenberg, and she gave a friendly but distant hello to Roman Polanski. "Madame," said Roman, "I remember you. I love your dress."

The following afternoon Barbra augmented her tour wardrobe by shopping at Ungaro. She spent four hours buying clothes while eighty-six paparazzi stood outside on the street. "How do we know that there were eighty-six photographers?" columnist Suzy asked. "Someone took a Polaroid snap out the window and we counted."

In Rome, Streisand also gave the back of her head, and her hand, to their feisty lensmen. First off she was furious at the Italian press. Upon her arrival one leading magazine published an unauthorized photograph of her wearing a frumpy one-piece bathing suit that revealed gorgeous cleavage but also a slight pot belly. "We asked and asked for some recent shots," the editor of the magazine stated. "We also requested an interview, but her employees gave us nothing." Her bodyguards, however, gave the rough arm to two street photographers, bruising their bones and breaking their cameras, and were promptly arrested by the Italian police.

In Hamburg, at a meeting with reporters, Barbra spoke of her fervent desire to play Shakespeare, Ibsen, the classics. "Everything from Hedda Gabler to Medea." "But, Fraulein," one learned journalist asked, "you've been saying that for twenty years. *When* are you going to do it?" The actress responded with a glare that could have pulverized the Führer's bunker.

And in Tel Aviv—her last stop—when reporters arrived for a scheduled press conference, they sat for two hours, but no Barbra. Eventually they were told she was elsewhere, having a glass of tea with Yitzhak Shamir, the Prime Minister.

In retaliation, that evening some of the Israeli media boycotted the premiere of *Yentl,* and the press who did appear chastised her for being a no-show. "Darlings," Barbra responded as the TV cameras rolled, "I only wrote, directed, and starred in the movie. I did not arrange these festivities."

"Attagirl!" this Streisand fan responded, watching the proceedings on television in America. "Make them kneel, have them beg, let 'em eat cake." I mean, how often would they get to see a real-life legend, up close?

You know?

Chapter 35

Jon Peters: *"What we need for this project is a shvartzer."*
Stephen Silverman: *"Huh?"*
Jon Peters: *"A prominent shvartzer."*

KINDRED SPIRITS PART

By 1982 Jon Peters had realized his ambition to become a "mogul"—of establishing an entertainment complex to encompass records, publishing, management, television, and movies. Following the dismal returns on *Eyes of Laura Mars,* Jon produced the wildly successful *Caddyshack,* and he had a hand, or a finger or two, in the productions of *Missing* and *Flashdance.* In December of 1982, at a New York screening of his latest movie, *Six Weeks,* he spoke to *New York Post* reporter Stephen Silverman about his plans to move next to Broadway, to produce straight plays and musicals. Silverman at that time was writing the book and the lyrics for a musical based on *Amos n' Andy,* using the popular black characters from the 1930s radio serial. Jon Peters was interested in this project, and at the postscreening party at the Hilton Hotel he asked the reporter to sit at his table. "Barbra was with him," said Silverman, "and throughout our entire conversation she kept her eyes down, staring at her salad. Jon, who was very buddy-buddy, kept saying to me, 'We've got to do this musical *together.'* I mentioned the possibility of a problem with CBS Broadcasting. Their radio division claimed they owned the rights to *Amos n' Andy,* which wasn't true. Jon also dismissed the problem. 'CBS?' he said. 'I can handle them. You see this man next to me? This is Walter Yetnikoff, the president of CBS Records, Barbra's record label. He will take care of everything.'"

In the period that followed, Peters read Silverman's script and came through with encouragement. "I liked him," said Stephen. "He had a lot of energy. And some strange ideas about producing. From time to time he would say to me, 'What we need for this project is a *shvartzer.*' And I didn't know if he meant for the cast or as a coproducer. Then one day he brought it up again. 'We need a *shvartzer;* a prominent *shvartzer.*' And I said, 'Well . . . how about Coretta King?'"

With time Silverman began to realize that Jon was taking over his show. "One day he called and said, 'I don't know what your credit will be on this musical, but you'll be involved.' And I said, 'Hey wait a minute, Jon. This is *my* project. I wrote it.' But he said his partner, Peter Guber, had had the idea for years. 'Great,' I replied. 'Then there will be two shows, yours and mine.' With that Jon got a little nervous. 'No, *buddy,*' he said, 'we're doing this together. I like you, and I think you like me.' 'I do, Jon,' I replied, 'I like you in *spite* of your bad press.' And he started yelling, '*My* bad press? Why, you ----ing ----sucker!'"

One year later there was another screening of a Jon Peters production in New York. By this time he and Barbra had broken up. Some say the split began when he failed to show enough faith in her fifteen-year odyssey, *Yentl.* Others claimed the trouble was caused by Jon's roving eye. "Every time Barbra left L.A. to work on *Yentl,* Jon had women arriving at the ranch," said a co-worker. He was seen holding hands with model Lisa Taylor at a disco in New York. There was also a romance on his home turf, with a real-estate lady from Malibu. When Barbra heard about that she erected a fence at the ranch, separating his house from hers. One night when Jon came home and parked his car on her side of the property she had it towed away.

"There is no question that there is still something deep between Jon and Barbra," said columnist Liz Smith, referring to the night in 1983 when Jon's film *D.C. Cab* opened in Manhattan. "They had a dinner party at Wally's, this conservative theater restaurant. I liked the movie and thought it would be a nice gesture to go over to him and say hello, which is something I rarely ever do. We didn't know each other. We spoke on the phone a few times. But I introduced myself, and he was sitting at this table with these very flashy women, who had their hair done just like Barbra's. He didn't introduce me to *anyone*. And he didn't stand up. He left me standing there and said, 'Well, yeah,' and 'Okay,' and 'I'm glad you liked the film.' I began to feel embarrassed, until I eventually said, 'Well good luck,' and I walked away, *furious* with myself. I was later told by some people at my table that he was nervous or afraid that I would print something about him being with other women, and that Barbra would read it. But I wasn't thinking about writing about that. I *never* blow the whistle on anyone. People would have to be standing on their heads, nude, in Times Square, before I'd mention it. But he was rude, and I thought, Hey, you ---hole, if you had just stood up and said, 'Hi, Liz, so nice to meet you,' what would it cost? So the next day I ran the item."

"I first saw Barbra in Philadelphia, at the opening of I Can Get It for You Wholesale. When she rolled down the footlights in her secretary's chair, we all gasped. I was jealous. Later I saw her on Broadway in Funny Girl. Ray Stark the producer insisted I go backstage to meet her. I'll never forget it. Walking across the dressing room to shake her hand, she shrank away from me. She was very cold. Looking back on that evening and who we thought we were —all of us—and how we related to people, this evening seems very special to me. Barbra's voice has become very special to me, to all of us. She is a national treasure. I think she's come a long way."

Jane Fonda, introducing Barbra Streisand at an award ceremony in Beverly Hills, June 1984

When Streisand returned from Europe in the late spring of 1984 she and Jon Peters parted as roommates. She moved from the ranch in Malibu to her house in Holmby Hills; and he bought Mary Tyler Moore's house on Palm Drive in Beverly Hills for $2 million (spending another $1 million on renovations). Peters continued to manage Streisand's career, however. "Barbra is smart in that regard," said a William Morris agent. "She never lets sentiment or romance stand in the way of business. She also knows that Jon always delivers the best deals."

With *Yentl* gone and forgotten by most, Jon concentrated on getting his number-one client back into the recording studio. During April there was a report that she was going to record an album of standards similar to Linda Ronstadt's *What's New?* Barbra denied this. "I'm not moving backwards, but forwards," she said. In May rumors of possible duets with Mick Jagger, Lionel Ritchie, and Boy George surfaced, but Jon Peters had another superstar coupling in mind. He and Charles Koppelman wanted Michael Jackson to sing with Streisand, and to produce the duet, they called upon the producer, arranger, and co-composer of *Thriller*, Quincy Jones. But Quincy, with the 30 million–plus sales of Jackson's *Thriller*, was already being courted by every big name in the business. Diana Ross, Julio Iglesias, and Frank Sinatra were almost camping on his front lawn, pleading with him to produce their next LPs. Again, Jon Peters had a fast lead over the competition. For openers he owned the movie rights to *The Color Purple*, and he hired Quincy Jones as a consultant and the executive music producer for the film. Then he commissioned the composer to write a theme for a special Peters-Guber LP entitled *The Official Music of the XXIII Olympiad, Los Angeles, 1984.*

This album was the idea of Gary Le Mel, Barbra's former publishing executive. He suggested to Jon that he put together an album of original themes for the key events of the forthcoming Olympics in Los Angeles. Peters secured the sanction of the Olympics committee; made a deal with Walter Yetnikoff of CBS Records; then called in twelve writers and performers to contribute to the album. Included were Giorgio Moroder, Toto, Christopher Cross, Bob James, and Quincy Jones, who was asked to write the official gymnasts' theme, which he called "Grace."

On June 13, 1984, a month before the Olympics began in California, the album and the single of "Grace" were released by CBS Records. With the release came the news that "Grace" would soon be recorded by none other than Barbra Streisand, with special lyrics added by Marilyn and Alan Bergman. There was also a strong possibility that Barbra would sing the song live at the opening night's ceremonies.

But then she chickened out. That old bugaboo stage-fright prevented her participation in the ceremonies. It was also said that the actress was still angry at the entire Los Angeles community for their snub of her *Yentl* during the recent Oscar voting season. Closer to the truth was a fact supplied by Marilyn and Alan Bergman. Two weeks before the Olympics were to begin, they told this reporter that they still had not written the lyrics to the song and it was doubtful if they would get to them until after the games were over.

Without "Grace" Streisand lost Quincy Jones as a producer (and Michael Jackson for duets). Not to worry, Barbra was told. Jon Peters and Charles Koppelman had a higher concept in mind for her next album. They intended to put her with a galaxy of hot-rock star writers, performers, and producers—different ones for every cut on the LP.

In all some twenty-five top talents were approached to work on the new Streisand album. Some said no—including Bruce Springsteen. "Bruce and Barbra would have been wonderful together," said John Hammond, "but the recording and editing on just one single would take months. He's just as much a perfectionist as she is." John Cougar Mellencamp agreed to write with Barbra, but he would not sing on the session. Then Kim Carnes was recruited; the Pointer Sisters came in with their "Jump" producer, Richard Perry; and in lieu of Springsteen two members of his E Street Band agreed to perform on "Left In The Dark," a song written and produced by Jim ("Total Eclipse Of The Heart") Steinman.

"Left In The Dark" was to be the first single released from the new album; and to keep tempo with the MTV times Barbra announced she was going to make her first rock video.

Although the lyrics to "Left In The Dark" told of a woman lying in bed, waiting for her cheating lover to come home and kiss her blind, Barbra said she had to change the scenario for the video. "I would never be passive," she said. "I would never wait in bed for anyone I *knew* was cheating on me." The man had to appear as the loser. She would be "a lounge singer and 1950's actress" who, when she finds her lover in bed with another woman, leaves him in the dark, staring forlornly from a window as she drives off in a 1951 Ford convertible.

When old friend Kris Kristofferson agreed to play her one-minute lover, shooting on the video commenced on September twenty-fourth 1984 at the Zoetrope Studios in Los Angeles. With her call set for nine-thirty A.M., Barbra showed promptly at ten fifteen her hair newly frizzed and bleached a pale blond. After a minimum of suggestions to Jonathan Kaplan, the director *(Heart Like a Wheel)*, and to the lighting designer, she fell into the accelerated pace of video production.

On September twenty-sixth, the eve of Rosh Hashanah, the single of "Left In The Dark" was released by Columbia Records. The video, as planned, would come one month later when the single was sailing into the Top 20 and needed that extra push to jettison it to the number-one position. On October twenty-fifth, however, when the video was "world-premiered" on *Entertainment Tonight,* "Left In The Dark" was sailing *backward* on the record charts. It only made number fifty in *Billboard* and then began to drop. The video was shown sporadically; then it, too, vanished.

Barbra's new album, *Emotion,* fared better in sales, but not with the critics. *"Emotion* is Streisand's latest attempt to appear hip, and one must wonder why she bothers," said *USA Today.* It "strains in a much more mundane way towards contemporary commerciality," said Stephen Holden in the Sunday *New York Times;* and *People* magazine questioned the need for so many producers: "It's like hiring nine drivers to drive a bus two blocks. You can get where you're going, but there sure is a lot of confusion."

By November twenty-sixth the album had reached the number 19 position in *Billboard;* but a week later it slipped back to 22 and the trade magazine which originally hailed the LP as containing "half a dozen gems" were now tolling its demise. "Here's the dish," said *Billboard* columnist Paul Grein: *"Emotion* is Streisand's first studio album to fall short of the Top Ten since *Songbird* peaked at number 12 in 1978 (That was the one with the dog on the cover and Streisand's note, 'Sorry, couldn't find a bird.'). If it doesn't rebound (and fast!) it will go down as Streisand's lowest-charting studio album in more than 15 years."

In late December, in an effort to boost sales, a second single, "Make No Mistake He's Mine," Streisand's duet with Kim Carnes, was released. It peaked at number 51 and faded shortly thereafter. At this time Barbra's speaking voice was heard loud and clear over the telephone lines from Aspen, Colorado, where she was vacationing with new beau, Richard Baskin (the heir to the Baskin-Robbins ice cream fortune). She called Charles Koppelman and CBS chief Walter Yetnikoff in New York, demanding to know why her new records were not selling at the volume she was accustomed to. "No one had the guts to give her an honest answer," said a CBS executive. "She was carrying on, saying that CBS was ignoring her, favoring Cyndi Lauper and Bruce Springsteen instead. Which was ridiculous, because she considered herself in that class. Her album was called 'hot rock,' but in reality it was 'hot-flash rock'; menopausal, so to speak. Most of the songs she and executive producer Charles Koppelman chose were tired, insipid. 'Left In The Dark' was written by Jim Steinman *five* years ago and passed over by Bonnie Tyler. Barbra also let her ego get in the way of the production. She hired these first-rate producers, Maurice White and Albhy Galuten. After they edited the sessions she and Koppelman went back into the studios and remixed some of the tracks. She had the most popular group of the year, the Pointer Sisters, singing with her on one song; but she put them so far back on the track they could have been the Lennon Sisters for all anybody knew. Nobody could hear them."

In February CBS made one last attempt to resuscitate *Emotion* by releasing a third single, the title song, with the corresponding video co-starring Roger Daltrey and Mikhail Baryshnikov, codirected by boyfriend Richard Baskin. The video this time out was a popular success on MTV, but it did little to raise sales in record stores. The "Emotion" single stayed on the charts for one week, then vanished. The album lingered longer, until it, too, faded into oblivion. Other portents seemed to be saying that the days of Barbra the Rocker were over. In March she failed to make *Playboy*'s Top 10 Best Pop Female Vocalist poll (she had been number one in 1979), and in a *Newsweek* cover story on women in rock, which featured such veterans as Linda Ronstadt, Carly Simon, and Joni Mitchell, Streisand's name drew not even a mention.

"Why is she singing that type of music?" composer Jule Styne asked. "Barbra has a very special gift, one of the greatest voices of this century. Why is she wasting it?"

"She can sing whatever she wants," said lyricist Marilyn Bergman in rapid defense. "Her genius should not be limited."

"There is an entire generation of fans who have never seen Barbra Streisand in person," said singer Margaret Whiting. "Why doesn't she come back to Broadway or do concerts?"

"I would pay five hundred dollars to see her perform live," said super-fan Randy Emerian. "I know others who would pay more."

"I doubt if Barbra will ever do concerts again," said Howard

Rosenman. "She is terrified of audiences. The last live performance she gave was at a benefit for the Bergmans, and she had to have the help of a yoga instructor [Alan Finger] to get her onstage." "It is sad," said another close source, "but Barbra believes that the only way she can perform is within an isolated environment. Unless she has total control of the circumstances the thought of singing paralyses her with fear."

"She has these people around her that encourage her insularity and her craziness," said Liz Smith. "They are serving their own best interests in keeping her isolated from the realities. I think Barbra has a great future ahead of her; she can act, sing, direct, do whatever she wants to. But she should leave Hollywood for a while. I spoke my piece to her last year. I said, 'Come back to New York; visit Brooklyn; interact more with people. You should not become the Garbo of your day.'"

"That's part of the myth she's built up," said the late Arthur Bell, "and I'm not sure if it's a deliberate defense. Barbra doesn't need anyone to protect her. She plays the power game better than anyone else and she always wins. She is not Judy Garland or Marilyn Monroe; she is tough, a survivor."

"She is not crazy and not drugged out and hasn't killed herself," Kenny Solms agreed, "because she has a strong base, a strong soul. Barbra's only destructive streak is that she eats too much ice cream. And she likes to shop."

In April 1985 former Streisand costar Robert Redford told a reporter in Salt Lake City that there was a possibility he and Barbra would be reunited in the future for a sequel to *The Way We Were*. The new movie could incorporate unused footage from the original and be updated to be called *The Way We've Changed*. When queried directly, Streisand's press agent, Lee Solters, said this was one of many movie projects being considered by his client. According to other reports these include two films with Jane Fonda; a film with Goldie Hawn, entitled *Sisters,* written by Patricia Resnick of *9 to 5;* a film musical of *They're Playing Our Song* with ex-husband Elliott Gould ("It's definite," said Gould. "I've heard about it," said the score's composer and male character model, Marvin Hamlisch, "but I swear to God no one has spoken to me yet"); a remake of *The Captain's Paradise* with Streisand playing the Alec Guinness role of a ship's cruise director with a husband in every port; a film remake of *Gypsy* with Barbra as Mama Rose ("We're talking about it," said Jule Styne. "I don't *want* to make another movie of *Gypsy,*" said writer Arthur Laurents. "One was done already. It was bad. If it's done again it should be for cable TV"); *Macbeth* with Marlon Brando; a film about Margaret Bourke White, the *Life* photographer; *The Merry Widow* with Placido Domingo; and a film based on the life of Ruth Snyder, the first woman put to death in the electric chair. "I can see why Streisand would like to do that role," said the late Truman Capote to interviewer Lawrence Grobel. "She really is something. She's always got something up her skirts."

So it continues—the quotes, the speculation, the abiding interest in the life and career of Barbra Streisand. For twenty-five years she has been an object of praise and derision; she has been exalted, feared, admonished, dismissed, redeemed, distrusted, regenerated, and eventually elevated to the stature of superstardom. To a public starved for authentic stars, she is the genuine article. To the media she is always news, simply because she is seldom available. Through the course of writing this book many attempts were made to talk to Streisand directly. Although her sanction was not required, and the provocative reports of her temperament and frugality, the creative disjunction and deception, were confirmed by different sources, it was only fair, I believed, that Barbra be allowed to add her side to the story. She *would* talk, I was told by Lee Solters, Miss Streisand's personal representative. It was a matter of time and place. Yet for over fifteen months, despite repeated requests, Barbra remained silent, almost secluded, behind the walls of her Holmby Hills mansion. She ventured forth infrequently: to the movies in Westwood, to a Prince concert, disguised in dark glasses and assorted headgear. After she was invited to be a part of the U.S.A. for Africa all-star chorus for the "We Are the World" recording session, and begged off, citing "other commitments," a final attempt was made to reach the star through Lee Solters. The answer to one question was sought. It concerned a prime focus of this book: her music. Like many others I have always believed that Barbra's greatest gift is her voice. Her singing has brought immense joy to millions of people; but apparently not to Barbra. In the past she has dismissed that phenomenal talent as "second class," favoring her acting. "I hate to sing," she said early in her career. "I never do it in the bath. I do it only for the money." Did that conviction hold today?

The answer never came.

AND HOW RICH IS SHE?

In March of 1985 *People* magazine published a list of the top money makers in Hollywood for the previous year. Included were Sally Field ($1.5 million for *Places in the Heart),* Tom Selleck ($4.8 million for *Magnum P.I.)* and Dolly Parton ($6 million for *Rhinestone Cowboy* and a concert tour with Kenny Rogers). Absent from the tally was Barbra Streisand, who, although she did not make a movie, appear on TV, or perform in concert for the entire year, grossed close to $8 million from record royalties, film rentals, and cassette sales, and from careful, shrewd investments.

To date Streisand has made thirteen movies, which have brought her an up-front salary of $20 million. She has also received a percentage of the profits from 11 of these films, which, according to the *Variety* of January 16, 1985, have brought in receipts of $230 million, domestic, to the studios. Double that figure for worldwide grosses—$460 million; subtract negative and distribution costs of $140 million; and the studios' net came to approximately $320 million. Take a conservative ten percent of that for Barbra (reportedly she received thirty percent of the profits for *A Star Is Born* and *The Main Event);* add it to her salary; the resulting income: $52 million from her films alone.

Regarding record royalties: Streisand has recorded forty-one albums. Twenty of these have gone gold (in excess of 500,000 copies sold); six have gone platinum (1 million copies sold); one has gone triple Platinum *(Yentl*—3 million sold) and two—*A Star Is Born* and *Guilty*—have sold 6 million each. That adds up to 31 million albums sold, which, when mutiplied by an average royalty of one dollar per LP (she received a two-dollar royalty for *Yentl* and *Emotion)* puts her share at $31 million. On top of that CBS Records has released seventy-two Streisand singles, which have sold approximately 10 million copies; at ten cents a disc, these have brought the star another $1 million. All of which means that for a secondary profession—her singing—the star has received compensation of approximately 32 *million* dollars. (And CBS Records, who were initially reluctant to sign the singer, have reaped in excess of $125 million for their participation.)

In addition to her movies and records, Barbra has also worked in nightclubs, on concert tours, in Vegas, and on television in guest spots and star solos (but *never* in commercials). A conservative estimate of this supplementary income is $8 million. Deducting the cost of production expenses, management and agent fees, taxes, puts her net earnings from all entertainment activities at $22 million.

> *"Barbra has always lived in a bubble; a bubble she fears is going to break at any second. So when she buys, it's always three of everything."*
>
> Fred Glaser

INVESTMENTS AND REAL ESTATE HOLDINGS

In 1962, when she was making fifty dollars a week singing in miniature cabarets, Streisand bought her clothes in thrift shops. From time to time, when her budget allowed, she also purchased *"tsatskes"*—porcelain eggs, cameo brooches—which were later appraised as objets d'art, increasing in value. From 1964 onward, when she was a star on Broadway, Barbra became a frequent fixture at art galleries and antique stores throughout Manhattan, Long Island, and Bucks County. "She bought paintings, fine furniture, and Aubusson rugs by the *ton,*" said one curator. "I wanted Louis, Louis—as much as I could lay my hands on," she told *Architectural Digest,* "and I got it: bronzes, porcelains, satins, moiré. Later I became far more sophisticated."

Later meant "discovering the pleasures" of Victorian and Second Empire furniture, followed by her art nouveau and art deco period, when she acquired Gallo sculptures, no end of Tiffany glass, and the largest private collection of Erté prints, sketches, and silkscreens. "She kept buying and buying, never discarding anything," said a close friend. "When she ran out of room she had the older pieces crated and put in a warehouse. Today she must have over two million dollars' worth of stuff sitting on the floor at Manhattan Storage." "It drives me crazy to think some of my things are moldering away in storage," said Streisand. "I guess at heart

I'm a compiler of inventories. I would like to document everything I own—every pair of shoes, every antique fan . . . all my objects. I'd like to have it all photographed and bound in volumes." "Her collection today is worth at least twenty million dollars," said Fred Glaser, not counting the value of her furs and jewelry. "I am *mad* for jewelry," said the actress in 1966. "It's a better investment than clothes. They increase in value and don't wear out from dry cleaning."

There are also stocks, tax-free portfolios, and extensive real estate holdings. Her penthouse apartment in Manhattan, overlooking Central Park, is estimated to be worth $3 million on the current market; her house in Holmby Hills with four and a half acres (purchased for $240,000 in 1970) could easily fetch $6 million; with another $5 million coming in for her three houses in Malibu. She also owns commercial buildings and apartments in Los Angeles, New York, and Florida; four music-publishing firms; and her own production company, Barwood—which holds the rights to numerous creative properties, including Broadway plays, best-selling books, and various remakes. Last summer Barwood and Barbra signed an exclusive contract with Warner Bros. Communications. The pay for the package, for starring, producing, and/or directing three films, is said to be $20 million. Add that sum to her assets, and a modest estimate of Streisand's wealth falls between $70 and $80 million, with an additional $1.2 million coming in each year (from royalties and investments), even if she *never* works another day in her life.

Yet according to friends she still has visions of the poorhouse. "Enough is never enough when you've been poor as a child," said Bob Schulenberg. "Barbra still thinks the wolves are at her door when in fact today she *owns* the wolves."

On a side street in mid-Manhattan the branch office of a relatively small bank is located. The bank specializes in making loans and conserving the savings of New York's working classes. One of these accounts was opened in 1960 by a switchboard operator named Barbara Joan Streisand. "I still got that account," the most popular performer in the world said recently. "I started it just before I took the third a out of my name. I put money in it only when I feel it's really mine, like the seven hundred fifty dollars my mother gave me when I married Elliott. I think I have seventeen thousand dollars there now. I feel really rich. If ever I have to escape, if I ever want to leave this life, I'd take the money out of that account."

Afterword

"I really can't stand listening to pop music, although I know I should. I don't even keep in close touch with Broadway anymore."

Streisand to The New York Times, November, 1985

THE BROADWAY ALBUM

In the summer of 1985, in a bid to lift her waning popularity and record sales, Streisand recorded *The Broadway Album*. To produce and arrange the bulk of the score she called upon Peter Matz, who was largely responsible for the success of her first LP in 1963.

"Barbra and I had been out of touch for quite a few years," said Matz. "When she called and mentioned the type of material she wanted to sing, I thought it was a step in the right direction. I had no idea of course how successful the album would become."

There was some initial trepidation on Streisand's part, Matz added. "Most of the songs she wanted to sing were Broadway standards. This threw her into a panic. She was afraid that by singing familiar songs people would consider her old-fashioned."

To modernize and tailor the Broadway material to her form, the singer called composer Stephen Sondheim and asked him to rewrite three of his more famous songs for her. "I didn't know how he would react," said Barbra, "but he was so cute." Pop composers Paul Jabara and Bob Esty were also hired to arrange and produce a medley from *The King and I;* and to do work on "Somewhere," from *West Side Story.* According to Marilyn and Alan Bergman, who wrote the liner notes, Barbra "envisioned the song in an electronic setting and asked David Foster *(St. Elmo's Fire)* to place it in a new environment: space." (Floating off into orbit themselves, the Bergmans said of the arrangement: "There's a glimpse of infinity in it. Like this album.")

In July of 1985 recording on *The Broadway Album* began at the A&M studios in Hollywood. The sessions were done "live," meaning that Barbra sang with the orchestra present, while the feed was being captured on three 24-track machines, for later remixing.

In all, eighteen songs were recorded over nine weeks. "Originally we were supposed to be recording a two-album set," said Peter Matz, "but then CBS Records got nervous. They felt the market wouldn't go for a double album at twice the price." During the first elimination, five completed songs were discarded. They included "Home" from *The Wiz;* "Being Good (Isn't Good Enough)" from *Hallelujah Baby;* "Unusual Way" from *Nine;* "Adelaide's Lament" from *Guys and Dolls* (later included in the compact disc release); and "Shall We Dance?" from *The King and I* medley. " 'Shall We Dance?' was done with a whimsical Latin arrangement," said Paul Jabara, "but after it was edited Barbra decided she didn't want the song in the medley. She said it lowered the integrity of the album. I reminded her that Broadway musicals were about singing *and* dancing *and* comedy. 'Adelaide's Lament' was also adorable, but Barbra didn't want any humor on this album."

In September one final song was abandoned. "I Know Him So Well," from the forthcoming London musical *Chess* was already a hit single in England by Elaine Paige and Barbara Dickson. For her version Streisand initially considered recording the song with either Olivia Newton John or Dionne Warwick. Upon deliberation Barbra decided the duet would best be served with herself on both vocals. Arranged and produced by David Foster, her performance was "magical," but since *Chess* was not yet on Broadway they would have to drop the song or change the title of the album.

Having conceived and completed the project in its entirety in California, a semblance of Broadway was added to the package when Barbra opted to pose for the album's cover onstage in an empty theater in Times Square. While on the East Coast she also took time to indulge in her latest passion: the acquisition of Early American Folk Art. "I am interested in primitive furniture, especially painted pieces," she explained. "It's the antithesis of Art Nouveau; very crude, very simple." One shopping spree to Vermont and Massachusetts provided the following item in *Arts and Antiques* magazine: " 'Whole Berkshire villages can now retire and go to Florida,' claims an art insider who witnessed the singer raid Massachusetts for country furniture." Later, wearing black Reeboks and carrying a checkbook, Barbra was first in line when the Fall Antiques Show opened in Manhattan. To house her spreading collection, the star confided that she built a barn on her forty-acre ranch in Malibu.

On October 5th *The Broadway Album* was released to the public. "I will be disappointed if it sells less than two million," said Barbra. Reviewers shared her optimism. "The album of a lifetime," said *The New York Times,* giving special honors to "If I Loved You" from *Carousel* and "Can't Help Lovin' That Man," from *Showboat.* "More please! More!" said *People* magazine. While *Rolling Stone* found some songs to be "tritely up-to-date, with synthesizers, computerized drumming, and wailing saxes," overall it felt the album "works somehow, if only as a reminder of what a neglected wealth of riches Broadway offers, and what a marvelous singer Streisand is when she's not trying to pass herself off as a rock star."

Within four weeks *The Broadway Album* had bounded onto *Billboard*'s charts, eventually landing into the number-one position and staying there. Close to four million copies were sold, but again the star's triumph took its toll on contributors. For Peter Matz, who produced and arranged most of the album, it meant the end of a twenty-two-year relationship. "Going in we had an agreement on credits and royalties," said Matz. "There was a handshake and a deal memo. At the end of the project I was told that Barbra wanted to cut my royalties in half. She also threatened to take my name off the LP unless I shared my producing and arranging credit with her."

"She did the same thing with us," said Paul Jabara. "She asked if she could list her name on our credits because the others agreed. We said O.K., not realizing that she intended to put her name *first.* Then she didn't pay me. We worked for three months on her songs and she wanted to give me $1650 and eight-tenths of a point for a royalty."*

"What really saddens me," said Peter Matz, "is that after all these years I believed that Barbra and I were friends. Now I know we are not. There was considerable deception involved."

"She's like a spoiled child who wants all the candy," said Jabara in closing. "I feel like a fool for having cared too much, for too long. It's almost as if she knows that and she's thinking: 'Ha-ha—fooled you.'"

"I am a mass of contradictions. I am simple, complex; generous, selfish; unattractive and beautiful; lazy and driven. The contradictions used to be more polarized, now they're sort of growing towards the center. I'm simply complex."

**Barbra Streisand to Barbara Walters,
in the fall of 1985.**

SOME PUBLIC APPEARANCES

By January of 1986, with the success of *The Broadway Album,* Streisand had recaptured most of the nation's ear; now it was time to reclaim their eye—with some prudently arranged public appearances.

A year previously, when the album was at its inception, a memo went from Streisand's management team to her personal press representative, Lee Solters. The memo said the album would be recorded live before an audience (paying $1,000 per ticket, for charity). The evening would be taped for "pay-per-view cable sale," then later "assembled for normal sale to HBO, for a European theatrical release, and on video cassette for commercial sale." Not too long after this, when details of the concert appeared in the press, Streisand had already abandoned all thoughts of performing live before an audience. She had also changed managers. Jon Peters, anxious to devote full time to his producing career, was replaced by Sandy Gallin (who also represented Dolly Parton). Gal-

---

* For the work involved that sum does seem low; especially when it appeared that producer Richard Baskin, Barbra's boyfriend, received $20,000 as a "consultation" fee.

lin, in turn, allegedly weary of the constant midnight crisis calls from Streisand, stayed but a short time on the job and was replaced by former representative Marty Erlichman (ousted by Jon Peters, back in 1976, during the heat of Jon's affair with Barbra). "Age has worked well for both of us," said Erlichman, happy to be back on the superstar circuit. Task number one would be the marketing of an HBO special entitled *Barbra Streisand Putting It Together: The Making of* The Broadway Album.

Although the show was billed as "an exclusive music special," some of the footage had been shot and used five months earlier for a Barbara Walters TV special on ABC. "We wanted to film Barbra in the recording studio," said Nick Lombardo, an associate producer with the Walters show. "Barbra was willing, as long as she could choose the shots and keep the film afterwards. As a part of ABC News we could not agree to that, so Barbra hired her own crew to photograph the sessions." Six hours of footage was shot. Five minutes went to Barbara Walters. The rest of the film was edited down by Barwood Films, augmented with still photographs, a video of "Somewhere," and an interview with video director William Friedkin. The autogenous package was then sold to HBO, who heralded its January broadcast as "a big event—marking the actress-singer's return to the TV special format for the first time in twelve years."

Reviewers of the show were not as taken with the uniqueness of the format. "At its worst it's a gooey salute," said *USA Today.* "At its best the documentary is a testament to celebrity, to power, to art, to diva divine Barbra." "The Streisand package doesn't even make a gesture towards being objective," said John J. O'Connor of *The New York Times.* "This is 'The Streisand Show' and don't anybody dare rain on her parade." In closing Mr. O'Connor noted that interviewer Mr. Friedkin brought "new dimensions to the art of fawning. He tells the star that, just as she directed the film *Yentl,* she seems to be directing 'sound pictures on her new album.' 'That's nice, Billy,' Miss Streisand says sincerely."

The following month, dressed in black, Barbra made an appearance as a presenter at the Grammy awards in Los Angeles. The month after that, dressed in white, she showed up on the Oscar telecast. At both events stringent arrangements were made to ensure that the proper distance be kept between the superstar and her public. At the Grammys, dispensing with the offer of a private dressing room, she asked that a trailer be set up in the parking lot, with armed guards on hand to escort her to and from the stage. At the Oscars she declined to sit in the audience and arrived at the festivities in a motor home, very close to the moment that she was scheduled to present the Best Director award to Sydney Pollack for *Out of Africa*. After the Oscar ceremonies she used the motor home to drive her and escort Richard Baskin to Swifty Lazar's Oscar bash at Spago. Again, outwitting the press and her fans, Barbra entered the restaurant through a side door, and was already seated at a table, mid-meal, before her host knew she was on the premises.

THE COVER OF *LIFE*

On April 24, 1986, Streisand turned forty-four. That evening lyricists Marilyn and Alan Bergman threw a surprise birthday party for her at their home in Bel-Air. The guests included Burt Bacharach and his wife Carole Bayer Sager; Barbra's mother; her sister Roslyn; nineteen-year-old son Jason; boyfriend Richard Baskin; manager Marty Erlichman; and actor Walter Matthau with his wife Carol. Arriving on the arm of record producer Richard Perry was another former nemesis: Elizabeth Taylor, looking slim and gorgeous, and causing Barbra's mother to be a little tongue-tied in her presence. "I was nervous talking to such a big, big star," Mrs. Kind remarked the following day.

During the month of April, Streisand also appeared on the cover of *LIFE,* along with Jane Fonda, Sally Field, Jessica Lange, and Goldie Hawn. "These were the five women who had real clout in getting movies made," said *LIFE*'s entertainment editor, Jim Watters. When he went out to Hollywood in the fall of 1985 to talk to stars about being featured in the magazine's Spring movie issue, he had the concept for the cover in mind. "I knew there might be some difficulty in getting these five women to pose together," said the well-traveled editor, "but I decided to appeal to their sense of sisterhood. Actually the only one I anticipated reluctance from was Streisand. I was willing to get down on my knees to beg her to participate, but it never came to that."

With the consent of the five stars secured, a problem of scheduling came not from ego but from impending motherhood. "When I went to see Jessica Lange she was already six or seven months pregnant," said Watters, "and she felt, quite naturally, that she didn't want to be photographed in that condition. I told her we had a deadline of March 1 for the cover. 'My baby is due in January; can we shoot after that?' Jessica asked. I agreed, but at Christmas I found out that Goldie Hawn was also expecting. I thought: 'Well, there goes the cover.' But Goldie said there would be no problem. She felt that being pregnant was one more real sense of being a full, productive woman, I guess. We scheduled the cover for February, but that was bumped because Jessica's baby arrived late. Eventually, with limited time to spare, we set another date of March 2. Meanwhile I kept my fingers crossed."

The second of March was a Sunday and all five women were asked to be at the photographer's studio at 1:00 P.M., ready to shoot, with hairstyles and makeup in place. "We didn't have space to accommodate two or three attendants for each person," said Watters, "so we paid to have people fix them up at home. We also supplied the wardrobes—black sweaters or blouses for the cover, and assorted tops and jeans for the informal inside shots." Sally Field arrived first, followed by Jessica Lange, Goldie, and Fonda. By 1:00 P.M. everyone was in place but Barbra. "She was late and Jane [Fonda] started looking at her watch. She had a rehearsal with Jeff Bridges and Sidney Lumet scheduled for four o'clock. 'Is there going to be a problem here?' Jane asked. I checked with Barbra's press agent. He said Barbra was coming from Carolwood, not Malibu, so she should be there any second. She showed up not long after that—ten minutes past, at the most—which to me isn't late at all."

First on the agenda for the stellar group was the cover portrait. Their positions had already been marked and lit, using stand-ins. Barbra asked to be on the far right; which the photographer had anticipated. "He worked fast. Using a Hasselblad he shot five rolls of twelve exposures in a very short time. Then a break was called and I asked everyone to relax for the candid shots. Goldie and Sally were the life of the party. They kept horsing around. They would hug and kiss, pull their hair and cross their eyes. Barbra and Jessica Lange were more subdued. 'I never have been a joiner. I never even had fun at recess in grade school,' Barbra said. She looked great; they *all* looked great. And I think they enjoyed themselves. I know I did, although I wouldn't believe I had anything good until I saw the shots come out of the lab."

When the cover shot for *LIFE* was selected, Watters had the photograph blown up, framed with the logo, and air-expressed to Los Angeles for viewing by the principals. "No one had kill rights," he said. "There was not even a discussion about approval. Pat Kingsley, who represents Sally Field, saw the shot and liked it. Barbra also got a look, and the word that got back to me was that she was 'thrilled.'"

NUTS

"Do you want the best? I am not talking about some little black Alabama whore you find outside the Port Authority Bus Terminal. I am talking about a piece of ass like you have never seen. I am talking about good times, darlin'."

From the Broadway play Nuts, by Tom Topor.

Nuts—Streisand's tentative next film—opened on Broadway in April of 1980. The plot—that of a deserted housewife turned hooker (and part-time law student) who murders a customer, then insists on a sanity hearing so she can stand trial for manslaughter —seemed implausible to reviewers, although the leading performance by actress Anne Twomey drew unanimous raves. The play ran for two months, with subsequent productions staged in Philadelphia, Toronto, and Los Angeles. The movie rights were picked up by Universal Pictures (who backed the play) and the producer-director at inception was Mark Rydell, whose credits included *Cinderella Liberty* and Bette Midler's *The Rose*.

From 1981 to 1985 Rydell piloted *Nuts* through numerous script changes and production delays. During this time he also directed *On Golden Pond,* with Henry Fonda and Katharine Hepburn, and worked on a film adaptation of *The White Hotel.* The latter, a D. M. Thomas novel about a patient of Sigmund Freud who has strange sexual dreams and hallucinations, was being scripted for Barbra Streisand. According to Rydell, she had first refusal, which she took. Then the idea of her doing *Nuts* came up. The script at this juncture was, according to *Variety,* being "sought after by some of the leading actresses in Hollywood," including Cher and Debra Winger. As the story goes, when Streisand heard of their interest she said to the director, "Why not *Nuts* for me?" "Why not indeed," Rydell reportedly answered, and on October 1, 1985, columnist Army Archerd announced that the film had shifted from the Universal lot to Warner Bros., where Streisand's production company resided. The package, once planned as a low-budget film, now entered "the high-rent district," with Barbra receiving a reported $5 million-plus for the strictly dramatic role. When asked whether the play's theme of incest, prostitution, etc., would be part of the film version, Rydell told Army: "Yes. And it makes me feel deeply responsible."

Once at Warners the script of *Nuts* proceeded to undergo some drastic changes. In the original play, Streisand's character did not make any discernible physical impact until Act Two. For the movie Barbra wanted more of herself from the beginning, via the use of flashbacks and fantasies. Mark Rydell objected, holding firm to his original concept and his original start date of mid-February. After all, she may be the star, but he was the producer and the director and he *owned* the property. But Warners, who were putting up the cash for the production, and who had made a bundle from three previous Streisand films (including *A Star Is Born* and *The Main Event)* sided with their star-in-residence. *Nuts* was postponed; additional story conferences were scheduled; arguments ensued, followed by a crisscross of arbitrative calls between lawyers, agents, and studio executives. On the weekend of March 3 an agreement was reached. Included with the settlement was a press release, assembled and approved by the principals. On Monday morning the release was copied and hand-delivered to the editors and columnists of the leading Hollywood trade papers. The essence of the statement was that Rydell, after working five years on *Nuts,* had quit the picture.

The parting was amicable, the press release emphasized. "If I have any regrets it is that I will not be able to work with Barbra Streisand, an immense talent with whom I have enjoyed an exciting work relationship," said Rydell, avoiding any mention of the severance pay involved.* When queried directly, Streisand also said that any talk of her taking over as director was "totally premature." Two weeks later a new director, Marty Ritt, was on the

---

* Reported to be over $500,000, plus a percentage of the gross take, Rydell's press reps, Rogers and Cowan, would not confirm or deny this sum.

picture, as well as a new producer. "Streisand is now also producing," said *Variety* on April 2.

A LEADING MAN

Due to the secrecy and the camouflage of releases being issued on the shift in studios and directors, little notice was paid in the press to who would co-star with Barbra Streisand in *Nuts*. The role of Aaron Levinsky, a defense attorney who wins an acquittal for his client in exchange for the $18,000 she earned in whoredom, was thought to be secondary, but by May of 1986 the part was being bounced between two leading Academy Award winners—Richard Dreyfuss and Dustin Hoffman. Dreyfuss was first in line. He read the script for Barbra, Marty Ritt, and the Warner executives. The part was his until early May, when Barbra flew to New York to accept an award and to discuss another film project, *The Normal Heart*, with Dustin Hoffman. Over dinner at an East Side restaurant the actress spoke to her old friend about *Nuts*. For input she asked Hoffman to read the script. He obliged, not only offering a critique, but expressing his willingness to play the role of the defense attorney. Ecstatic, Streisand flew back to Los Angeles in the company jet. She told the Burbank brass they now had *two* blockbuster stars for their movie. Warners naturally asked about the previous commitment to Richard Dreyfuss: no contract had been signed with the actor, but a verbal offer had been made.

"Dreyfuss says Nuts to Role," was Marilyn Beck's column headline on May 11. He was bowing out of *Nuts* she said, to play the lead in *Tin Men*, a Disney movie about aluminum-siding salesmen. Lamenting their loss, *Nuts* director Marty Ritt told Beck that he and Warners were starting the search all over again for a leading man, seemingly oblivious to the fact that the previous day in New York, another reporter, Suzy, told her readers that Dustin Hoffman was locked into the role. "The gossip is," said Suzy, "that *Nuts* is already running a budget of $45 million—and they haven't even started filming. There's no business like ---- -------- (Fill in the blanks.)." A week later, on May 19, director Ritt acknowledged that he and Warners were "absolutely interested" in Hoffman, that a deal was in the works. "Don't dress for the premiere," another Hollywood source advised, doubting if negotiations between Streisand and Hoffman would ever be finalized.

Dustin, like Barbra, was a super-perfectionist about his work. Certainly Warner Bros. knew that. Back in 1978 he sued them, First Artists (co-owned by Barbra), *and* his agent, for seizing two of his films *(Agatha* and *Straight Time),* therein denying him his contractual right to a final edit. The subsequent brilliance of *Kramer vs. Kramer* and *Tootsie* was due in part, it was said, to his performance, his directors, and to his constant creative vigilance on each film, before, during, and *after* production. So if Barbra and Ritt and Warners wanted his participation in *Nuts* they would have to come up with his salary (currently $6 million-plus) and give him creative approval every step of the way.

"Warners says Nuts to Dustin" Marilyn Beck announced on June 5. The studio turned down his demands, and were now talking to Paul Newman, Al Pacino, and Marlon Brando, all of whom were interested in the role. "That's what I was told by a high-placed executive," said Beck in an update for this chapter. "Then I learned that Newman was *not* interested in *Nuts,* and that I was being used as a casting tool."

"It's back to square one," Liz Smith reported two weeks later. Richard Dreyfuss was, once again, Barbra's leading man. Production on *Nuts* would now commence in October of 1986.

Acknowledgments

This book represents two years of research and some 125 hours of interviews with people who worked with Barbra Streisand on her stage performances, her recordings, her nightclub performances, TV specials, concerts, and on her films. By request, some of these people cannot be mentioned by name. Those who can include: Ron Alexenburg, John Berg, Marilyn and Alan Bergman, Mike Berniker, Abba Bogin, Jim Brown, Elinor Bunin, Sammy Cahn, Mario Casilli, Bob Cato, Peter Daniels, Clive Davis, Nancy Donald, Marty Erlichman, Myra Friedman, Fred Glaser, Jack Gold, Wally Gold, Greg Gorman, Ed Graham, Marvin Hamlisch, Don Hunstein, Paul Jabara, Glenn Jordan, Dave Kapralik, the late John Kurland, Frank Laico, Tony Lane, Arthur Laurents, Tony Lawrence, Michel Legrand, Gary Le Mel, Mickey Leonard, Nan Leone, Terry Leong, Bruce Lundvall, Peter Matz, Bob Merrill, Bob Mersey, Tom Noonan, Marty Paich, Gail Parent, Peter Reilly, Howard Rosenman, Milton Schafer, Steve Schapiro, Robert Scheerer, the late Nat Shapiro, Tom Sheppard, Andrew Smith, Jule Styne, Virginia Team, Ed Thrasher, Warren Vincent, Ken Welch, Tom Wilkes, Toni Wine, Neil Wolfe, and David Wynshaw.

For additional interviews, quotes, and anecdotes, I am grateful to Carol Burnett, David DeSilva, Gary Guthrie, John Hammond,

Candy Leigh, Jim Lowe, Tommy Makem, Mitch Miller, Sandra Morbeck, Dick Riddle, Sheila Schandler, Bob Schulenberg, Kenny Solms, Elly Stone, Chuck Taggert, Michaele Vollbracht, and Billie Wallington.

Special thanks to the journalists, editors, reviewers, and publicists who provided other leads and dimensions. They include the late Arthur Bell; Liz Smith of the *Daily News;* Harvey Mann; Chris Chase; Arthur Gelb, Stephen Holden, Judy Klemesrud, and Anna Quindlen of *The New York Times;* Guy Flatley of *Cosmopolitan;* and Bob Colacello, Kitty Kelley, Grover Lewis, Stephen Silverman, Lee Solters, and William Raidy.

For help with research and referrals I am indebted to Bob Altshuler and the CBS Records publicity staff; to Barbara Flannery of the CBS Records Legal Department; to Josephine Mangiaracina; Tina McCarthy Vinces and Beatrice Beamud; Donna Cuervo; the staff of the theater, film, and music departments at Lincoln Center Library of the Performing Arts in New York; to Randy Emerian of Fresno, California, who supplied audio tapes of Streisand performances and interviews; and to Eve Babitz, Brett Bacchus, Dorothy Dicker, Eugene Ferrara of the *Daily News,* Joseph Goodwin, Paula Green, Mikey Harris, Annette Hirn, Rick Ingersoll, Pat Landis of Wide World/AP, Bruce Mandes, Renee Mayson, Chris Nelson, Bill Townley, Kate Nolan, and Marsha Tyronis of *Playboy,* and to Ray Whelan of Globe Photos.

Cheers also to agent Julia Coopersmith, who sold the book in outline form; to Chuck Adams at Delacorte Press, who bought it; to Jim Judge of Southampton, who edited the first draft; to Marie Considine, who typed some of the next-to-last pages; to my brother Pat Considine, who copied them; to Niamh and Anne Marie for the "type-out"; to Eileen Tuohy for her help in Los Angeles; to Lilda Lando for the same in Washington, D.C.; to David Weitzman at Delacorte Press, and my lawyer Rich Heller; to Kaye Hart McDonald and Jean Halbert for their long-term friendship and encouragement; to Ken O'Keefe of Harper Restaurant, for the good food and messenger service; to Kathy and "Peg" Judge for their grandiose plans and enthusiasm; and to Nell Connaire for her intercessions to St. Jude.

Shaun Considine
New York City
August 1, 1985

Bibliography

Bacon, James. *Hollywood Is a Four Letter Town.* New York: Avon Books, 1977.

Barry, Stephen B. *Royal Service.* New York: Avon Books, 1983.

Burke, Tom. *Burke's Steerage.* New York: G. P. Putnam's Sons, 1976.

Collins, Joan. *Past Imperfect.* New York: Simon and Schuster, Inc., 1984.

Crist, Judith. *Take 22.* New York: Penguin, 1984.

Davis, Clive, with James Willwerth. *Clive.* New York: Ballantine Books, Inc., 1977.

Engel, Lehman. *This Bright Day.* New York: Macmillan Publishing Co., Inc., 1974.

Friedman, Myra. *Buried Alive.* New York: William Morrow and Co., Inc., 1973.

Goldman, Albert. *Elvis Presley.* New York: McGraw-Hill Book Co., 1981.

Goldman, William. *Adventures in the Screen Trade.* New York: Warner Books, Inc., 1983.

Goldman, William. *The Season.* New York: Harcourt, Brace and World, Inc., 1969.

Graham, Sheilah. *Confessions of a Hollywood Columnist.* New York: William Morrow and Co., Inc., 1969.

Griffin, Merv, and Peter Barsocchini. *Merv.* New York: Simon and Schuster, Inc., 1980.

Grobel, Lawrence. *Conversations with Capote.* New York: New American Library, 1984.

Halberstam, David. *The Powers That Be.* New York: Dell Publishing Co., Inc., 1979.

Hallowell, John. *The Truth Game.* New York: Simon and Schuster, Inc., 1969.

Hammond, John, with Irving Townsend. *On Record.* New York: Penguin Books, Inc., 1982.

Hirschorn, Clive. *Gene Kelly.* London: W. J. Allen, 1974.

Huston, John. *John Huston: An Open Book.* New York: Alfred A. Knopf, Inc., 1979.

Jordan, Rene. *The Greatest Star: The Barbra Streisand Story.* New York: G. P. Putnam's Sons, 1975.

Katkov, Norman. *The Fabulous Fanny Brice.* New York: Alfred A. Knopf, Inc., 1953.

Lewis, Grover. *Academy All the Way.* New York: Straight Arrow Books, 1974.

Logan, Joshua. *Movie Stars, Real People, and Me.* New York: Dell Publishing Co., Inc., 1978.

McClintock, David. *Indecent Exposure.* New York: William Morrow and Co., Inc., 1982.

Page, Tim, ed. *A Glenn Gould Reader.* New York: Alfred A. Knopf, Inc., 1984.

Paley, William. *As It Happened.* New York: Doubleday and Co., Inc., 1975.

Pavarotti, Luciano, with William Wright. *Pavarotti—My Own Story.* New York: Doubleday and Co., 1981.

Picon, Molly. *Molly!* New York: Simon and Schuster, Inc., 1980.

Reed, Rex. *Do You Sleep in the Nude?* New York: New American Library, 1968.

Ritz, David. *Marvin Gaye: Divided Soul.* New York: McGraw-Hill Book Co., 1985.

Sharif, Omar. *Omar Sharif: The Eternal Male.* New York: Doubleday and Co., Inc., 1977.

Silverman, Stephen. *Public Spectacles.* New York: E. P. Dutton, 1981.

Teti, Frank, with Karen Moline. *Streisand: Through the Lens.* New York: Delilah Books, 1982.

Torme, Mel. *Judy Garland: The Other Side of the Rainbow.* New York: William Morrow and Co., Inc., 1970.

Zec, Donald, and Anthony Fowles. *Barbra.* New York: St. Martin's Press, Inc., 1981.

◄ 405 ►

◄ 410 ►

You're invited to a reunion well worth attending

College classmates Emily, Chris, Daphne, and Annabel will be there. Friends from their days at Radcliffe in the 50s, they found glamorous careers, married "perfect" men, and expected to have "perfect" children. They played by the rules —sort of—but the rules changed midway through their lives.

You'll meet them first in Rona Jaffe's wonderful **Class Reunion**. And catch up with these remarkable women 25 years after graduation in **After the Reunion.**

R o n a   J a f f e

_____	CLASS REUNION	11288-5-43	$4.50
_____	AFTER THE REUNION	10047-X-13	4.50

SAMUEL SHEM, M.D.

Our author, the doctor, is back with another hilarious novel. Enjoy!

_____ **FINE** 12510-3-17 $3.95

What happens to a misfit genius whose grade-school teacher thinks he's retarded and whose government picks his brains? He becomes a shrink, of course! And has it all—marriage, friendship, a successful psychiatric practice—until Fine's over-zealous pursuit of a career clashes with his most important relationships. You'll laugh at, love, and cry over Fine's crazy, comic, glittering glory.

_____ **HOUSE OF GOD** 13368-8-26 $3.95

Revel in this modern, underground classic of humor, with its unforgettable, "catch-22" portrait of doctors. A wonderful and witty gem!